ᔥ The Engaged Historian ᔦ

MAKING SENSE OF HISTORY

Studies in Historical Cultures
General Editor: Stefan Berger
Founding Editor: Jörn Rüsen

Bridging the gap between historical theory and the study of historical memory, this series crosses the boundaries between both academic disciplines and cultural, social, political and historical contexts. In an age of rapid globalization, which tends to manifest itself on an economic and political level, locating the cultural practices involved in generating its underlying historical sense is an increasingly urgent task.

Recent volumes:

Volume 37
The Engaged Historian: Perspectives on the Intersections of Politics, Activism and the Historical Profession
Edited by Stefan Berger

Volume 36
Contemplating Historical Consciousness: Notes from the Field
Edited by Anna Clark and Carla L. Peck

Volume 35
Empathy and History: The Context of Historical Understanding in Re-enactment, Hermeneutics and Education
Tyson Retz

Volume 34
The Ethos of History: Time and Responsibility
Edited by Stefan Helgesson and Jayne Svenungsson

Volume 33
History and Belonging: Representations of the Past in Contemporary European Politics
Edited by Stefan Berger and Caner Tekin

Volume 32
Making Nordic Historiography: Connections, Tensions and Methodology, 1850–1970
Edited by Pertti Haapala, Marja Jalava and Simon Larsson

Volume 31
Contesting Deregulation: Debates, Practices and Developments in the West since the 1970s
Edited by Knud Andresen and Stefan Müller

Volume 30
Cultural Borders of Europe: Narratives, Concepts and Practices in the Present and the Past
Edited by Mats Andrén, Thomas Lindkvist, Ingmar Söhrman and Katharina Vajta

Volume 29
The Mirror of the Medieval: An Anthropology of the Western Historical Imagination
K. Patrick Fazioli

For a full volume listing, please see the series page on our website:
http://www.berghahnbooks.com/series/making-sense-of-history

THE ENGAGED HISTORIAN

Perspectives on the Intersections of Politics, Activism and the Historical Profession

Edited by Stefan Berger

berghahn
NEW YORK • OXFORD
www.berghahnbooks.com

First published in 2019 by
Berghahn Books
www.berghahnbooks.com

© 2019, 2025 Stefan Berger
First paperback edition published in 2025

All rights reserved. Except for the quotation of short passages
for the purposes of criticism and review, no part of this book
may be reproduced in any form or by any means, electronic or
mechanical, including photocopying, recording, or any information
storage and retrieval system now known or to be invented,
without written permission of the publisher.

Library of Congress Cataloging in Publication Data
A C.I.P. cataloging record is available from the Library of Congress
Library of Congress Cataloging in Publication Control Number:
2019003775

British Library Cataloguing in Publication Data
A catalogue record for this book is available from the British Library

ISBN 978-1-78920-199-4 hardback
ISBN 978-1-80539-740-3 paperback
ISBN 978-1-80539-917-9 epub
ISBN 978-1-78920-200-7 web pdf

https://doi.org/10.3167/9781789201994

To Georg G. Iggers (1926–2017),
an engaged historian in the best sense

Contents

Introduction
Historical Writing and Civic Engagement: A Symbiotic
Relationship   1
Stefan Berger

Chapter 1. Engagement: Metahistorical Considerations on a
Disputed Attitude in Historical Studies   33
Jörn Rüsen

Chapter 2. The Ideal of Justice and Its Significance for Historians
as Engaged Intellectuals   44
Martin Wiklund

Chapter 3. Committed Writing: History and Narrative
Communication Revisited   63
Kalle Pihlainen

Chapter 4. The Historian-King: Political Leaders, Historical
Consciousness and Wise Government   79

Appendix 1: List of Historically Informed Political Leaders
(1900–2018)   98

Appendix 2: Writings about Heads of State and
Government as Historians   101

Appendix 3: Historians as Nobel Peace Prize Laureates
and Nominees   106
Antoon De Baets

Chapter 5. Historians with a Cause: Refugees' Memory and Historical Practices in Interwar Greece — 118
Emilia Salvanou

Chapter 6. The Making of the Zhanguo Ce Clique: The Politicization of History Knowledge in Wartime China — 136
Xin Fan

Chapter 7. The Historicization of World War II in Greece after the Civil War: Looking Back on the Public Debate over a Lecture by British Historian C.M. Woodhouse — 151
Manos Avgeridis

Chapter 8. Historians as Dissidents: Intellectual 'Eros' in Action — 163
Nina Witoszek

Chapter 9. The *Social Movement History* as a Social Movement in and of Itself — 185
Michihiro Okamoto

Chapter 10. Professional Historical Writing and Human Rights Engagement in the Twenty-First Century: Innovative Approaches and Their Dilemmas — 205
Nina Schneider

Chapter 11. Using the Past: The Brazilian Cinema between Censorship and Representation — 221
Meize Regina de Lucena Lucas

Chapter 12. Historians and the Trauma of the Past: The Destruction of Security Files on Citizens in Greece, 1989 — 237
Vangelis Karamanolakis

Chapter 13. Historians and/in the New Media — 250
Effi Gazi

Chapter 14. Street History: Coming to Terms with the Past in Occupy Movements — 261
Antonis Liakos

Afterword
The Historian as an Engaged Intellectual: Historical Writing and Social Criticism – A Personal Retrospective — 277
Georg G. Iggers

Index — 301

INTRODUCTION

Historical Writing and Civic Engagement

A Symbiotic Relationship

STEFAN BERGER

Professional historians have never been just that. The rise of the historical profession from the second half of the eighteenth century onwards was accompanied by the idea of the historian as public intellectual. Yet notions of professionalization have at times sat awkwardly with the willingness of historians to be political and social activists. The ghosts of 'objectivity' and a 'value-free science' haunted a profession that gained phenomenal authority from the belief that their professionalism made them the only ones who could speak authoritatively about the past.[1] Those historians unwilling to give up their civic engagement and unable to draw a clear line between their historical profession and their political commitment had to find methodological and theoretical justifications for their engagement. This book will give a range of examples of how such justifications worked and what kinds of engagement have been prominent among historians. But the book will also give several examples of historians who were not professional historians and did not have a job at the university or the academy. Whether they were politicians, journalists, publicists or earned their money elsewhere, many people of diverse backgrounds had either some training as a historian or wrote history without such training. Sometimes their histories were far more influential than those of professional historians. Especially

---

Notes for this section begin on page 22.

when we discuss forms of engaged history writing it would be difficult just to concentrate on professional history writing.

Historians, who decided to act as engaged intellectuals, had to position themselves within a wider societal memory discourse about the past. They became memory agents and through their historical expertise and their professionalism spoke with special authority within broader memory discourses. Even those historians who stuck to their professional work and were reluctant to become engaged in wider societal debates were, through their work on the past, contributing to memory discourses. History thus should not be seen as counter-opposite to memory, a view prominently put forward by Maurice Halbwachs,[2] but it has to be regarded as having been part and parcel of memory discourses.[3] The voices of professional historians were particularly important in memory discourses, where their authoritative historical work spoke to the memory in question. In fact, François Bedarida has argued that historians have a special responsibility in addressing those topics that are particularly troubling for the public and which provide the source of a great deal of moral uncertainty. If historians often have a particular authority in memory discourses, they do not stand apart from them. In fact it makes more sense to see historians as one particular group of memory activists (among others) whose views on the past influence memory discourses.[4]

Positioning the topic of the historian as engaged intellectual between the fields of history of historiography, social movement studies and memory studies also means that future researchers on this topic will have to familiarize themselves with all three areas of research. So far, there is little systematic scholarship on this topic. True, biographies of historians often also contain information on their political and social activism, in so far as it was prominent,[5] but the dedicated study of the interrelationship between such activism and history writing is still in its infancy. Some books on the historical profession have also dealt with the topic of the engaged intellectual.[6] Taking his cue from contemporary US (and British) debates in the 1990s and early 2000s about the impact of overspecialization, multiculturalism and the fragmentation of history on the profession, allegedly leading to a lack of public influence, Ian Tyrrell has traced the public influence of historians in American society from the 1890s to the 1970s.[7] In his history of the decline of public intellectuals in the US, Richard Posner also recalls the work of many public historians, including Gertrude Himmelfarb, whose famous intervention against the impact of 1968 on US American culture has had such strong political repercussions among the political Right in the US.[8] Marcel vom Lehn has examined West German and Italian historians' pubic intervention in the media to discuss the fascist and National Socialist past in the post-World War II period – highlighting national differences such as the greater professionalization of both the historical science and the media in West Germany, their greater (traditional) state orientation and the weaker debating culture in West Germany that can be related to a less polarized political public sphere (exacerbated by the fact that there were two Germanies after 1949).[9] Some historical journals – among them the *Radical History Review* and *History Workshop Journal* – have at times celebrated the link between historical studies and political engagement.[10]

The notion of public history includes an element of political engagement of the historian who perceives his role as that of communicating the past to a wider public and thereby fulfilling a social function in society that goes beyond that of a traditional professional historian.[11] Of course, there are a great many varieties of public history. Any aspect of the past that is communicated within public spheres belongs to public history. Historical museums and monuments present the past to the public, as do a variety of different media, including newspapers, radio, television, film and digital media. Historical commissions discuss usually problematic aspects of the past in order to shed more light on the past or work towards reconciliation. Public history also provides fascinating synergies between social movement studies and the history of historiography, precisely because intellectuals played a major role in social movements, often providing important repertoires of ideas and discourses that empowered social movements.[12] The nineteenth-century labour movement already drew support from a range of intellectuals supporting the demands for social reform and revolution. Sidney Webb and his engagement of the Labour Party is a good example of a labour movement intellectual.[13] Later on, communist parties attracted many intellectuals to their ranks, and the fascist movements also were supported by a range of intellectuals. Whilst social democratic parties post-World War II often sought alliances with intellectuals in their respective countries, the new social movements that emerged from the 1970s onwards also often sought to capitalize on the support of intellectuals. Amongst social movement intellectuals, historians have at different times and places been prominent, as the past was a vital resource for social movements and their political struggles.[14]

If historians have been prominent intellectuals for a long time, it is intriguing to note that histories of intellectuals rarely engage with historians.[15] In his book on nineteenth-century intellectuals, Christoph Charle has pointed out that the famous Dreyfus affair in France was not so much the starting point of political intervention by intellectuals than an end point of a long formation process.[16] Charle also warns not to generalize from a very French notion of 'intellectual', and indeed we do have different ideas of precursors to the modern intellectual in the French concept of the 'philosophes', the English concept of the 'men of letters' and the German concept of the 'Bildungsbürger'.[17] It is notoriously hard to define intellectuals, as their meaning depends invariably on the context in which they are being discussed, and I am not sure whether it is actually helpful to try and find firm definitions, but their rise in European society has a lot to do with the extension of a public sphere from the nineteenth century onwards. Karl Mannheim and Pierre Bourdieu, two sociologists, who have worked extensively on intellectuals, have both argued that their independence of mind is one of their crucial trademarks.[18] But even here, I am not so sure. After all, many intellectuals were serving those with political, economic or social power and were legitimating forms of rule. Of course, we have many intellectuals who did the opposite – they opposed the powerful and, in the famous dictum, spoke truth to power, regardless of the consequences. Joseph Schumpeter described intellectuals as a 'potential irritating factor for any ruling order',[19] and Max Weber thought of them as 'switch operators' of different systems of intellectual thought.[20] Intellectuals could be oppositional, but they could also be the handmaidens of those firmly in power. From the second half of the nineteenth century onwards, an inexorably rising public sphere provided the means for a group of intellectuals, who were living of their criticism in the new urban conurbations that were a hub for contesting ideologies and social organizations. They were journalists and literary figures, and quite a few belonged, after 1900, to an ever-growing academic proletariat, who lived of their pen. It is because of the rise of this class that those working in a professional capacity, be it as historians or as representatives of other sciences or the civil service or other professions, were increasingly not seen, or at least not primarily seen, as intellectuals. Yet these groups, as will be exemplified in this volume with regard to professional historians, often played an important role also as intellectuals.

In this introduction I shall provide a brief outline of the relationship between professional historical writing and civic engagement from the Enlightenment to the present day, highlighting several strands of research that need to be developed further in years to come. Last but not least I shall also weave into this historical tapestry of the concept and practice of the historian as engaged intellectual brief summaries of the chapters in this volume, which shed light on diverse aspects of this topic. As the subsequent chapters only provide glimpses of certain aspects of the manifold relationships, there are certain gaps in the comprehensive treatment of this complex topic that will at least be highlighted in this outline. The chapters are ordered according to chronology: following some theoretical and general considerations regarding the relationship between engagement and historical writing, we have a range of case studies highlighting particular aspects of that relationship in different parts of the world. They should be seen as throwing a spotlight on diverse aspects of the complex relationship between commitment and scholarship. Hopefully they can serve as inspiration for others to explore this subfield in the history of historiography further. It is for future work in this field to fill some of the many gaps that still remain.

It is appropriate to begin the volume with some general conceptual considerations about the relationship between historical scholarship and political engagement, and Jörn Rüsen's contribution here fits the bill perfectly. The equation of a 'scientific' (wissenschaftlich) practice of history with a non-political one is false, he argues. Doing 'scientific' history has many potential implications for political engagement, in the past and in the present. But, he continues, it may be necessary to distinguish forms of political engagement and their way of doing history from other modes of doing the same history. As historical thinking is always related to needs of orientation in time and space, and as such orientation often has a political dimension, this function of historical thinking is closely related to political engagement. However, how the past is understood as history, what rules are being followed in disclosing the perception of the past, how the interpretations of the past are represented and how these representations are used in the wider historical culture differs enormously and is intimately related to diverse forms of political commitment emanating from historical scholarship at specific times and in specific places. The historical sciences, Rüsen contends, are never neutral but position themselves in a wider politics in which they take up either self-conscious or unconscious positions informed by history. Such a wider politics has to do with normative horizons of expectations grounded often in particular moral universes of which historians as citizens and human beings are a part. Geoffrey Barraclough, in a famous lecture delivered at Chatham House in the late 1950s, admitted that moral issues are always linked to political judgements but still insisted that one must 'be careful to avoid confusing the position of the historian and the citizen'.[21] Yet his assumption that historians can avoid in their writings personal horizons of expectations and normative assumptions has to be questionable. Indeed, as Herman Paul has observed, it is impossible for the historians to leave out of the equation of their history writing their scholarly selves, which incorporate moral dimensions and ethical choices.[22] Historians are therefore never objective but invariably engaged in an intersubjective search for historical truth that in turn has political implications. Rüsen warns of ideological commitments for historians, as they tend to lead them to search in history for legitimation of their ideologies rather than approach history with the willingness to let their research hypotheses be falsified. Hence historians need to be prepared to devise research designs that allow them to be surprised by their own findings.[23]

Martin Wiklund's chapter provides another entry point into exploring the relationship between the professional historian and political engagement. He argues that the ideal of justice is eminently important for historians in their roles as engaged intellectuals. In his view justice is the crucial element in what he calls a 'new ethics ... for the use of history'. Public struggles over the past, he argues, resemble a court of justice situation, in which the historian as engaged intellectual can be public prosecutor, defence lawyer or judge depending on which position is best suited in concrete historical situations to enhancing justice. He warns, however, against the historian to be both public prosecutor and judge as this carries the danger of secretly imposing the claims of the prosecutor with the authority of the judge and thus short-circuiting the critical evaluation of the claims of the prosecutor.[24]

A final chapter dealing with the general relationship between historical scholarship and political engagement is Kalle Pihlainen's attempt to deconstruct the fallacy of many practising historians' beliefs that their epistemological commitments conflict with any potential political commitment. The political in this perception becomes tainted with the brush of being ideological. Instead both the aestheticization of history and its strong commitment to empiricism led, in Pihlainen's view, to its depoliticization. Thus, the enormous energies invested by historians to distinguish 'facts' from 'fiction' are, above all, an attempt to avoid political commitment.[25] A range of historians and philosophers discussed by Pihlainen, from Jean-Paul Sartre to Michel Foucault and further to Hayden White, have all problematized this avoidance strategy of historians for political commitment and instead posited a moral imperative for the historian to become a politically active, engaged intellectual.[26]

The chapters by Rüsen, Wiklund and Pihlainen all investigate to what extent and how historians can and shall be engaged intellectuals. The following chapter by Antoon De Baets reminds readers of the important relationship between historical consciousness and political wisdom, which philosophers of history have dealt with time and again. Assembling a list of political leaders with strong historical consciousness, De Baets contrasts this with another list of 'wise leaders' – as expressed in nominations for the Nobel Peace Prize. Checking these lists against each other, he arrives at a list of only four historian politicians who he regards as wise leaders because of their historical consciousness: Woodrow Wilson, Thomas Masaryk, Jawaharlal Nehru and Mikhail Gorbachev.[27]

De Baets also reminds us that politicians with a close interest in history were often more interested in power than in wisdom. There is no shortage of dictators who had a strong historical consciousness, and the latter is neither related to inclinations for democracy nor for peace. In fact, as De Baets has pointed out elsewhere, historians who were murdered because of political circumstances count in their hundreds. Many more were imprisoned, suffered relegation and censorship or were threatened with any one of these measures in the light of their political engagement. Oppositional political engagement also often resulted in historians having to flee their country and seek political refuge somewhere else. Hence the topic of the historian as engaged intellectual is closely related to the topic of the exile historian who produces his histories in exile and stands between his former country that he fled and his new host country.[28] Nevertheless, we should state at the beginning that we are dealing here with a small phenomenon within the historical profession as a whole. Most professional historians were content with pursuing their historical work and did not think of getting politically involved or playing a political role, even if their professional work had political implications. Yet professionalization meant, above all, specialization, and a highly specialized historical profession included many members whose work had few immediate political repercussions and was not particularly relevant for everyday politics.[29] However, there always were prominent exceptions where historical work did have direct political implications and where the politics had led historians to pursue particular historical investigations. Of course, we also find the case of the historian who was a specialist in a particular field of history that had little relation to politics and who became politically active out of a general sense of civic duty or out of a wider historical understanding that did not specifically have to do with his concrete specialism. There are then many different scenarios in which historians became politically active and in which they played roles as public intellectuals, and this volume is an attempt to explore some of those circumstances.

The modern research university, as we know it today, started its rise during the second half of the eighteenth century when the material culture of academia became characterized by processes of rationalization, bureaucratization, commodification and the move towards meritocratic principles. Exams, dissertations and publications became more and more important as did public lecturing and research seminars. The professor was endowed with a certain charisma that allowed him to become a research leader and develop his school of thought – training 'pupils' who were to follow in his footsteps.[30] This first happened at universities in the German lands, such as Halle, Wittenberg and Göttingen, from where the idea of the research university spread globally and became adapted in a plethora of different ways. It coincided with the age of the Enlightenments, and Enlightenment values were prominently represented at the new research universities.[31]

One of these values was the belief in civic engagement. A famous political protest happened at the University of Göttingen in 1837. The so-called Göttingen Seven, seven professors, amongst them two historians, Friedrich Christoph Dahlmann and Georg Gottfried Gervinus, protested against the changes introduced to the constitution of the Kingdom of Hannover by its ruler Ernst August. They were dismissed from the university, and three of them, amongst them the two historians, had to leave the country. Yet their action had become a powerful symbol for the constitutional struggle across the German lands, and it became itself the stuff of legend. The memorial culture of Germany makes frequent references to the Göttingen Seven to this day, and their bronze statues can be found near the parliament of Lower Saxony in Hannover.[32]

Elsewhere, Enlightenment historians were known for their fierce public criticism of religion and superstition, their championing of the progress of human civilization down the ages and their promotion of rationalism, tolerance, liberty, freedom and constitutionalism. All of these were hotly contested and made many Enlightenment historians into public intellectuals. At the same time as they promoted particular moral and political projects, Enlightenment historians were also crucial in freeing history from the remaining shackles of theology. Up until the eighteenth century, history in many universities was only taught in theology departments. The setting up of separate history departments became the norm at European institutions of higher education only towards the second half of the eighteenth and the early nineteenth century. The new secular history was intensely interested in the emergence of great global civilizations. Historians were influenced by Jean Jacques Rousseau's notion that the age of discoveries had been a wasted opportunity for mankind, as the European conquerors had failed to appreciate the civilizations they encountered.[33] In many Enlightenment histories, the place of God was now taken by the spirits and customs of peoples and civilizations. The Enlightenment historians often became engaged intellectuals qua their moral and normative ideas about individuals and their rights and liberties that clashed with the absolutism of their age.[34]

Whilst Enlightenment historians looked for universal values in history, both in the universal and the national histories they penned, the subsequent generation of Romantic historians were more and more concerned with national specifics and nation states.[35] The nationalizing tendencies in historiography often went hand in hand with nationalist political commitments. The German historian Heinrich von Treitschke and the entire Prussian school of historiography became synonymous with the championing of a small German nationalism through history writing. When that nation state came into being in 1871, the Prussian historians felt vindicated, and some promoted ever more aggressive forms of German nationalism in imperial Germany.[36]

Elsewhere in Europe, historians were often important in providing historical legitimation to aspiring national movements. Mykhailo Hrushevsky in the Ukraine was not only a major organizer of Wissenschaft but also a political campaigner who promoted federalism in pre-revolutionary Russia and promoted the Ukrainian cause abroad. A staunch opponent of imperialism and a promoter of democratic federalism, his politics marched alongside his historical work throughout his long and distinguished career.[37] Those historians whose political commitments lay with nations that had not (yet) got their nation state tended to hang their narratives on a history of the people and their alleged oppression by a state described as foreign. By contrast, those historians who already lived in a nation state often promoted state nationalism in a variety of different ways. In Tsarist Russia the state orientation of many historians was legendary. Sergej Michajovič Solovev, who held the chair in Russian history at the University of Moscow after 1835, not only penned a twenty-nine volume *History of Russia from the Oldest Time*, he also worked tirelessly as a public intellectual to promote the idea that the state was the major factor in constructing the Russian nation. His justification of strong statism went hand in hand with sympathies for liberal reforms and liberal ideas that he had encountered during his travels to Western and Central Europe, where he met fellow historians such as François Guizot, Jules Michelet and František Palacký.[38]

Many nineteenth-century historians thought of themselves as public intellectuals in the service of their respective nation. The Greek historian Spyridon Lambros remarked that the pen of the historian was more important for nation-building than the guns of the military.[39] The very first issue of the *Revue Historique*, published in Paris in 1876, stated very clearly a political calling for professional historians. History, the editors wrote, was 'to give to our country the unity and moral strength it needs', in particular for the revenge for 1871 and the recovery of the 'lost lands' of Alsace and Lorraine.[40]

Professional historians became festive speakers, political speech writers and the authors of articles in popular media, especially newspapers and journals. They were politically committed not just to the nation but to a variety of different causes next to historiographical nationalism and strongly intertwined with imperialism. In Britain, John Robert Seeley promoted a 'greater Britain', extending the nation to incorporate all white settler societies that were part of the British Empire. His *Expansion of England*, published in 1883, was very much written as a public intellectual for a wide audience, and his political-cum-historical role was recognized by a knighthood, awarded in 1894. Seeley's writings were not just promoting a new understanding of an imperial Britain within the British Isles and the empire, but his works also had a major influence on other historians of empire in other empires, most notably Russia.[41]

Throughout much of the nineteenth century, nationalism and imperialism were strongly allied to liberalism. Many historians were political

Liberals, championing ideas of constitutional rule and the political participation of the educated and propertied middle classes. This political commitment provided another vast area for the engagement of historians in wider civil society. Nineteenth-century Whig historiography, as represented by Thomas Babington Macaulay's *History of England* was the archetypal liberal-national-imperial historiography, promoting a view of the long forward march of constitutionalism, parliamentarism, liberty and the rule of law.[42] Variants of English Whig historiography can be found in many parts of Europe. Thus, for example, in Hungary Mihály Horváth championed the alleged 'original liberty' of the Magyars, and much of nineteenth-century Polish historiography retained a fascination with the Polish constitution of 1791, which had made Poland the alleged homeland of liberty in Europe.[43]

Political commitments also extended to democratic and socialist historians, although they rarely managed to find a position within European university systems in the nineteenth and early twentieth centuries. Louis Blanc, for example, became one of the most prominent historians of class, for whom the French revolution of 1789 was a class history that represented the precondition for the emergence of socialism.[44] Around 1900 a thriving autodidactic tradition of historical writing within the nascent European labour movement gave rise to strong class perspectives on modern European history. European socialists, such as Jean Jaures, Eduard Bernstein, Filippo Turati, Robert Grimm and many others wrote history as a way of affirming a particular historical mission for their respective parties. History became a powerful weapon in the class struggle and the attempt to grab political power from the hands of the bourgeoisie.[45]

Apart from direct political commitments, many historians also engaged themselves in the promotion of their Christian beliefs. They championed the history of Christianity in their own writings. British nineteenth-century historians, for example, often described the church as the saviour of the state in medieval England. Later, Protestantism supposedly gave rise to individual liberty, which in turn became the anchor of English national identity.[46] Where there existed a strong relationship between church and state we find the strong involvement of the clergy in the writing of history and in the promotion of Christian historical narratives.[47] The pastor historian was by no means an exception in nineteenth-century Europe.[48] And Catholic historiographies were as publicly engaged as their Protestant counterparts. In Hungary, for example, the Catholic historical master narrative contributed to the public cult surrounding King Stephen, the first king of Hungary in the eleventh century and a Catholic saint.[49] In the German lands, Protestant historians became champions of the Luther cult, whilst their minoritarian Catholic counterparts sought to develop a similar national cult around the figure of St Bonifaz.[50]

A final example from a long list of possible engagements and commitments of nineteenth- and early twentieth-century historians comes from the nascent women's movement. Women had been prominent historical authors in many parts of Europe in the eighteenth and early nineteenth centuries. In England, Catherine Macaulay published an eight-volume History of England between 1763 and 1783 that amounted to a rallying cry of liberty against tyranny. Her republicanism made her a strong public intellectual in eighteenth-century historical-political discourses.[51] Yet with the onset of the institutionalization and professionalization of historical studies, they were pushed to the margins, as the profession became overwhelmingly male.[52] Even thereafter, however, women continued to play a prominent role as non-professional 'amateur' writers and as spouses/partners of professional male historians.[53] And in some cases women historians became prominent champions of women's rights and women's emancipation. Thus, for example, Irish female historians established a strong tradition of a politically committed engaged history on behalf of women's rights from the mid nineteenth century onwards.[54]

Whilst the political engagement of historians was manifold, it was the strong nationalist commitment of historiography that produced major tragedy for millions of people, as it contributed to the legitimation of forms of ethnic cleansing, genocide and war – fully coming into its own in the first half of the twentieth century. Emilia Salvanou in her chapter in this volume deals with the Ottoman Greeks, in particular the Thracian Greeks, who were forced to flee their homeland in the interwar period, after the failure of the Greek Megali idea (the idea of a greater Greece including the former western parts of the Greek settlement of the Ottoman Empire) at the end of World War I. In interwar Greece the refugees were widely associated with national shame, and their memories were excluded from the national imaginary. Yet representatives of those refugees were steadfastly seeking ways of representing their traumatic past within a wider Greek national historical narrative. They did so by forming history associations in which intellectuals, often associated with the refugee milieu, sought to progress memory and history work aimed at integrating the refugees' experience with broader Greek history and memory. Salvanou pays special attention in her chapter to the concept of nostalgia and argues that it was important to the refugees, as it allowed them to construct the past as one of 'cancelled potentials'. Overall, she contends that the refugees succeeded in integrating their history into the wider national history the more historians were ready to interpret the trauma of the Ottoman Greeks as a trauma of the entire Greek nation. The nationalization of history and memory alike thus not only produced the trauma in the first instance; it ironically also helped people to deal with it.[55] The Ottoman Greek diaspora in Greece is only one of several cases of forced migration and ethnic cleansing that have produced a string of politically committed historical accounts penned by historians keen to lend their pens to public forms of intervention.

So far this account of the relationship between political engagement and the historical sciences has been very Eurocentric. Yet, both history as a 'science' (in the sense of the German 'Wissenschaft') and nationalism were hugely successful export articles of the imperialist European states in the late nineteenth and early twentieth centuries.[56] Neither were adopted wholesale and straightforwardly copied in the non-Western world. Instead they were adapted and reformulated in complex processes of transnational receptions that still deserve far more attention in both the histories of historiography and the histories of nationalism. And the non-Western world would in turn write back and begin to influence Western understandings of historical writing and nationalism, most notably through the subaltern school of historians emanating from India in the 1980s and through the diverse reconceptualizations of the national idea and nationalism present in the processes of decolonization beginning in the interwar period and coming fully into their own in the post-World War II period.[57] In Egypt, for example, Cairo and the Ain Shams University became the undisputed centre of scholarly historical writing in the years after 1945, but the historians who worked there were at the same time politically committed and engaged. Their anti-colonialist nationalism had different ideological shades, and their political convictions differed, but they were in agreement on their perception of history being important beyond the academic ivory tower.[58]

In the present volume Xin Fan is dealing with one such case of the adaptation of Western historical and nationalist ideas in China. Focusing on the historian Lei Haizong and the so-called 'Zhanguo Ce Clique', he analyses their intellectual development in the light of the emergence of greater intellectual freedoms following the end of the Quing Empire in 1911. Although the tradition of writing history is a very old one in China, the 1910s and 1920s saw a strong reception of Western ideas of historical scholarship leading to processes of professionalization and institutionalization of historical studies in urban centres like Shanghai or Beijing. According to Xin Fan, the scholars most closely involved with those processes also adopted Western ideas, including nationalism, liberalism and modernity. In their history writing, they sought to trace and support the forces that were in line with their new-found *Weltanschauung*. Like in the West, notions of academic autonomy sat at best uneasily with ideas of political commitment, the latter especially to the force of nationalism. Fan exemplifies this through Lei Haizong, who was trained as a professional historian in China and the US, receiving his PhD from the University of Chicago before returning to China. Initially not enamoured by Chinese culture, he came to endorse strong nationalist ideas, including notions of the superiority of Chinese culture, in the context of the war against Japan in the 1930s and 1940s. He was, like other members of the 'Zhanguo Ce Clique', intellectually influenced by cyclical ideas of history championed by Oswald Spengler, and their strong political commitment found expression in support for Chiang Kai-shek.[59] Whilst the nationalist historiography continued to flourish under the Kuomintang in Taiwan after 1949, the victory of communism on the Chinese mainland meant that Marxist-Leninist and, increasingly, Maoist perspectives on history ruled supreme amongst communist historians in China. The Cold War had produced two historiographical traditions that are currently engaged in an intriguing dialogue about the future of Chinese historical thinking.[60]

In Europe, like in China, the memoryscape of World War II was very differently reconfigured by the Cold War in different parts of the continent. In communist Eastern Europe, it was contextualized within the anti-fascist struggle led by communist parties who fought in fascism the most aggressive political form of the economic system of capitalism. That the Soviet Union was during a brief period allied to the most aggressive form of fascism, National Socialism, and had agreed with its representatives the carving up of spheres of interest in Eastern Europe was comprehensively silenced both in the general memory discourse and in the more specific historiographical discourse during the Cold War.[61] In the capitalist West, by contrast, the history of World War II was seen within the dominant paradigm of totalitarianism. In this narrative, beleaguered liberal democracies of the interwar period had a hard time fighting both totalitarian temptations – that of fascism and that of communism. During World War II the fascist variant could only be defeated by an alliance of the strongest and most stable liberal democracies of the West with Soviet communism, but after the war, the remaining totalitarianism, that of communism, became the new adversary of the liberal democratic order of the West.[62]

Yet before the establishment of such a clear Cold War binary world, many European countries witnessed major economic and social challenges to existing liberal-democratic capitalist orders at the end of World War II.[63] Nowhere did those challenges result in a regime change, not least because the liberal capitalist West invested heavily in keeping those regions, where the Red Army was not in control, outside of the influence of communism. In Greece this led to a protracted and bloody civil war that followed World War II and in which the strong communist resistance to the fascist occupation of Greece in the World War II was defeated by those in favour of a liberal capitalist restitution after the war. Manos Avgeridis's chapter in this volume draws attention to the case of the historian and public intellectual Christopher Montague Woodhouse. His manifold publications on

Greece during World War II and the immediate postwar period stressed the insignificance of the Greek resistance to the outcome of World War II. Furthermore, he underlined the importance of the British intervention in Greece, starting from 1944, for the eventual defeat of communism and for keeping the country within the realm of the 'liberal West'. His theses provoked a huge debate in Greece, which is examined in detail by Avgeridis. It is interesting to note that Woodhouse's championing of a professional, 'objective' history jarred badly with his own very partisan political engagement as a historian.

The case of Woodhouse is an intriguing one, not just because of what it tells us about the construction of wider Cold War historical narratives but also because it points to the continued existence and importance of the 'amateur' or 'half professional' in European history writing during the second half of the twentieth century. Woodhouse can be regarded as a professional historian, having studied history and later filling the post as general director at the Royal Institute for Foreign Affairs in London. Yet he had also been at different points in his life a diplomat, a member of parliament (for the Conservative Party) and a businessman. He was thus not a million miles removed from many nineteenth-century historians who were also multitaskers, occupying a vast range of professional positions during their lifetimes, including those of journalists, politicians, diplomats, even bishops and government ministers. The histories of the professionalization of the historical discipline emphasize that these existences of nineteenth-century historians who fulfilled many roles and inhabited a range of different professions during their lifetimes gave way to the fully professionalized historians who, after having received theirtraining at university, underwent a lengthy cursus honorum that would set them on their paths to becoming professional historians with their own distinct habitus and their own communities, networks and institutions. The movement between professions allegedly became increasingly rare. Whilst this is on balance a fair description of professionalization and its consequences, we still often find that historians engaged as intellectuals defied this trend and continued to occupy multiple roles in society. In the light of this finding, it would merit further investigation as to what extent the decisions of historians to become public intellectuals worked against their sole definition as members of a professional and institutionalized community.

During the Cold War, historians as public intellectuals could be found on both sides of the Iron Curtain. Nina Witoszek in her contribution to the volume discusses the role of Polish historians such as Bronisław Geremek, Adam Michnik and Jacek Kuroń, in the Polish revolution of the 1980s. Contributing in a major way to the oppositional Workers' Defence Committee (KOR) in communist Poland, they came to exemplify how intellectuals could support a humanist agenda. In 1976, when the KOR was founded, it began to erect a 'parallel polis' and a 'republic of friendship' in Poland, including a Flying University. Without its historians as engaged intellectuals, Witoszek argues, Solidarnosc might well have just remained a workers' strike movement, as it had already occurred in Poland before. Public intellectuals like Kuroń pushed the movement further, in the direction of fighting tyranny. They established dialogic orientation in the parallel polis of Solidarnosc, which, Witoszek argues, amounted to an actualization of the res publica literarum of the Renaissance.[64]

The appearance of Solidarnosc marked and was itself a symbol of a deep political crisis in Polish society. The political engagement of historians is often particularly prominent at times of political crisis. When a specific political movement appears that raises prominent political demands, historians feel called upon to react and either oppose or support those movements with historical expertise that can justify or undermine those movements. In the nineteenth century, as we have seen above, the synergies between national movements and history writing were considerable. Many historians identified wholeheartedly with various forms of nationalism. In the twentieth century, the world wars as well as the political battles between liberal democracies, fascisms and communisms also were moments of mobilization for historians as political intellectuals. In England, liberal historians such as George Trevelyan wrote political speeches and campaigned in public for the liberal political values that they saw enshrined in British history and endangered on the European continent.[65] In France, the father figures of the Annales, Lucien Febvre and Marc Bloch, as well as their admired Übervater, Henri Pirenne, also defended a republican and liberal political ideal against the temptations of a deeply nationalist and right-wing historiography that ruled the day in much of interwar Europe. Pirenne had already called on the historical profession to 'unlearn' history from the Germans after World War I, as he was shocked by the nationalist commitments of German historians in that war.[66] Bloch joined the Resistance during World War II and was killed by the Gestapo for his political choice. He also penned a number of reflections on the historian's craft that have retained their inspirational value to this day.[67]

Yet many historians in the interwar period also committed themselves to the causes of fascism, right-wing authoritarianism and communism – all claiming to supersede the liberal ideas of the nineteenth century. Whilst few historians in Germany were committed National Socialists, many failed to oppose the dictatorship. Some might have been glad at the end of an unloved Weimar Republic; some might have felt proud of the foreign policy successes of the National Socialists in the 1930s; not a few were enamoured by the early successes of the German Wehrmacht in World

War II. The conservative mainstream of the German historical profession had accommodated themselves to the dictatorship, supporting it in parts and paying lip service to the National Socialist regime, performing its historical 'services' where required. A younger group of historians, committed to *Volksgeschichte*, went further in their support for the regime. Historians involved in German Ostforschung and German Westforschung were part and parcel of the National Socialist attempt to restructure the map of Europe in the context of World War II, and they helped the regime to plan and execute ethnic cleansings and expansionist schemes.[68]

Like in National Socialist Germany, in fascist Italy we also find few out-and-out apologists for fascism, even if many historians had sympathies for the regime and were happy to cooperate with it.[69] Historians also supported the right-wing authoritarian dictatorships that were established in the Iberian peninsula in the interwar period. In Portugal, under the military dictatorship and the Estado Novo, they promoted a traditionalist vision of the nation's past, celebrating the Age of Discoveries and Portugal's golden age whilst silencing the traditions of Portuguese liberalism.[70] In Francoist Spain, those regarded as disloyal to Francoism were purged from the universities in 1939. It is estimated that about one third of all historians lost their job, and many of them had to go into exile. Those in support of Franco promoted a history writing that emphasized the positive role of Catholicism in Spanish history – betraying the strong influence of the ultra-Catholic Opus Dei on higher education in Spain during the Franco years.[71]

After 1917, the victory of Bolshevism in the Soviet Union saw the complete restructuring of the Russian historical profession in the 1920s and 1930s. Historians loyal to the communist regime saw history as a weapon in the struggle for communism and developed a position according to which historians had to be partisan and on the side of the progressive forces in history. The old idea of objectivity was replaced with that of partisanship. Bourgeois historians, critical of Bolshevism, were purged, exiled, imprisoned and killed. Under Stalin, the historical profession was further streamlined, and the critical methodological and theoretical arsenal of Marxist thought became a dull and simplistic ideological straitjacket.[72] Outside of the Soviet Union, Marxist thought inspired a range of historians who tended to combine their historical work with political engagement on behalf of communism and allied causes. The Communist Party Historians' Group in Britain, including the likes of, among others, Eric Hobsbawm, E.P. Thompson, Dona Torr and Raphael Samuel is a good example of more productive forms of Marxism in historical writing, as is the work of French historians of the Great Revolution, like Albert Soboul.[73]

In the post-1945 world, the chiffre of 1968 signifies another key moment of political crisis in which historians were again prominent, albeit to very different degrees and under very different circumstances in diverse parts of the world.[74] In the West, critical historians aimed at increasing their influence over the Academy and promoted the writing of an engaged history as part and parcel of a strong intervention of historians in civil society.[75] Although it could at times appear as though they were more concerned with internal factional struggles between different shades of Marxism and the New Left, 1968 undoubtedly saw a strong mobilization of engaged leftwing intellectuals.[76] In the communist East, 1968 as a crisis year had entirely different connotations from its meanings in the capitalist West. Yet, if we take the example of 1968 in Czechoslovakia, it was also a time of intense historical debate when historians decided to take a stance in favour of political reform. Many of them paid a heavy price when that reform movement was crushed by Soviet tanks. The memory of 1968 was in fact so divisive in Czech history circles that the post-1989 transition saw the settling of many old scores in what often became very ugly public debates about individual historians and their implication in relegations and other discriminations suffered by Czech historians after 1968.[77]

In this volume Michihiro Okamoto discusses the case of Japan, where a group of young historians aligned themselves with the student protest movement, and in founding the journal *Social Movement History* (*SMH*) sought to contribute to their political struggles. They influenced the turn of Japanese historiography to everyday life history and to anthropological perspectives. Furthermore, they played an important role in importing Western ideas, including Annales scholarship from France and critical Marxist approaches, such as those championed by E.P. Thompson in Britain. Okamoto's chapter brings to the fore the issue of how historical work itself can be a contribution to political struggles. A particular way of seeing the past, analysing it and making it visible have political implications that go far beyond the realm of scholarship. It is not by chance that many of the leading historians of the Annales have been for many generations also the lead commentators on politics in French newspapers and other media, whilst the role of E.P. Thompson as a transnational peace activist is another prominent example of the direct relationship between historical work and political action.[78]

Historians as engaged intellectuals have at times been in the forefront of protest movements, mobilizing dissent, but they were also at times known for their role as bridge-builders between different ideologies and in diverse political conflicts. I can think of a no more impressive example of both forms of political engagement than Georg G. Iggers, who provides to this volume what he calls a 'personal retrospective' to his own life as a historian and engaged intellectual. A refugee from National Socialist Germany at the age of twelve, he effectively made his life and his career in North America, where eventually he ended up as a distinguished professor of history, writing books that have become classics and that are widely respected and admired among his peers. Always in close partnership with his wife, Wilma Iggers, herself a distinguished historian of the Czech and Slovak lands, he also performed the role of the historian as engaged intellectual, first by supporting the civil rights movement and the anti-Vietnam War campaign in the US[79] and later by building bridges between East and West German historiography during the Cold War. Well into his 80s, he was one of the first American historians to build bridges to the historical profession in Cuba, for so long isolated from the West. It is particularly intriguing to observe in his contribution how he relates his historical research to particular ethical and normative positions that also guided his political activism. Although he was not a historian of the civil rights movement, the anti-Vietnam War movement, the Cold War or Cuba, his work, first on democratic socialism and later on German historiography, was informed by similar sentiments and motivations that guided his political work, in particular his strong humanistic and democratic convictions.[80]

Throughout his life, Iggers has been a strong champion of human rights. In this respect, there is a firm connection between his chapter and that of Nina Schneider, who discusses the entanglements of professional historical writing and human rights activism in the twenty-first century. She refers to the case of Elazar Barkan, a contemporary leading scholar on human rights, who has consistently demanded that historians 'abandon their ivory towers' and become involved in the 'cause of reconciliation'. He believes that scholars, who are also historical activists, could promote a 'shared narrative' that would form the basis for reconciliation in conflicts involving contestation about the past. Based on Barkan's assumptions, Schneider investigates Brazil as a country divided by historical memory of the military dictatorship that ruled between 1964 and 1985. The Brazilian case, in her view, shows how problematic Barkan's notion of history work as work of reconciliation is, for what Brazil needs is not a shared narrative between former perpetrators and former victims but an engaged history that is both truthful and begins to acknowledge the victims' struggle against the dictatorship. In particular, she assesses the work of the truth commission (2012–2014) against the background of a benchmark that sees historical writing as supporting human rights, even if she has to admit that she herself is not sure how to narrativize such historical writing.

Meize Lucas's chapter also deals with the Brazilian dictatorship and its censorship of history in historical films. She shows how the anti-communist framework of the Brazilian state and its obsession with 'national unity' had implications for which representations of the past were allowed to show up on the big screen. Any references to religious and social conflicts tended to be cut out by the censors, who were also not shy to ban whole films, including those produced outside of Brazil. Lucas gives us several intriguing examples of how popular histories, represented through film, were seen as a major threat to the dictatorship, underlining to what extent public history was seen as a resource for politics by representatives of the dictatorial state in Brazil.

Truth commissions, such as the one in Brazil, deal with traumatic pasts in the hope that their work will bring about some form of reconciliation. The past is brought out in the open. Testimonies are heard from victims, bystanders and perpetrators, and the public discussions that ensue are thought of as contributing to some form of societal healing process. It is interesting to note that many truth commissions have not included historians in the list of those who are being heard. Historical evidence as the basis of some sort of historical truth is apparently not part of the remit of truth commissions.[81] This indicates that history might not in fact work in the direction of healing but rather in the direction of keeping historical wounds open.

The recognition that history might in fact stand in the way of reconciliation has led to the conscious destruction of historical archives seen as holding unpalatable and unwanted knowledge of the past. It is a well-known fact that failed governments who see themselves under threat of being deposed or overthrown have, time and again, tried to destroy archives and files, mostly in order to prevent knowledge of things that would reflect badly on the government or individuals working for it. Wars and civil wars have repeatedly led to the loss and destruction of archives.[82] One of the most comprehensive undertakings was the destruction of files by the East German state in the midst of the East German revolution of 1989 and the toppling of its communist regime. The reaction of the post-revolutionary state can also be regarded as one of the most noteworthy in history. It decided to invest considerable resources and energy in trying to put together again hundreds of thousands of documents that had been destroyed by the East German secret police and other government agencies.[83] Yet it is one thing for a failed government to destroy archives and quite another for a successor government of a failed one to order the destruction of archives seen as endangering national reconciliation. In this volume, Vangelis Karamanolakis is analysing just such a case that happened in Greece in 1989, precisely the year in which the East German files were destroyed.

But in Greece this did not happen in the midst of a revolution and under secrecy but following a very public debate on what to do with 17 million police and intelligence files that had been assembled on ordinary citizens during the years of the Greek dictatorship. The files had been closed to historians after the junta had come to an end in the 1970s and the country transitioned to democracy. In fact, as Karamanolakis points out, the post-dictatorship phase in Greek history was an extremely fruitful and energetic one for Greek history writing. Historians played a prominent role in public debates about national and social identities in Greek society. New history journals were established and the profession flourished. Professionalism was strong, with many historians feeling that after the distortions of history under the dictatorship, it was their task to return to a myth- and ideology-free history that would reliably inform the public about the past. However, there were also, especially among Greek left-wing historians, prominent ideas about history as an emancipatory idea that would help bring about social change in Greek society. Greek historical culture saw lively debates on twentieth-century Greek history, including its history during World War II and the Greek civil war. The topic of the military junta was also a prominent one, although it is interesting to observe that the debate on what to do with the secret police files only erupted with a delay of almost fifteen years. Furthermore, it was the government and not the historians starting the debate with the decision to destroy these files. They were seen as endangering social peace in Greece, as they contained information that was deeply upsetting to millions of Greek citizens. As Karamanolakis writes, historians were the main opposition to the burning of those files. They argued that they were a unique source for Greek history under the dictatorship. Whilst they accepted that access should perhaps be prohibited for some time to come and whilst they also agreed that access would have to be strictly limited and controlled, they argued that national reconciliation would not be possible without those files, as they contained access to many rifts that had gone through many Greek families and the entire fabric of Greek society during the years of the dictatorship. Yet, as Karamanolakis also observes, the historians lost the public debate. Opinion polls clearly indicate that a majority of Greek citizens were in favour of the proposed government action, fearing misuse of the files and the return of a past that many were happy to repress. The case detailed here raises many interesting questions, not least about the extent to which history can help or hinder reconciliation and how it may perform a useful function in processes of coming to terms with traumatic memory.

The loss of archives is definitely a major problem for historical research. After all, archives are an integral part of social memory and form the basis on which contestation over the past can be fought out authoritatively. The archivist is a key 'activist in the production of (historical) knowledge'.[84] Arguably, another problem is the enormous proliferation of archives in the digital age. The impact of digitalization, also, has important consequences for historians as engaged intellectuals, as Effi Gazi argues in her chapter. Digital media make it much easier to intervene in society and bring history into political debates. They have also produced a step change in how historians do, present and perform historical research. Digital archives have their own challenges and problems with regard to decisions about what is going to be saved and uploaded in the digital repositories of the future. The consequences of all this are highly contested: while some commentators declare the 'democratization of history', others bemoan the end of 'concrete historical narratives'. Undoubtedly, the digital revolution poses new questions regarding 'usable' and 'disposable' pasts and the relationship of history with memory.[85]

Several contributions to this volume make reference to public uses of history that go far beyond professional history discourses, even if they are often influenced by them. The chapter by Antonis Liakos discusses a particularly prominent example of public history in the recent past, namely the use of history by the Occupy movement. With special reference to Greece and the Greek financial crisis between 2008 and 2011, Liakos analyses political slogans and visual images, such as graffiti in public spaces. He points out how images were often transferred from earlier protest movements to the present one, providing the Occupy movement with memoryscapes of past movements and mobilizations on which it could build.[86] The memory of past struggles allowed the Occupy movement to construct political traditions and create a usable past for its present political struggles. Quite apart from the transfer of images and slogans from past protest movements, Liakos also points to the contemporary transfer of political slogans and images from other antiglobal protest movements. He points out that one of the strongest resources for protesters was the national past, which was reinterpreted to support the protesters' arguments. Analogical historical thinking was strongly present in the protests. Thus past political enemies tended to be equated with present ones; for example, in the identification of the troika with the military junta in Greece. Overall, he concludes the uses of history allowed the protesters to construct an alternative vision of the future. The present was endowed with utopian energy by reference to the past.

All contributions to this volume highlight how the practitioners of history have contributed as public intellectuals to historically informed political debates in various contexts. History was and continues to be an important resource for political agendas and mobilizations, and those whose job it is to interpret the past therefore have felt or have been called upon to engage with those agendas and mobilizations. Historians cannot ignore politics, nor can politics ignore historians. However, the most powerful way in which history is politically and socially engaged may not be through an overt political commitment but simply by, as Richard Rorty has suggested, following its disciplinary guidelines in an honest way.[87] In a similar fashion, Jo Tollebeek has hailed a certain aimless historicist curiosity as the most effective political intervention, as it allows the historian to fully consider the otherness of the past that might well work as a potent criticism of the present, avoiding the presentist desire to put the contemporary frameworks of reference as absolute.[88]

Stefan Berger is Professor of Social History and Director of the Institute for Social Movements at Ruhr University, Bochum, in Germany. He is also executive chair of the Foundation History of the Ruhr and an Honorary Professor at Cardiff University in the UK. He has published widely on the history of historiography, historical theory, memory studies, the history of social movements and the history of deindustrialization as well as the history of British-German relations. Among his most recent books are *History and Belonging: Representations of the Past in Contemporary European Politics* (Berghahn, 2018, edited with Caner Tekin) and *Palgrave Handbook of Research in Historical Culture and Education* (Palgrave Macmillan, 2017, edited with Mario Carretero and Maria Grever).

Notes

1. On professionalism and professionalization of the historical sciences see Torstendahl, *The Rise and Propagation of Historical Professionalism*. On scientificity in historical studies see also Feldner, 'The New Scientificity in Historical Writing around 1800', 3–21.

2. Halbwachs, *On Collective Memory*.

3. On the relationship between history and memory see Lorenz, 'Blurred Lines: History, Memory and the Experience of Time', 73–90; see also Lorenz, 'Drawing the Line: "Scientific History" between Myth-Making and Myth-Breaking', 35–55.

4. Kansteiner, 'Postmoderner Historismus'; Bédarida, 'The Historians' Craft, Historicity and Ethics', 69–76.

5. See, for example, Brown, *An Intellectual Biography*; Joyce and Zinn, *A Radical American Vision*.

6. Banner, *Being a Historian: An Introduction to the Professional World of History*, 158–66; Yerxa (ed.), *Recent Themes on Historians and the Public: Historians in Conversation*.

7. Tyrrell, *Historians in Public: The Practice of American History, 1890–1970*.

8. Posner, *Public Intellectuals: A Study of Decline*, chapter 8.

9. Vom Lehn, *Westdeutsche und italienische Historiker als Intellektuelle? Ihr Umgang mit Nationalsozialismus und Faschismus in den Massenmedien 1943/45–1960*.

10. DuBois, 'Long Live Radical History!', 91–92.

11. The literature on public history has exploded in recent years. See, for example, Lyon, Nix and Shrum, *Introduction to Public History: Interpreting the Past, Engaging Audiences*.

12. Zald and McCarthy, 'Organizational Intellectuals and the Criticism of Society', 97–120; Borg and Mayo, *Public Intellectuals, Radical Democracy and Social Movements: A Book of Interviews*; Baud and Rutten, *Popular Intellectuals and Social Movements: Framing Protest in Asia, Africa and Latin America (International Review of Social History Supplement 12)*; specifically on the relationship between labour movement historians and the construction of particular pasts as a form of political engagement see Irving and Scalmer, *Labour Historians as Labour Intellectuals: Generations and Crises*.

13. Morgan, *The Webbs and Soviet Communism*.

14. With relation to the American labour movement, see Green, *Taking History to Heart: The Power of the Past in Building Social Movements*.

15. See, for example, Hübinger and Hertfelder, *Kritik und Mandat: Intellektuelle in der deutschen Politik*, which is an outstanding volume, but it does not discuss a single historian.

16. Charle, *Naissance des Intellectuels: 1880–1900*; see also idem, *Les Intellectuels en Europe au XIX Siècle: Essai d'Histoire Comparée*. For a specifically French tradition see also Ory and Sirinelli, *Les Intellectuels en France dans l'Affaire Dreyfus à nos Jours*; for Britain see Collini, *Absent Minds: Intellectuals in Britain*; for Germany see Bering, *Die Intellektuellen: Geschichte eines Schimpfworts*; idem, *Die Epoche der Intellektuellen, 1898–2011: Geburt, Begriff, Grabmal*.

17. Hübinger, 'Die politischen Rollen europäischer Intellektueller im 20. Jahrhundert', 30–44.

18. Mannheim, *Ideologie und Utopie: Wissenssoziologische Untersuchungen*; Bourdieu, *Satz und Gegensatz: Über die Verantwortung der Intellektuellen*.

19. Schumpeter, *Kapitalismus, Sozialismus, Demokratie*, 237.

20. Weber, *Schriften 1915–1920: Die Wirtschaftsethik der Weltreligionen: Konfuzianismus und Taoismus*, 101.

21. Barraclough, 'History, Morals, and Politics', citation on p. 3.

22. Paul, 'The Epistemic Virtues of Historical Scholarship; or, the Moral Dimensions of a Scholarly Character', 371–87.

23. See also Rüsen, *Evidence and Meaning: A Theory of Historical Studies*.

24. On the intricate relationship between the judge and the historian and their common attempts to look at evindence, proof and testimony, see also the inspirational book by Ginzburg, *The Judge and the Historian: Marginal Notes on a Late Twentieth-Century Miscarriage of Justice*.

25. See also Pihlainen, *The Work of History: Constructivism and a Politics of the Past*.

26. See in particular White, *The Practical Past*. On Foucault's analysis of power as a basis for political engagement see Bové, *Intellectuals in Power: A Genealogy of Critical Humanism*, 209–37.

27. De Baets's *Responsible History* is an excellent discussion of how history was abused by politics and how historians carried out their professional duties and what they saw as their duty as citizens in the face of such abuses. See also De Baets, *Censorship of Political Thought: A World Guide, 1945–2000*, which documents the impact of censorship on historical and political thought. And De Baets, *Crimes against History*.

28. A recent special issue of *Storia della Storiografia* that goes back to a session held at the 2015 world historical congress engages with exile historiographies in different parts of the world. See Berger and De Baets, 'Reflections on Exile Historiographies', 11–26.

29. On the professionalization of the historical sciences in Europe see also Porciani and Raphael, *Atlas of European Historiography: The Making of a Profession, 1800–2005*; Porciani and Tollebeek, *Setting the Standards: Institutions, Networks and Communities of National Historiography*.

30. Clark, *Academic Charisma and the Origins of the Research University*.

31. I follow here John Pocock's suggestion to speak of Enlightenments rather than Enlightenment in order to highlight the simple fact that this movement had a very different character in different places. See Pocock, *Barbarism and Religion, vol. 1: The Enlightenments of Edward Gibbon 1737–1764*, 12. On the development of the European universities from the Enlightenment onwards, see Anderson, *European Universities from the Enlightenment to 1914*.

32. Von See, *Die Göttinger Sieben: Kritik einer Legende*.

33. Rousseau, 'Discourse on the Origins and Foundations of Inequality among Men', 84–86.

34. Abbatista, 'The Historical Thought of the French Philosophes', 406–27; Oz-Salzberger, *Translating the Enlightenment: Scottish Civic Discourse in Eighteenth-Century*

Germany; Grell, *L'histoire entre erudition et philosophie: étude sur la connaissance historique à l'âge des Lumières*; Reill, *The German Enlightenment and the Rise of Historicism*.

35. Berger and Conrad, *The Past as History: National Identity and Historical Consciousness in Modern Europe*, chapters 2 and 3.

36. Iggers, *The German Conception of History: The National Tradition of Historical Thought from Herder to the Present*; Gerhards, *Heinrich von Treitschke: Wirkung und Wahrnehmung eines Historikers im 19. Und 20. Jahrhundert*.

37. Plokhy, *Unmaking Imperial Russia: Mykhailo Hrushevsky and the Writing of Ukrainian History*; Prymak, *Mykhailo Hrushevsky: The Politics of National Culture*.

38. Tolz, *Russia: Inventing the Nation*, 172.

39. Cited in Gazi, 'Theorizing and Practising "Scientific History" in Southeastern Europe: Spyridon Lambos and Nicolae Iorga', 198.

40. Monod and Fagniez, 'Avant-Propos', 4.

41. Mycock and Loskoutova, 'Nation, State and Empire: The Historiography of "High Imperialism" in the British and Russian Empires', 233–58; Semyonov, 'Mirrors of Imperial Imagination in the Early Twentieth-Century Russian Empire', 139–52.

42. Blaas, *Continuity and Anachronism: Parliamentary and Constitutional Development in Whig Historiography and in the Anti-Whig Reaction between 1890 and 1930*; Hall, *Macaulay and Son: Architects of Imperial Britain*.

43. Von Klimó, *Nation, Konfession, Geschichte: Zur nationalen Geschichtskultur Ungarns im europäischen Kontext (1860–1948)*, 37; Fiszman, *Constitution and Reform in Eighteenth-Century Poland: The Constitution of 3 May 1791*; on variants of liberal political commitment of historians in East-Central Europe see also Báar, *Historians and Nationalism: East-Central Europe in the Nineteenth Century*.

44. Loubère, *Louis Blanc: His Life and His Contribution to the Rise of French Jacobin-Socialism*, chapter 14.

45. Deneckere and Welskopp, 'The "Nation" and "Class": European National Master Narratives and their Social "Other"', 135–70.

46. Bentley, *Modernizing England's Past: English Historiography in the Age of Modernism*, 45–69.

47. Hermann and Metzger, 'A Truculent Revenge: The Clergy and the Writing of National History', 313–29.

48. Den Boer, 'Deux aspects de l'historiographie aux Pays-Bas et en France vers 1900: le rôle des facultés de théologie et la non-intervention de l'État', 117.

49. Klimó, *Nation*, 92–130.

50. Weichlein, '"Meine Peitsche ist die Feder": Populäre katholische Geschichtsschreibung im 19. und 20. Jahrhundert', 227–58.

51. Hill, *The Republican Virago: The Life and Times of Catherine Macaulay, Historian*.

52. B.G. Smith, *The Gender of History: Men, Women and Historical Practice*.

53. Melman, 'Gender, History and Memory: The Invention of Women's Past in the Nineteenth and Early Twentieth Centuries', 5–41; Porciani, *History Women*, special issue of *Storia della Storiografia* 46.

54. N.C. Smith, *A 'Manly Study'? Irish Women Historians 1868–1949*.

55. For the context of the development of Greek historiography, see Gazi, *Scientific National History: The Greek Case in Comparative Perspective*.

56. Berger, *Writing National Histories: A Global Perspective*.

57. Majumdar, *Writing Postcolonial History*; Chatterjee, *Nationalist Thought and the Colonial World: A Derivative Discourse*.

58. Gorman, *Historians, State and Politics in Twentieth-Century Egypt: Contesting the Nation*, 43f.

59. See also Schneider, *Nation and Ethnicity: Chinese Discourses on History, Historiography and Nationalism (1900s to 1920s)*.
60. Weigelin-Schwiedrzik, 'Chinese Historical Writing since 1949', 615–36.
61. Antohi, Trencsényi and Apor, *Narratives Unbound: Historical Studies in Post-Communist Eastern Europe*.
62. Friedrich and Brezinski, *Totalitarian Dictatorship and Autocracy*; for the impact on West Germany see Fellner, 'Nationales und europäisch-atlantisches Geschichtsbild in der Bundesrepublik und im Westen in den Jahren nach dem Ende des Zweiten Weltkriegs', 213–26.
63. Berger and Boldorf, *Social Movements and the Change of Economic Elites in Europe after 1945*.
64. Zuzowksi, *Political Dissent and Opposition in Poland: The Workers' Defence Committee KOR*.
65. Hernon, 'The Last Whig Historian and Consensus History: George Macaulay Trevelyan 1876–1962', 66–97.
66. Schöttler, 'After the Deluge: The Impact of the Two World Wars on the Historical Work of Henri Pirenne and Marc Bloch', 404–25.
67. Bloch, *The Historian's Craft*.
68. There is, by now, an extensive literature on the political commitment of German historians under National Socialism. See, among others, Schönwälder, *Historiker und Politik: Geschichtswissenschaft im Nationalsozialismus*; Haar and Fahlbusch, *German Scholars and Ethnic Cleansing 1919–1945*.
69. Fogu, *The Historic Imaginary: Politics of History in Fascist Italy*.
70. Matos, *História, mitologia, imaginário nacional: a História no Curso dos Liceus (1895–1939)*.
71. Marin, *Los historiadores españoles en el franquismo 1948–1975*; Pasamar, *Apologia and Criticism: Historians and the History of Spain, 1500–2000*, chapter 3.
72. Banerij, *Writing History in the Soviet Union: Making the Past Work*.
73. Kaye, *The British Marxist Historians: An Introductory Analysis*; Kroll, *Kommunistische Intellektuelle in Westeuropa: Frankreich, Österreich, Italien und Grossbritannien im Vergleich 1945–1956*.
74. For 1968 as a global social movement see Horn, '1968: A Social Movement Sui Generis', 515–42.
75. For the US, see Dubermann, *Howard Zinn: A Life on the Left*, 155–80.
76. Green, 'Intellectuals and Activism: The Dilemma of the Radical Historian', 3–5, 28.
77. Rupnik, 'The Politics of History-Writing in Czechoslovakia', 166–68; Kolář and Kopeček, 'A Difficult Quest for New Paradigms: Czech Historiography after 1989', 173–310.
78. On the Annales, see Raphael, *Die Erben von Bloch und Febvre: Annales Geschichtsschreibung und nouvelle histoire in Frankreich, 1945–1980*; on E.P. Thompson, see Berger and Wicke, 'A Very Rooted Cosmopolitanism: E.P. Thompson's Englishness and His Transnational Activism'.
79. Also very interesting are the reflections by Michael Adas that all the historical expertise on Vietnam and South Asia had virtually no influence at all on the political decisions taken by the US government during the Vietnam War. This indicates that more than scholarship is needed to make historical knowledge productive in political contexts. See Adas, 'In Defence of Engagement: The Social Use of History in a Time of Intellectual Abdication', 141–56.
80. See also G. and W. Iggers, *Two Lives in Uncertain Times: Facing the Challenges of the Twentieth Century as Scholars and Citizens*.
81. Scheuzger, 'Truth Commissions and the Politics of History: A Critical Appraisal'.

82. International Council on Archives, *Memory of the World at Risk: Archives Destroyed, Archives Reconstituted*; Spurr, 'Iraqi Libraries and Archives in Peril', 273ff.
83. For details see http://www.bstu.bund.de/DE/Archive/RekonstruktionUnterlagen/_node.html (last accessed 11 August 2017).
84. Blouin and Rosenberg, *Processing the Past: Contesting Authority in History and the Archives*, chapter 8.
85. See also Weller, *History in the Digital Age*; Rosenzweig, *Clio Wired: The Future of the Past in the Digital Age*.
86. On the concept of memoryscapes see Phillips and Reyes, *Global Memoryscapes: Contesting Remembrance in a Transnational Age*.
87. Rorty, 'Afterword', 197–204.
88. Tollebeek, '"Italian" History versus French Heritage: Cultural Criticism, Positivism, and Political Commitment in Taine', 125–40.

Bibliography

Abbatista, G. 'The Historical Thought of the French Philosophes', in J. Rabasa, M. Sato, E. Tortarolo and D. Woolf (eds), *Oxford History of Historical Writing*, vol. 3 (Oxford: Oxford University Press, 2012), 406–27.
Adas, M. 'In Defence of Engagement: The Social Use of History in a Time of Intellectual Abdication', in J. Leerssen and A. Rigney (eds), *History* (Amsterdam: Amsterdam University Press, 2000), 141–56.
Anderson, R.D. *European Universities from the Enlightenment to 1914*. Oxford: Oxford University Press, 2004.
Antohi, S., B. Trencsényi and P. Apor (eds). *Narratives Unbound: Historical Studies in Post-Communist Eastern Europe*. Budapest: Central European University Press, 2007.
Báar, M. *Historians and Nationalism: East-Central Europe in the Nineteenth Century*. Oxford: Oxford University Press, 2010.
Banerij, A. *Writing History in the Soviet Union: Making the Past Work*. New Delhi: Social Science Press, 2008.
Banner, J.M. *Being a Historian: An Introduction to the Professional World of History*. Cambridge: Cambridge University Press, 2012.
Barraclough, G. 'History, Morals, and Politics', *International Affairs* 34(1) (1958), 1–15.
Baud, M. and R. Rutten (eds). *Popular Intellectuals and Social Movements: Framing Protest in Asia, Africa and Latin America* (*International Review of Social History* Supplement 12). Cambridge: Cambridge University Press, 2004.
Bédarida, F. 'The Historians' Craft, Historicity and Ethics', in J. Leerssen and A. Rigney (eds), *Historians and Social Values* (Amsterdam: Amsterdam University Press, 2000), 69–76.
Bentley, M. *Modernizing England's Past: English Historiography in the Age of Modernism*. Cambridge: Cambridge University Press, 2005.
Berger, S. (ed.). *Writing National Histories: A Global Perspective*. Basingstoke: Palgrave Macmillan, 2007.
Berger, S. and M. Boldorf (eds). *Social Movements and the Change of Economic Elites in Europe after 1945*. Basingstoke: Palgrave Macmillan, 2018.
Berger, S. and C. Conrad. *The Past as History: National Identity and Historical Consciousness in Modern Europe*. Basingstoke: Palgrave Macmillan, 2015.
Berger, S. and A. De Baets. 'Reflections on Exile Historiographies', *Storia della Storiografia* 69 (2016), 11–26.

Berger, S. and C. Wicke. 'A Very Rooted Cosmopolitanism: E.P. Thompson's Englishness and His Transnational Activism', in S. Berger and S. Scalmer (eds), *Transnational Activism and Social Movements: A History*. Basingstoke: Palgrave Macmillan, 2018.

Bering, D. *Die Intellektuellen: Geschichte eines Schimpfworts*. Stuttgart: Klett-Cotta, 1982.

———. *Die Epoche der Intellektuellen, 1898–2011: Geburt, Begriff, Grabmal*. Berlin: Berliner Universitätsverlag, 2010.

Blaas, P.B.M. *Continuity and Anachronism: Parliamentary and Constitutional Development in Whig Historiography and in the Anti-Whig Reaction between 1890 and 1930*. The Hague: Martinus Nijhoff, 1978.

Bloch, M. *The Historian's Craft*. New York: Alfred A. Knopf, 1954.

Borg, C. and P. Mayo (eds). *Public Intellectuals, Radical Democracy and Social Movements: A Book of Interviews*. Bern: Peter Lang, 2007.

Blouin, F.X, Jr and W.G. Rosenberg. *Processing the Past: Contesting Authority in History and the Archives*. Oxford: Oxford University Press, 2011.

Bourdieu, P. *Satz und Gegensatz: Über die Verantwortung der Intellektuellen*. Frankfurt am Main: Suhrkamp, 1993.

Bové, P. *Intellectuals in Power: A Genealogy of Critical Humanism*. New York: Columbia University Press, 1986.

Brown, D.S. *R. Hofstadter: An Intellectual Biography*. Chicago: University of Chicago Press, 2006.

Charle, C. *Naissance des Intellectuels: 1880–1900*. Paris: Les Editions de Minuits, 1990.

———. *Les Intellectuels en Europe au XIX Siècle: Essai d'Histoire Comparée*. Paris: Le Seuil, 2012.

Chatterjee, P. *Nationalist Thought and the Colonial World: A Derivative Discourse*. London: Zed Books, 1986.

Clark, W. *Academic Charisma and the Origins of the Research University*. Chicago: The University of Chicago Press, 2006.

Collini, S. *Absent Minds: Intellectuals in Britain*. Oxford: Oxford University Press, 2006.

De Baets, A. *Censorship of Political Thought: A World Guide, 1945–2000*. Westport, CT: Greenwood Press, 2002.

———. *Responsible History*. Oxford: Berghahn, 2009.

———. *Crimes against History*. London: Routledge, 2019.

Den Boer, P. 'Deux aspects de l'historiographie aux Pays-Bas et en France vers 1900: le rôle des facultés de théologie et la non-intervention de l'État', *Revista di Storia della Storiografia Moderna* 95(16) (1995), 117–25.

Deneckere, G. and T. Welskopp. 'The "Nation" and "Class": European National Master Narratives and their Social "Other"', in S. Berger and C. Lorenz (eds), *The Contested Nation: Ethnicity, Class, Religion and Gender in National Histories* (Basingstoke: Palgrave Macmillan, 2008), 135–70.

Dubermann, M. *Howard Zinn: A Life on the Left*. New York: The New Press, 2012.

DuBois, E.C. 'Long Live Radical History!' *Radical History Review* 79(1) (2001), 91–92.

Feldner, H. 'The New Scientificity in Historical Writing around 1800', in S. Berger, H. Feldner and K. Passmore (eds), *Writing History: Theory and Practice*, 2nd ed. (London: Bloomsbury, 2010), 3–21.

Fellner, F. 'Nationales und europäisch-atlantisches Geschichtsbild in der Bundesrepublik und im Westen in den Jahren nach dem Ende des Zweiten Weltkriegs', in E. Schulin (ed.), *Deutsche Geschichtswissenschaft nach dem Zweiten Weltkrieg, 1945–1965* (Munich: Oldenbourg, 1989), 213–26.

Fiszman, S. (ed.). *Constitution and Reform in Eighteenth-Century Poland: The Constitution of 3 May 1791*. Bloomington: Indiana University Press, 1997.

Fogu, C. *The Historic Imaginary: Politics of History in Fascist Italy*. Toronto: University of Toronto Press, 2003

Friedrich, C.J. and Z.K. Brezinski. *Totalitarian Dictatorship and Autocracy*. Cambridge, MA: Harvard University Press, 1956.

Gazi, E. *Scientific National History: The Greek Case in Comparative Perspective*. Frankfurt am Main: Peter Lang, 2000.

———. 'Theorizing and Practising "Scientific History" in Southeastern Europe: Spyridon Lambos and Nicolae Iorga', in S. Berger and C. Lorenz (eds), *Nationalizing the Past: Historians as Nation Builders in Modern Europe*. Basingstoke: Palgrave MacMillan, 2010.

Gerhards, T. *Heinrich von Treitschke: Wirkung und Wahrnehmung eines Historikers im 19. und 20. Jahrhundert*. Paderborn: Ferdinand Schöningh, 2013.

Ginzburg, C. *The Judge and the Historian: Marginal Notes on a Late Twentieth-Century Miscarriage of Justice*. London: Verso, 1999.

Gorman, A. *Historians, State and Politics in Twentieth-Century Egypt: Contesting the Nation*. London: Routledge, 2003.

Green, J. 'Intellectuals and Activism: The Dilemma of the Radical Historian', *The Activist: A Student Journal of Politics and Opinion* 11(2) (1970–1971), 3–5.

———. *Taking History to Heart: The Power of the Past in Building Social Movements*. Amherst: University of Massachusetts Press, 2000.

Grell, C. *L'histoire entre erudition et philosophie: étude sur la connaissance historique à l'âge des Lumières*. Paris: Presses Universitaires de France, 1993.

Haar I. and M. Fahlbusch (eds). *German Scholars and Ethnic Cleansing 1919–1945*. Oxford: Berghahn, 2005.

Halbwachs, M. *On Collective Memory*. Chicago: The University of Chicago Press, 1992.

Hall, C. *Macaulay and Son: Architects of Imperial Britain*. New Haven, CT: Yale University Press, 2012.

Hermann, I. and F. Metzger. 'A Truculent Revenge: The Clergy and the Writing of National History', in I. Porciani and J. Tollebeek (eds), *Setting the Standards: Institutions, Networks and Communities of National Historiography* (Basingstoke: Palgrave Macmillan, 2012), 313–29.

Hernon, J.M, Jr. 'The Last Whig Historian and Consensus History: George Macaulay Trevelyan 1876–1962', *American Historical Review* 81 (1976), 66–97.

Hill, B. *The Republican Virago: The Life and Times of Catherine Macaulay, Historian*. Oxford: Oxford University Press, 1992.

Horn, G.-R. '1968: A Social Movement Sui Generis', in S. Berger and H. Nehring (eds), *The History of Social Movements in Global Perspective: A Survey* (Basingstoke: Palgrave Macmillan, 2017), 515–42.

Hübinger, G. 'Die politischen Rollen europäischer Intellektueller im 20. Jahrhundert', in G. Hübinger and T. Hertfelder (eds), *Kritik und Mandat: Intellektuelle in der deutschen Politik* (Stuttgart: DVA, 2000), 30–44.

Hübinger, G. and T. Hertfelder (eds). *Kritik und Mandat: Intellektuelle in der deutschen Politik*. Stuttgart: DVA, 2000.

Iggers, G.G. *The German Conception of History: The National Tradition of Historical Thought from Herder to the Present*, revised ed. Middletown, CT: Wesleyan University Press, 1983.

Iggers, G. and W. Iggers. *Two Lives in Uncertain Times: Facing the Challenges of the Twentieth Century as Scholars and Citizens*. Oxford: Berghahn, 2006.

International Council on Archives. *Memory of the World at Risk: Archives Destroyed, Archives Reconstituted*. Munich: De Gruyter, 1996.

Irving, T. and S. Scalmer (eds). *Labour Historians as Labour Intellectuals: Generations and Crises*. Melbourne: Melbourne University Press, 1999.

Joyce, D.D. *Howard Zinn: A Radical American Vision*. New York: Prometheus, 2003.

Kansteiner, W. 'Postmoderner Historismus: Das kulturelle Gedächtnis als neues Paradigma der Kulturwissenschaften', in F. Jäger and J. Straub (eds), *Handbuch der Kulturwissenschaften*, vol. 2: *Paradigmen und Disziplinen*, Stuttgart: Metzler, 2004, 119–139.

Kaye, H.J. *The British Marxist Historians: An Introductory Analysis*. Cambridge: Cambridge University Press, 1994.

Kolář, P. and M. Kopeček. 'A Difficult Quest for New Paradigms: Czech Historiography after 1989', in S. Antohi, B. Trencsényi and P. Apor (eds), *Narratives Unbound: Historical Studies in Post-Communist Eastern Europe* (Budapest: Central European University Press, 2007), 173–310.

Kroll, T. *Kommunistische Intellektuelle in Westeuropa: Frankreich, Österreich, Italien und Grossbritannien im Vergleich 1945–1956*. Cologne: Böhlau, 2007.

Lorenz, C. 'Drawing the Line: "Scientific History" between Myth-Making and Myth-Breaking', in S. Berger, L. Eriksonas and A. Mycock (eds), *Narrating the Nation: Representations in History, Media and the Arts* (Oxford: Berghahn, 2008), 35–55.

———. 'Blurred Lines: History, Memory and the Experience of Time', in S. Berger and J. Seiffert (eds), *Erinnerungsorte: Chancen, Grenzen und Perspektiven eines Erfolgskonzeptes in den Kulturwissenschaften* (Essen: Klartext, 2014), 73–90.

Loubère, L.A. *Louis Blanc: His Life and His Contribution to the Rise of French Jacobin-Socialism*. Evanston, IL: Northwestern University Press, 1961.

Lyon, C.M., E.M. Nix and R.K. Shrum (eds). *Introduction to Public History: Interpreting the Past, Engaging Audiences*. Lanham, MD: Rowman & Littlefield, 2017.

Majumdar, R. *Writing Postcolonial History*. London: Bloomsbury Academic, 2010.

Mannheim, K. *Ideologie und Utopie: Wissenssoziologische Untersuchungen*. Frankfurt am Main: Suhrkamp, 1985 [1929].

Marin, M.A. *Los historiadores españoles en el franquismo 1948–1975*. Zaragoza: IFC, 2005.

Matos, S.C. *História, mitologia, imaginário nacional: a História no Curso dos Liceus (1895–1939)*. Lisbon: Livros Horizonte, 1990.

Melman, B. 'Gender, History and Memory: The Invention of Women's Past in the Nineteenth and Early Twentieth Centuries', *History and Memory* 5 (1993), 5–41.

Monod, G. and G. Fagniez. 'Avant-Propos', *Revue Historique* 1(1) (1876), 1–4.

Morgan, K. *The Webbs and Soviet Communism*. London: Lawrence & Wishart, 2006.

Mycock, A. and M. Loskoutova. 'Nation, State and Empire: The Historiography of "High Imperialism" in the British and Russian Empires', in S. Berger and C. Lorenz (eds), *Nationalizing the Past* (London: Palgrave Macmillan, 2010), 233–58.

Ory, P. and J.-F. Sirinelli. *Les Intellectuels en France dans l'Affaire Dreyfus à nos Jours*. Paris: Armand Colin, 1986.

Oz-Salzberger, F. *Translating the Enlightenment: Scottish Civic Discourse in Eighteenth-Century Germany*. Oxford: Oxford University Press, 1995.

Pasamar, G. *Apologia and Criticism: Historians and the History of Spain, 1500–2000*. Bern: Peter Lang, 2010.

Paul, H. 'The Epistemic Virtues of Historical Scholarship; or, the Moral Dimensions of a Scholarly Character', *Soundings: An Interdisciplinary Journal* 91(3/4) (2008), 371–87.

Phillips, K.R. and G. Mitchell Reyes (eds). *Global Memoryscapes: Contesting Remembrance in a Transnational Age*. Tuscaloosa: The University of Alabama Press, 2011.

Pihlainen, K. *The Work of History: Constructivism and a Politics of the Past*. London: Routledge, 2017.

Plokhy, S. *Unmaking Imperial Russia: Mykhailo Hrushevsky and the Writing of Ukrainian History*. Toronto: University of Toronto Press, 2005.

Pocock, J.G.A. *Barbarism and Religion, vol. 1: The Enlightenments of Edward Gibbon 1737–1764*. Cambridge: Cambridge University Press, 1999.

Porciani, I. (ed.). *History Women*, special issue of *Storia della Storiografia* 46 (2004).

Porciani, I. and R. Lutz (eds). *Atlas of European Historiography: The Making of a Profession, 1800–2005.* Basingstoke: Palgrave Macmillan, 2010.

Porciani, I. and J. Tollebeek (eds). *Setting the Standards: Institutions, Networks and Communities of National Historiography.* Basingstoke: Palgrave Macmillan, 2012.

Posner, R.A. *Public Intellectuals: A Study of Decline.* Cambridge, MA: Harvard University Press, 2001.

Prymak, T.M. *Mykhailo Hrushevsky: The Politics of National Culture.* Toronto: University of Toronto Press, 1987.

Raphael, L. *Die Erben von Bloch und Febvre: Annales Geschichtsschreibung und nouvelle histoire in Frankreich, 1945–1980.* Stuttgart: Klett-Cotta, 1994.

Reill, P.H. *The German Enlightenment and the Rise of Historicism.* Berkeley: University of California Press, 1975.

Rorty, R. 'Afterword', in R. Rosenzweig (ed.), *Clio Wired: The Future of the Past in the Digital Age.* New York: Columbia University Press, 2011, 197–204.

Rousseau, J.J. 'Discourse on the Origins and Foundations of Inequality among Men', in R.D. Masters and C. Kelly (eds), *The Collected Writings of Rousseau* (Hannover, NH: Dartmouth College Press, 1993), 84–86.

Rupnik, J. 'The Politics of History-Writing in Czechoslovakia', *History Workshop Journal* 11 (1981), 166–68.

Rüsen, J. *Evidence and Meaning: A Theory of Historical Studies.* Oxford: Berghahn, 2017.

Scheuzger, S. 'Truth Commissions and the Politics of History: A Critical Appraisal', in B. Bevernage and N. Wouters (eds), *Palgrave Handbook of State-Sponsored History after 1945.* Basingstoke: Palgrave Macmillan, 2018.

Schneider, J.C. *Nation and Ethnicity: Chinese Discourses on History, Historiography and Nationalism (1900s to 1920s).* Leiden: Brill, 2017.

Schönwälder, K. *Historiker und Politik: Geschichtswissenschaft im Nationalsozialismus.* Frankfurt am Main: Campus, 1992.

Schöttler, P. 'After the Deluge: The Impact of the Two World Wars on the Historical Work of Henri Pirenne and Marc Bloch', in S. Berger and C. Lorenz (eds), *Nationalizing the Past* (London: Palgrave Macmillan, 2010), 404–25.

Schumpeter, J. *Kapitalismus, Sozialismus, Demokratie.* Tübingen: Mohr, 1993 [1942].

Semyonov, A. 'Mirrors of Imperial Imagination in the Early Twentieth-Century Russian Empire', in A. Nowak (ed.), *Imperial Victims – Empires as Victims – 44 Views.* Cracow: IPN, 2010, 139–52.

Smith, B.G. *The Gender of History: Men, Women and Historical Practice.* Cambridge, MA: Harvard University Press, 1998.

Smith, N.C. *A 'Manly Study'? Irish Women Historians 1868–1949.* Basingstoke: Palgrave Macmillan, 2006.

Spurr, J. 'Iraqi Libraries and Archives in Peril', in P.G. Stone and J. Farchakh Bajjaly (eds), *The Destruction of Cultural Heritage in Iraq.* Woodbridge: The Boydell Press, 2008.

Tollebeek, J. '"Italian" History versus French Heritage: Cultural Criticism, Positivism, and Political Commitment in Taine', in J. Leerssen and A. Rigney (eds), *Historians* (Amsterdam: Amsterdam University Press, 2000), 125–40.

Tolz, V. *Russia: Inventing the Nation.* London: Arnold, 2001.

Torstendahl, R. *The Rise and Propagation of Historical Professionalism.* London: Routledge, 2015.

Tyrrell, I. *Historians in Public: The Practice of American History, 1890–1970.* Chicago: University of Chicago Press, 2005.

Vom Lehn, M. *Westdeutsche und italienische Historiker als Intellektuelle? Ihr Umgang mit Nationalsozialismus und Faschismus in den Massenmedien 1943/4–1960.* Göttingen: Vandenhoeck & Ruprecht, 2012.

Von Klimó, Á. *Nation, Konfession, Geschichte: Zur nationalen Geschichtskultur Ungarns im europäischen Kontext (1860–1948)*. Munich: Oldenbourg, 2003.

Von See, K. *Die Göttinger Sieben: Kritik einer Legende*. Cologne: Winter, 2000.

Weber, M. *Schriften 1915–1920: Die Wirtschaftsethik der Weltreligionen: Konfuzianismus und Taoismus*, vol I, 19. Tübingen: Mohr, 1989.

Weichlein, S. '"Meine Peitsche ist die Feder": Populäre katholische Geschichtsschreibung im 19. und 20. Jahrhundert', in W. Hardtwig and E. Schütz (eds), *Geschichte für Leser: Populäre Geschichtsschreibung in Deutschland im 20. Jahrhundert* (Stuttgart: Franz Steiner Verlag, 2005), 227–58.

Weigelin-Schwiedrzik, S. 'Chinese Historical Writing since 1949', in A. Schneider and D. Woolf (eds), *The Oxford History of Historical Writing, vol. 5: Historical Writing since 1945* (Oxford: Oxford University Press, 2011), 615–36.

Weller, T. (ed.). *History in the Digital Age*. London: Routledge, 2013.

White, H. *The Practical Past*. Evanston, IL: Northwestern University Press, 2014.

Yerxa, D.A. (ed.). *Recent Themes on Historians and the Public: Historians in Conversation*. Columbia: University of South Carolina Press, 2009.

Zald, M.N. and J. McCarthy. 'Organizational Intellectuals and the Criticism of Society', in M.N. Zald and J. McCarthy (eds), *Social Movements in an Organizational Society: Collected Essays*. New Brunswick: Transaction, 1987, 97–120.

Zuzowksi, R. *Political Dissent and Opposition in Poland: The Workers' Defence Committee KOR*. London: Praeger, 1992.

CHAPTER 1

Engagement

Metahistorical Considerations on a Disputed Attitude in Historical Studies

Jörn Rüsen

A Misleading Idea of Engagement

The juxtaposition of engaged and non-engaged forms of historical thinking is a usual way of perceiving and interpreting historiography.[1] A 'non-engaged' procedure is commonly understood as 'neutral' or 'scientific' (in the broader meaning of the word). It indicates a higher level of claiming for truth, and quite often it is understood as 'objective'. But since the concept of objectivity has been discredited and the role of subjectivity in bringing about historical knowledge cannot be denied, it has become rather unclear what the contrary of engagement really means in historiography.

But, nevertheless, the juxtaposition is still in use and can be proven by a lot of historical examples. In the classical German historicism of the nineteenth century, a typical case is the difference between Ranke (1795–1886) and Gervinus (1805–1871). Ranke's slogan that he only wanted to find out 'how it really was'[2] has become a very famous statement. It indicates the widespread opinion of professional historians that their way of doing history by methodical research can claim higher plausibility than all other ways of historical thinking. They expressed this claim by defining their profession as science, as *Wissenschaft*. Ranke characterized this logical status as an elimination of subjectivity in representing the past. His well-known statement rings in our ears: that it is his intention, so to speak, 'to relinquish

---

Notes for this section begin on page 41.

his subjectivity and give voice to the facts'.[3] He claims non-partisanship and total objectivity.[4]

In contrast to this attitude, Gervinus is representative of the historian's intense commitment to political partisanship. His slogan that the historian is a 'partisan of destiny' was famous in his time. His partisanship was an identification with democratization as a general process in modern history. When he had to witness the Bonapartism of the new German Reich in 1871, which did not fulfil his hopes for a democratic German national state, he felt personally devastated: 'as if all roots of my national existence were cut off or pulled out'.[5] This example shows that engagement has existential roots and consequences. Gervinus was aware of this, and so were his contemporary colleagues, but this existential factor reaches deeply into the unconscious regions, where it is much more difficult to identify and criticize it.

Another example is the controversy between Hans-Ulrich Wehler and Thomas Nipperdey over Wehler's book *Das Deutsche Kaiserreich*.[6] One of the main points of Nipperdey's criticism is Wehler's thesis that historical studies have to be committed to a set of norms. By him, historical studies are ascribed to a task:

> the emancipatory task: to break through the fog of inherited legends in an ideology-critical way, to dissolve stereotypical misunderstandings, to precisely carve out the effects of realized decisions or the social costs of omitted ones, and therefore to augment the chances of rational orientation for our practical lives, embedding them in a horizon of carefully checked historical experiences.[7]

Wehler tried to realize this task, and by doing so he stirred up the German public. Against this political commitment, Nipperdey defended the academic ethics of objectivity.[8]

Both examples show the same strategy of academic discourse: commitment is understood as running against basic rules of academic neutrality; against this neutrality the idea is upheld that history is based on normative presuppositions and that academic historiography has a normative function of cultural orientation.

The different way of presenting the past is evident, but is the juxtaposition of objectivity versus engagement convincing? In both cases it is rather easy to demonstrate that both representatives of objectivity, nevertheless, show political inclinations and that their controversy reflects different political standpoints in the context of their work. Ranke, for example, explicated in his 1836 inaugural lecture in Berlin that historical knowledge and political practice are systematically interrelated.[9]

So we have to accept that the difference of attitudes exists, but it does not represent mutually excluding principles of historical thinking. If this is true, we need a new understanding of engagement and its specific mode of doing history in contrast to other modes of doing the same history.

The Logic of Historical Thinking

In order to bring about such a new understanding, it is necessary to analyse the logic of historical thinking – that is, to ask for the basic principles of historically making sense of the past. Before I thematize historical studies and its related historiography, I would like to descend to a deeper level, namely to five fundaments of historical thinking in general:[10]

- the need for orientation in the temporal dimension of human life, particularly in coming to terms with the experience of contingency;
- to understand the concept of the past as history;
- to understand the rules for disclosing perceptions of the past;
- to learn the forms of representing an interpretation of the past;
- to learn the functions of using the representation of the interpreted past in the historical culture of the present.

Every single principle is necessary and the interrelationship is a dynamic reciprocity. Realizing this complexity explains why engagement in the form of being entangled in practical life is a constitutive element of historical thinking in general. It starts with orientation needs and ends with guidelines for the practical use of historical knowledge, thus placing individuals and peoples in the temporal dimension of their lives. One of the most important procedures of this orientation is related to the identity of the people: historical thinking is a necessary element for answering questions about who we are. In this broad and fundamental context, engagement as a specific way of doing history refers to partisanship in historically describing topical conflicts. Engagement has often meant one-sidedness and as such it is generally criticized as violating fundamental truth criteria and the moral standards of the historian.

Practice and Cognition – The Rationality of Historical Studies

In the context of academization and professionalization of historiography, engagement has received its specific modern meaning as fundamentally running against basic standards of historical thinking. The decisive factor of this 'scientific' way of doing history is the method of historical research. It brings methodical rationality into historical thinking, and with it the five principles of making sense of the past change their character:

- need for orientation changes into interests in cognition;
- concepts of historical understanding change into (reflected) frames of interpretation ('theories');

- rules for disclosing sources change into methods of historical research;
- forms of representation integrate rational explanations;
- functions of orientation gain elements of practical reason.

Does this 'rationalization' of historical thinking exclude any engagement? Professional historians have tended to claim 'objectivity', thus answering this question with a clear 'no!' In being 'objective' they understand that their statements about the past can be intersubjectively tested by empirical evidence and logical coherence of explanation. This claim for intersubjectivity has good reasons, but it does not bring about neutrality of historical knowledge in its relationship to practical life.[11] Neutrality would mean that the interrelationship between the five factors of historical meaning would be split in half: need for and function of orientation on the one hand and the task of the last three factors on the other. But this split is logically impossible, since historical thinking, even in its academic form, remains rooted in practical life, although it furnishes more distance from it. Therefore the term of 'neutrality' is misleading. Instead, the term 'intersubjectivity' is more adequate: intersubjectivity does not negate engagement but gives it a specific form. It subjugates it under the rule of giving reason for its normative (mainly political) claims, and this reason is embedded in historical knowledge as a result of methodical research.

History as a matter of methodical research is an issue of cognition. Historical studies distinguishes itself from other practices of doing history by an elaboration of rationality. But the complex interrelationship of the five constitutive factors of historical meaning shows that this rationality is only one dimension of making sense of the past besides others. There are others that cannot be denied in understanding what historical studies are about.

Five Dimensions of Historical Culture

These further dimensions come into view when we go back to the fundamental constitution of historical sense generation. They are displayed depending on the perspective within which historical thinking is used and reflected. Let me enumerate the five (most) important ones:[12]

- in the cognitive dimension, history is done as an issue of thinking, guided by the idea of truth;
- in the aesthetical dimension, history is an issue of sensual perception, guided by the idea of beauty;
- in the political dimension, history is an issue of power and domination, guided by the idea of legitimacy;

- in the ethical dimension, history is an issue of evaluation (normative assertiveness), guided by the idea of good and evil;
- in the religious dimension, history is an issue of belief, guided by the idea of resurrection.

All these dimensions are interrelated. In modern times, the religious dimension is confronted with a strong secularism in civil society. But it has not vanished; instead it has recruited different manifestations. One of them is a secular (inner-worldly) form of resurrection (like Marxism).[13] In the academic field of historical thinking, secularism is necessary but is open to the experience of and reference to transcendence.[14]

Vis-à-vis these manifold dimensions and their interrelatedness, 'engagement' gains a manifold meaning. In general it is no more than a qualification of the interrelatedness in which one of the dimensions dominates the others. Traditionally, the *political* one stands out. In this case, engagement might lead to political partisanship as a dominant factor in the web of the complex procedure of making sense of the past. Cognition and representation could serve political aims; cognition might become one-sided or even ideological; the form of historical representation might come close to propaganda, and the forces of religious belief might become weapons in the struggle for power.

An historical example for this one-sidedness in historical thinking is Johann Gustav Droysen's *Geschichte der preußischen Politik*.[15] When working with the sources for this work, Droysen refused to use non-Prussian archives.[16] He deliberately chose the Prussian standpoint in order to support the foundation of the German national state under the leadership of Prussia. This is a clear case of violating basic methodical rules of getting solid knowledge out of the relicts of the past in favour of legitimating a strategy of politics by historical argumentation.

Political commitment is only one form of engagement. Another one is the *cognitive* form. Here knowledge and cognition and related truth-claims dominate historical thinking despite and even against all other qualifications. Therefore, it rather often may go along with a boring presentation,[17] an apolitical attitude, a lack of moral commitment and ignorance concerning the role of transcendence in human life. Encyclopaedias[18] are good examples of this dominance of knowledge in presenting the past.

By the *aesthetic* commitment, the work of making sense of the past concentrates on the formal quality of presenting it. It may lead to an aestheticism that does not care very much about the solidity of facts and the explanatory power of interpretation, thus ignoring the political relevance of historical thinking. This is very often the case when history is presented in the cinema. The well-known film *Schindler's List* (1993), for example, changed the character of one of its heroes (Itzhak Stern) against all facts and only for rules of entertainment in order to present a clear-cut black and white painting of friend and foe. Remarkable cases of aesthetizing history are the films by Hans-Jürgen Syberberg (especially *Hitler, ein Film aus Deutschland* from 1977).[19]

Ethical commitment strengthens the normative elements in historical thinking. In this case, historical experiences may mainly function as a source for insight into the effectiveness and applicability of ethical rules in and for practical life. It may reduce empirical evidence to a mere illustration of the validity of these rules and give political attitudes a moralistic form, thus ignoring the proper weight of politics with its fundamental difference from morality. It also may dissolve religion into the normative dimension of inner-worldly human life, thus ignoring its fundamental reference to a divine transcendent world.

The dominance of ethics in historical interpretation characterizes a widespread type of making sense of the past: the exemplary one. Cicero characterized it by the slogan '*historia vitae magistra*'.[20] A recent example for ethical commitment (and its inclination to one-sidedness) is Fritz Fischer's book *Griff nach der Weltmacht* (1961),[21] in which the politics of Germany are made responsible for the outbreak of World War I. This book can be understood as a German historian's moral self-accusation; he wants to compensate for his earlier commitment to the Nazi regime.

Religious commitment stresses the role of history in articulating the belief in transcendent factors in human life-orientation. It introduces the sacred into the experience and interpretation of the past. Examples of this engagement (to a very different extent) can be found in church history written by theologians. Outside this academic level, religious commitment may suffer from a much higher degree of one-sidedness. It might set aside the other sense criteria in favour of theocracy in politics, dogmatism in cognition and rhetorical constraints in representation.

As a result of this differentiation of engagement, I would like to emphasize the fact that the usual juxtaposition of engaged and not engaged historiography is too simple. This is true for the academic historical discourse as well. In a certain sense, every historical presentation is engaged, since it includes a constitutive relationship to practical life – in a more or less mediated way. It depends upon the extension and the way of this mediation as to whether we address it as engaged or not engaged ('neutral' would be a misleading notion, since it ignores the rootedness of historical thinking in practical life and the constitutive role that points of view play in the tensions of this life when it comes to making sense of the past by presenting it as history).

The traditional contrast between engaged and non-engaged historiography is an indicator of the extent to which the political dimension of doing history is explicated or hidden. A strict refutation of politics in general is logically impossible, since political points of view are always effective in the conceptualization of the framework of historical interpretation and in the forms of representing historical knowledge. This applies as well to addressing orientation problems in the context of historical thinking.

Nevertheless, it makes sense to use the distinction between engaged and non-engaged historiography. It can be used to characterize an *unbalanced relationship between the different dimensions*. I have already described this specific constellation in my presentation of the five dimensions. But what does 'unbalanced' mean? There is no sixth (meta-)dimension that determines the relationship of the other five. All the dimensions have their own role in doing history. There is a 'natural' tendency of the sense criteria, which constitute the single dimension as dominant or sub-dominant; and this tendency is effectively realized in different forms of historical representation in the wider and complex field of historical culture. But being dominant can be realized in (logically) different ways: either at the cost of others or by respecting their sense-making peculiarity.

The problematic side of engagement becomes visible if one dimension limits, hinders or even contradicts the deployment of sense and meaning in the others. This is even possible when the cognitive dimension is dominating. In this case it is possible that cognition becomes ideology (e.g. by changing political legitimacy into cognitive truth, aesthetics into propagandistic forms, morality into ideology, and religious desires into inner-worldly predictions.

The Role of Historical Studies in Historical Culture

Historical studies are committed to the dominance of cognition. If it avoids the possibility of ideological engagement and does not suppress the sense criteria of its political, moral and aesthetic dimensions it can contribute to the historical culture of its time in different ways.

Firstly, it is able to accomplish the knowledge of the past by research. Research brings about new knowledge, and its method of interpretation enriches this knowledge with explanatory power. By this knowledge it introduces an element of intersubjective plausibility into the politics of memory. Second, it enables people to use this knowledge to criticize problematic historical legacies, and it empowers the argumentative forces in the minds of its addressees by the discursive dynamics of reasoning. So it may strengthen the power of reason in cultural orientation.

One of the most problematic practical functions of historical thinking is its ethnocentric formation, by which it might support and strengthen the self-esteem of those people to which the historians themselves belong. Engagement can be observed as a means of ethnocentrism. Concerning this danger, historical studies very often serves the needs of an unbalanced historical identity. Its methodical rationality includes the issue of forming historical identity, which belongs to the constitutive factors of historical sense making. The ruling (methodical) idea of intersubjectivity can be applied to the way in which history thematizes the concept of identity. Doing so, it may overcome the unbalanced relationship between self and the other. There is always the danger of ethnocentrism lurking to give this relationship an asymmetrical structure. This might lead to aggression and violence in the process of self-asserting one's own people in its relationship to other. The idea of intersubjectivity brought into historical culture may overcome this dangerous potential when using history for the practical purpose of identity formation.

Counter-engagement

Engagement seems to be the historians' activity when using history for practical (mostly political) purposes. Its one-sidedness, therefore, needs an antidote: a more careful observance of the past. But this is only one perspective in which engagement in history has to be analysed and treated. A completely different one has not yet been granted the attendance it needs: it occurs when historical thinking is 'moved by the past'.[22] Now engagement is the consequence of the determination of present-day thinking about the past by the past itself. This determination has not taken place in the past, but it has done so under conditions of present-day culture as the result of past developments. In this context, historical thinking may be seen as an outcome of repetition compulsion (to use the psychoanalytical term).

Unsolved problems, open wounds and traumatic events in the past condition historians' viewpoint of them in a more or less unconscious way. So it might happen that the history of this past reproduces the one-sidedness of people in conflicts of the past. An example is the distinction of perpetrators and victims. This distinction is necessary, of course, to characterize a constellation of people in past events (besides the bystanders, profiteers, opponents and other groups). But when writing a history of this constellation by using it as a determination of the perspectives of its interpretation, we reproduce it. Thus, the past becomes transported into the present and located and established here so that the chance of overcoming this old distinction for a more complex and mediated perspective is neglected. The general tendency of victimization in the historical culture of today can be defined as such a one-sidedness. In order to avoid this kind of engagement, a broader and deeper reflection of its logic is necessary.

Jörn Rüsen is Senior Fellow at the Kulturwissenschaftliches Institut (Institute for Advanced Study in the Humanities) at Essen and Professor emeritus at the University of Witten/Herdecke. He was Professor of modern history with special respect to history didactics at the Ruhr-University of Bochum; Professor for general history with special respect to theory of history at the University of Bielefeld; director of the Zif (centre for interdisciplinary study) in Bielefeld; President/director of the Kulturwissenschaftliches Institut (Institute for Advanced Study in the Humanities) at Essen; and head of the research project on 'Humanism in the Era of Globalisation – An Intercultural Dialogue on Humanity, Culture, and Values' at the Kulturwissenschaftliches Institut (Institute for Advanced Study in the Humanities) at Essen. His fields of research include: theory and methodology of history, history of historiography, didactics of history, historical culture, strategies of intercultural comparison and humanism in a globalizing world. Among his recent publications are: *Historik: Theorie der Geschichtswissenschaft* (Böhlau Verlag, 2013), translated into Portuguese and English, with Chinese translation forthcoming and *Approaching Humankind: Towards an Intercultural Humanism* (V&R unipress, 2013).

Notes

1. I dedicate this chapter to Hans-Georg Soeffner on the occasion of his 75th birthday, with gratitude for his never-ending engagement for reason and humanity in our academic work.
2. Von Ranke, *Geschichten der romanischen und germanischen Völker von 1494–1514: Sämtliche Werke*, VIII; see Von Ranke, *The Theory and Practice of History*; Mommsen, *Leopold von Ranke und die moderne Geschichtswissenschaft*.
3. Von Ranke, *Englische Geschichte, vornehmlich im 17. Jahrhundert*, 103.
4. Von Ranke, *Vorlesungs-Anleitungen*, 80 sq.
5. Letter to Manuel 1 April 1867; Wagner, 'Gervinus über die Einigung Deutschlands', 376. See J. Rüsen, 'Der Historiker als Parteimann des Schicksal – Georg Gottfried Gervinus', 157–225; Hübinger, 'Georg Gottfried Gervinus: Geschichtsdenken zwischen Wissenschaft, Publizistik und Politik im 19. Jh', 271–92; Hübinger, *Georg Gottfried Gervinus: Historisches Urteil und Politische Kritik*; Wagner, *Germany's 19th Century Cassandra: The Liberal Federalist Georg Gottfried Gervinus*; Alfaix Assis, *What is History For? Johann Gustav Droysen and the Functions of Historiography*, esp. 159 sq.
6. Wehler, *Das Deutsche Kaiserreich 1871–1918*; Nipperdey, 'Wehlers "Kaiserreich" – eine kritische Auseinandersetzung', 539–60.
7. Wehler, *Kaiserreich*, 12.
8. Nipperdey, 'Kann Geschichte objektiv sein', 218–34.
9. Von Ranke, *Über die Verwandtschaft und den Unterschied der Historie und der Politik: Sämtliche Werke*, vol. 24: *Abhandlungen und Versuche*, 280–93.

10. See Rüsen, *Historik: Theorie der Geschichtswissenschaft*, 68 sqq.
11. See Haskell, *Objectivity is not Neutrality: Explanatory Schemes in History*.
12. This distinction is a 'construction'. It is easily possible to present other dimensions like the ideological or the psychological one (the latter with the important factor of unconscious elements and factors of making sense of the past). See Rüsen and Straub, *Die dunkle Spur der Vergangenheit: Psychoanalytische Zugänge zum Geschichtsbewußtsein* (English edition *Dark Traces of the Past: Psychoanalysis and Historical Thinking*; Klüners, *Geschichtsphilosophie und Psychoanalyse*.
13. Küenzlen, *Der neue Mensch: Eine Untersuchung zur säkularen Religionsgeschichte der Moderne*.
14. Rüsen, 'Zivilgesellschaft und Religion – Idee eines Verhältnisses', 227–39.
15. Droysen, *Geschichte der preußischen Politik*.
16. Nippel, 'Zum Kontext von Droysens Geschichtstheorie', 337–391, esp. 369.
17. Like many PhD theses.
18. I mention only one: Cancik, Schneider and Landfester (eds), *Der Neue Pauly: Enzyklopädie der Antike, Jubiläumsausgabe*.
19. Friedländer, *Kitsch und Tod: Der Wiederschein des Nazismus* (English original: *Reflections on Nazism: An Essay on Kitsch and Death*).
20. De Oratore II, 36.
21. Fischer, *Griff nach der Weltmacht: Die Kriegszielpolitik des kaiserlichen Deutschland 1914/18*.
22. Runia, *Moved by the Past: Discontinuity and Historical Mutation*.

Bibliography

Alfaix Assis, A. *What is History For? Johann Gustav Droysen and the Functions of Historiography*. New York: Berghahn, 2014.
Cancik, H., H. Schneider and M. Landfester (eds). *Der Neue Pauly: Enzyklopädie der Antike, Jubiläumsausgabe* (*Das klassische Altertum und seine Rezeptionsgeschichte*: 13 vols *Altertum A–Z*; 5 vols *Rezeptions- und Wissenschaftsgeschichte*; 1 vol.), Register. Stuttgart: Metzler Verlag, 2007.
Droysen, J.G. *Geschichte der preußischen Politik*, 14 vols, Berlin: Verlag von Veit, 1855–1886.
Fischer, F. *Griff nach der Weltmacht: Die Kriegszielpolitik des kaiserlichen Deutschland 1914/18*. Düsseldorf: Droste Verlag, 1961.
Friedländer, S. *Reflections on Nazism: An Essay on Kitsch and Death*. Bloomington: Indiana University Press, 1984.
———. *Kitsch und Tod: Der Wiederschein des Nazismus*, Munich: Hanser Verlag, 1986.
Haskell, T.L. *Objectivity is not Neutrality: Explanatory Schemes in History*. Baltimore, MD: The Johns Hopkins University Press, 1998.
Hübinger, G. *Georg Gottfried Gervinus: Historisches Urteil und Politische Kritik*. Göttingen: Vandenhoeck & Ruprecht, 1984.
———. 'Georg Gottfried Gervinus: Geschichtsdenken zwischen Wissenschaft, Publizistik und Politik im 19. Jh', *Archiv für Hessische Geschichte und Altertumskunde* 45 (1987), 271–92.
Klüners, M. *Geschichtsphilosophie und Psychoanalyse*. Göttingen: V&R unipress, 2013.
Küenzlen, G. *Der neue Mensch: Eine Untersuchung zur säkularen Religionsgeschichte der Moderne*. Frankfurt am Main: Suhrkamp, 1997.
Mommsen, W.J. (ed.). *Leopold von Ranke und die moderne Geschichtswissenschaft*. Stuttgart: Klett-Cotta, 1988.

Nippel, W. 'Zum Kontext von Droysens Geschichtstheorie', in S. Rebenich and H.-W. Wiemer (eds), *Johann Gustav Droysen: Philosophie und Politik – Historie und Philologie*. Frankfurt am Main: Campus Verlag, 2012, 337–91.

Nipperdey, T. 'Wehlers "Kaiserreich" – eine kritische Auseinandersetzung', *Geschichte und Gesellschaft* 1(4) (1975), 539–60.

———. 'Kann Geschichte objektiv sein' (first published 1979), reprinted in *Nachdenken über die deutsche Geschichte: Essays*, T. Nipperdey (ed.), 2nd ed. (Munich: C.H. Beck, 1986), 218–34.

Runia, E. *Moved by the Past: Discontinuity and Historical Mutation*. New York: Columbia University Press, 2014.

Rüsen, J. 'Der Historiker als Parteimann des Schicksals – Georg Gottfried Gervinus', in J. Rüsen (ed.), *Konfigurationen des Historismus: Studien zur deutschen Wissenschaftskultur* (Frankfurt am Main: Suhrkamp, 1993), 157–225.

———. 'Zivilgesellschaft und Religion – Idee eines Verhältnisses', in J. Rüsen (ed.), *Kultur macht Sinn: Orientierung zwischen Gestern und Morgen* (Cologne: Böhlau, 2006), 227–39.

———. *Historik: Theorie der Geschichtswissenschaft*. Cologne: Böhlau, 2013.

Rüsen, J. and J. Straub (eds). *Die dunkle Spur der Vergangenheit: Psychoanalytische Zugänge zum Geschichtsbewußtsein* (*Erinnerung, Geschichte, Identität*, vol. 2). Frankfurt am Main: Suhrkamp, 1998.

———. *Dark Traces of the Past: Psychoanalysis and Historical Thinking*. New York: Berghahn, 2010.

Von Ranke, L. *Geschichten der romanischen und germanischen Völker von 1494–1514: Sämtliche Werke*, vol. 33. Leipzig: Duncker & Humblot, 1855.

———. *Englische Geschichte, vornehmlich im 17. Jahrhundert*, vol 2. (*Sämtliche Werke*, vol. 15). Leipzig: Duncker & Humblot, 1877.

———. *Über die Verwandtschaft und den Unterschied der Historie und der Politik: Sämtliche Werke*, vol. 24: *Abhandlungen und Versuche*. Leipzig: Duncker & Humblot, 1877.

———. *Vorlesungs-Einleitungen: Aus Werk und Nachlaß*, vol. IV, V. Dotterweich and W.-P. Fuchs (eds). Munich: Oldenbourg Verlag, 1975.

———. *The Theory and Practice of History* (edited with an introduction by Georg G. Iggers). London: Routledge, 2011.

Wagner, J.F. 'Gervinus über die Einigung Deutschlands, Briefe aus den Jahren 1866–1870', *Zeitschrift für die Geschichte des Oberrheins*, NF 82 (1973), 376.

———. *Germany's 19th Century Cassandra: The Liberal Federalist Georg Gottfried Gervinus*. New York: Lang, 1995.

Wehler, H.-U. *Das Deutsche Kaiserreich 1871–1918*. Göttingen: Vandenhoeck & Ruprecht, 1973.

CHAPTER 2

The Ideal of Justice and Its Significance for Historians as Engaged Intellectuals

Martin Wiklund

Introduction

What is a proper role for historians as engaged intellectuals? Is it possible to formulate any kind of guiding ideals for such a role? In the twentieth century, intellectuals typically assumed the role of a 'public conscience', acting as prosecutors criticizing wrongs in society and violations of fundamental rights and norms. The paradigmatic model for this kind of intellectual protest is of course Émile Zola's 'J'accuse...!', an open letter addressed to the president of France to expose the unfair treatment of Alfred Dreyfus. In it, the intellectual takes up the role of an independent prosecutor acting in the name of truth and justice.[1]

Since the days of Zola, however, it has become more complicated for intellectuals to make such high claims of authority, whether these are based on historical research or moral and ideological values. Should there be definitive scientific truths and universally accepted norms in society to which to refer, it would be easier for engaged scholars to publically raise their voice in the name of truth and justice, but, in reality, conflicts of historical interpretation exist within the scientific community just as in the public sphere. Moreover, the historical controversies in which historians participate as public intellectuals typically deal with questions not only of truth but also of identity, evaluation of the past and future orientation.

Notes for this section begin on page 59.

The expectations of the general public that professional historians speak out on controversial historical issues, combined with the aspirations of professional historians to influence public debate in particular political directions, can easily entice historians to instrumentalize history in ways that end up distorting it, with harmful consequences not only for public debate but also for the legitimacy of history as a discipline. It is nonetheless important that historians engage in public conflicts of historical interpretation. Consequently, there seems to be a need for a new ethics of intellectual engagement and for guidelines for the use of history that go beyond the standards of scientific truth and politico-ideological convictions.

In this chapter, 'justice' is put forward as an element of such an ethics as a value-rational ideal guiding historical interpretation and judgment-making. How can 'justice' be understood and conceptualized in a way that is relevant for historical thinking? What role ought historians to play in order to further justice with regard to historical interpretations and judgments? These are the main questions guiding the analysis. The analogy of a 'court of justice' will be used to place the role of the intellectual-as-prosecutor in its context consisting of a number of complementary roles and in that way throw light on the risks and responsibilities pertaining to the role of historians acting as intellectuals. Since some of the problems related to the role of the historian as an engaged intellectual have to do with inherited notions of 'the intellectual', I will first make some initial remarks about common ideas of 'the intellectual'. After that, I describe the analogy of the court of justice, explain the meaning of the ideal of justice and, finally, draw some conclusions about the implications of this ideal for historians acting as public intellectuals.

Intellectuals, Intellectuality and the Quality of Engagement

Intellectuals are sometimes depicted as critical heroes and enlightened demythologizers with a mission to liberate the oppressed. The role of the intellectuals as defended, for instance, by Edward Said in his 1993 Reith Lectures displays a number of characteristics that reflect this conception.[2] Such intellectuals are typically those who take sharp, radical normative positions in the public sphere and are anti-establishment and negative rather than affirmative. There are, however, good reasons for relativizing this conception and leaving room for other ones.[3] With the privilege of hindsight, it is easy to see, for instance, that many 'demythologizers' have also themselves been myth creators, formulating enchanting myths of the Enlightenment and modernity or simply misinterpreting the past. Several of the great champions of scientific rationality relied on what today must reasonably be judged as overly narrow concepts of rationality (e.g. functionalist and economistically reductionist explanations of human behaviour). Moreover, we now know that even critical minds can cherish naive dreams of ideal societies, which they project onto some remote place on the other side of the globe (e.g. the visions of China among Western Maoist intellectuals in the 1960s and 1970s).[4] Some projects of liberation have actually turned into projects of oppression, as in the case of, for instance, the Russian Revolution or the postcolonial regime in Zimbabwe. Critical intellectuals committed to these projects have sometimes ended up legitimizing oppression, tyranny and terrorism, by dismissing criticism and evidence contradicting their ideological identifications and perceived patterns of conflict (e.g. the rejection of reports of the genocide in Cambodia as anti-communist propaganda). Furthermore, being anti-establishment or an outsider is not the equivalent of being independent or 'free-floating', two qualities otherwise often ascribed to intellectuals.[5] The anti-establishment identity of intellectuals has often been related to more particular viewpoints: bohemian, anti-bourgeois, anti-conventionalist, anti-capitalist and, during the postwar era, predominantly left-wing.[6] The anti-conventionalist, anti-establishment identity makes intellectuals reluctant to support positions embraced by the majority in society and, in an almost compulsory fashion, tends to push them towards oppositional and sometimes also extremist standpoints. Insights such as these should not, however, be used as warrants for self-congratulatory condemnations of past intellectuals but ought rather to provoke thinking about other possible roles for intellectuals that take these negative experiences into account. For anyone seriously interested in critical thinking, it would surely be unwise to dismiss such experiences as mere reactionary propaganda.

The role of the intellectuals described above, which can be characterized as avant-gardist or modernist, was generally based on grand narratives about modernity that legitimized the 'new' over the existing, identified a particular direction of development as 'progress' and presented certain perspectives as 'scientific' or 'realistic'. Radicalism as a virtue for intellectuals depended on the validity of the norms, ideals and truths guiding the actions of the avant-gardist intellectuals. When, however, neither historical research nor ideological values or other normative convictions provide any solid foundation, the rationality and ethical value of such radicalism must be put into question. The point is not that 'conservative' or less radical projects are preferable but that the lack of certainty has implications for the role of the intellectual.

It seems that the different ideas we have of the task of the intellectual correspond to different notions of practical reason. What kind of rationality is suited for handling issues of common political and cultural concern, and how can intellectuals promote the process this entails?[7] If there is a specific task for historians as intellectuals, an important question to ask is how the kind of knowledge and competences that historians possess can contribute to issues of practical reason. Consequently, the usual characterization of intellectuals as amateurs, as opposed to experts and disengaged researchers,[8] is to some extent misleading, even if it is true that in acting as an intellectual the historian must transcend the role of a mere professional expert. Historians can, to be sure, enter the public arena just like any other citizen, but for them to be able to act as intellectuals *as historians*, they should also be more than just amateurs. The specific value of historians' engagement in public discourse derives, precisely, from their specific competences as historians.[9]

In the same vein, engagement as such has no specifically *intellectual* quality, regardless of whether it is understood as ideological commitment or as implying activity in the public sphere. Football hooligans, militant fundamentalists and neo-Nazi street thugs, too, can be notably engaged, in the sense of fighting for what they believe in and having strong ideological convictions or a passionate commitment to a particular political standpoint. Those actively participating in the public arena do not always contribute to an improved quality of public debate – indeed, they sometimes lower it. Accordingly, the engagement and the contribution of historians as engaged intellectuals ought, in the first place, to be understood in terms of historical knowledge and historical thinking, something that gives their engagement in the public sphere a specifically intellectual quality.

The intellectuality of the engaged intellectuals depends not on the strength or the radical nature of their ideological and political convictions but on their ability to apply their knowledge and intellectual powers to issues of common concern. Intellectuality in the context discussed here should, preferably, be associated with virtues such as flexibility of mind, facility to understand perspectives different from one's own (as opposed to insularity and arrogance) and ability to take new information and opponents' arguments into account (as opposed to rigid self-righteousness). The critical and reflective faculties that define intellectuality ought to include critical inquisitiveness (as opposed to taking things for granted) and an increased ability to discern problems and shortcomings (as opposed to gullibility). Compared to more narrowly focused specialists, intellectuals should also be able to discuss broad perspectives and large issues, which, in the case of the historians, requires an ability to discuss the significance of more specific historical knowledge in relation to the larger questions involved. All these virtues, to be sure, have the character of ideals rather than actual, empirical competences that all historians possess; yet, there would be no point with virtues if they only described how people behave de facto.

Historical controversies deal with questions not only about what happened in the past but also about what political and ideological conclusions should be drawn from historical facts and phenomena. These questions cannot be answered merely by referring to findings from historical research, as if research could decide for us that we have to reject (or return to) the ideas of '1968', for example. Nor should such practical questions be settled simply with reference to ideological commitments ('as a committed socialist historian, I advocate conclusions that support socialism').[10] If what historians can add to conflicts of historical interpretation are merely their personal ideological convictions – something that can be provided by many non-historians as well – there is no particular need for historians as engaged intellectuals. In order to throw some light on the different roles that historians-as-intellectuals can play, it is useful to place the paradigmatic role of the intellectual as prosecutor in the context of the other roles implied by the analogy of the court of justice. This analogy also helps to make the problematic connection between facts about a controversial past and normative judgments of the historical phenomenon discussed more obvious.

The Symbolic Court of Justice

In the last couple of decades, major public debates around a problematic past have emerged in many countries. Accusations have been made, for example, about 'forgotten' political crimes in Spain, about aboriginal groups being discriminated by the public memory in Australia, about the false picture heroic narratives present of the role of countries such as France, Denmark and Sweden during World War II.[11] In such debates and in related historical research, metaphors belonging to the legal sphere have frequently been resorted to, such as perpetrators and victims, accusations and witnesses, guilt and responsibility, trials and judges.[12] While the historical controversies in question have at times evolved in relation to actual legal processes, what needs to be emphasized is that it is the *symbolic* model of a court of justice that I am interested in here, taking it as a suitable analogy for discussing certain uses of history and the role of historians as intellectuals engaged in historical controversies.[13] The fact that history is easily abused in real-life courts of justice, as Rousso has maintained in regard to the Papon trial in France,[14] and that, as many historians have been eager to point out, there are important differences between history and law, does not in any way preclude the possibility of deriving useful insights from the application of the analogy.

One of the benefits of the analogy of a court of justice is the plurality of roles to which it refers. Apart from the role of the prosecutor, it addresses also other key roles, including the judge, the defence lawyer, the accused, the plaintiff, different witnesses and the jury. The role of the critical intellectual as discussed above resembles most of all the role of the prosecutor. We may admire the courage of the critical intellectual in 'speaking truth to power' and publicly calling attention to injustices perpetrated.[15] In a trial situation, however, it would be a cause of concern for us were the case to be decided by the prosecutor and based only on his or her argument. It is therefore vital not to confuse the role of the prosecutor with that of the judge (or the jury). When the prosecutor has made his or her case, we do not think of the case as in any way settled yet but expect other voices to be uttered still and taken into consideration.[16]

Something similar applies also to historians-as-researchers, as it is perfectly possible for them to act as 'pure' scholars disseminating regular research results to the general public while still taking on the roles of both the prosecutor and the judge. How so? As convincingly demonstrated by so-called 'speech act theory', language does not only describe but also *does* things with words. Statements can be descriptive and at the same time, for example, function as an accusation, an excuse, an attempt to justify actions, a rejection of an accusation, or an appeal to extenuating circumstances.[17] Instances of such language use that can be employed in both a legal context and a historical discourse would, for example, be: 'It was the police who shot the student,' 'The student was already dead when the police arrived,' 'The police were threatened by an armed group of students,' and 'The students had tried to negotiate with the authorities, but all of their claims were rejected.'

The typical speech acts of a historian can thus be descriptive while at the same time functioning as accusations or as reasons given to justify certain judgments. Consider, for instance, the following utterances: 'Twenty million people were killed by communist regimes,' 'The Swedish welfare state forced 10,000 people to be sterilized,' 'Capitalist conditions of production are the main cause of economic exploitation and inequality in modern society,' 'Modern Western society is fundamentally characterized by instrumental rationality, which also governed the Nazi project to exterminate the Jews.' The point here, to make it clear, is not whether such statements are true or false but that they can be descriptive in form *while at the same time* delivering an accusation, be this against an ideology, a particular state, some political movement, a certain kind of social structure, an entire civilization, or something else of the kind. Given that the statements historians put forth in their role as scholars can also and at the same time serve as accusations or justifications for certain normative judgments while still claiming the authority of a scholar whose work follows commonly recognized standards of historical research, the critical historian-as-prosecutor can easily be confused with a judge that settles the case. In the same way, when truth commissions deliver their statements and interpretations, these can be perceived as judgments closing the case, since the truth about the past has then been investigated by experts, even if their report rather resembles the argument of a defence lawyer or a prosecutor.

Historians who question the judgments of prosecuting intellectuals by contextualizing and explaining the events described can easily appear as opponents of justice and the righting of wrongs. While the role of engaged intellectuals acting as defence lawyers is hardly accompanied by the kind of rhetorical charisma typically surrounding the critical intellectual, in the symbolic court of justice the role of the defence lawyer nevertheless remains a vital one in ensuring that the rights of those accused are respected and the interpretations of the historians acting as prosecutors are subjected to a system of checks and balances. In this sense, the constellation of the defence lawyer and the other key roles of the court of justice can be understood as a means to further more *just* judgments, or at least less unjust judgments, and to diminish the degree of arbitrariness in judgments. The prosecutor's claims are not automatically confirmed as verdicts, since the defence should be given the opportunity to question the accusations. The controversial claims of fact have to be supported by evidence, the accusations and witness statements should be subjected to scrutiny, and the judgments need to be justified.

Sometimes, however, a much more humble role has been suggested as the proper one for historians, a role that resembles that of the witness: to tell the truth while leaving the judgment to others. Leaving aside the question of the credibility of witnesses and the difficulties of establishing 'what actually happened', the most pertinent aspect to notice in this context is that the account given by a witness yields not just facts in general but provides pieces of information that are *relevant to the court case* at hand. The claims about circumstances surrounding the events under discussion often supply reasons either for or against specific judgments and in that way function much like the speech acts of an implicit prosecutor or defence lawyer, albeit one speaking with the humble voice of a witness. Something similar applies to historical explanations and contextualizations: they, too, can support or weigh against a specific judgment. As argued above, speech acts belonging to the 'truth game' often also function as actions in the games of normative evaluation, accusation and justification. When historians step forward to act as witnesses instead of judges and prosecutors, it is of vital importance, therefore, to pay attention to how their statements concerning the historical circumstances of the case affect the discussion of possible judgments and evaluations of the past. That the analogy of the court of justice makes such problems with the truth-telling roles of the witness and the expert more obvious demonstrates its usefulness.

Who, however, is the judge? In one sense, the judge is the one who determines the judgment. Translated into the sphere of historical thinking, this could be understood as referring to the agents that have the ability to determine which historical judgments and evaluations become entrenched in public memory. In public historical controversies, public opinion quite obviously plays an important role in this regard, but not necessarily that of a good judge. Where that opinion, however, plays the role of the judge, it is imperative that historians contribute to the debate to enable more just judgments to emerge. In this effort, another dimension of the judge's role, moreover, becomes important. The judge does not speak in the voice of the petitioner or in the voice of the accused but tries to incorporate all the different pieces of information and argument into a coherent whole in order to be able to arrive at a balanced, fair and well-informed judgment. In performing this task, the role of the judge is, admittedly, not a humble one, and since, in historical thinking, there is much less to guarantee that the judge's judgment is just, there must always be room left for criticism and reconsideration of the judgments of 'the judge' and the established judgments entrenched in public memory.

To summarize, not only the role of the prosecutor but also the other roles prescribed by the court of justice analogy are important for the furtherance of justice in the sense of more just judgments and interpretations. For this reason, they are also relevant for historians acting as engaged intellectuals. The role of the intellectual as a critical prosecutor is certainly valuable, especially in calling attention to problems and injustices, so long as the prosecutor's claims are not confused with the judge's final judgment. Vis-à-vis other agents and users of history acting as prosecutors in the public sphere, it may, however, be crucial for historians to assume the role of the defence lawyer or a defence witness, or to pursue in their interventions some of the virtues of a good judge. In this regard, it seems useful to consider the different roles pertaining to the analogy of the court of justice in relation to one another and in relation to the ideal of justice.

The Ideal of Justice

If the court of justice is supposed to further more *just* judgments, what does 'justice' mean? More specifically, how can justice be interpreted in a way that is relevant for historical thinking? In this section, I consider certain key aspects of justice in this regard, pointing out some risks of distortion that historians as engaged intellectuals run, especially in their role as a prosecutor.[18] These risks expose corresponding responsibilities that historians need to observe. Articulating such responsibilities enables us to move towards an ethics of intellectual engagement that is not restricted to the cognitive truth dimension or to politico-ideological convictions.

To talk of 'justice' of historical judgments may appear as exceedingly idealistic or naive. Even sceptics of justice, however, are usually willing to acknowledge the possibility of *injustice*, so I will begin from that angle. In what sense can historical interpretations, the established memory and the judgments inscribed in that memory be unjust?

To say, for instance, that the radical Left of the 1960s and early 1970s in Sweden supported totalitarian states such as that of Mao's China is correct but only for part of the radical Left. As a general characterization of the country's radical Left of that period, the statement is very one-sided. Telling the truth does not automatically result in just interpretations. A historian can present interpretations that are well-founded on the level of facts but still very unjust because of their one-sidedness. This is a typical hazard for critically engaged historians who strive to make the effect and the moral point of their story as strong as possible. In order to promote radical political change, for example, it might be tempting to describe the history of the present in purely negative terms. Indeed, revolutionary and utopian movements have often interpreted the historical developments of the recent past in apocalyptic terms – 'the world as we know it is coming to an end' – in order to justify the revolutionary conclusions to be drawn from the narratives they advocate.[19] The negative past provides fuel for change and action in the present, and it is tempting to step a bit on the gas.

For the prosecutor or the critical intellectual, one-sidedness may, however, be appropriate or even necessary to some extent, to help clarify the point of one's critique. Yet, if the voice of the historian-as-prosecutor is confused with the voice of the judge, even legitimate critique tends to produce one-sided and unwarranted interpretations and conclusions. To counter this one-sidedness, it is often helpful to consider the aspect of desert: does 'the accused' actually *deserve* the judgment? What are the positive and negative merits of the historical phenomenon or agent in question? In public conflicts of historical interpretation, these questions also usually concern the distribution of praise and blame between the parties involved. In the debates about '1968' in Sweden, for instance, the prosecutors have typically focused only on the shortcomings and alleged 'crimes' of the Left, without paying any attention to what one might view as the positive outcomes of the Left movements of the time. Not to consider positive merits is thus a form of injustice in the sense of not allowing something to be judged as deserved. A clearer example still is a situation where someone is accused of and condemned for wrongs never even committed. This illustrates why the dimension of 'truth' and facts must remain important for any administration of justice: who did what, against whom, how, with what intentions and under what circumstances. Truth, to be sure, is valuable in this context not as an end in itself but for the sake of the justice of historical judgments.

However, even when the historical judgment is based on established wrongs committed and there are no particular positive merits to take into account, it may still be unjust if it shows lack of *proportion*. With this we are confronted with yet another aspect of justice: is the pronounced judgment proportional to the wrong committed? In the Swedish debates about '1968', for example, it was, quite correctly from this perspective, observed that it would be most unfair to judge the Western supporters of Mao the same way one would judge Mao himself.

The aspects of desert and proportion often become even more apparent in cases involving *discrimination*. In these cases, one party is treated differently from other parties owing merely to this party's membership in a category not accorded equal status. This may be so, for example, when the wrongs committed against one group are met with harsh judgments while similar wrongs committed against other groups are belittled or entirely overlooked. The kind of discrimination in question is based not only on the categories of race, ethnicity, nationality and gender but also on other categorical distinctions such as between the political Left/political Right, working class/ middle class, secular/religious, 'modernist'/ 'antimodernists' and so on. The treating of like cases alike and equality before the law are fundamental principles of justice. These principles are indirectly acknowledged when comparisons are made between different cases whose similarities are then referred to as reasons for judging case A similarly to case B. An example would be to claim that communism and fascism are both totalitarian systems and that therefore communism should be judged as equally evil as fascism.

There is, moreover, a corresponding principle, the treating of different cases differently, that requires us to pay attention to relevant differences between cases and take them into consideration in the judgment. It does not contradict but supplements the principle of treating like cases alike. In the debate around communism and totalitarianism it has, for example, been claimed that communism ought to be judged differently from fascism because communism represented an attempt to create an equal society and fascism a hierarchical and racist society (whether that is a good argument or not is not the issue here).

A further principle of justice related to non-discrimination is *impartiality*. Ever since the wave of criticism of positivist philosophy and scientific objectivity in the 1960s and 1970s, impartiality has, however, come to be seen as a naive ideal, and sometimes not even as an ideal at all. In its stead, there has been a widespread acceptance of a pluralism of different forms of partiality. If history is always written under some presuppositions, how can one avoid being 'biased'? How can there be any neutrality if historical interpretations, for strictly theoretical (and not merely psychological or sociological) reasons, are necessarily based on certain epistemological, ontological and normative presuppositions? Moreover, does neutrality not imply indifference – and how could that be an ethical ideal? It seems, however, that we often confuse impartiality with neutrality and equate normativity with partiality. Is it not possible, in principle, to be normative but impartial? In fact, both of these dimensions are usually considered to be essential aspects of the concept of justice. Impartiality, as part of the concept of justice, does not imply value neutrality, since it involves normative laws and judgments. Therefore, justice can function as a normative ideal that favours impartiality without implying indifference or value neutrality. Impartiality as an ideal does not preclude engagement but can rather be understood as an *engagement for impartiality*, as part of one's engagement for justice. Furthermore, to be 'partial' in the sense of favouring some principles rather than others is different from being partial in relation to the parties in a conflict. Taking a stand against oppression is not the same as taking a stand in favour of a particular group. Nationalistic and racist historiography provides numerous examples of the latter kind of partiality, of favouring one group to the detriment of its enemies.

But is it not the case that the typical critical intellectual is often committed to a particular group and thus antagonistic towards its opponents or oppressors? Is not such a partisan commitment a sign of a commitment for justice rather than of discrimination? Again: it is necessary to make a distinction here between, on the one hand, taking a general stand against oppression (or in favour of some general principle or value) and, on the other hand, acting in a partial manner towards a particular group or a party in a conflict. The first type of commitment does not run counter to the idea of impartiality. The reason why a commitment to a particular group can be understood as a commitment for justice is either that the distinction stressed above is overlooked or that the particular group in question is understood as the embodiment of a general interest, as, for example, in the case of the proletariat in the Marxist philosophy of history. Even in the latter case, there is thus an overarching principle of impartiality and universality – the general interest of humankind – that justifies one's support of the interests of a particular group. Whether it was ever really plausible to interpret those particular interests as representing the universal interest of humanity is, of course, a different question.

Commitment to a particular group and the conflict in which the group is involved sometimes becomes an important dimension of a critical intellectual's identity. This is the case, for example, with strong identifications with the labour movement and the political Left as opposed to the 'bourgeois' society and its representatives and supporters. Such identifications can easily result in reified forms of partiality, leading one to overlook aspects and facts contradicting one's accusations against the oppressor while idealizing or victimizing the group one favours. Commitments of this kind do not tend to further the cause of justice in the sense of bringing about more just historical judgments but, instead, run the risk of fostering discrimination between the different parties involved, due to biased treatment of a particular group.

As a general rule, then, like cases ought to be treated alike. Correspondingly, different cases should be treated differently but only for relevant reasons such as desert and proportion, as discussed above. Comparison with other cases and how one would handle them is often enlightening in this regard. Some historians who condemn the 'fellow travellers' of communism in other cases reject condemnations of historical phenomena as expressions of an unhistorical attitude and, instead, emphasize the need for understanding and historical contextualization of the past. Similarly, some historians who generally condemn the United States and its actions in Latin America and Vietnam in other situations dismiss negative judgments aimed at the 'crimes' of communist regimes as unhistorical.[20]

Yet another dimension of justice concerns the rightness and appropriateness of the norms guiding the judgment. Impartial and balanced judgments may still be fundamentally unjust if these norms are inappropriate or false. The justness of just judgments also depends on the validity or *rightness*[21] of the content of the 'laws' and the norms, not only on how the historical phenomenon in question is formally treated. Should the Left movements of the 1960s be condemned for not being racist enough, most people would certainly consider the judgment as unreasonable, even when other political movements were treated the same way and according to the same norm: the judgment only makes sense if racism is considered a valid norm to be observed. Consequently, the question of the validity or 'rightness' of the norms that guide historical judgments will usually be an essential aspect of historical controversies.

These norms, however, must also be *appropriate* in relation to the historical phenomenon being discussed, so that they can throw light on relevant aspects of it. Do the norms used allow taking both positive and negative aspects of the phenomenon into consideration? Are they able to do justice to the phenomenon? The relevance of the norms in the sense of their being appropriate depends not only on the historical phenomenon itself but also on what the historical controversy being waged in the present is about. For example, new conflicts in relation to the Enlightenment, focusing on, say, the Enlightenment's implication in the colonial project and modern racism rather than on the issue of freedom versus totalitarian utopianism, make it relevant to change the norms or at least include also other norms. That, in turn, makes it pertinent to introduce new empirical aspects of the phenomenon into the discussion. This relationship between which empirical factual aspects are deemed relevant and which norms are judged as relevant is dialectical in character.[22]

In historical thinking, as opposed to real-life legal processes, there are no given norms or laws to refer to but that does not make the validity or 'rightness' of norms an irrelevant issue. It is still an indispensable dimension of historical judgments and will thus have to play a part in any controversy. The justification of the norms is thus part of the justification of the judgment, which means that historians acting as engaged intellectuals should pay attention also to this aspect.

The question of the rightness of norms raises yet another question: that of the historicity of judgments and the historical distance to the past. A typical criticism directed at the idea of making judgments about the past is that one then looks at the past through the lenses of today's norms and knowledge. 'But they had other values at the time!' and 'Back then, they did not know what we know now!' are typical objections raised in this regard. It is therefore necessary, it is claimed, to historicize.[23] The general idea behind such claims, however, can be explained as a concept of *justice* rather than a notion of truth, objectivity or understanding. What is claimed is that one should not judge historical actors and phenomena according to historical conditions other than those of their own; doing otherwise would be to treat these actors and phenomena unjustly. This aspect of historical justice entails a need to take into account the historical conditions and circumstances of the phenomena and actors considered. A judgment leaving such relevant circumstances out of consideration can, consequently, be criticized for being *unjust*. Historicization, or historical contextualization, does thus not have to be viewed as the opposite of making historical judgments; instead, it can be understood as a way of furthering more just historical judgments.[24]

What renders the norms of the prosecuting critical historian valid and appropriate in relation to the phenomenon, the context and the parties involved? The answer can hardly be that the norms correspond to that historian's own ideological convictions. Again, as argued above, for the purpose of furthering more just judgments, there is a need for engaging also other roles suggested by the analogy of a court of justice, since the judgments and norms of the prosecutor need to be put to the test. To be able to engage productively in conflicts between ideological standpoints typical of historical controversies, an overarching idea is needed that transcends the different positions expressed. With such an idea, a possibility for arriving at new ideological insights and drawing new ideological conclusions is created, since an effort to do justice to the historical phenomenon, and the dialectical interaction with it that this involves, makes it possible for the phenomenon to challenge normative judgments and ideological convictions in the present.

To counteract the risks of political and ideological instrumentalization of history, there is a need for a value-rational ideal that is independent of any particular ideological standpoint or political purpose, something akin to an ethics of ideological thinking and intellectual engagement. Truth and objectivity, which used to serve the function of such value-rational ideals, are not sufficient for handling the kind of normative questions typically involved in historical controversies, as I have tried to show above. What is more, as I have also pointed out, even truth can be instrumentalized for political purposes. Neither truth nor objectivity or any particular political or ideological standpoint will thus suffice on its own to engage productively with the normative character of conflicts of historical judgments. The different aspects of justice as outlined above together form an overarching idea that transcends partiality and particular standpoints. The analogy of the court of justice is, in the first place, applicable to cases where the question is about historical judgments of the past. Even if it does not automatically cover other important dimensions of historical thinking such as understanding, reflection and orientation, the ideal of justice and the different roles of the analogy are nevertheless, as a rule, relevant also when such other dimensions of historical thinking are concerned.

Conclusion: The Roles of the Engaged Intellectual and Historians' Engagement for Justice

What are, then, the implications of the ideal of justice for historians acting as engaged intellectuals? Instead of striving for any particular preconceived political outcome or pursuing a commitment to some specific ideology or group, they should pursue a broader commitment to *justice* or justness of historical judgments and interpretations. The problems noted above as intrinsic to the role of the historians as engaged intellectuals ought, however, not be understood as implying a rejection of the idea of historians as critics, or a denial of the importance of the role that historians can play as prosecutors. The role of the critical prosecutor remains a vital one, although perhaps not so much in the sense of an intellectual engaging in political protests or fighting for particular political outcomes but, rather, as one important part of historians' task to identify and help make visible hitherto unseen problems, injustices and moral wrongs. The problems highlighted above in this chapter should, thus, be interpreted as so many aspects of responsibility that historians need to be mindful of as engaged intellectuals.

To better be able to work through the questions that historians (and others) raise in their role as prosecutor, there is a need also for other roles as suggested by the analogy of the court of justice. In order to contribute to more just historical judgments and a more just public memory, historians as engaged intellectuals sometimes need to act in the role of a defence lawyer or a judge. Which of the different roles the historian ought to play in each particular case will, amongst other things, depend on how history is used by other parties in the debate and on the current pattern of established public narratives. Some of the general considerations here could be: how can historians contribute to more just judgments in light of the different aspects of justice and the risk of distortion as described above? Do the dominant narratives of public memory express exculpation, self-legitimation and ideological rationalization? Do they imply condemnation and exclusion of certain groups or projection of blame on scapegoats? Do they correspond to the role of a prosecutor or rather to that of a defence lawyer? How are the parties involved treated by the narratives? In searching for an answer to the question of the proper role for historians as engaged intellectuals, it would thus be useful not to focus merely on the role of the critical intellectual-as-prosecutor but, rather, to assess the situation in each case against the whole spectrum of roles entailed by the analogy of the court of justice.

From the point of view of the ideal of justice, neither the role historians play as experts concerned with diffusing results from historical research nor their involvement as critical intellectuals inspired by political projects appear as sufficient. If intellectuals, according to the classical model, had the role of the conscience of society, then also that conscience clearly needs some kind of conscience. As Finkielkraut has put it in his critical remarks on the role of intellectuals in the twentieth century, '[i]t is much more comfortable, in fact, *being* a conscience than *having* one.'[25] The idea of justice, as a self-transcending ideal, can provide historians acting as a conscience and performing the different roles pertaining to the court of justice analogy with just such a conscience. Historians as engaged intellectuals should, accordingly, try to recognize, listen to and serve this self-transcending ideal of justice rather than treating the norms of critique as a matter of ideological conviction and using history as an instrument for pursuing the attendant purposes.

Martin Wiklund is currently working as Assistant Professor in the History of Ideas, Stockholm University. He has published monographs and articles on functions and uses of history, theory of history, the crisis of historicism, historical argumentation and narratives of modernity. Among his publications are *I det modernas landskap: Historisk orientering och kritiska berättelser om det moderna Sverige mellan 1960 och 1990* (Symposion, 2006), *Historia som domstol: Historisk värdering och retorisk argumentation kring '68'* (Nya Doxa, 2012), editorship of several anthologies and more recently 'Ett ansvarslöst ansvar? Om historikerns ansvar för historiska lärdomar' (*Historiens hemvist*, Vol. II, Makadam 2016) and 'Rüsen's Response to the Crisis of Historicism' (*Intelligere*, 3/2017).

Notes

The text was written as part of the research project 'The Use and Abuse of Historical Lessons: Instrumentalization, Contingency and the Ethics of Historical Lessons', financed by the Swedish Research Council. The language of the text was improved by the language editor Timo Lyyra.

1. Zola, 'J'Accuse...! Lettre au Président de la République'; Winock, *Le Siècle des Intellectuels*, 17–27.
2. Said, *Representations of the Intellectual: The 1993 Reith Lectures*; See also Walzer, *The Company of Critics: Social Criticism and Political Commitment in the Twentieth Century*, 3–28.
3. For examples of other roles of intellectuals in a longer historical perspective, see Charle, *Vordenker der Moderne: Die Intellektuellen im 19. Jahrhundert*, 25f., 60–69; Juliá, *Historias de las dos Españas*.
4. Hollander, *Political Pilgrims: Travels of Western Intellectuals to the Soviet Union, China, and Cuba 1928–1978*.
5. For a discussion of these commonly ascribed qualities, see S. Collini, *Absent Minds: Intellectuals in Britain*, 61–64; Walzer, *Interpretation and Social Criticism*, 31–33.
6. Several aspects of this identity can be related to what Calinescu has termed 'aesthetic modernity' standing in opposition to 'bourgeois modernity'; see Calinescu, *Five Faces of Modernity: Modernism, Avant-Garde, Decadence, Kitsch, Postmodernism*, 40–44.
7. In his discussion of social criticism and the role of the critic, Walzer distinguishes between three different ways of doing moral philosophy: the path of discovery, the path of invention and the path of interpretation. These paths roughly correspond to three different models of practical reason. The role of the modernist or avant-gardist intellectual follows the path of invention. For a more detailed discussion of the three paths, see Walzer, *Interpretation and Social Criticism*, 4–17.
8. The distinction is referred to in, e.g., Said, *Representations of the Intellectual*, 49–63.
9. For a similar argument about the role of sociology as a 'public science', see Calhoun, 'Social Science for Public Knowledge', 299–318.
10. For a discussion of the problems of 'ethics of conviction' in relation to the role of public intellectuals, see Scott, 'Between Autonomy and Responsibility: Max Weber on Scholars, Academics and Intellectuals', 45–64.
11. The literature on such historical controversies is vast. See, e.g., Andersson and Tydén, *Sverige och Nazityskland: Skuldfrågor och moraldebatt*; Bernecker and Brinkmann, *Kampf der Erinnerungen: Der spanische Bürgerkrieg in Politik und Gesellschaft 1936–2006*; Bock and Wolfrum, *Umkämpfte Vergangenheit*; Bryld and Warring, *Besættelsestiden som kollektiv erindring*; Macintyre and Clark, *The History Wars*; Rousso, *The Haunting Past: History, Memory, and Justice in Contemporary France*.
12. See, e.g., Barkan, *The Guilt of Nations: Restitution and Negotiating Historical Injustices*; Bensaïd, *Qui est le Juge? Pour en finir avec le tribunal de l'Histoire*; Delgado and Fusi, *Franquismo:*

El juicio de la historia; Jones, Östberg and Randeraad, *Contemporary History on Trial: Europe Since 1989 and the Role of the Expert Historian*.

13. Different legal systems to some extent express different legal ethics. The adversarial system emphasizes competition of arguments and the protection of individual rights, whereas the inquisitorial system aims at impartial truth and reconstruction by the investigating judge and at 'letting justice be done' to the culprit. The analogy of the court of justice as described in this chapter is not explicitly based on either one of these systems, since the point is not to imitate the actual functioning of the judicial system but to throw light on historical thinking. To that end, aspects from both systems have been included where it has seemed useful. It should, however, be noted that the roles of the prosecutor, the judge and the defence lawyer in this chapter are more akin to those in the adversarial system. The ideal of justice, on the other hand, makes the constellation of roles here as a whole more similar to that in the inquisitorial system. See Nagorcka, Stanton and Wilson, 'Stranded between Partisanship and the Truth? A Comparative Analysis of Legal Ethics in the Adversarial and Inquisitorial Systems of Justice', 448–77.

14. Rousso, 'Justiz, Geschichte und Erinnerung in Frankreich: Überlegungen zum Papon-Prozeß', 141–63.

15. Said, *Representations of the Intellectual*, 63ff.

16. Here the role of the prosecutor is based on the adversarial model of the trial and not the inquisitorial one.

17. For a more extensive analysis of such speech acts, see Wiklund, *Historia som domstol: Historisk värdering och retorisk argumentation*, 31–40. Speech act theory was developed by John Austin (Austin, *How to Do Things with Words*) and by John Searle (Searle, *Speech Acts: An Essay in the Philosophy of Language*). For an analysis of speech acts connected to some of the different roles in a legal process, see Hoffmann, 'Zur Pragmatik von Erzählformen vor Gericht', 28–63 and Hoffmann, *Kommunikation vor Gericht*.

18. The aspects of justice discussed here derive mainly from the principles analysed in Hart, *The Concept of Law*; and Perelman, *The Idea of Justice and the Problem of Argument*. For a more elaborate discussion of the relevance of these aspects to historical thinking, see Wiklund, *Historia som domstol*, 233–74.

19. See, e.g., Löwy, *Redemption and Utopia: Jewish Libertarian Thought in Central Europe: A Study in Elective Affinity*, 18f, 118–23, 140–47.

20. The German Historikerstreit and the debates around *The Black Book of Communism* (Courtois) provide examples of such attitudes.

21. Robert Alexy, who has drawn attention to the need to make a distinction between formal legality and normative validity, uses the concept *Richtigkeit* for the latter dimension. According to Alexy, the application of law makes a claim not only to legality but also to a certain degree of validity or 'rightness' (*Anspruch auf Richtigkeit*). Merely following the law can result in extreme injustice, as Gustav Radbruch argued after World War II with reference to the racial discrimination sanctioned by law during the National Socialist regime in Germany. Alexy, *Begriff und Geltung des Rechts*, 64–69, 90f.

22. The dialectical interdependence determining which factual (empirical) aspects and which norms are deemed relevant at each given moment makes it problematic to uphold the idea that historians should limit themselves to just describing, explaining or understanding a case and then leave it to others to evaluate it normatively. Historians can only discern which facts and empirical aspects are relevant to include in an interpretation with an idea of what *normative* aspects are relevant for the controversy, given that conflicts of interpretation are not merely about what happened in the past but also about how to judge the historical phenomenon. The sharp distinction Marc Bloch made between the role of the scholar and that of the judge, where the scholar describes and explains what has happened and the judge also passes judgment, has been reiterated by many contemporary historians, although it is actually

based on the implausible idea of knowledge as positive science and an assumption about an ontological gap between normative and descriptive judgments: 'For we can neither condemn nor absolve without accepting a table of values which no longer refers to any positive science' (Bloch, *The Historian's Craft*, 138f, 193).

23. The need for this kind of historicization was emphasized by historicist historians such as J.G. Herder and L. v. Ranke against external normative standards used in the historical thinking of the Enlightenment.

24. See Rüsen, 'Die Historisierung der Nationalsozialismus', 217–62.

25. Finkielkraut and Sloterdijk, *Les battements du monde*, 230 (my translation). The distinction between having and being a conscience (*Gewissenhaben* and *Gewissensein*) has earlier been made with regard to modern philosophy of history in Marquard, *Schwierigkeiten mit der Geschichtsphilosophie*.

Bibliography

Alexy, R. *Begriff und Geltung des Rechts*. Freiburg/Munich: Verlag Karl Alber, 2011.
Andersson, L. and M. Tydén (eds). *Sverige och Nazityskland: Skuldfrågor och moraldebatt*. Stockholm: Dialogos, 2007.
Austin, J. *How to Do Things with Words*. Oxford: Oxford University Press, 1962.
Barkan, E. *The Guilt of Nations: Restitution and Negotiating Historical Injustices*. New York: W.W. Norton & Company, 2000.
Bensaïd, D. *Qui est le Juge? Pour en finir avec le tribunal de l'Histoire*. Paris: Fayard, 1999.
Bernecker, W.L. and S. Brinkmann. *Kampf der Erinnerungen: Der spanische Bürgerkrieg in Politik und Gesellschaft 1936–2006*. Nettersheim: Graswurzelrevolution, 2006.
Bloch, M. *The Historian's Craft*. New York: Vintage Books/Random House, 1953.
Bock, P. and E. Wolfrum (eds). *Umkämpfte Vergangenheit*. Göttingen: Vandenhoeck & Ruprecht, 1999.
Bryld, C. and A. Warring. *Besættelsestiden som kollektiv erindring*. Roskilde: Roskilde Universitetsforlag, 1998.
Calhoun, C. 'Social Science for Public Knowledge', in S. Eliaeson and R. Kalleberg (eds), *Academics as public intellectuals* (Newcastle: Cambridge Scholars, 2008), 299–318.
Calinescu, M. *Five Faces of Modernity: Modernism, Avant-Garde, Decadence, Kitsch, Postmodernism*. Durham, NC: Duke University Press, 1990.
Charle, C. *Vordenker der Moderne: Die Intellektuellen im 19. Jahrhundert*. Frankfurt am Main: Fischer Verlag, 2001.
Collini, S. *Absent Minds: Intellectuals in Britain*. Oxford: Oxford University Press, 2006.
Courtois, S. et al. (ed.). *The Black Book of Communism*. Cambridge, MA: Harvard University Press, 1999.
Delgado, J.L.G. and J.P. Fusi (eds). *Franquismo: El juicio de la historia*. Madrid: Ediciones Temas de Hoy, 2000.
Finkielkraut, A. and P. Sloterdijk. *Les battements du monde*. Paris: Pauvert, 2003.
Hart, H.L.A. *The Concept of Law*. Oxford: Clarendon Press, 1961.
Hoffmann, L. 'Zur Pragmatik von Erzählformen vor Gericht', in K. Ehlich (ed.), *Erzählen im Alltag* (Frankfurt am Main: Suhrkamp, 1980), 8–63.
———. *Kommunikation vor Gericht*. Tübingen: Gunter Narr Verlag, 1983.
Hollander, P. *Political Pilgrims: Travels of Western Intellectuals to the Soviet Union, China, and Cuba 1928–1978*. Oxford: Oxford University Press, 1981.
Jones, H., K. Östberg and N. Randeraad (eds). *Contemporary History on Trial: Europe Since 1989 and the Role of the Expert Historian*. Manchester: Manchester University Press, 2007.

Juliá, S. *Historias de las dos Españas*. Madrid: Taurus, 2004.

Löwy, M. *Redemption and Utopia: Jewish Libertarian Thought in Central Europe: A Study in Elective Affinity*, trans. H. Heaney. Stanford, CA: Stanford University Press, 1992.

Macintyre, S. and A. Clark. *The History Wars*, Melbourne: Melbourne University Press, 2004.

Marquard, O. *Schwierigkeiten mit der Geschichtsphilosophie*. Frankfurt am Main: Suhrkamp, 1982.

Nagorcka, F., M. Stanton and M. Wilson. 'Stranded between Partisanship and the Truth? A Comparative Analysis of Legal Ethics in the Adversarial and Inquisitorial Systems of Justice', *Melbourne University Law Review* 29(2) (2005), 448–77.

Perelman, C. *The Idea of Justice and the Problem of Argument*. London: Routledge & Kegan Paul, 1963.

Rousso, H. 'Justiz, Geschichte und Erinnerung in Frankreich: Überlegungen zum Papon-Prozeß', in N. Frei, D. van Laak and M. Stolleis (eds), *Geschichte vor Gericht: Historiker, Richter und die Suche nach Gerechtigkeit*. Munich: C.H. Beck, 2000, 141–63.

———. *The Haunting Past: History, Memory, and Justice in Contemporary France*. Philadelphia: University of Pennsylvania Press, 2002.

Rüsen, J. 'Die Historisierung der Nationalsozialismus', in J. Rüsen (ed.), *Zerbrechende Zeit: Über den Sinn der Geschichte* (Cologne: Böhlau, 2001), 217–62.

Said, E. *Representations of the Intellectual: The 1993 Reith Lectures*. London: Vintage, 1994.

Scott, A. 'Between Autonomy and Responsibility: Max Weber on Scholars, Academics and Intellectuals', in J. Jennings and T. Kemp-Welch (eds), *Intellectuals in Politics: From the Dreyfus Affair to Salman Rushdie* (New York: Routledge, 1997), 45–64.

Searle, J. *Speech Acts: An Essay in the Philosophy of Language*. Cambridge: Cambridge University Press, 1969.

Walzer, M. *Interpretation and Social Criticism*. Cambridge, MA: Harvard University Press, 1987.

———. *The Company of Critics: Social Criticism and Political Commitment in the Twentieth Century*. New York: Basic Books, 1988.

Wiklund, M. *Historia som domstol: Historisk värdering och retorisk argumentation*. Nora: Nya Doxa, 2012.

Winock, M. *Le Siècle des Intellectuels*. Paris: Éditions du seuil, 1997.

Zola, É. 'J'Accuse…! Lettre au Président de la République'. *L'Aurore* (13 January 1898).

CHAPTER 3

Committed Writing

History and Narrative Communication Revisited

Kalle Pihlainen

History and Literature – One More Try

Historians still, by and large, appear to assume that they can write fairly unproblematically about past reality. Even the strong anti-foundationalist, linguistically or textually focused debate during recent decades has done little to diminish this belief. In many respects, it has perhaps rather only strengthened historians' commitments to a truth that is somehow 'out there' – and as a consequence the position of theory in historical writing has become increasingly problematic. The current and, to me, still largely undertheorized move away from what are viewed as the 'extremes' of textualism and linguistic-turn-type thinking and towards an emphasis of 'presence', 'materialities' or some form of practical realism, for instance, appears to have held out hope of reasons for returning to quite naive positions regarding the nature of historical representation. This is not to say that historians are necessarily unaware of the theoretical difficulties inherent in what they do but, rather, that – because of a general aversion to theory – they have in many cases decided to leave their own theoretical commitments unexamined. From a theoretical perspective, it seems that in doing so they have also largely had to abandon the idea of political commitment because their epistemological beliefs conflict with the political in simplistic, 'realist' formulations of this relation.[1] It is particularly the issue of political commitment that I wish to revisit here.

Notes for this section begin on page 76.

Contemporaneous with the linguistic turn and attendant phenomena, a similar broad move away from political issues can be claimed to have taken place in contemporary literature. Consequently, many who deal with literature assume a conflict to exist between artistic ambitions and the political. Importantly, however, these parallel intuitions concerning the political within the disciplines of history and literature can be claimed to move in opposite directions: in history, the political is seen as being an ideological, additional component, whereas in literature, the political is often still seen to relate to the 'real' (or the real-world or referential) dimension of the text. Given this difference and complexity, would it not be useful to discuss history's relation to literature in terms of three categories – the epistemological, the aesthetic and the ethicopolitical? Or should discussions continue primarily in terms of only fact and fiction as has most often been the case? My aim in the first part is to show that an alternative way of approaching the issues raised by the fact-fiction debate could bring significant benefits. Or, to put it differently, I hope to suggest that moving beyond such claims against relativism as to continue to assume that meaning (aesthetic-ethical-political) is somehow grounded or groundable in the epistemological is a necessary step to take.[2] Importantly, changing the terms of the debate in this way is not intended to suggest that the problems involved would themselves somehow go away. Yet – and although a full separation of the dimensions of epistemology, aesthetics and the ethicopolitical is impossible – such a distinction is crucial as a heuristics for a useful examination of historical writing, one that might be conducted outside the current deadlock.

The aestheticization of history as well as of literature – to the extent to which it makes sense to speak so of literature – has in both cases been taken to also lead to its depoliticization. Yet it seems that aestheticization and depoliticization should not be understood as synonymous, at least without first giving further thought to the matter. Much of the reason why constructivist theorists of history tend to equate the ethicopolitical with the aesthetic resides in what they take to be a central function of narrative form: the narrative, whether historical or literary, imposes closure on the subjects of the representation. In order to achieve its effects, this closure has to be ethical – always in the sense of the ethicopolitical; as, that is, governed by some sense and question of responsibility – and not only aesthetic. Hayden White has famously emphasized this valuative nature of closure: 'When it is a matter of recounting the concourse of real events, what other "ending" could a given sequence of such events have than a "moralizing" ending? What else could narrative closure consist of than the passage from one moral order to another?'[3]

The closure imposed by narratives necessarily introduces judgement (ethical or aesthetic), since those are part and parcel with the representational form. And, following narrative constructivists like White, it would be challenging to distinguish aesthetic from ethical closure in these impositions of form. The totalization effected by form presents its contents or substance as forming a whole, as being in some sense 'complete', and thus it creates an artificial space where evaluation can *and must* take place. Since there seems to be broad agreement on this, it is the nature and the site of this evaluation that should be considered. I will return to these questions in a moment. Before doing so, however, it will be useful to briefly consider the role of stories – and especially of historical or 'factual' stories – as instruments of what might best be termed therapy and recreation. It seems that the only way to prevent the ethical and aesthetic imposition of meaning, the moral of the story, as it were, from automatically also being a political matter is to keep stories away from issues that might be seen as politically significant. Following this strategy, the desire to 'have meaning' has, one might argue, led – when theorizing on the matter has not ended in an outright denial of 'doing history' – to a proliferation of microhistories, stories with an abundance of details that are mainly meaningful only for the subjects of the past described.[4] On the other hand, for literature, shying away from the political has in some cases meant an emphasis on fantasy and a general turning away from the real world. The value of storytelling in a very traditional fashion has thus also been rediscovered, albeit often with an ironic or fantastic twist. Naturally, sensibilities regarding such questions continue to change too. Perhaps comparably to the backlash towards 'reality' in history, there now appears to be a growing interest in historical novels too.

There is another, more theoretically significant alternative for history that has continued to be the mainstay of much contemporary, 'modernist' literature (and of popular culture too), however. This is the attempt to do away with the moral of the story altogether; with texts leaving readers to conclude that the only lesson remaining is that stories hold no real answers for life and – the reverse side of this – that life is nothing but a freely chosen story, a matter of redescription, as also the extreme anti-foundationalist argument would have it. In other words, the challenge posed by the political has, in such literary writing, been met by an attempt – which I will here call *poststructuralist* – to subvert representation.[5] In more radical interpretations, this amounts to a denial of truth – even if that may appear to be a misplaced requirement for literature for those who take 'fiction' to be capable of relativism only vis-à-vis ethical but not epistemological issues.

Where an emphasis on storytelling in the mode of the fantastic and a desire to avoid the closure imposed by narrative representation are certainly not essentially mutually excluding, it needs to be noted that the objectives involved lie in opposing directions. While literature can avoid taking a moral stance by moving away from reality into fantasy, this choice expresses a desire to be apolitical. In remaining political – yet at the same time breaking away from traditional ideological positionings – literature can only make itself unavailable for habitual moral evaluation or 'therapy' through refusing closure. Here, the challenge of politics is not to be met by simple avoidance but by a destabilization and rejection of interpretive categories and capacities. This latter possibility also seems to be the driving force behind the majority of theoretical appeals for history to become more literary. The kind of radical history that White advocates is a case in point.[6]

With reference to history especially, and as opposed to literature, it is useful to note that emphasis on the epistemological dimension *per se* – that is, on the evidentiary nature and abundance of the material used regardless of its significance for us – clearly turns attention away from political commitment. Since, by its agreed-upon nature, 'by definition' as it were, history cannot avoid the political by retreating into fantasy, the empirical provides the only available avenue of escape from this kind of responsibility. (One can think again of the importance – almost a fetishization – of empirical detail in many microhistories or historians' attempts at 'thick description'.) On the other hand, an express awareness of the fact that material concerning past reality could also turn attention from the world of 'narrative-as-escape' to the world of 'narrative-as-possibility' – that is, from passivity and (feigned?) detachment to reflection and responsibility – offers new prospects and may potentially call up an attitude of involvement. At the same time, empathy and the assumption of some (albeit most often vague and undefined) 'ethical responsibility' for the subjects in the past are virtues that historians easily identify with, simply as a consequence of their dealing with real people. Indeed, it seems that appeals to 'truth' and 'authenticity' are enough to evoke such optimistic positionings, even if they are not always sufficient to lead to substantial articulations of what is in fact entailed. Certainly these sentiments do not always translate into action. As they are so prevalent in historians' justifications, such motives should not, despite their going against my main argument here, be completely discounted, however.[7]

In debates concerning fact and fiction in historiography as well as in the relatively few historical works that have attempted to really accommodate such theoretical considerations, the second politically viable alternative of refusing to impose interpretive closure on available material – the alternative that I here refer to as a poststructuralist one – has unfortunately rather often gone hand in hand with a visible turn to fantasy. Here, when the attempt to banish the moral of the story from historical narrative tries to follow the literary course (by adopting similar stylistic means: complexity, repetition, ambiguity, juxtapositions, contradiction and fragmentation, for example), it easily simultaneously slides into the anything-goes relativism narrative constructivist theorists of history have so often been accused of advocating.

In other words, the potential political questioning offered up by use of the imagination in literature with regard to form (and hence meaning) is confused with a literary use of imagination with regard to subject matter (facts), which only returns attention to the fact-fiction dualism. Thus the usual lesson derived *by historians* from literature and discussions of the literariness of history seems to remain focused more on epistemological detail than on aesthetic form. And, if that is indeed the case, it can be said that, despite all good intentions, the fact-fiction debate within historical theory as it now stands describes an escape from commitment and a withdrawal to the politically detached either-or of literary fantasy *or* historical empiricism. Brought across genre boundaries, the means for constructing political commitment seem to undermine each other.

Why Poststructuralist History?

Although I have in mind here quite different thinkers under the reductive rubric of 'poststructuralism', it seems justified to suggest that there is something to such a positioning that can be summarized in terms of a broad resistance to representation. Thus poststructuralism and history seem an unlikely fit from the outset. Yet, against this general sentiment, Todd May, for instance, has offered a convincing reorientation of any total denial of representational practices. May has taken up the challenge of defining a common 'ethics' for poststructuralist thinkers and – following his lead – it can, I would say, be argued that the central responsibility in all social action for poststructuralists is to resist representation *if and when* doing so does not run counter to ethical responsibilities that have been ascribed greater value. On this view, representation would still be perfectly justifiable when it increases people's freedom for self-definition, for instance; something that is certainly a potentially suitable goal for historians – in addition to being an interpretation that fits in nicely with the general 'textualist' or narrative constructivist theorizing about history that I have so far discussed. The specific implications that such a textualist or poststructuralist position has for history writing (and indeed for any justifications for continuing with history at all) will need to be further investigated, however.[8] From my perspective at least, White's narrative constructivism is the best point of entry for articulating some form of poststructuralist history. Because of poststructuralism's problematic relation to representation, any attempt to do so will require negotiation.

For Dominick LaCapra – despite his being on many counts, I think, a poststructuralist – a commendable approach to history is 'one that attempts to work out the "dialogical" connection between past and present through which historical understanding becomes linked to ethicopolitical concerns.'[9] Other theoretically minded commentators on history echo this same idea in various forms. For Joan Scott, for instance, the task of the historian is not primarily to examine what has taken place in the past but how the terms used in talking about those events have come about. As she puts it: 'The story is no longer about the things that have happened to women and men and how they have reacted to them; instead it is about how the subjective and collective meanings of women and men as categories of identity have been constructed.'[10]

In this (quite limited) way, then, the past is not removed from everyday concerns but 'lives on' in us as well as in our social discourses and practices. What remains of the past inhabits a space that is temporally removed from us only in the strictest of senses.[11] Thus the 'present past' in this weaker (discursive) sense is very much a factor to be accounted for when discussing history in terms of the aesthetic and the ethical. In this formulation, the emphasis placed by the historian on the empirical becomes not only a matter of the standards of the discipline but also a matter of more far-reaching ethical significance. To reiterate this key point: since meaning is not 'out there' – in reality or in the facts – historical facts are significant only in how they can limit and refute interpretations and not because they might provide some unmediated access to a more robust pastness.

Following such textualist inclinations, it is perhaps possible to be more precise about the idea of this present past, then. In daily experiences, the connection between past and present is located in memory, in language, in various material and social practices and customs, and so on. In the field of history, this connection resides firstly in the social space opened up by the genre (just as with historical meaning, the historical past is not 'out there' for experiencing, after all) – or, in any single instance, in a particular narrative's communicative potential in evoking the 'historical' in these broader discourses. It is within this same communicative or *narrative space*[12] produced in the aesthetic process that the valuative 'content of the form' is also created. The reason that this fictional space – 'fictional' in the sense of imaginary as well as in the sense of being fashioned by the narrative – is the place where any pastness can be constructed is that it is the only available forum for the *present*ation of the temporal nature of the connection (again, I say this with all necessary caveats). The historical past can only present itself through the aesthetic, through imagination, and, once present, brings into existence a comparison: the present is seen in terms of the potential for things to be different. Thus, by default, this introduces the idea of future change also. In doing so, it simultaneously establishes the basis for the ethicopolitical. A question that I think needs to be considered, then, is: if the 'present-ing' of temporal difference in the narrative space of history – an instance where the epistemological is mediated by the aesthetic – leads to ethical considerations, what, then, of the difference marked by the imaginary other of literature? What more could this comparison reveal?

The dynamics that I have attempted to outline here so far have a clear parallel in the thought of Jean-Paul Sartre. Indeed, the mutual recognition of freedoms, which is necessarily also a recognition of otherness as opposed to objectification, and which Sartre sees as manifested in literature, will form the basis for my definition of narrative space. According to Sartre, at least at the time of his advocacy of committed literature, the presence of an ethical relation in literature is undeniable. As he writes:

> ... at the heart of the aesthetic imperative we discern the moral imperative. For, since the one who writes recognizes, by the very fact that he takes the trouble to write, the freedom of his readers, and since the one who reads, by the mere fact of his opening the book, recognizes the freedom of the writer, the work of art, from whichever side you approach it, is an act of confidence in the freedom of men.[13]

In expressing this confidence, the work of art creates a space where writer and reader can meet. This space is free of any epistemological worries, since these are already removed by the mutual trust facilitating the encounter.[14] At the same time, and while epistemological issues are marginalized in literary fiction, it needs to be remembered that there still are at least implied connections to reality and truth through the reality of this encounter that are responsible for a work's ethicopolitical impact.

The question that makes all of this of particular interest to historians, I think, is whether such encounters can take place through historical narratives – that is, can and should the historical narrative create a space where we are free from doubt? Further, since the historical narrative is – by its form – implicitly involved in a process of forgetting much of what continues beyond the artificial ending it imposes, can historical narratives inspire confidence and trust when they do create such a space? Or are they working too strongly against their other commitments in doing so?

In thinking these things, it is necessary to keep vigilant and remember that the commitments of historical narratives are very different to those of literary ones. While questions of what is true are certainly political in historical narratives, it is only the introduction of the fictive that makes them so. In other words, it is only through their aestheticization that epistemological considerations become political ones for historical narratives. If we did not need to consider the very basic idea that facts have no meaning *within* them – that is, that there are no entailments from reality to values and that values thus always have to be imposed – it would be possible to naively assume that histories simply represented 'things as they are'. In this way truth – 'as such' – carries no consequences.

Given that narratives necessarily aestheticize, it can be said, then, in parallel with Sartre's claims for literature, that, for historical narratives, at the heart of the epistemological imperative lies the moral imperative. And this raises some interesting questions: is the process of historical writing also a recognition of the freedom of readers in the same way as the process of writing literature? Do historians write for readers whose participation is an affirmation of trust? Or do they write for readers who can disregard the epistemological commitment of the text? As far as I can see, this is the point on which the poststructuralist history project hinges.

So what is involved in the writer-reader relationship of historical narratives? Or, perhaps more cynically: what are the dynamics connecting producers and consumers of history? This depends on how the genre agreement between historians and their readers is defined, of course. And, again, this is also a very Sartrean question: *for whom does the historian write?* Or again more cynically: what exactly is it that prompts historians to do what they do? But let me focus on the reading contract in the ideal rather than the actual, 'capitalized' situation for now ... Given historians' general disregard for theory, it can safely be assumed that historians do not write for theorists. Rather, like most writers, they write for readers who they expect will read with trust and (an attempt at) understanding. Readers who disrupt the 'mutual recognition of freedoms' are not the intended audience. Thus, when other historians examine historical texts, they too are assumed to enter into this relation. Importantly, the relation of trust does not exclude, in the case of historical narratives, the possibility of objections concerning either empirical issues or interpretations, since these are both formative in bringing about the space where the relation exists. It does, however, exclude abuse of trust as well as criticisms of doing so. So revisionism and propaganda, for instance, are easily dealt with since none of what I have said so far implies that debates about accuracy or even interpretation do not continue to be relevant.

The space opened up by different attitudes towards the communicative function of historical narratives and the nature of the narrative can best be illustrated with a concrete example: according to less theoretically elaborated views, the case of historical writing *simply is* different from that of literature. Here, and worth quoting at length, since he crystallizes some very basic prejudices, is Keith Windschuttle on Simon Schama's *Dead Certainties* (1991). Windschuttle claims that:

> ... once some of a book of history is discovered to be fabricated, the reader can never be sure that it is not *all* made up. Under these conditions, how could we have any confidence that the composite version itself is at all accurate or authentic? When a writer presents what he or she says is history, then the reader takes it on faith that the writer is at least trying to tell the truth. Once

the writer admits that some of what he or she has written is fiction, the reader not only feels a justified sense of betrayal but is bound to suspend judgement about the credibility of everything the writer has written. ... being mistaken is a world away from deliberately inventing fictionalised passages.[15]

One might respond to Windschuttle by asking a very basic theory question – what does it mean for a composite, a complex representation, to be 'authentic or accurate'? That, by itself, might be enough to demonstrate how far he in fact strays in this critique. But, in light of what I have said already, this prompts the more important question: how justified is such a sense of betrayal in terms of the rules of this narrative space? Admittedly, this kind of action goes against the 'historian's promise' understood in a traditional, very narrow sense. A great deal hinges on the characterization of 'the writer ... [as] at least trying to tell the truth' and on the near absolute opposition between truth and fiction that Windschuttle presents. Schama, more in line with narrative and constructivist theory of history, is obviously doing his best to tell some kind of truth rather than simply regaling us with factual details. Indeed, from a moderate textualist point of view, concepts like 'fictional truth' or 'metaphorical insight' seem to offer the most promising avenues for reaching the 'real' – for reaching something beyond linguistic free play and appropriation. Thus, these notions also offer the most promising objects for a historian's commitment. It is no surprise that narrative constructivists operate with a different conception of truth to Windschuttle's here.

There is a lot more packed into Windschuttle's objection, however. His conclusion is that history loses its meaning once the reader suspends judgement about the credibility of the text. Yet such a situation should perhaps – by many contemporary theoretical accounts, at least, and certainly by those that I have defended here – be seen as a desirable one. Suspension of judgement regarding the epistemological is exactly what the narrative space created by historical narratives can ideally afford, since readers are thus given better opportunities for making up their own minds about the *implications* of what is said. This too might be posited as a crucial part of the generic agreement for histories. Centrally, at stake is not an epistemological issue, since readers most often also have an alternative perspective or access to the material the text discusses – since, that is, texts, and especially historical texts, cannot and do not operate in a vacuum. Nor are historical narratives ever left in a vacuum with respect to their to-truthness, since the discipline works the way it works. To put all this differently, the fact that a text is not 'true' is not enough to deny its referentiality. Indeed, it must still be predicated on some idea of reference even for the criticism of fictionality to make sense.

There is a deeper, implicit ideological valuation here too, then. Windschuttle's view of readers is clearly dismissive. He supposes that readers are simply docile and unreflective consumers of texts. On the other hand, Hayden White's insistence on historical accounts in the style of 'anti-narrative non-stories' and 'postmodern parahistorical representations' envisions readers who have already moved on from such innocent or naive attitudes.[16] Quite naturally, such different views of readers' capacities lead also to different mindsets regarding history.

The Situation of the Historian in 2018?

Since historical and literary explanations hold such privileged cultural positions today, it is essential that their authority be viewed in the context of their responsibilities. As noted, an understanding of history as having an ideological or political dimension concerned with the legitimation of both present and future practices in addition to the more obvious and largely academic dimension of dealing with the past has become an informing force for much current theory of history. As Michel de Certeau has famously put it, it is time to recognize that 'history is a system at the general locus of society' and not only a subject for academic research. On this view, both private and shared ways of negotiating the world are based on this 'system that organizes by means of "histories" all social communication and everything that makes the present habitable.'[17]

To create some transparency, history thus appears to be faced with the need to embrace its presentist derivation. In realizing this presentism, by accepting their valuative role, historians cannot then any longer claim that historical method or the discipline is enough to shelter them from the assumption of responsibility for the consequences of their representational practices. And here literature could provide some guidance. As discussed already, the extremes of empiricism and 'postmodernism' both reject totality.[18] Hence either history 'in the extreme' – the option of material without commentary, albeit largely a theoretical option – or literary experimentation taken to similar extremes – aleatory techniques, estrangement, and so on – would not provide the kind of satisfaction required in terms of 'answers' that would improve the present 'for life'. Because historical questions have become questions that readers need to be able to make up their own minds about, they demand a particular kind of space to do so; a space in which communication becomes possible. Again, the idea of clear – but redefined – generic commitments and the relation of trust that these facilitate is central.

Simon Schama's admission of writing fiction in *Dead Certainties* repeats a strategy utilized by the later Sartre and quite notoriously by Michel Foucault as well. Commenting on his biography of Gustave Flaubert, *L'Idiot de la Famille* (1971–72), Sartre admits:

> Writing on Flaubert is enough for me by way of fiction – it might indeed be called a novel. Only I would like people to say that it was a true novel. I try to achieve a certain level of comprehension of Flaubert by means of hypotheses. Thus I use fiction – guided and controlled, but nonetheless fiction.... My hypotheses are in this sense a sort of invention of the personage.[19]

Despite what seem greatly exaggerated philosophical differences between their commitments, Sartre's method in *The Family Idiot* bears strong affinities to poststructuralism and particularly to Foucault's radical empiricism; Foucault, after all, presented his histories equally provocatively as 'fictions'.

For sure, *The Family Idiot* easily accommodates the concerns that poststructuralism raises with regard to representation. There is often claimed to be one crucial difference in world views, however: Sartre's humanism is generally not seen to agree with the 'anti-humanism' of the poststructuralists. On the level of terminology, a conflict between the two is painfully obvious. Such conflict is equally expected, of course, if poststructuralism is viewed as a movement directed forcefully against, among others, Sartrean existentialism. But *The Family Idiot* provides little justification for such a strong separation. At this late stage in Sartre's thought, subjectivity is curtailed by the facticity of the world and individuals are fully socialized, becoming what they are only through first internalizing and then re-externalizing their conditions. That is, subjects make the best use they can of a world that is given, both world and process having made them what they are. It is thus a small theoretical step from the later Sartre to poststructuralism – or at least to the forms that poststructuralism takes in Foucault's histories (if it in fact has much weight at all there). As May puts it: 'What is of interest to the poststructuralists is neither the constituting interiority of the subject nor the constituting exteriority of structures, but instead the interlocking network of contingent practices that produces both "subjects" and "structures".'[20] While there naturally remain differences between Sartre and poststructuralism, these differences relate more to the capacity of subjects for self-determination and self-definition than to the process of their constitution.

In examinations of historical narrative, focus would, then, by extension of such ideas, be neither on the author nor reader, nor on 'truth', but on the text itself as broadly construed (that is, on both a specific text and on the textual context that that text introduces) and on the narrative space where the significance of 'doing history' can be argued to reside. Indeed, it might be that readers' expectations and world views have in fact already changed in parallel with these and other similar theoretical sensibilities. There certainly seems to be support for such a claim in the contemporary and changing emphases of literary studies. As a consequence, and if they are to continue fulfilling a communicative function, historical narratives also need to change. By opening up a differently conceived and defined communicative or narrative space, historical narratives could better aid people in the present and participate in their projects of understanding the world as well as in their efforts at self-definition.

Greater emphasis on the empirical alone or even an abstention from unnecessary interpretation is not enough to counter the harmful effects of representation – by which I again refer to the ideological fixing that traditional and habitual emplotment and closure effect. Strategies of allowing sources to speak for themselves, however, are clearly in line with the general political commitments of contemporary theories, but difficulties concerning motivation and usefulness appear if the subjects presented only speak of matters that have little or no bearing on readers' lives. So the reconceived genre agreement also needs to include some kind of reward, as it were, some promise of entertaining. For issues of the past to have bearing they must first be moved into the realm of the aesthetic or that of the ethical. Only once past events or processes come be seen as 'beautiful', 'inspiring' or 'just', for example, can they be said to have any broader significance. Facts in themselves, without such interpretation, hold no interest except for those with a purely antiquarian interest in the past. In fact, I would maintain, this kind of 'pure' antiquarianism is more a rhetorical construct than a potential position at all.

As readers, we generally seem to want answers from what we read; hence some compromise is surely needed. What are our questions like at those times? Are they opposed to the possibilities open to writers? Are historians faced by different constraints than literary authors in answering these questions? Writing on literature already in 1947, Sartre claimed:

> The questions which our age puts to us and which remain *our* questions are of another order. How can one make himself a man in, by, and for history? Is there a possible synthesis between our unique and irreducible consciousness and our relativity; that is, between a dogmatic humanism and a perspectivism? What is the relationship between morality and politics? How, considering our deeper intentions, are we to take up the objective consequences of our acts?[21]

Considering the collusion of conventional forms of history with conservative values, the co-option of history to consumer culture, and so on, the challenge to histories today needs, I think, to be articulated in precisely those terms that Sartre used in presenting his idea of committed literature – terms that also offer some prescriptive content:

> *Is* one what one *does*? ... *What* should one do, what end should he choose *today*? What are the relationships between ends and means in a society based on violence? The works deriving from such preoccupations cannot aim first to please. They irritate and disturb. They offer themselves as tasks to be discharged. They urge the reader on to quests without conclusions. They present

us with experiences whose outcomes are uncertain. ... They will give not a world 'to see' but to change.²²

The contrast between the kinds of works Sartre defends here and conventional historical narratives surely requires no underscoring? For histories to 'irritate and disturb', for them to present as tasks and responsibilities rather than explanations and justifications for the way things are, for them to foster uncertainty, and so on, runs forcefully counter to their disciplinary function.²³ In this light, the political motive of White's argument for 'modernist' and experimental forms can hardly be overlooked. These questions that Sartre posed to literature would seem to be the kind of questions that many theorists of history more broadly too might want historians to include on their agendas today.

In lieu of any more programmatic conclusion, some further thoughts on commitment and the genre of history: factual and fictional accounts differ, it is most often suggested, with respect to their material. Or, rather, they differ with respect to the status of this material vis-à-vis truth. Accepting that this difference lies not so much in their material, their epistemological standing, as in their commitments, their ethical commitment to truth as necessarily mediated by aesthetic form, can provide much more leeway for historical narratives in selecting representational strategies. While this undeniably introduces a 'fictional' element, the usual objections can be met in the standard way by noting that the fictional is present in any representation regardless of our wanting it there or not. The crux of the issue lies, then, in the question of whether the historian's commitment to truth is sufficient justification for accepting these stories as historical, or not. On this level, the fact-fiction debate is ultimately about one issue only: whether or not the historian's commitment to truth is to be taken seriously; whether, that is, that commitment is enough even when the problematic nature of historical representation is recognized. The commitment can, of course, be conceived of in differing ways. For the more empirically minded, it concentrates on some vaguely expressed responsibility for the past or, in a worst-case scenario, simply a responsibility for 'getting the story straight' – in which case it may not be sufficiently met by such 'fictional' representations as long as it is the issue of fictionality that is held to be decisive – whereas those who understand the problematic of truth and the presentist nature of meaning will have an easier time appreciating that it is the commitment and not the results that decide the issue. Either way, the outcome or upshot of the debate is a political one: histories either continue to serve the status quo or they become vehicles of change.

In much the same way that historians ultimately fall back on claims about imagination and empathy in dealing with subjects of the past – with these claims implicating them in a reconstruction or re-enactment of some kind because the relationship is not really dialogical in the sense of active engagement and because the actor in the past is ultimately excluded from the (fictional) relation – the historian and reader can be seen to constitute a relation that is based on a combination of both absence and trust. What is more, the trust that the reader places in the author is not an epistemological one – 'this is true' – but moderated by the other dictates of the narrative space, ideally involving trust in the writer's good intentions and generic commitments more broadly. For that reason alone, those intentions and the specifics of the genre should not be blindly assumed but instead deliberately chosen and shaped by each and every historian.

Kalle Pihlainen is a senior research fellow in Cultural Theory at the School of Humanities at Tallinn University, Estonia (funded by the Estonian Research Council [PUT1150]), and editor of *Rethinking History: The Journal of Theory and Practice*. His research focuses on the theory and philosophy of history as well as literary and historical culture, with particular emphasis on the ethics and politics of historical representation, embodiment and existential phenomenology. His recent book, *The Work of History: Constructivism and a Politics of the Past* (Routledge, 2017), explores current theory debates and their implications for writing history today.

Notes

1. The problems articulated by the narrative constructivist theory of history have met with a great deal of resistance for what seems a curious reason: overly eager supporters as well as opponents of narrative constructivism or 'the fictionalization of history' have contributed such extreme views that discussion concerning fictionality between the majority of historians and theorists has become near-impossible.

2. A central difficulty with the fact-fiction focus is that it easily justifies an opposition where one might also see a continuum. This hankering for oppositions reflects the extent to which relativist debates have revolved around simplistic ontological questions like 'is the past real?' (simply a historical variant of the more common 'does the world exist?') as well as more involved issues of qualia or representation, for example.

3. White, *The Content of the Form: Narrative Discourse and Historical Representation*, 23.

4. I realize that this is a simplification in that it perhaps somewhat unfairly glosses over some of the (at least early) commitments of microhistory. My admittedly very broad concern regarding microhistory is, however, that through an exaggerated emphasis on the epistemological, historians lose sight of their responsibilities to the present. For an elaboration of this argument, see Pihlainen, 'The End of Oppositional History?', 463–88.

5. For more on this, see, e.g., May, *The Political Philosophy of Poststructuralist Anarchism*.

6. For more on this, see White, *Figural Realism: Studies in the Mimesis Effect*. Also, on 'experimental' history, see, e.g., Munslow and Rosenstone, *Experiments in Rethinking History*.

7. I will not go into the carry-over from the epistemological to the ethical in the case of empathy here, since it would only confuse the issue.

8. For more on the question of a poststructuralist ethics, see May's *Political Philosophy* as well as *The Moral Theory of Poststructuralism*; also, see my essay, 'The End of Oppositional History?'

9. LaCapra, *History, Politics, and the Novel*, 9–10.

10. Scott, *Gender and the Politics of History*, 6.

11. I adopt this terminology of 'living' here quite intentionally to address recent concerns within the theory of history regarding presence, experience and materiality. Hopefully, such a formulation might serve to better underline the fact that poststructuralism's emphasis on textuality is not intended to deny the 'reality' of the past but to highlight the difficulty of making any claims about accessing it. The crucial takeaway here is that there are concrete limits on accessing 'collective' experience, and that these kinds of currently fashionable parallels between subjective experiences and history (that is, representations of a non-subjective past) should be examined critically.

12. I do not intend 'narrative space' as a technical term, although my usage is similar to Gérard Genette's. I place greater emphasis, however, on narrative as a communicative site where the temporal concerns of the material, author and reader can perhaps meet and be jointly appreciated (which is not to be taken strictly literally of course!), and hence focus less here on the deployment of narrative as a representational tool.

13. Sartre, *What is Literature?*, 63.

14. Thomas Flynn, for instance, sees Sartre relying strongly on the goodwill and honesty of the actors in any attempt at understanding: 'What is noteworthy for our purposes is his view of *comprehension as practical*, not merely speculative, *and as involving commitment*' (Flynn, *Sartre, Foucault, and Historical Reason: Toward an Existentialist Theory of History*, 51; my emphasis).

15. Windschuttle, *The Killing of History: How Literary Critics and Social Theorists are Murdering Our Past*, 230.

16. See White, *Figural Realism*. Now, if the historical narrative is no longer defined as historical by its empirical standing alone but by its generic *commitment* to truth, a better understanding of the dimensions of the epistemological and the political can be reached. To be fair, Windschuttle does leave some room for this commitment, but his emphasis remains on its objectivist nature as evidenced by his repeated appeals to 'proper scientific methodology'. See, e.g., Windschuttle, *Killing of History*, 245.

17. De Certeau, *Heterologies: Discourse on the Other*, 205.

18. See, e.g., Perry, *Marxism and History*, 86. Foucault's histories and their 'radical empiricism' well illustrate this shared characteristic of empiricism and anti-foundationalism when put into practice.

19. Sartre, *Between Existentialism and Marxism*, 49. This kind of Sartrean (and I would say also poststructuralist) controlled fiction is essential for opening up the narrative space. The recognition and foregrounding of fictional elements as a justified method produces necessary trust, leads to readers' critical attitudes, and so on. Nancy Partner has also advocated a notion of 'controlled fiction' in Partner, 'Historicity in an Age of Reality-Fictions', 21–39. To me, Sartre's attitude certainly lends itself well to a discussion of 'the content of the form' à la White, perhaps more clearly describing the constraints on fiction too. As Sartre much later writes – in connection with his interpretation of Flaubert in *The Family Idiot* – the reconstruction of Flaubert's life project as a whole 'will be the test of that rediscovered childhood and will determine in retrospect its resemblance to reality'. This overall life project is, I would argue, one formulation of the narrative or metaphorical truth that such reconstructions can create. See Sartre, *The Family Idiot* vol. 1, 46.

20. May, *Political Philosophy*, 78.

21. Sartre, *Literature*, 223.

22. Sartre, *Literature*, 236–37.

23. For a very convincing elaboration of realism and the ways in which realist form supports the status quo, see Jameson, *The Antinomies of Realism*.

Bibliography

De Certeau, M. *Heterologies: Discourse on the Other*. Minneapolis: University of Minnesota Press, 1986.
Flynn, T. *Sartre, Foucault, and Historical Reason: Toward an Existentialist Theory of History*, vol. 1. Chicago: University of Chicago Press, 1997.
Jameson, F. *The Antinomies of Realism*. London: Verso, 2013.
LaCapra, D. *History, Politics, and the Novel*. Ithaca, NY: Cornell University Press, 1987.
May, T. *The Political Philosophy of Poststructuralist Anarchism*. University Park: Pennsylvania State University Press, 1994.
———. *The Moral Theory of Poststructuralism*. University Park: Pennsylvania State University Press, 1995.
Munslow, A. and R. Rosenstone (eds). *Experiments in Rethinking History*. London: Routledge, 2004.
Partner, N. 'Historicity in an Age of Reality-Fictions', in F. Ankersmit and H. Kellner (eds), *A New Philosophy of History* (Chicago: University of Chicago Press, 1995), 21–39.
Perry, M. *Marxism and History*. New York: Palgrave, 2002.
Pihlainen, K. 'The End of Oppositional History?' *Rethinking History* 15(4) (2011), 463–88.
Sartre, J.-P. *What is Literature?* New York: Philosophical Library, 1949.
———. *Between Existentialism and Marxism*. London: NLB, 1974.
———. *The Family Idiot*, vol. 1. Chicago: University of Chicago Press, 1981.
Scott, J.W. *Gender and the Politics of History*. New York: Columbia University Press, 1988.
White, H. *The Content of the Form: Narrative Discourse and Historical Representation*. Baltimore, MA: Johns Hopkins University Press, 1987.
———. *Figural Realism: Studies in the Mimesis Effect*. Baltimore, MA: Johns Hopkins University Press, 1999.
Windschuttle, K. *The Killing of History: How Literary Critics and Social Theorists are Murdering Our Past*. New York: The Free Press, 1996.

CHAPTER 4

The Historian-King

Political Leaders, Historical Consciousness and Wise Government

A<small>NTOON</small> D<small>E</small> B<small>AETS</small>

> Wisdom too often never comes, and so one ought not to reject it merely because it comes late.
> —Justice Felix Frankfurter,
> Henslee v. Union Planters Bank (1948)

Once upon a time, Plato distinguished four cardinal virtues: wisdom, justice, courage and moderation.[1] He believed that wisdom could play an important role in politics, where it is scarce and sought after. In *The Republic*, he expounded his idea of what a wise ruler ought to be: a philosopher-king. In his words:

> Unless … either philosophers become kings … or those whom we now call our kings and rulers take the pursuit of philosophy seriously … and there is a conjunction of these two things, political power and philosophic intelligence …, there can be no cessation of troubles … for our states, nor … for the human race either.[2]

Plato's proposal has been fiercely debated over the centuries, sometimes by studying real-life examples of philosopher-kings such as Marcus Aurelius, Ashoka or Frederick the Great. In 1795, Immanuel Kant expressed reservations about Plato's ideal:

Notes for this section begin on page 108.

> It is not to be expected that kings will philosophize or that philosophers will become kings; nor is it to be desired, since the possession of power inevitably corrupts the free judgment of reason.[3]

Kant thought that power stood in the way of wisdom. In 1945 Karl Popper went a step further. In *The Open Society and Its Enemies*, he convincingly argued that Plato, when writing about the philosopher-king, had a completely different understanding in mind than we have. According to Popper, Plato's philosopher-kings were supposed to love the truth and yet they were allowed to lie and censor; they strived for justice only if it served state interests, their wisdom boiled down to secret or rigid knowledge and not to humanism, and their politics were intrinsically conservative and discriminatory. On top of this, Plato had only one candidate in mind for the job: himself.[4] The idea of the philosopher-king received a fatal blow.

Meanwhile, writing in 1820, Georg Wilhelm Friedrich Hegel took a different path. He maintained that wisdom spread its wings only with the fall of dusk: 'The owl of Minerva takes its flight only when the shades of night are gathering.'[5] He meant that the wisdom of philosophy is not a matter of foresight – as implied in Plato's proposal and assumed by many today – but of hindsight. This was a new perspective: is wisdom an ability to look into the future or an ability to look into the past and then learn its lessons for the future? How can wisdom be advanced, by the seer or the storyteller? If the latter, in addition to philosophers other candidates for wisdom emerge. One could think of wise judges (King Solomon) or wise legislators (Hammurabi, Lycurgus, Solon).

Cultural historian Jacob Burckhardt gave his personal twist to this new perspective. While firmly rejecting Hegel's philosophy of history because of its 'false premises', he saw a role for history. In 1868, he wrote:

> With this, the phrase 'history is the teacher of life' gets a deeper and at the same time humbler meaning. Through experience we hope to become not so much smart (for the next time) as wise (forever).[6]

He argued that wisdom increased with experience and historical consciousness. And this is precisely what I want to investigate here. The idea was not new and, of course, Burckhardt was acutely aware of this because he referred to Cicero's saying, '[H]istory, the witness of time, the light of truth, the life of memory, the teacher of life, the herald of antiquity.'[7] Before Cicero, Aeschylus believed that memory was the mother of all wisdom, and Thucydides argued that history was 'philosophy teaching by examples'.[8] After Cicero, Friedrich Schlegel orated that the historian was a 'prophet looking backward',[9] and Søren Kierkegaard wrote in 1843: 'It is quite true what philosophy says: that life must be understood backwards. But then one forgets the other principle: that it must be lived forwards.'[10]

Could historical consciousness be the mother of wisdom? This is the question addressed here. Historical consciousness has two dimensions: a sustained sensitivity to the past as expressed in memory and knowledge[11] and, furthermore, an ability to recognize the epochal quality of a current event and to see it, as it were, with the eyes of future generations.[12] Is Burckhardt's version of the wise ruler – which we may perhaps call the 'historian-king' – plausible? In particular, are political leaders known for their distinct historical consciousness wiser than others? And, conversely, are rulers famous for their wisdom notable for their historical consciousness? I proceed in two steps: first, I identify the political leaders who display a distinct historical consciousness and within this group try to mark those with a reputation for wisdom. Then I look at the career of these wise leaders in the hope of extracting some of their secrets.

Historically Informed Political Leaders

If I talk about '(political) leaders' or rulers, I exclusively mean heads of state and government. Leaders are called 'leaders with a distinct historical consciousness' or 'historically informed leaders' or 'historically oriented leaders' if they meet one or more of the following criteria before, during or after their political career:

- They received a formal history education.
- They wrote a historical work.
- They gave important speeches with substantial historical content.
- They displayed a sustained interest in history in other demonstrable ways.

Applying these criteria, I compiled a list of 188 leaders in 86 countries for the period 1900–2018, reproduced as Appendix 1. Each of these leaders clearly developed a sustained form of historical consciousness, often in a compelling fashion.[13] Winston Churchill, for example, was a gifted writer and historian before, during and after his career as British prime minister. In 1953, he received the Nobel Prize in Literature for his six-volume history of the Second World War.[14] Or take Eric Williams, author of the seminal *Capitalism and Slavery*, who published a *History of the People of Trinidad and Tobago* on 31 August 1962, the day that he led his country to independence as its prime minister. The book was the first national history of his country and a gift to his people.[15] Sometimes a quip is enough to make people reflect on historical perspectives. British Prime Minister and historian Gordon Brown, for example, once remarked: 'In establishing the rule of law, the first five centuries are always the hardest.'[16]

Although the list of leaders was the result of a systematic search during two decades,[17] undoubtedly many leaders are still lacking, especially for the first decades of the twentieth century. In addition, some cases on the list are probably false positives while other cases that were investigated but do not figure on the list would appear to be false negatives on closer scrutiny. I am convinced that the list can be contested in more than one case. Hence, this survey should start with a warning: as its analysis is comparative and its grasp wide, I did not study in depth any of the leaders discussed below, although, evidently, I documented each of my assertions. I lean on authorities who studied the lives of these leaders in greater detail. I believe, nevertheless, that these circumstances do not affect the following impressions that emerge almost spontaneously after a glance at the list.

First of all, the expression 'leaders with a distinct historical consciousness' has to be qualified in several ways. The possession of a history degree, for example, was no guarantee that political leaders subsequently developed an elaborate view of history or even that history played a role of some significance in their world view, ideology or policy. Julius Nyerere is an example: a historian by training, he did not refer to the past very often, except to talk about a romanticized traditional Africa. In addition, several professional historians who became presidents or prime ministers were mediocre leaders by most standards. Think of Aleksandr Lukashenko in Belarus or Laurent Gbagbo in Ivory Coast, both educated as historians. Known as 'Europe's Last Dictator', Lukashenko in 2013 received the so-called Ig Nobel Peace Prize, a prize awarded since 1991 to 'honor achievements that first make people laugh, and then make them think'. Lukashenko received it for making it illegal to applaud in public.[18] Until early 2019, Gbagbo was on trial before the International Criminal Court for crimes against humanity committed during the 2010–2011 post-election crisis. When interviewed by a British journalist, he lamented: 'It's difficult for us to make history … We have to carry out our own French Revolution with Amnesty International peering over our shoulder.'[19]

History and politics have a tense relationship, as the former demands patient research and past-oriented reflection while the latter requires future-oriented actions and decisions. If political leaders continuously take into account the wider scope of current and past events, it may become an ingrained personality trait that implicitly influences state stewardship. Inevitably, however, this also slows down the pace of political decisions, and not everybody is happy with such delays. Looking at the world around him, the Italian philosopher and historian Benedetto Croce, in 1938, contrasted historians and politicians, arguing that they belonged to different spheres of life.[20]

Because both the development of a distinct historical consciousness and the occupation of political office take so much time, leaders who developed a historical consciousness *before* embarking on a political career had a clear advantage from our perspective. Others – certainly a Nehru, probably a Mandela and a Havel – developed their sense of history because they spent long years in prison. Still others cultivated a historical consciousness when fate brought them exile or temporary dismissal. Bertram Wolfe touched this nerve when he contrasted Stalin – who edited a history book while in office, the *History of the All-Russian Communist Party (Bolsheviks): Short Course* in 1938 – with other leaders:

> [I]n contradistinction to a Napoleon ... or even a Churchill, who wait to turn their energies into the writing of history until defeat has deprived them of the opportunity of making it, Stalin engaged in the writing of history as one of the means by which he climbed to power.[21]

The list of 188 leaders is also illustrative because it represents only a fraction of the total. In his book about heads of states and governments, Harris Lentz counted over 2,300 leaders between 1945 and 1992 alone. The number of leaders without proven interest in history is far higher, which surely indicates that a distinct historical consciousness is not a necessary condition for political leadership. It should come as no surprise, then, that many leaders are unencumbered by the burdens of historical consciousness. When President Lyndon Johnson heard from an assistant that the Pentagon was working on a top-secret history of American involvement in Vietnam between 1945 and 1968 (the notorious *Pentagon Papers*), he reacted surprised: 'What the hell are they writing history for? I thought they're supposed to be out winning the war.'[22] And Israeli President Shimon Peres, talking to historian Benny Morris, confessed:

> But history [meaning the writing of history] in my eyes is not that important. I have reached the conclusion that a leader who worries about how he will go down in history will not be a great leader. He must give up his place in history in order to make history ... That's the difference between us. You write history – I have to make history.[23]

As far as I see, most leaders with a weak interest in history tolerated the appeal to history that their collaborators made. For maximum effect, official ideology always needs historical context and historical legitimacy. Rarely does one see leaders without any interest in history at all. Undoubtedly, some leaders who are not on the list had an aversion to history. Others may have regarded their lack of a distinct historical consciousness as a defect, especially because political office – despite its hectic agenda – induces historical reflection in two exceptional senses: sooner or later leaders are compelled to ask themselves how their own performance compares to what their predecessors did *and* how they will be remembered. Philippine President Ferdinand Marcos mused:

> I often wonder what I will be remembered in history for. Scholar? Military hero? Builder? The new constitution? Reorganization of government? Builder of roads, schools? The green revolution? Uniter of variant and antagonistic elements of our people? He brought light to a dark country? Strong rallying point, or a weak tyrant?[24]

We are also reminded of Churchill's saying: 'For my part, I consider that it will be found much better by all parties to leave the past to history, especially as I propose to write that history myself.'[25] This curious combination of shortage of time, abundance of well-documented action, excitement of being at the centre of history and desire to safeguard a reputation inspires many a leader to take notes or keep a diary as a prelude to, or part of, writing their memoirs. As David Ben Gurion reportedly once remarked: 'Anyone who believes you can't change history has never tried to write his memoirs.'[26] Some developed a keen sense of the passage of time and invoked the 'court of history' for a final verdict about their actions.[27] Strictly speaking, however, leaders developing a strong historical consciousness *after* their political term are less interesting for our analysis because it is centred on the impact of historical consciousness on leadership.

Many historically oriented leaders used history frequently in the symbols and rituals that accompany the staging of political power. Most were men: the list contains a mere seven female leaders (in itself telling on account of the gender-biased recruitment of political talent). And many of these men were adherents of the theory that history was made by Great Men. This posed a problem for leaders of the communist brand, who had to profess the power of structural forces in history. Be that as it may, most historically oriented leaders invoked a canon of simple, often outdated and distorted historical knowledge to increase their legitimacy.[28] By and large, they confirm Kant: their historical insights served power rather than wisdom.

Given their long genealogies and vested interest in tradition, monarchs could have been expected to figure prominently on the list. In fact, only a small minority of the 188 leaders were monarchs: I counted 11. This is a surprisingly low number given the strong interest of monarchies in multigenerational continuity: apparently, the throne – or the prospect of the throne – does not automatically invite historical reflection. But let us look beyond monarchies. The number of those interested in history but not bound by the discipline of elections is far higher. This elicits another comment: there is no correlation between historical consciousness and regime type. Historical consciousness clearly did not deter political leaders from establishing or continuing dictatorships. Several of them picked powerful historical figures as their predecessors. For Mao Zedong, these were Qin Shihuangdi and the Hongwu emperor; for Saddam Hussein, Nebuchadnezzar and Saladin; for Islam Karimov it was Tamerlane, for Juan Domingo Perón, José de San Martín. The Central African Republic's dictator Jean-Bédel Bokassa was an exception: he crowned himself in Napoleonic style in 1976.

Stalin was often compared to the Tsars, but, apparently, he did not like this. During a talk in 1931, the German writer Emil Ludwig asked him: 'Do you think a parallel can be drawn between yourself and Peter the Great? Do you consider yourself a continuer of the work of Peter the Great?' Stalin responded: 'In no way whatever. Historical analogies are always risky. There is no sense in this one.'[29] Nevertheless, he had huge admiration for the strong leadership of sixteenth-century Tsar Ivan the Terrible. He also 'appointed' court historians: he used historians Wilhelm Knorin, Yemelyan Yaroslavsky, Pyotr Pospelov and 'a whole collective farm of assistants' as ghostwriters for his *Short Course*, but he did the final editing himself.[30]

The predilection for selected predecessors usually came with an intolerance for other options. Some leaders were so wary of the danger of rival historical representations that they singled out the historical profession for repression. Numerous leaders publicly attacked historians and sued, imprisoned or killed them because their views deviated from the official one and threatened the leader's legitimacy at its core.[31] Let me give three quick Soviet examples. When the writer Maxim Gorky asked Lenin for clemency for the Grand Duke Nikolas Mikhailovich Romanov, a historian and member of the Tsarist family, he replied: 'The Revolution does not need historians.'[32] The Grand Duke was shot in 1919. When historian A.G. Slutsky dared to question Lenin's credentials, Stalin retorted in 1931: 'Who, except archive rats, does not understand that a party and its leaders must be tested primarily by their deeds and not merely by their declarations?'[33] On 5 May 1956 Nikita Khrushchev had a conversation with a French delegation inviting him to establish a Franco-Russian commission of historical research into each other's past. When a French delegation member remarked that it was the historians' profession to analyse the past, Khrushchev replied: 'Historians too must be directed.'[34] It sounds paradoxical, but it is not: the zeal of leaders to censor history is proof a contrario for their historical consciousness.

Paradoxically, even leaders who unleashed an iconoclastic fury to destroy as much of the past as possible needed a view of history, either to present the post-iconoclastic era as the restoration of some golden past age or to contrast it with the epochs that had disappeared. When the Khmer Rouge took over Phnom Penh in 1975, their spokesman proclaimed that 'two thousand years of history had ended.' The year zero had begun. Khmer Rouge leader and former history teacher Ieng Sary declared: 'The Khmer revolution has no precedent. What we are trying to do has never been done before in history.'³⁵ Nevertheless, Pol Pot saw himself as a vehicle of History, and the Khmer Rouge obstinately referred to the twelfth-century Khmer culture of Angkor Wat. Other iconoclastic leaders – Mao, Ceauşescu, Saddam – had an elaborate view of history. This did not prevent them from mercilessly choking their own historical consciousness when it suited them.³⁶

These preliminary observations are sobering. A leader's 'distinct historical consciousness' is not necessarily one supporting democracy or peace nor one justified by scientific standards. Yes, it is probable that the exercise of political power in itself awakens a manifest desire for historical consciousness – but that was not our question. All in all, at first sight, there is no evidence that rulers who display distinct historical consciousness are necessarily wiser than their counterparts who lack such outspoken awareness. Archaeologist Bogdan Filov became Bulgaria's prime minister during World War II and collaborated with the Nazis. After the war, he was sentenced to death and shot by the new communist government. At that occasion, *Time* wrote: 'The parade to the execution wall included … ex-Premier Professor Bogdan Filo[v], Bulgarian expansionist, who preferred making history to teaching it …'³⁷ The precise impact of writing history on making history remains a mystery.

Wise Historically Informed Political Leaders

What to do? Maybe we can consult a list of wise leaders, compare it with our list of historically oriented leaders and discuss the overlap. Unfortunately, no such list of wise political leaders exists.³⁸ Therefore, I will create one, starting from the following premise: the Nobel Peace Prize, if awarded to a head of state or government, is often considered to be an internationally accepted empirical indicator of wise government.³⁹ A list of leaders who won the Nobel Peace Prize could then serve as a proxy for a list of wise leaders. This hypothesis has a weak point at its core: it equates wisdom with peace. Undoubtedly, both have much in common: it is difficult to see how a warmongering leader can be wise. On the other hand, certainly not all Noble Peace Prize winners were pacifists.⁴⁰ Few will disagree with the just war doctrine that, as a last resort, it is morally justified to revolt against tyrants or start a war of self-defence against aggressors rather than peacefully and passively abiding one's time. This principle is even recognized in the preamble of the Universal Declaration of Human Rights. In short, it will be imperative to bear the distinction between peace and wisdom in mind.

The plan to compile a list of leaders who won the Nobel Peace Prize comes with a few additional practical biases that can only be partly remedied. First of all, until the 1970s, the Nobel Peace Prize had almost exclusively been awarded to highly educated white men from Europe and the United States.[41] Until then, female and non-Western laureates were underrepresented among the prize winners but not necessarily among the peace brokers or wise leaders. We cannot change the list of laureates, but we can remedy these two biases by widening our scope to include the prize nominees. This constitutes a considerable enlargement. While since 1901 the Nobel Peace Prize has been awarded 99 times, to 130 laureates, the number of nominations from 1901 (the year of the first prize) to 1967, for example, was 4,425. Or, to give another idea of the wide scope: there were 331 candidates for the 2018 prize (216 individuals and 115 organizations).

The scope narrows down again, however, due to two problems, the first of which is that the official website of the Norwegian Nobel Committee (nobelprize.org) blocks information about nominees for 50 years.[42] At the time of writing, the nomination database was only accessible for 1901–1967. For 1967–2001, the data is scarce. Those for the most recent period (from 2002) are gathered via shortlists drafted by other organizations than the Norwegian Nobel Committee and then based only on those nominations that had become public.[43] Another problem is that a one-time nomination is obviously a weaker indicator than repeated nominations from various origins. In order to rule out chance nominations, I only selected leaders who had accumulated at least ten nominations.[44] The list of those nominated less than ten times is very heterogeneous and at times disconcerting because occasionally even warmongers and mass murderers were nominated – and at moments when this should have been clear to all.

There is another thing we should know before we embark upon our analysis: experts tell us that the Nobel Peace Prize assignment pattern between 1901 and 2018 seems to show four trends: from 1901 to 1914, most prizes went to pioneers of the organized peace movement; in the interwar years, they tended to go to active politicians who sought to promote peace by means of diplomacy and international agreements; after 1945 campaigns in disarmament, peace negotiation, and democracy and human rights were more often singled out; and after 2000 efforts to limit the harm done by man-made climate change and environment threats were embraced.[45] From our perspective, this would imply that the period 1918–1945, with its emphasis on active politicians, is slightly overrepresented – which may indeed be the case.

In the following table, I list all the Nobel Peace Prize laureates and nominees who were also on the list of historically informed leaders. For comparative reasons, I also present those historians who won the Nobel Peace Prize or were nominated for it at least ten times in Appendix 3.

Table 4.1 Historically informed political leaders and the Nobel Peace Prize (1901–2018).

Laureates (7)	
1906 | Theodore Roosevelt – United States	(7x nominee in 1906)
1919 | Woodrow Wilson – United States	(1919 prize awarded in 1920, 22x nominee in 1918–1920)
1957 | Lester Pearson – Canada	(2x nominee in 1952–1957)
1990 | Mikhail Gorbachev – Soviet Union	
1993 | Nelson Mandela – South Africa	
2002 | Jimmy Carter – United States	
2009 | Barack Obama – United States	
Nominees with at least ten nominations (2)	
Tomáš Masaryk – Czechoslovakia (17x nominee in 1913–1937)	
Jawaharlal Nehru – India (13x nominee in 1950–1961)	

Notes:

1. For discussion, see text.
2. In 1919 no prize was awarded; Wilson was awarded the 1919 prize in 1920.
3. Only pre-1967 data are available for nomination frequencies, making them unknown for Gorbachev, Mandela, Carter and Obama.
4. Leaders with a distinct historical consciousness but nominated less than ten times for the Nobel Peace Prize (attention: only pre-1967 data are available for nomination frequencies, making them unknown or speculative for many nominees): Mustafa Kemal Atatürk (1x), Habib Bourguiba (1x), George W. Bush (3x), Fidel Castro (1x), Hugo Chávez (3x), Jacques Chirac (2x), Winston Churchill (2x), Bill Clinton (3x), Dwight Eisenhower (9x), Václav Havel (4x), Adolf Hitler (1x), John Howard (x2), John Kennedy (1x), Helmut Kohl (4x), Pierre Mendès-France (1x), Angela Merkel (1x), Benito Mussolini (2x), Mohammed Reza Pahlavi (2x), Juan Domingo Perón (2x), Vladimir Putin (4x), Franklin Roosevelt (5x), Leopold Sédar Senghor (2x), Joseph Stalin (2x), Dominique de Villepin (1x), Kaiser Wilhelm II (3x), Xi Jinping (1x), Victor Yushchenko (1x).

Sources:

1. List of historically informed political leaders (1900–2018): Appendix 1.
2. Information about the Nobel Peace Prize laureates and nominees at https://www.nobelprize.org.

Historically Informed Leaders as Nobel Peace Prize Laureates

We are ready to look at the leaders themselves. Seven historically informed leaders were laureates of the Nobel Peace Prize. I realize that acting as a judge for the wisdom displayed by persons with such impressive track records has more than a few ironic overtones. In trying to make my assessment as objective as possible, I will use a method of exclusion: in evaluating the 'wisdom levels' of the laureates, I shall look first at the indicator value of the prize (its general appreciation as an index of wisdom in the particular instance), then at other factors.

If we assess the extent to which the prize indicates wisdom, we should first of all exclude Roosevelt and Obama, but for different reasons. Known as a voracious reader, Theodore Roosevelt was the author of works about the history of the American navy. He helped flesh out the 'frontier thesis' elaborated by Frederick Jackson Turner. It is likely that his romanticized and moralistic view of history played a role in the decisions he took as a president. When he gave his keynote address before the American Historical Association in 1912, after his presidency, he told his audience that the purpose of the historian was to be a 'great moralist' and to 'thrill the souls of men with stories of strength and craft and daring'.[46] Despite the fact that a comprehensive report by Halvdan Koht, a historian who advised the Norwegian Nobel Committee, had been rather critical, Roosevelt was awarded the prize in 1906 for his encouragement of international arbitration (he was instrumental in strengthening the Permanent Court of Arbitration in The Hague) and in particular for his mediation during the Russian-Japanese war of 1904–1905 leading to the 1905 peace treaty. The award was much disputed because Roosevelt was not exactly known as a peace apostle. Above all, he did not shun imperialism in the Caribbean. The *New York Times* called him 'the most warlike citizen of these United States'.[47] The more controversial the laureate was, the less the prize's predictive value for noble and wise statesmanship. For that reason, Roosevelt is excluded.

Barack Obama received the prize 'for his extraordinary efforts to strengthen international diplomacy and cooperation between peoples'. He was particularly inspired by his predecessors Abraham Lincoln, Theodore and Franklin Roosevelt, and John Kennedy. Despite his considerable attempts to draw attention to the diversity of the American people by designating national monuments to many neglected groups, he does not seem to have had a full-fledged view of history.[48] In addition, there is widespread consensus that the prize, awarded less than nine months after he took office, came too early. Everybody, including Obama himself, was surprised: the award was more an expression of the tremendous worldwide hope that his election had aroused than a decision based on past performance. For that reason, he should be excluded as well.

Different considerations lead to the exclusion of Lester Pearson and Nelson Mandela. If we only concentrate on sitting heads of state and government, we are obliged to drop them because in contrast to the other laureates they received the prize *before* their terms as head of government and state respectively. Pearson became prime minister six years after winning the prize; Mandela president less than a year later. That would be a silly reason to exclude them, however, as this early recognition qualifies them even more as candidates for wisdom. As the Canadian Minister of Foreign Affairs, Pearson won support for sending a United Nations Emergency Force to the Middle East in 1956 to separate the warring parties in the Suez Crisis. Later, he embarked on a widely lauded career as prime minister. Mandela and his co-laureate F.W. de Klerk had worked 'for the peaceful termination of the apartheid regime, and for laying the foundations for a new democratic South Africa'. There are no immediate indications that Pearson's training as a historian and Mandela's strong interest in history played an important role in their political views.[49] Especially for Mandela this needs a little elaboration. His younger years were coloured with an interest in history. After the Sharpeville massacre of 1960, he lost confidence in peaceful solutions to apartheid and co-founded the paramilitary wing of the African National Congress, Umkhonto we Sizwe. Sentenced on sabotage charges in 1964, he spent more than a quarter of a century in prison, mostly on Robben Island.[50] To his formidable credit, the country embarked on a largely peaceful reckoning with the apartheid past before and during his presidency, mainly through the establishment of a Truth and Reconciliation Commission, which operated from 1995 to 1998. Inspired by its Latin American predecessors, this truth commission set the standard for many to follow. When Mandela received its report in 1998, he referred to apartheid – 'this terrible period of our history' – as a system that 'committed a crime against humanity', but his speech mostly revolved around the non-recurrence theme ('never again') while dwelling on the past in succinct terms only.[51] Although both Pearson and Mandela can be called leaders with much political wisdom and imbued with a distinct historical consciousness at the same time, it is not clear whether there is a causal connection between both. Therefore, I exclude them.

American President Jimmy Carter is a difficult case. He was awarded the prize in 2002 'for his decades of untiring effort to find peaceful solutions to international conflicts, to advance democracy and human rights, and to promote economic and social development'. He is credited with having substantially contributed to the breakthrough of the idea of human rights during his presidency.[52] And among his many peace efforts, the 1978 Camp David agreement stands out. Carter relates the following about the negotiations that led to it:

> At the Camp David discussions with Begin and Sadat I didn't have to turn around to Vance [his Secretary of State] ... and say, 'Would you explain to me the history of this particular issue' ... because I knew it.[53]

In addition, he became the author of a historical novel in 2004, *The Hornet's Nest*, a story set in the South during the American Revolution. The Nobel

Prize expressed the fact that many of Carter's feats received an aura of wisdom in hindsight: it was awarded twenty-two years after his presidential term. He was called 'the best ex-president we ever had.' That sounds unfair: if recognition came too early for Obama, it perhaps came too late for Carter. After much hesitation, I still exclude Carter, not because of this belated recognition but because the connection between his impressive achievements during and after his presidency and his historical views seems not strong enough.

Mikhail Gorbachev received the Nobel Peace Prize for 'his leading role in the peace process'. Like Khrushchev before him, he showed an intense interest in history only when forced to look it in the eye. Khrushchev had delivered a secret speech in 1956; it was a lengthy attack on Stalin and the crimes of the past.[54] In the same vain, Gorbachev had to confront the past so as to make his plea for urgent change inescapable in his book, *Perestroika: New Thinking for Our Country and the World* (1987). In addition, he gave a further speech about Soviet history and Stalin's crimes in the same year. In 1990, he signed a decree exonerating all the victims of Stalin's repressions. Even after his fall, he defied plans of the Constitutional Court to bring the Communist Party to trial and 'put our history in the dock'. When an interviewer in 2009 asked him how he saw his place in history, he growled: 'Don't consign me to history.'[55] While the wisdom of his international performance is undisputed (and, therefore, the prize deserved), judgments about the domestic consequences of his policies for the Soviet successor states are complex and they diverge. Gorbachev's pronounced historical consciousness is undeniable, but it was prompted by the Soviet Union's problematic circumstances in the first place. His historical consciousness was reactive rather than proactive – and thus a weaker index of wisdom. He unintentionally encouraged the unprecedented and unanticipated explosion of popular interest in the past that was the consequence of his glasnost and perestroika policies, but he reasoned within the bounds of a Leninist framework, cautiously and daringly at the same time.[56] In normal circumstances, the jury would be out for Gorbachev, but the circumstances in the Soviet Union's last years (1985–1991) were exceptional. On balance, I count him in.

The only laureate left is Wilson. Like Roosevelt, Wilson was an active professional historian before his political career began; like Roosevelt he received the prize during his presidency; and like Roosevelt, he led the American Historical Association after his presidency (he passed away before the completion of his term).[57] A biographer of George Washington (1897) and the author of a five-volume *History of the American People* (1902), Wilson revealed himself as a literary rather than scientific historian. Fully convinced of the power of individuals in history and of the duty of historians to morally judge them, he embraced the English historian Edward A.

Freeman's maxim, 'History is past politics and politics present history.'[58] He specialized in political and constitutional history to discover both the lessons of history for the present and the mission of the United States in the future. While president of his country, he had to tackle the challenges imposed by the Great War. In January 1918, he unfolded his postwar settlement, the famous *Fourteen Points*. This declaration eventually led to the incorporation of a covenant to establish the League of Nations into the 1919 peace Treaty of Versailles. The United States Senate, however, never approved American membership of the League. For this reason there was some disagreement in the Norwegian Nobel Committee, until a majority decided to award him the prize. All in all, the influence of Wilson the history professor on Wilson the statesman and subsequently on Wilson the peacemaker is not immediately obvious.[59] Nevertheless, he clearly belongs on my shortlist.

Historically Informed Leaders as Nobel Peace Prize Nominees

Two historically oriented leaders were nominated for the prize ten times or more: Masaryk (17 nominations in 24 years) and Nehru (13 nominations in 11 years). A philosopher by training and historically oriented by inclination, Masaryk had exposed the historical falsification for chauvinistic purposes behind the alleged 'rediscovery' of two medieval Bohemian manuscripts in 1886. He was interested in the relationship between historical understanding and morally inspired progress, and he developed a philosophy of history in his book *The Social Question* (1898). He rejected conflict-based historical views such as Marxism and radical variants of Darwinist evolutionism, and adopted an idealist view of history, always looking for the power of ideas and of individuals pursuing them.

Masaryk worked to improve the relations between Czechs and Germans both within and outside Bohemia. He defended the Slav peoples against Austrian-Hungarian imperialism and successfully mediated between Austria-Hungary and Serbia in 1912. The founding father of Czechoslovakia after the fall of the Habsburg Empire in 1918, Masaryk left a lasting impression as its first president. He thought that national self-determination was a universal principle compatible with humanitarian and democratic incentives. He was nominated for the Nobel Peace Prize because he promoted humanism, ethics and pacifism. Known as 'the Great Old Man of Europe,' he died a year before the 1938 Munich Agreement and the Nazi occupation of his country. After 1948, the communists erased Masaryk from public tributes, to be rehabilitated only, hesitantly and unofficially, 50 years after his death, in 1987, when the system was almost on the verge of collapse.[60]

A philosopher by profession and a statesman by career, he came nominally closest to the Platonic ideal of the philosopher-king.[61] As in Wilson's case, however, it remains complicated to pinpoint the precise impact of historical views on his leadership. On balance, I select him.

Meanwhile, in British India, Jawaharlal Nehru spent nine years in prison because of his pro-independence activities. In various jails, he read and wrote as a self-educated historian about Indian and world history. Between 1930 and 1933, he sent almost 200 letters on world history to his daughter, Indira Gandhi, from different prisons. Their publication in 1934 as *Glimpses of World History* – a book of 1,000 dense pages – made Nehru one of the first non-western world historians of modern times. As late as 1989, a re-edition of *Glimpses* was published to commemorate the hundredth anniversary of Nehru's birth. Another of his historical works, *The Discovery of India* (1946), was written in Ahmadnagar Fort Prison Camp between April and September 1944 during a prison term that totalled almost three years.[62] Praised for his fair judgment and lack of resentment and nationalist bigotry, Nehru thought that India could only be properly understood if situated amid other civilizations. His works offer a fascinating insight into his titanic efforts to understand his own times and India's place in them. Mesmerized by the broad sweep of events, though, the past interested him only insofar as it could throw light on the present.

Nehru was influenced by three philosophical currents: Marxism, Mahatma Gandhi's thoughts on non-violence and non-cooperation in the struggle for freedom, and above all by a liberal and secular humanism. His sophisticated judgment regarding events in the history of India and the world were testimony to his deeply engrained humanism. His nominators praised him for his role in the independence of India, his confidence in parliamentary democracy, his neutral foreign policy and his affinity with Gandhi.[63] Few other statesmen delved so deeply and so critically into the past of their country. Historian and diplomat K.M. Panikkar sums up Nehru's approach:

> Nehru's interest in history has affected his position as a statesman. Anyone who studies his work as the Prime Minister of India can easily see that ... he is dominated by a sense of history. The sense of urgency in dealing with India's ... problems arises from his knowledge of India's past failures ... His approach to international affairs is equally dominated by his sense of historical forces working in our time ... Thus, transcending the politician's approach to these problems as something to be dealt with ad hoc, he views them as parts of a unified whole ... In fact, even on contemporary events he brings to bear a historian's mind.[64]

More than anybody else, Nehru tried to construct a historical synthesis. His interest in history transcended its potentially political use. He definitely belongs on my shortlist.

Discussion

Not all historically informed leaders are wise. Not all wise leaders are historically informed. Not all historically informed leaders who are wise are historically informed *because* they are wise. Not all wise leaders who are historically informed are wise *because* they are historically informed. Leaders who are wise *because* they are historically informed are rare. Only four statesmen turned out to be entitled to this powerful combination: Wilson, Masaryk, Nehru and Gorbachev. I will not rank these leaders in order of wisdom: judging wisdom is already precarious, but ranking leaders on a wisdom index is outright frivolous and a demonstration of lack of wisdom itself. If these four men were philosopher-kings – Masaryk literally, Wilson and Nehru in the metaphorical sense, Gorbachev moulded by pressures he mobilized himself – this is good news: the specimen is capable of surviving and thriving everywhere, as the four come from very different corners of the globe. They worked in exceptional circumstances: Wilson sought a new world order after the Great War; Masaryk and Nehru built newly independent states while resisting old frameworks (supranational and colonial respectively); Gorbachev presided involuntarily over the demise of a multinational empire. They had to find new solutions and for inspiration turned to the past as example or counter-example.

Gorbachev is a special case because, as the months in 1987 crept by, his view of history, limited and distorted as it was, suddenly looked progressive when compared with both his predecessors and many contemporaries. The other three tried to develop a consistent and comprehensive view of history. Ostensibly better than other leaders, they knew to place current and past events in a larger framework. They had at least two things in common: all three were humanists (Wilson's and Masaryk's brand was inspired by Christianity, Nehru's was secular-minded) and all three were literary historians who loved the broad sweep of events and the larger context. If humanism is the central common feature of these three, then their wisdom lies in the recognition that humanity should not repeat all the follies of the past and in the sense of urgency they derived from it. Somehow, this is a disappointing conclusion, as it is more or less what one could have expected without research. Context-sensitive? Yes! A broad grasp of events? Certainly! Humanism? Of course! To make things worse, solid evidence for a beneficial direct influence of these four leaders' distinct historical consciousness upon their decisions is missing or very difficult to pinpoint.

Moral Judgment and Age

Two pairs of factors impede firm conclusions. The first pair, the fluctuating character of moral judgments and the problematic association of wisdom and age, varies with the leaders under consideration. Our moral judgment – and therefore our judgment about a person's wisdom, which is part of it – can shift quickly when we suddenly learn how leaders acted or failed to act at certain moments in their political careers. Aung San Suu Kyi was adored for two decades, earning the Nobel Peace Prize in 1991, but she attracted criticism later for lacking the moral courage to speak out against the violations to which the Rohingya were subjected in Myanmar. Churchill, twice a Noble Peace Prize nominee, was accused in 2018 of a series of purported war crimes in at least seven countries.[65] Likewise, Wilson was criticized in 2015 – 91 years after his death – because as the president of Princeton University in 1902–1910 he was a supporter of racial segregation. Many have pointed to the complex legacies that historical personalities leave behind. Anne-Marie Slaughter, a former Princeton professor and State Department official, tweeted about Wilson: '... *All* our idols have feet of clay. All our heroes have dark sides; but they can also do [great] things.'[66]

The age factor is even more complicated. The natural life cycle complicates the argument: typically, historical consciousness is acquired in younger years, the need for it increases during the active political career while simultaneously its cognitive growth probably stalls due to time constraints, while 'noble rule' is a characteristic of elder statesmen (or elder stateswomen for that matter). It is a fact that several political leaders ended up on the list of historically informed leaders partly or entirely for activities they undertook when their active political career was over; in other words, when their distinct historical consciousness could not impact on the quality of their decisions anymore (with Carter being the exception that proves the rule). Not only does the development of a distinct historical consciousness take much time, the ability to apply it at the right moment, mainly by seeing current events in a historical context, has to be practised as well. This art of applying concentrated experience and mature historical knowledge humanely at the right moment is itself a bit mysterious. I speculate that Plato's three other cardinal virtues – courage, moderation and justice – contribute in unison to it: to be wise requires courage and moderation in its activation, and justice in its application.

Psychologists investigating wisdom leave open the impact of age: on the one hand, age may transform wisdom into something profound; on the other, wisdom may crumble under its weight. Gerard Brugman was pessimistic: '[O]ne needs to be old and wise to see that wisdom does not come with age.'[67] Awareness of one's failing wisdom makes one wiser. Among the factors mitigating or inhibiting the impact of wisdom at a later age are an increasing rigidity and a risk of illness. The stroke that Wilson suffered in October 1919 is reported to have intensified his rigidity and may have affected, if not eliminated, the hope that the Senate would approve

American membership of the League of Nations. '[I]llness can make leaders unpredictable, limit their attention spans, shorten their time horizons, and diminish their cognitive capacities.'[68] Nehru's health began declining steadily after the Sino-Indian War of October–November 1962. Arnold Toynbee testified how China tormented him.[69] Nehru died 18 months later, in May 1964, and many attributed this to his surprise over the war. His overwhelming passion for history could have had contradictory effects: he understood the historical background of India's problems better, but at the same time, he may have been taken aback, even paralyzed by the sheer complexity of problems. And, naturally, there was always the risk that he overestimated the historical sensitivity of his allies and opponents. In his own words:

> The burden of the past, the burden of both good and ill, is over-powering, and sometimes suffocating, more especially for those of us who belong to very ancient civilizations like those of India and China. As Nietzsche says: 'Not only the wisdom of centuries – also their madness breaketh out in us. Dangerous it is to be an heir.'[70]

The Lucas Critique and the Fischhoff Critique

The second pair of factors that stand in the way of convincing conclusions consists of structural biases. I shall call them the Lucas critique and the Fischhoff critique. Is wisdom the product of foresight as is commonly accepted, or of hindsight as Hegel contended? The foresight theory is dubious, as it presupposes a clairvoyance that leaders all too eagerly claim to possess. Is the hindsight theory more plausible? Can we create wisdom by looking backward and distil lessons from the past? Even that can be doubted on account of a critical reasoning inspired by the theory of rational expectations developed by Robert Lucas, initially a historian by training and in 1995 the laureate of the Nobel Prize in Economics.[71] It is, in fact, a negative application of that theory, and it can be summarized as follows. If we were rational and really able to learn from negative historical events (such as war), we would seek to reduce their impact and avoid them. And if we could have avoided these negative historical events long enough, they would have been largely eliminated by now. In other words, the lessons learned about negative historical events would have a self-cancelling effect, meaning that historical information would become useless for predicting the future. Because we still repeat many of these negative historical events, however, we should conclude that we are not so rational and do not learn from them. In itself, the Lucas critique is deadly but not completely sufficient to cast doubt on the capacity to learn from the past, as wise leaders are typically more clear-eyed than others.

Equally fundamental is the doubt that we can distil any useful lessons from the past at all. A persistent bias clouds our historical judgment. The psychologist Baruch Fischhoff called this the hindsight bias.[72] He wrote that:

> Searching for wisdom in historic events requires ... a belief in the existence of recurrent patterns waiting to be discovered. Searching for wisdom in the behavior of historical characters requires a ... confidence that our predecessors knew things we do not know.[73]

Aside from the painful but not impossible fact that in certain respects we may well know less than our ancestors, as Fischhoff suggests here, the existence of the hindsight bias corrupts historical knowledge at its core: 'Thus the very outcome knowledge which gives us the feeling that we understand what the past was all about may prevent us from learning anything about it.'[74] On top of these biases identified by Lucas and Fischhoff, the usual, distorting partialities and passions in approaching the past should be added. The conclusion is ineluctable: Popper buried the philosopher-king; Lucas and Fischhoff buried the historian-king.

Afterword

When all is said and done, after leaders bury their axes, smoke their peace pipes and cultivate their gardens, do they gratefully recall and apply the lessons of their ancestors? It would surprise me if wise leaders – with the dust of the past on their shoes while boldly looking into the future – really exist and, if they do, if their magic has a secret recipe. Kant wrote that one could not possess wisdom, only feel love for it. Wisdom informed by history is a North Star.

Antoon De Baets is Professor of History, Ethics and Human Rights by special appointment of the Foundation Euroclio at the University of Groningen, The Netherlands. He is the author of 185 publications, including *Responsible History* (Berghahn, 2009), and the coordinator of the Network of Concerned Historians. His most recent book is *Crimes against History* (Routledge, 2019).

Appendix 1: List of Historically Informed Political Leaders (1900–2018)

Note: Leaders are called 'historically informed political leaders' if they meet one or more of the following criteria before, during or after their political career:
- They received a formal history education.
- They wrote a historical work.
- They gave important speeches with substantial historical content.
- They displayed a sustained interest in history in other demonstrable ways.

Disclaimer: The author does not necessarily share the views, historical or otherwise, or approve the actions of the persons on this list.

Source: Compiled by Antoon De Baets.

Albania: Enver Hoxha, Aleksander Meksi
Argentina: Bartolomé Mitre Martínez, Juan Domingo Perón
Armenia: Levon Ter-Petrosian
Australia: Alfred Deakin, Paul Hasluck, Gough Whitlam, Paul Keating, John Howard, Kevin Rudd
Azerbaijan: Abulfaz Elchibey, Haydar Aliyev, Ilham Aliyev
Belarus: Aleksandr Lukashenko
Bolivia: Carlos Mesa Gisbert
Brazil: Jânio Quadros, Dilma Rousseff
Bulgaria: Ivan Geshov, Bogdan Filov, Todor Zhivkov, Nikolai Todorov, Zhelyu Zhelev, Georgi Parvanov, Sergey Stanishev
Burma: U Nu
Cambodia: Norodom Sihanouk, Pol Pot
Canada: Lester Pearson, Joe Clark, Justin Trudeau
Chile: Luis Barros Borgoño
China: Sun Yat-sen, Chiang Kai-shek, Mao Zedong, Zhou Enlai, Hu Yaobang, Xi Jinping
Colombia: Eduardo Santos
Costa Rica: Cleto González Víquez, Luis Guillermo Solís Rivera, Carlos Alvarado Quesada
Croatia: Franjo Tudjman
Cuba: Alfredo Zayas y Alfonso, Fidel Castro Ruz
Cyprus: Demetris Christofias
Czechoslovakia: Tomáš Masaryk, Gustav Husák
Czech Republic: Václav Havel, Petr Pithart
Denmark: Niels Neergaard, Margrethe II
Dominican Republic: Juan Bosch
Egypt: Gamal Abdel Nasser
Estonia: Lennart Meri, Mart Laar
Ethiopia: Haile Selassie
France: Jean Jaurès, Louis Barthou, Pierre Mendès-France, Charles de Gaulle, Maurice Couve de Murville, François Mitterrand, Edouard Balladur, Jacques

Chirac, Dominique de Villepin, Emmanuel Macron
Germany: Wilhelm II, Adolf Hitler, Konrad Adenauer, Theodor Heuss, Walter Ulbricht, Willy Brandt, Helmut Kohl, Richard von Weizsäcker, Angela Merkel, Joachim Gauck
Greece: Eleftherios Venizelos, Spyridon Lambros, Themistocles Sophoulis, Panayotis Kanellopoulos, Spyridon Markezinis, Kostas Karamanlis
Grenada: George Brizan
Guatemala: Jacobo Árbenz Guzmán
Guyana: Cheddi Jagan
Haiti: Jean-François Duvalier, Leslie Manigat
Hungary: József Antall, Viktor Orbán
Iceland: Kristján Eldjárn, Guðni Johannesson
India: Jawaharlal Nehru, Rajendra Prasad, Indira Gandhi
Indonesia: Sukarno
Iran: Mohammed Reza Pahlavi, Haji Ali Razmara, Ruhollah Khomeini
Iraq: Saddam Hussein
Ireland: Douglas Hyde
Israel: David Ben Gurion, Itzhak Ben-Zvi, Ariel Sharon
Italy: Benito Mussolini, Luigi Einaudi, Amintore Fanfani, Giovanni Spadolini
Ivory Coast: Laurent Gbagbo
Jamaica: Michael Manley
Japan: Yoshihito, Yasuhiro Nakasone, Shinzō Abe
Kenya: Jomo Kenyatta, Mwai Kibaki
Korea, North: Kim Il-Sung, Kim Jong-il
Kosovo: Hashim Thaçi
Laos: Katay Don Sasorith
Libya: Muammar al-Qaddafi
Lithuania: Vytautas Landsbergis
Malawi: Hastings Kamuzu Banda
Maldives: Kenereege Mohamed Nasheed
Mali: Alpha Konaré
Malta: Ugo Mifsud Bonnici
Mexico: José López Portillo
Netherlands: Jan Peter Balkenende, Willem-Alexander van Oranje, Mark Rutte
New Zealand: Bernard Fergusson
Pakistan: Mohammad Ali Jinnah, Benazir Bhutto
Palestinian Authority: Mahmoud Abbas
Panama: Ricardo Joaquín Alfaro Jované
Paraguay: Cecilio Baez González, Juan Natalicio González Paredes
Philippines: Ferdinand Marcos
Poland: Henryk Jabłoński, Mieczysław Rakowski, Lech Kaczyński, Donald Tusk
Portugal: António Salazar, Marcelo Caetano, Mário Soares
Romania: Nicolae Iorga, Nicolae Ceaușescu
Russia: Vladimir Putin
Senegal: Leopold Sédar Senghor
Serbia: Stojan Novaković
South Africa: Nelson Mandela
Spain: Niceto Alcalá-Zamora y Torres
Sweden: Nils Edén, Gustav VI Adolf
Tajikistan: Emomali Rahmonov
Tanzania: Julius Nyerere

Trinidad and Tobago: Eric Williams
Tunisia: Habib Bourguiba
Turkey: Mustafa Kemal Pasha, Şemsettin Günaltay, Bülent Ecevit, Turgut Özal, Recep Tayyip Erdoğan
Ukraine: Mykhailo Hrushevsky, Victor Yushchenko
United Kingdom: George V, Elizabeth II, Winston Churchill, Margaret Thatcher, Gordon Brown
United States: Theodore Roosevelt, Woodrow Wilson, Franklin Roosevelt, Harry Truman, Dwight Eisenhower, John Kennedy, Jimmy Carter, Bill Clinton, George W. Bush, Barack Obama
Uruguay: Eduardo Víctor Haedo
USSR: Vladimir Lenin, Joseph Stalin, Nikita Khrushchev, Mikhail Gorbachev, Gennady Yanayev
Uzbekistan: Islam Karimov
Vatican: Pius XII
Venezuela: José Gil Fortoul, Hugo Chávez Frías
Vietnam: Tran Trong Kim, Ho Chi Minh

Appendix 2: Writings about Heads of State and Government as Historians

Shinzō Abe: Yi Man-yol, 'Prime Minister Abe's Incorrect View of History', *Korea Focus* (26 April 2012) [http://www.koreafocus.or.kr/design2/layout/content_print.asp?group_id=104730].

Mustafa Kemal Atatürk: Nusret Baycan, 'Atatürk as a Historian', *Revue internationale d'histoire militaire*, no. 50 (1981), 265–74; Eric-Jan Zürcher, 'De politicus als geschiedschrijver, de historicus in de politiek: over de "Nutuk" (de zesdaagse rede) van Mustafa Kemal Pasha', in Ed de Moor (ed.), *Elf wijzen van interpreteren* (Nijmegen: Mandara, 1992), 127–37.

Hugo Chávez: Irene Caselli, 'Putting Bolívar on the Map', *Index on Censorship*, 47 no. 1 (Spring 2018), 62–63.

Winston Churchill: Maurice Ashley, *Churchill as Historian* (London: Secker & Warburg, 1968); Martin Gilbert, 'Churchill, Winston Spencer', in John Cannon (ed.), *The Blackwell Dictionary of Historians* (Oxford: Blackwell, 1988), 79–81; Robert Messenger, 'Last of the Whigs: Churchill as Historian', *The New Criterion* (October 2006) [https://www.newcriterion.com/issues/2006/10/last-of-the-whigs-churchill-as-historian]; David Reynolds, *In Command of History: Churchill Fighting and Writing the Second World War* (London: Penguin, 2005); Algis Valiunas, *Churchill's Military Histories: A Rhetorical Study* (Lanham, MD: Rowman & Littlefield, 2002).

Mikhail Gorbachev: Aleksandr Nekrich, 'General Secretary Gorbachev and History', in Idem, 'Perestroika in History: The First Stage', *Survey: A Journal of Soviet and East European Studies*, 30 no. 4 (1989), 23–27.

Adolf Hitler: Alexander Demandt, 'Klassik als Klischee: Hitler und die Antike', *Historische Zeitschrift*, 274 no. 2 (April 2002), 281–313; Timothy Ryback, *Hitler's Private Library: The Books that Shaped His Life* (New York: Knopf, 2008) (including 'Hitler's History of the Second World War', 208–22).

Saddam Hussein: Jan Ballast, 'Het verleden in dienst van de toekomst: Saddam Husayn en de geschiedenis in Ba'thi Irak', *Groniek: historisch tijdschrift*, 27 no. 125 (June 1994), 42–52 [https://rjh.ub.rug.nl/groniek/issue/view/2393]; Amatzia Baram, *Culture, History and Ideology in the Formation of Ba'thist Iraq* (Basingstoke: Macmillan, 1991); Paul Cooper, 'Saddam's "Disney for a Despot": How Dictators Exploit Ruins', *BBC News* (20 April 2018) [http://www.bbc.com/culture/story/20180419-saddam-disney-for-a-despot-how-dictators-exploit-ruins]; Stefan Wild, 'Der Generalsekretär und die Geschichtsschreibung: Saddam Husayn und die irakische Geschichtswissenschaft', in Ibrahim El Sheikh, Aart van den Koppel, Ruud Peters (eds), *The Challenge of the Middle East: Middle Eastern Studies at the University of Amsterdam* (Amsterdam: University of Amsterdam Institute for Modern Near Eastern Studies, 1982), 161–72.

Nicolae Iorga: Maurice Pearton, 'Nicolae Iorga as Historian and Politician', in Dennis Deletant and Harry Hanak (eds), *Historians as Nation-Builders: Central and South-East Europe* (London: Macmillan, 1988), 157–73.

Jean Jaurès: Helmut Hirsch, *Jean Jaurès as Historian* (Laramie, WY: [University of Wyoming], 1944); Helmut Hirsch, 'Jean Jaurès als Historiker', in Idem, *Denker und Kämpfer: Gesammelte Beiträge zur Geschichte der Arbeiterbewegung* (Frankfurt am Main: Europäische Verlagsanstalt, 1955), 149–81; Valérie Lecoulant, *Jaurès, historien de la révolution française* (Montreuil: Éditions du musée d'histoire vivante, 1993).

Helmut Kohl: Christian Wicke, 'Kohl as Nationalist Historian', in Idem, *Helmut Kohl's Quest for Normality: His Representation of the German Nation and Himself* (New York and Oxford: Berghahn, 2015), 170–206.

Vladimir Lenin: A.M. Sakharov, M.E. Naidenov and V. Ya. Zevin, 'Lenin as Historian, Soviet Treatment of', in Joseph Wieczynski (ed.), *The Modern Encyclopedia of Russian and Soviet History* (Gulf Breeze, FL: Academic International Press), no. 49 (1988), 210–21.

Mao Zedong: Frans de Boer, 'De geschiedvisie van Mao Zedong', *Groniek: historisch tijdschrift*, 27 no. 125 (June 1994), 22–31 [https://rjh.ub.rug.nl/groniek/issue/view/2393]; Howard Boorman, 'Mao Tse-tung as Historian', in Albert Feuerwerker (ed.), *History in Communist China* (Cambridge, MA: Massachusetts Institute of Technology Press, 1968), 306–29.

Tomáš Masaryk: R.R. Betts, 'Masaryk's Philosophy of History', *Slavonic and East European Review*, 26 no. 66 (November 1947), 30–43; Milan Hauner, 'The Meaning of Czech History: Masaryk versus Pekař', in Harry Hanak (ed.), *T.G. Masaryk (1850–1937)*, vol. 1, *Thinker and Politician* (Basingstoke: Palgrave Macmillan, 1990), 24–42; Karel Kučera, 'Masaryk and Pekař: Their Conflict over the Meaning of Czech History and its Metamorphoses', in Stanley Winters (ed.), *T.G. Masaryk (1850–1937)*, vol. 1, *Thinker and Politician* (Basingstoke: Palgrave Macmillan, 1990), 88–113.

Benito Mussolini: Rients Verschoor, 'Tussen socialist en fascist: Een analyse van de historische retoriek van Mussolini', *Groniek: historisch tijdschrift* no. 198 (2013), 97–108 [https://rjh.ub.rug.nl/groniek/issue/view/2572].

Gamal Abdel Nasser: Bert Zengerink, 'Historische fundamenten voor de Egyptische Revolutie', *Groniek: historisch tijdschrift*, 27 no. 125 (June 1994), 53–61 [https://rjh.ub.rug.nl/groniek/issue/view/2393].

Jawaharlal Nehru: Balkrishna Gokhale, 'Nehru and History', *History and Theory*, 17 no. 3 (October 1978), 311–22; David Kopf, 'A Look at Nehru's *World History* from the Dark Side of Modernity', *Journal of World History*, 2 no. 1 (1991), 47–63; Saul Padover, *Nehru on World History* (Bloomington: Indiana University Press, 1962); K.M. Panikkar, 'As a Historian', in Rafiq Zakaria (ed.), *A Study of Nehru* (Bombay: Times of India Press, 1959), 404–7; Eric Williams, 'A Tribute to Nehru' (1964), in Paul Sutton (ed.), *Forged from the Love of Liberty: Selected Speeches of Dr. Eric Williams* (Port of Spain: Longman Caribbean, 1981), 229–33.

Stojan Novaković: Dimitrije Djordjević, 'Stojan Novaković: Historian, Politician, Diplomat', in Dennis Deletant and Harry Hanak (eds), *Historians as Nation-Builders: Central and South-East Europe* (London: Macmillan, 1988), 11–69.

Julius Nyerere: John Meijerink, 'De omgang van Nyerere met het verleden', *Groniek: historisch tijdschrift*, 27 no. 125 (June 1994), 62–70 [https://rjh.ub.rug.nl/groniek/issue/view/2393].

Barack Obama: Jennifer Schuessler, 'Lessons Taught: Obama's Legacy as a Historian', *New York Times* (18 January 2017) [https://www.nytimes.com/2017/01/18/arts/barack-obama-legacy-historian.html?smid=fb-share&_r=1]; Steven Sarson, *Barack Obama: American Historian* (London and New York: Bloomsbury, 2018).

Juan Domingo Perón: Jan Blaauw, 'Speurtocht naar de grootstheid', *Groniek: historisch tijdschrift*, 27 no. 125 (June 1994), 80–88 [https://rjh.ub.rug.nl/groniek/issue/view/2393]; Alberto Ciria, 'Angels and Demons', *Index on Censorship*, 14 no. 6 (December 1985), 46–49.

Vladimir Putin: Andrei Kolesnikov, 'Putin's Politicization of Soviet History', *Carnegie Endowment for International Peace* (11 October 2017) [https://carnegie.ru/commentary/73341]; Shaun Walker and Andrew Weiss, 'Putin and the Politics of History', *Carnegie Endowment for International Peace* (16 January 2018) [http://carnegieendowment.org/2018/01/16/putin-and-politics-of-history-event-5790].

Theodore Roosevelt: William Wunder, 'Historian Theodore Roosevelt: The History Career of the Twenty-Sixth President' (10 October 2008) [https://web.archive.org/web/20090104102151/http://politicians.suite101.com/article.cfm/historian_theodore_roosevelt]; Jean Yarbrough, 'History

Lessons: Roosevelt's America', in Idem, *Theodore Roosevelt and the American Political Tradition* (Lawrence, KS: University Press of Kansas, 2012), 50–83.

Mark Rutte: Janna Overbeek Bloem, 'Rutte was voorbeeldige geschiedenisstudent', *Historisch Nieuwsblad* (5 August 2010) [https://www.historischnieuwsblad.nl/nl/nieuws/14042/rutte-was-voorbeeldige-geschiedenisstudent.html].

Joseph Stalin: David Brandenberger, 'Stalin as Historian-in-Chief', in Idem, 'Ideological Zig-Zag: Official Explanations for the Great Terror, 1936–1938', in James Harris (ed.), *Terror: Political Violence under Stalin* (Oxford: Oxford University Press, 2013), 154–57; Christopher Hill, 'Stalin and the Science of History', *Modern Quarterly*, 8 no. 4 (1953), 198–212.

Sukarno: Bert Dijkstra, '"Een grootsch verleden": De visie van Soekarno op de geschiedenis', *Groniek: historisch tijdschrift*, 27 no. 125 (June 1994), 32–41 [https://rjh.ub.rug.nl/groniek/issue/view/2393].

Franjo Tudjman: Tomislav Dulić, 'Research Note: Mapping Out the "Wasteland": Testimonies from the Serbian Commissariat for Refugees in the Service of Tudjman's Revisionism', *Holocaust and Genocide Studies*, 23 no. 2 (Fall 2009), 263–84; Ivo Goldstein and Slavko Goldstein, 'Revisionism in Croatia: The Case of Franjo Tudjman', *East European Jewish Affairs*, 31 no. 2 (Summer 2002), 52–64.

Walter Ulbricht: Hermann Weber, *Ulbricht fälscht Geschichte: Ein Kommentar mit Dokumenten zum 'Grundriß der Geschichte der deutschen Arbeiterbewegung'* (Cologne: Neuer Deutscher Verlag, 1964).

Eleftherios Venizelos: Paschalis Kitromilides, 'Venizelos' Intellectual Projects and Cultural Interests', in Idem (ed.), *Eleftherios Venizelos: The Trials of Statesmanship* (Edinburgh: Edinburgh University Press, 2006), 377–88.

Eric Williams: Paul Sutton, 'The Historian as Politician: Eric Williams and Walter Rodney', in Alistair Hennessy (ed.), *Intellectuals in the Twentieth-Century Caribbean*, vol. 1 (London: Macmillan Education, 1992), 98–114; Paul Sutton, 'The Scholar: A Personal Appreciation', in Ken Boodhoo (ed.), *Eric Williams: The Man and the Leader* (Lanham, MD: University Press of America), 29–48.

Woodrow Wilson: Stockton Axson, 'The Literary Historian', in Idem, 'Woodrow Wilson as Man of Letters', *The Rice Institute Pamphlet*, 22 (October 1935), 195–270; Marjorie Daniel, 'Woodrow Wilson Historian', *The Mississippi Valley Historical Review*, 21 no. 3 (December 1934), 361–74; Marcia Synnott, 'Woodrow Wilson', in Clyde Wilson (ed.), *Dictionary of*

Literary Biography, vol. 47, *American Historians 1866–1912* (Detroit, MI: Bruccoli Clark and Gale Research, 1986), 342–57.

Xi Jinping: Alison Kaufman, 'Xi Jinping as Historian: Marxist, Chinese, Nationalist, Global', *The Asan Forum* (15 October 2015) [http://www.theasanforum.org/xi-jinping-as-historian-marxist-chinese-nationalist-global].

Notes to Appendix 2

1. Some writings discuss the historical views of heads of state and government who were not particularly interested in history, for example: *Pope Francis:* Bronwen McShea, 'Pope Francis as Historian', *First Things* (23 March 2017) [https://www.firstthings.com/web-exclusives/2017/03/pope-francis-as-historian]. *Daniël Malan*: Albert-Jan Bosch, 'Daniël François Malan: Het Boerenverleden als Zuidafrikaans toekomstbeeld', *Groniek: historisch tijdschrift* 27(125) (1994), 71–79 [https://rjh.ub.rug.nl/groniek/issue/view/2393]. *Donald Trump*: Ryan Walters, 'Trump as Historian', *The Abbeville Blog* (2 May 2017) [https://www.abbevilleinstitute.org/blog/trump-as-historian]. Several other articles about Trump's historical views are available, including at *History News Network* and *Politico*, and in *Time* and *The Washington Post*.

2. Some writings discuss the historical views of other influential political figures, for example: *Mahatma Gandhi:* Balkrishna Gokhale, 'Gandhi and History', *History and Theory*, 11(2) (1972), 214–25. *Leon Trotsky:* Peter Beilharz, 'Trotsky as a Historian', *History Workshop* 20 (1985), 36–55; Isaac Deutscher, 'Leon Trotsky as a Historian of Revolution', in Alex Simirenko (ed.), *Soviet Sociology: Historical Antecedents and Current Appraisals* (Chicago: Quadrangle Books, 1966), 150–67; Bertram Wolfe, 'Leon Trotsky as Historian', *Slavic Review* 20(3) (1961), 495–502.

Appendix 3: Historians as Nobel Peace Prize Laureates and Nominees

Below are thumbnail sketches of the historians who won the Nobel Peace Prize or were nominated for it. The list was initially compiled to detect possible overlap with the leaders' list.

Table 4.2 Historians and the Nobel Peace Prize (1901–2018).

Laureates (7)	
1906 | Theodore Roosevelt – United States	(7x nominee in 1906)
1919 | Woodrow Wilson – United States	(1919 prize awarded in 1920)
	(22x nominee in 1918–1920)
1921 | Christian Lange – Norway	(7x nominee in 1914–1921)
1927 | Ludwig Quidde – Germany	(35x nominee in 1924–1927)
1957 | Lester Pearson – Canada	(2x nominee in 1952–1957)
1973 | Henry Kissinger – United States	
1986 | Elie Wiesel – Romania/United States	
Nominees with at least ten nominations (4)	
Fyodor Martens – Estonia/Russia	(24x nominee in 1901–1908)
James Shotwell – United States	(19x nominee in 1927–1955)
Salvador de Madariaga y Rojo – Spain	(12x nominee in 1930–1965)
Richard Coudenhove-Kalergi – Austria	(54x nominee in 1931–1967)

Notes:

1. For discussion, see text.

2. Only pre-1967 data are available for nomination frequencies, making them unknown for Kissinger and Wiesel, and possibly incomplete for de Madariaga and Coudenhove-Kalergi.

3. Historians and history producers with less than ten Nobel Peace Prize nominations (attention: only pre-1967 data are available for nomination frequencies, making them unknown or speculative for many nominees): Hashem Aghajari (1x), Lyudmila Alexeyeva (2x), Rafael Altamira y Crevea (6x), Giulio Andreotti Institute and Secret Archives, and archivist Patrizia Chilelli (5x), Akram Aylisli (1x), Arthur Charles Frederick Beales (1x), Ismail Beşikçi (1x), Homer Boyle (2x), Winston Churchill (2x), Hans Viktor Clausen (1x), Mustafa Dzhemilev (x2), Arnaldo Fortini (1x), Svetlana Gannushkina (7x), Gabriel Hanotaux (1x), Ienaga Saburō (x2), Instituto Histórico-Geográfico Brasileiro (1x), International Committee of Historical Sciences (4x), Maxim Kovalevsky (1x), Memorial (6x), Peter Munch (4x), Sulak Sivaraksa (2x), Tiananmen Mothers (4x), Thich Quang Do (7x), Tong Zeng (1x), Toshitaka Onodera (1x), Leyla Yunus (1x).

4. Desmond Tutu, Nobel Peace Prize laureate in 1984, was a high school teacher of English and history in 1955.

Sources:
Information about historians as Nobel Peace Prize laureates and nominees at https://www.nobelprize.org/search/?query=historian.

There is overlap between the historians' list and the leaders' list for three laureates: Theodore Roosevelt, Woodrow Wilson and Lester Pearson – I have discussed their profiles in this chapter. The following are thumbnail sketches for the remaining eight historians. The Norwegian Christian Lange was awarded the prize in 1921 in his capacity as secretary-general of the Inter-Parliamentary Union. He studied history, was known for his solid historical knowledge and published a famous *Histoire de l'internationalisme* (his PhD history thesis) in 1919, barely two years before he won the prize.[75] The German Ludwig Quidde received the prize in 1927 for his lifelong work in the cause of peace. He had a strange career. As a medievalist, he was the founder of the *Deutsche Zeitschrift für Geschichtswissenschaft* and a respected editor of the *Deutsche Reichstagsakten*, but in the years 1894–1896, he was gradually excluded from the profession because he had published an extremely successful pamphlet about the Roman Emperor Caligula with satirical allusions to Kaiser Wilhelm II.[76] In the following decades, Quidde switched careers and became a renowned leader of the national and international peace movement.[77] His peace work earned him the Nobel Peace Prize in 1927. In 1933, when Hitler came to power, he went into exile in Geneva. Quidde's razor-sharp criticism of political leaders was memorable. Henry Kissinger was an American National Security Adviser (1969–1975) and Secretary of State (1973–1977). Technically a political scientist, he considered himself a historian. He was intensely interested in historical figures such as British Foreign Secretary Lord Castlereagh and State Chancellor of the Austrian Empire Klemens von Metternich. Together with Le Duc Tho, he won the prize in 1973 for negotiating the Paris Peace Accords that stopped the Vietnam War.[78] At the same time, Kissinger was associated with United States support for several repressive dictatorships. Most commentators in the international press, therefore, considered the award highly questionable.[79] Author and Holocaust survivor Elie Wiesel, who won the prize in 1986, was a historian in all but name. The Nobel Prize website observed: 'He made it his life's work to bear witness to the genocide committed by the Nazis during World War II. He was the world's leading spokesman on the Holocaust.'[80] From 1976 he was the Andrew Mellon Professor in the Humanities at Boston University where he taught 'Literature of memory'.[81]

Four historians were nominated at least ten times. Fyodor Martens was an Estonian jurist and legal historian operating in the service of the Tsar. He is celebrated in the history of human rights for formulating the so-called Martens Clause, which in 1899 introduced the fundamental idea that principles of humanity and public conscience offer residual protection for persons in times of war.[82] Canadian-born American historian and diplomat James Shotwell was an adviser to President Wilson. He edited the 150-volume *Economic and Social History of the World Wars* (1919–1929). He contributed, among others, to the Versailles Peace Conference (1919), to the foundation of the League of Nations (1920) and the International Committee of Historical Sciences (1926), and to the San Francisco Conference, which established the United Nations (1945).[83] Salvador de Madariaga was a leading Spanish liberal historian who was forced to live in exile for four decades during Francisco Franco's regime. He was the leader of the disarmament section of the Secretariat of the League of Nations. From the 1920s, the Austrian historian Richard Coudenhove-Kalergi led the Pan-European Movement and devoted his life to the idea of a 'United States of Europe'. Madariaga and Coudenhove-Kalergi were nominated intermittently during no less than thirty-five years. Coudenhove-Kalergi's score of fifty-four nominations was the highest. Curiously, many of the historians discussed here do not figure prominently in the histories of historical writing. This impressive parade of historians deserves wider recognition.

Notes

1. All websites mentioned in this chapter were last consulted on 31 December 2018.

2. Plato, 'The Republic', book V, 473c–d. (http://www.perseus.tufts.edu/hopper/text?doc=Perseus:text:1999.01.0168).

3. 'Daß Könige philosophieren, oder Philosophen Könige würden, ist nicht zu erwarten, aber auch nicht zu wünschen; weil der Besitz der Gewalt das freie Urteil der Vernunft unvermeidlich verdirbt', in Kant, 'Zum ewigen Frieden: Ein philosophischer Entwurf'. English version: 'Perpetual Peace: A Philosophical Sketch', 115.

4. Popper, *The Open Society and Its Enemies*, 150–69 ('The philosopher king'), 673–91 (notes).

5. '[D]ie Eule der Minerva beginnt erst mit der einbrechenden Dämmerung ihren Flug', in Hegel, *Grundlinien der Philosophie des Rechts*, 21.

6. 'Damit erhält auch der Satz Historia vitae magistra einen höheren und zugleich bescheideneren Sinn. Wir wollen durch Erfahrung nicht sowohl klug (für ein andermal) als weise (für immer) werden.' Originally from a course taught in 1868–1869, the text was published posthumously in 1905 in Jacob Burckhardt, *Weltgeschichtliche Betrachtungen*, 9. English version: *Force and Freedom: An Interpretation of History*, 78. Burckhardt's criticism of Hegel is at 72–73. See also Burckhardt's essay, 'The Great Men of History', based on three lectures delivered in 1870, in the same edition, 267–306. Burckhardt identified (at 288–306) a number of 'great men' (by which he meant 'irreplaceable men'), apportioning praise and blame to different historical figures in ways barely recognizable today. Interestingly, however, he also argues that great men are exceptions, not examples, and that, therefore, greatness is not a moral ideal (291, 294, 301).

7. Marcus Tullius Cicero, *De Oratore* (55 BCE), book II, section IX. For a study of the topos 'historia magistra vitae', one can start with the exchange of views between Holger Thünemann and Thomas Sandkühler, 'Historia Magistra Vitae? The Banality of Easy Answers' (https://public-history-weekly.degruyter.com/4-2016-3/historia-magistra-vitae-banality-easy-answers).

8. And, following him, Dionysius of Halicarnassus and Bolingbroke.

9. 'Der Historiker ist ein rückwärts gekehrter Prophet', in Schlegel, 'Fragmente', *Athenaeum*, Fragment 80. James Birren and Cheryl Svensson ('Wisdom in History', 16–18)

list 17 definitions of wisdom. To give one good example: 'Wisdom is expertise in the domain of fundamental life pragmatics, such as life planning or life review. It requires a rich factual knowledge about life matters, rich procedural knowledge about life problems, knowledge of different life contexts and values or priorities, and knowledge about the unpredictability of life.' (Quoted from Baltes and Smith, 'Toward a Psychology of Wisdom and Its Ontogenesis', 87–120). As may already be inferred somehow from the problem of defining wisdom with precision, the utility of the concept, although it has been around for millennia, is still disputed in philosophy. One major problem is that it presupposes that knowledge reflects perennial truths. See Osbeck and Robinson, 'Philosophical Problems of Wisdom', 61–64. Max Weber analysed the personal attributes needed by politicians; he did not single out wisdom but passion, responsibility and a sense of proportion, recommending a balance between an ethic of ultimate ends and an ethic of responsibility. See Weber, 'Politik als Beruf', 35–88. English translation: 'Politics as Vocation', 192–207, especially 198.

10. Kierkegaard, *Papers and Journals: A Selection*, 161 (reference to Danish original 1843. IV.A.164).

11. De Baets, 'Democracy and Historical Writing', 34–36 ('Democracy and historical awareness') (http://www.unizar.es/historiografias/numeros/9/debaets.pdf).

12. Philosopher Arnold Gehlen, as quoted in Schieder, 'The Role of Historical Consciousness in Political Action', 1.

13. The 2016 study 'Getting Political With Education: Evaluating the Educational Path to Congress and to the Presidency', *Trade Schools, Colleges and Universities* (11 October 2017) (https://www.trade-schools.net/learn/presidential-colleges.asp) showed that in the United States 'the most common presidential undergraduate degrees are in history, economics, international affairs, and political science.'

14. Many historians and historically oriented novelists were nominated for the Nobel Prize in Literature; a few were also awarded it (Theodor Mommsen, Romain Rolland, Winston Churchill, Boris Pasternak, Aleksandr Solzhenitsyn and Svetlana Alexievich).

15. Williams, *History of the People of Trinidad and Tobago*, vi–x.

16. I could not find the origin of this often mentioned quote, which possibly dates from around 1995. Another quip is attributed to Zhou Enlai, Premier of the People's Republic of China. During Nixon's visit to China in 1972, he was asked about the impact of the French Revolution, and answered: 'It is too early to say.' See Nicholas, 'Zhou Enlai's Famous Saying Debunked', *History Today* (https://www.historytoday.com/dean-nicholas/zhou-enlais-famous-saying-debunked) [link no longer available].

17. I first explored the topic in 'Herauten van een groots verleden: de geschiedvisie van Derde-Wereldleiders' [Heralds of a Glorious Past: The Historical Views of Third World Leaders], 6–21 (https://rjh.ub.rug.nl/groniek/article/view/16447/13937). In *Groniek's* special issue, I presented my insights as a prelude to seven leader studies carried out by my students. An early, concise version of the present text was published in Dutch as 'Het historisch besef van wijze leiders' [The Historical Awareness of Wise Leaders], 19–26. The present text has been thoroughly rewritten, expanded and updated. Its basis was a complete search of Lentz, *Heads of States and Governments: A Worldwide Encyclopedia of over 2,300 Leaders, 1945 through 1992*, supplemented with innumerable historical dictionaries, encyclopedias, biographies, memoirs, autobiographies, obituaries and commemorative addresses, ad hoc searches (since the early 1990s) and *Historical Abstracts* and *Wikipedia* searches.

18. See https://www.improbable.com/ig/winners. See also 'Belarus's Crackdown: No Applause, Please', *The Economist* (7 July 2011) (https://www.economist.com/europe/2011/07/07/no-applause-please). In 1996, French President Jacques Chirac received the Ig Nobel Peace Prize 'for commemorating the 50th anniversary of Hiroshima with atomic bomb tests in the Pacific'.

19. Quoted in S. Smith, 'The Story of Laurent Gbagbo', 10–12 (https://www.lrb.co.uk/v33/n10/stephen-w-smith/the-story-of-laurent-gbagbo). I thank Thijs Bouwknegt for alerting me to this quote.

20. Croce, 'Historians and Politicians', 175–78. For background, see D.M Smith, 'Benedetto Croce: History and Politics', 147–67.

21. Wolfe, 'Totalitarianism and History', 161. Like Stalin, Ceaușescu and Kim Il-Sung were also prolific authors of historical works while they stood at the helm of the state.

22. Johnson to John Roche as quoted in Wise, *The Politics of Lying: Government Deception, Secrecy, and Power*, 184.

23. Morris, 'Making History: Israeli President Shimon Peres Reflects on his Mentor, His Peace Partner, and whether the State of Israel Will Survive' (http://www.tabletmag.com/jewish-news-and-politics/40409/making-history).

24. Rempel, *Delusions of a Dictator: The Mind of Marcos as Revealed in His Secret Diaries*, xii; Curaming, 'Official History Reconsidered: The Tadhana Project in the Philippines', 237–53.

25. 'Speech in the House of Commons on 23 January 1948', UK House of Commons Hansard Archives, Foreign Affairs, volume 446, paragraph 557 (https://api.parliament.uk/historic-hansard/commons/1948/jan/23/foreign-affairs#S5CV0446P0_19480123_HOC_99).

26. I could not find the origin of this often mentioned quote. See the discussion at https://en.wikiquote.org/wiki/David_Ben-Gurion.

27. Examples are Sukarno in the Dutch East Indies (1930) and Fidel Castro in Cuba (1953) as prisoners during trials years before their accession to power; the Argentinian junta (1983) on leaving power; Japanese Prime Minister Hideki Tōjō while attempting suicide (1945); and Brazilian President Getúlio Vargas while committing suicide (1954). See Paget (ed.), *Indonesia Accuses! Soekarno's Defence Oration in the Political Trial of 1930*; Fidel Castro, 'History Will Absolve Me' (La historia me absolverá) (1953) (https://www.marxists.org/history/cuba/archive/castro/1953/10/16.htm). For the Argentinian junta, see *Documento final de la junta militar sobre la guerra contra la subversión y el terrorismo* (no place [Buenos Aires]; April 1983). For Tōjō, see Toland, *The Rising Sun: The Decline and Fall of the Japanese Empire, 1936–1945*, 872. For Vargas, see '1954: Brazilian President Found Dead', *BBC News* (24 August 1954) (http://news.bbc.co.uk/onthisday/hi/dates/stories/august/24/newsid_4544000/4544759.stm).

28. See for more analysis, De Baets, 'Herauten'.

29. Stalin, 'Talk with the German Author Emil Ludwig (December 13, 1931)', 106–25, here 106 (https://www.marxists.org/reference/archive/stalin/works/1931/dec/13.htm).

30. It had a print run of 15 million copies. Knorin was detained and eventually shot in July 1938 – during the very summer that Stalin was editing the final text. See Brandenberger, "Ideological Zig-Zag: Official Explanations for the Great Terror, 1936–1938', 143–57.

31. De Baets, *Crimes against History*, especially chapter 3 ('Public Attacks of Political Leaders on Historians').

32. Grand Duke Alexander of Russia, *Once a Grand Duke*, 371. For the context, see Cockfield, *White Crow: The Lives and Times of the Grand Duke Nikolas Mikhailovich, 1859–1919*, 242.

33. Stalin, 'Some Questions Concerning the History of Bolshevism: Letter to the Editorial Board of the Magazine "Proletarskaya Revolutsia"', 86–104, here 99 (https://www.marxists.org/reference/archive/stalin/works/1931/x01/x01.htm). See also Barber, *Soviet Historians in Crisis, 1928–1932*, 107–42, 174, 176.

34. 'Mais les historiens aussi ont besoin d'être dirigés'. Pivert, 'Problèmes du socialisme: quelques aspects théoriques des entretiens du Kremlin', 289 (http://chs.univ-paris1.fr/Voyages/probl%E8messoc.pdf).

35. Chandler, 'Seeing Red: Perceptions of Cambodian History in Democratic Kampuchea', 34.

36. De Baets, *Crimes against History*, chapter 4 ('Iconoclastic Breaks with the Past'). See also http://www.ohchr.org/Documents/Issues/CulturalRights/DestructionHeritage/NGOS/A.DeBaets.pdf.

37. '100 Death Sentences', *Time*, 45(7) (12 February 1945), 36.

38. See, however, the list in Weststrate, Ferrari and Ardelt, 'The Many Faces of Wisdom: An Investigation of Cultural-Historical Wisdom Exemplars Reveals Practical, Philosophical, and Benevolent Prototypes', 666. The thirteen nominees (in order of number of nominations) were: Mahatma Gandhi, Jesus Christ, Abraham Lincoln, Martin Luther King Jr, Winston Churchill, Thomas Jefferson, Socrates, Albert Einstein, Mother Teresa, Barack Obama, King Solomon, Benjamin Franklin and Nelson Mandela. Six were heads of state and government, with Lincoln, Churchill, Jefferson and Obama falling within the 'practical wisdom' category, Solomon falling within the 'philosophical wisdom' category and Mandela falling within the 'benevolent wisdom' category. Only Churchill, Obama and Mandela come within our ambit of research, and they are on my list of historically informed leaders (and the latter two also on my list of Nobel Peace Prizes). Etheredge, "Wisdom in Public Policy," in Sternberg and Jordan, eds., *Handbook of Wisdom,* 299, gives another list of wise leaders (loosely based on one compiled by historian Barbara Tuchman): Pericles, Marcus Aurelius, Ashoka, Charlemagne, Founding Fathers (United States), Franklin Roosevelt, Mikhail Gorbachev, and Nelson Mandela. All those falling within my scope (Roosevelt, Mandela, Gorbachev) are on my list of historically informed leaders (and the latter two also on my list of Nobel Peace Prizes). For Tuchman's observations, see her 'Pursuit of Policy Contrary to Self-Interest' and '"A Lantern on the Stern"', in Idem, *The March of Folly: From Troy to Vietnam* (London: Abacus, 1985), 2–40, 475–486 (her list of wise rulers is at 18–21).

39. I also checked other international prizes, such as the Stalin Peace Prize, the Lenin Peace Prize, the World Peace Council Prize, the Sakharov Prize, and the Right Livelihood Award, but none has the prestige and continuity of the Nobel Peace Prize.

40. For example, Theodore Roosevelt, Henry Kissinger and (the younger) Nelson Mandela. According to Etheredge ('Wisdom in Public Policy', 315) all the wise rulers on his list used violence.

41. Between 1901 and 2018, 17 women, 89 men and 24 organizations were awarded the prize. Since 1980, a total of 26 Nobel Peace Prize laureates has come from countries outside Europe and North America (https://www.nobelpeaceprize.org/Prize-winners). See, for an analysis, Tønnesson, 'Trends in Nobel Peace Prizes in the Twentieth Century', 433–42. I am very grateful to Øyvind Tønnesson, historian at Agder University (UiA), Norway, and previous editor of the official nobelprize.org website (1998–2000), for a long conversation on 2 June 2018 at UiA in which he answered many of my questions about the Nobel Peace Prize.

42. Each year, the Norwegian Nobel Committee extracts a shortlist from the list of nominees. These confidential shortlists are also inaccessible.

43. Most importantly, the director of the Peace Research Institute Oslo (PRIO) has offered a personal shortlist for the Nobel Peace Prize every year since 2002. For the complete series, see https://www.prio.org/About/PeacePrize. I thank former PRIO director and historian Stein Tønnesson for this information.

44. Multiple nominations per year are allowed. I took into account the absolute number of nominations over all the years but not the number of submitters per nomination or the latter's status. Those with the right to nominate are restricted to members of national assemblies and governments, current and former members of the Norwegian Nobel Committee, Peace Prize laureates, professors of certain disciplines, directors of peace research and foreign policy institutes and members of international courts.

45. https://www.nobelpeaceprize.org/Prize-winners.

46. Roosevelt, *History as Literature and Other Essays*, 19.

47. Tønnesson, 'Controversies and Criticisms' (https://www.nobelprize.org/prizes/themes/controversies-and-criticisms/). For John Hope Franklin's opinion about the 'aggressive-minded' Roosevelt, see his 'The Historian and Public Policy', 357.

48. In 2014, Obama said during a speech: 'But I promise you, folks can make a lot more, potentially, with skilled manufacturing or the trades than they might with an art history degree. Now, nothing wrong with an art history degree – I love art history. (Laughter.) So I don't want to get a bunch of emails from everybody. (Laughter.)'. The White House, 'Remarks by the President on Opportunity for All and Skills for America's Workers' (Waukesha, WI, 30 January 2014) (https://obamawhitehouse.archives.gov/the-press-office/2014/01/30/remarks-president-opportunity-all-and-skills-americas-workers).

49. In 2004, Mandela launched a memory project: 'Address by Nelson Mandela at launch of the Nelson Mandela Centre of Memory and Commemoration Project' (2004) (http://www.mandela.gov.za/mandela_speeches/2004/040921_memory.htm). One of Mandela's speechwriters was historian Carolyn Hamilton; former deputy director of National Archives Verne Harris was his personal historian and archivist from 2004.

50. See Bady, 'Robben Island University', 106–19. Mandela has sometimes been called 'a historian of human emancipation'. See Ndlovu-Gatsheni, *The Decolonial Mandela: Peace, Justice and the Politics of Life*, 6–7, 17–18, 25.

51. 'Statement by Nelson Mandela on Receiving Truth and Reconciliation Commission Report' (29 October 1998) (http://www.mandela.gov.za/mandela_speeches/1998/981029_trcreport.htm). Other leaders of emerging democracies also commented on the violent past of their countries. For example, during the presidential elections of November 1985, the later President of Guatemala, Vinicio Cerezo Arevalo, declared: 'We are not going to be able to investigate the past. We would have to put the entire army in jail.' Quoted in Americas Watch and Physicians for Human Rights, *Guatemala: Getting Away with Murder*, 1. Julio María Sanguinetti Coirolo, president of Uruguay in 1985–1990, ruled out mass trials of the military, reportedly saying: 'The best thing that can happen to the past is to leave it to the historians.' Quoted in Gillespie, *Negotiating Democracy: Politicians and Generals in Uruguay*, 219. And the first non-Communist President of Bulgaria, Zhelyu Zhelev, said around 1990: 'Before we turn the page, we should first read it.' Quoted in Todorov, 'The Evil that Men Do', 18.

52. Moyn, *The Last Utopia: Human Rights in History*, 4, 122, 149, 150–60, 216–17.

53. 'Jimmy Carter Oral History, President of the United States: Transcript', *Miller Center Presidential Oral Histories* (29 November 1982) (https://millercenter.org/the-presidency/presidential-oral-histories/jimmy-carter-oral-history-president-united-states).

54. Nikita Sergeyevich Khrushchev, 'Special Report to the 20th Congress of the Communist Party of the Soviet Union' (Moscow 1956) (http://novaonline.nvcc.edu/eli/evans/his242/Documents/Speech.pdf and https://www.marxists.org/archive/khrushchev/1956/02/24.htm).

55. Quoted in Beaumont, 'Mikhail Gorbachev: The Forgotten Hero of History', (https://www.theguardian.com/theobserver/2009/nov/08/observer-profile-mikhail-gorbachev).

56. See, among many sources, Davies, 'Soviet History in the Gorbachev Revolution: The First Phase', 42–44, 74–75; Nekrich, 'Perestroika in History: The First Stage', 23–27; Sherlock, 'Politics and History under Gorbachev', *Problems of Communism*, 16–17.

57. The American Historical Association has had a Theodore Roosevelt-Woodrow Wilson Public Service Award since 2003.

58. The quote is comparable to leading Soviet historian Mikhail Pokrovsky's famous dictum 'It is the essence of history … that it is the most political of all sciences.'

59. During World War I, Wilson twice appealed to Kaiser Wilhelm II (himself very interested in history, particularly Greek archaeology) to release imprisoned Belgian historians Henri Pirenne and Paul Frédéricq. See Lyon, *Henri Pirenne: A Biographical and Intellectual Study*,

237. Wilson once remarked: 'The history of liberty is a history of resistance.' Speech at New York Press Club (9 September 1912), in Link, *The Papers of Woodrow Wilson*, 124.

60. Betts, 'Masaryk's Philosophy of History', *Slavonic and East European Review*, 30–43; Schmidt-Hartmann, 'Forty Years of Historiography under Socialism in Czechoslovakia: Continuity and Change in Patterns of Thought', 300–24; Schieder, 'Role of Historical Consciousness', 11–12. About Masaryk's role in exposing historical falsification, see Renner, 'De oude handschriften uit Bohemen', 84–86.

61. Inspired by Masaryk, the dissident playwright and later president of Czechoslovakia and the Czech Republic Václav Havel was, in a sense, also a philosopher-king. See, for example, his 'Stories and Totalitarianism', 14–21. Another president with a background as philosopher was Zhelyu Zhelev (Bulgaria).

62. Nehru, *Glimpses of World History, Being Further Letters to His Daughter, Written in Prison, and Containing a Rambling Account of History for Young People*; Idem, *The Discovery of India*.

63. The Norwegian Nobel Committee considers the fact that Gandhi never received the prize its biggest mistake: it is certain that he would have received it in 1948, the year of his assassination. Between 1937 and 1948, he was nominated twelve times. The committee considered in earnest to award him the prize posthumously, and when that option was not chosen, the prize was not awarded in 1948. See Tønnesson, 'Mahatma Gandhi, the Missing Laureate' (https://www.mkgandhi.org/nobel/nobel.htm).

64. Panikkar, 'As a Historian', 406–7.

65. Tharoor, 'In Winston Churchill, Hollywood Rewards a Mass Murderer' (https://www.washingtonpost.com/news/global-opinions/wp/2018/03/10/in-winston-churchill-hollywood-rewards-a-mass-murderer/?utm_term=.5005c7dff1f8). Several commentaries have disputed Tharoor's claims. See also Heyden, 'The 10 Greatest Controversies of Winston Churchill's Career', *BBC News* (26 January 2015) (https://www.bbc.com/news/magazine-29701767).

66. Quoted in 'Princeton Considers Dropping Woodrow Wilson Name after Protests', *BBC News* (20 November 2015) (http://www.bbc.com/news/world-us-canada-34883289). Originally at https://twitter.com/SlaughterAM/status/667312627228389377. The quote has a biblical origin. See Book of Daniel 2: 31–33.

67. Birren and Svensson, 'Wisdom in History', 16, 17, 19. Quote on 19.

68. Mukunda, 'Don't Trust Anyone over 70: Why Old Leaders Are Dangerous' (http://foreignpolicy.com/2013/02/27/dont-trust-anyone-over-70/amp/?__twitter_impression=true).

69. Toynbee, 'Jawaharlal Nehru', 4.

70. Nehru, *Discovery of India*, 33–38 ('The Burden of the Past'), quote on 36. Original: 'Nicht nur die Vernunft von Jahrtausenden – auch ihr Wahnsinn bricht an uns aus. Gefährlich ist es, Erbe zu sein.' Nietzsche, *Also sprach Zarathustra – Ein Buch für Alle und Keinen*.

71. He was influenced by the views of Belgian historian Henri Pirenne. See 'Robert E. Lucas Jr. – Biographical' (https://www.nobelprize.org/nobel_prizes/economic-sciences/laureates/1995/lucas-bio.html).

72. Others have also pointed to the hindsight bias, while using other terms. David Hackett Fischer called it 'the historians' fallacy', 'the error of assuming that a man who has a given historical experience knows it, when he has it, to be all that a historian would know it to be, with the advantage of historical perspective'. Fischer, *Historians' Fallacies: Toward a Logic of Historical Thought*, 209–13 (definition on 209). Nassim Nicholas Taleb wrote about related terms such as the narrative fallacy, retrospective distortion, the illusion of posterior predictability and the reverse engineering problem. See his *The Black Swan: The Impact of the Highly Improbable*, 62–84, 304.

73. Fischhoff, 'For Those Condemned to Study the Past: Reflections on Historical Judgment', 83. An earlier version appeared as Fischhoff, 'Hindsight ≠ Foresight: The Effect of Outcome Knowledge on Judgment under Uncertainty', 288–99.

74. Fischhoff, 'For Those Condemned to Study the Past', 84.

75. Tønnesson, 'Christian Lous Lange (Peace, 1921)', 83–117. See Lange, *Histoire de l'Internationalisme*.

76. The affair became a complicated case of *lèse majesté*. For the pamphlet with the title *Caligula, eine Studie über römischen Cäsarenwahnsinn*, see Quidde, *Caligula: Schriften über Militarismus und Pazifismus*, 63–80 (originally in *Die Gesellschaft*, 1894, 413–30). Online version at http://gutenberg.spiegel.de/buch/caligula-7268/1. I analyse the episode in my *Crimes against History*, chapter 6 ('The Subversive Power of Historical Analogies').

77. Rürup, 'Ludwig Quidde', 144–45; 'Ludwig Quidde: Biographical', *Nobelprize.org* (http://www.nobelprize.org/nobel_prizes/peace/laureates/1927/quidde-bio.html).

78. Le Duc Tho refused the prize.

79. Tønnesson, 'Controversies'. In 2001, the journalist Christopher Hitchens published *The Trial of Henry Kissinger*, listing Kissinger's alleged war crimes and crimes against humanity.

80. 'Elie Wiesel – Facts', *Nobelprize.org* (https://www.nobelprize.org/nobel_prizes/peace/laureates/1986/wiesel-facts.html).

81. 'Elie Wiesel – Biographical', *Nobelprize.org* (https://www.nobelprize.org/nobel_prizes/peace/laureates/1986/wiesel-bio.html). See also 'Elie Wiesel – Nobel Lecture: Hope, Despair and Memory', *Nobelprize.org* (11 December 1986) (http://www.nobelprize.org/nobel_prizes/peace/laureates/1986/wiesel-lecture.html).

82. The Martens Clause first appeared in the preamble of the 1899 Hague Convention II – Laws and Customs of War on Land. It is echoed in the preamble of the Universal Declaration of Human Rights and repeated as article 15.2 of the 1966 International Covenant on Civil and Political Rights (and then meant to apply also in times of peace). *Professor Martens' Departure* (1984), a fictional memoir written by Jaan Kross (himself a Nobel Literature Prize nominee), recounts Martens's life.

83. About Shotwell, see Erdmann, Kocka and Mommsen, *Toward a Global Community of Historians: The International Historical Congresses and the International Committee of Historical Sciences, 1898–2000*, 75, 79, 84.

Bibliography

Americas Watch and Physicians for Human Rights. *Guatemala: Getting Away with Murder*. New York: Americas Watch, 1991.
Bady, A. 'Robben Island University', *Transition* 116 (2014), 106–19.
Baltes, P. and J. Smith, 'Toward a Psychology of Wisdom and Its Ontogenesis', in R. Sternberg (ed.), *Wisdom: Its Nature, Origins and Development* (Cambridge: Cambridge University Press, 1990), 87–120.
Barber, J. *Soviet Historians in Crisis, 1928–1932*. London and Basingstoke: Macmillan, 1981.
Beaumont, P. 'Mikhail Gorbachev: The Forgotten Hero of History', *The Guardian* (8 November 2009).
Betts, R.R. 'Masaryk's Philosophy of History', *Slavonic and East European Review* 26(66) (1947), 30–43.
Birren, J. and C. Svensson. 'Wisdom in History', in R. Sternberg and J. Jordan (eds), *Handbook of Wisdom: Psychological Perspectives* (Cambridge: Cambridge University Press, 2005), 3–31.
Brandenberger, D. 'Ideological Zig-Zag: Official Explanations for the Great Terror, 1936–1938', in J. Harris (ed.), *Terror: Political Violence under Stalin* (Oxford: Oxford University Press, 2013), 143–57.
Burckhardt, J. *Weltgeschichtliche Betrachtungen*. Berlin and Stuttgart: W. Spemann, 1910.

———. *Force and Freedom: An Interpretation of History*, J. Hastings Nichols (ed.). New York: Meridian Books, 1955.
———. 'The Great Men of History', in J. Hastings Nichols (ed.), *Force and Freedom: An Interpretation of History* (New York: Meridian Books, 1955), 267–306.
Chandler, D. 'Seeing Red: Perceptions of Cambodian History in Democratic Kampuchea', in D. Chandler and B. Kiernan (eds), *Revolution and Its Aftermath in Kampuchea: Eight Essays* (New Haven, CT: Yale University Press, 1983), 34–56.
Cockfield, J. *White Crow: The Lives and Times of the Grand Duke Nikolas Mikhailovich, 1859–1919*. Westport, CT: Praeger, 2002.
Croce, B. 'Historians and Politicians', in B. Croce, *History as the Story of Liberty*, *History as the Story of Liberty* (Chicago: Henry Regnery, 1970), 175–78 (originally Italian, 1938).
Curaming, R. 'Official History Reconsidered: The Tadhana Project in the Philippines', in B. Bevernage and N. Wouters (eds), *The Palgrave Handbook of State-Sponsored History After 1945* (Basingstoke: Palgrave-Macmillan, 2018), 237–53.
Davies, R.W. 'Soviet History in the Gorbachev Revolution: The First Phase', *The Socialist Register* 24 (1988), 37–78.
De Baets, A. 'Herauten van een groots verleden: de geschiedvisie van Derde-Wereldleiders', *Groniek: historisch tijdschrift*, 125 (June 1994), 6–21.
———. 'Het historisch besef van wijze leiders', in D. Bosscher and Y. van Hoef (eds), *Koning Nobel: Opstellen over goede en kwade leiders, en wat het verschil maakt – Liber amicorum voor Prof. dr. Hans Renner* (Groningen: University of Groningen, 2011), 19–26.
———. 'Democracy and Historical Writing', *Historiografías / Historiographies: The Journal of History and Theory* 9 (2015), 34–36.
———. *Crimes against History*. London: Routledge, 2019.
Erdmann, K., J. Kocka and W. Mommsen. *Toward a Global Community of Historians: The International Historical Congresses and the International Committee of Historical Sciences, 1898–2000*. New York and Oxford: Berghahn, 2005 (originally German, 1987).
Etheredge, L. 'Wisdom in Public Policy', in R. Sternberg and J. Jordan (eds), *Handbook of Wisdom: Psychological Perspectives* (Cambridge: Cambridge University Press, 2005), 297–328.
Fischer, D.H. *Historians' Fallacies: Toward a Logic of Historical Thought*. New York: Harper & Row, 1970.
Fischhoff, B. 'Hindsight ≠ Foresight: The Effect of Outcome Knowledge on Judgment under Uncertainty', *Journal of Experimental Psychology: Human Perception and Performance* 1(3) (1975), 288–99.
———. 'For Those Condemned to Study the Past: Reflections on Historical Judgment', in R. Shweder and D. Fiske (eds), *Fallible Judgment in Behavioral Research* (San Francisco: Jossey-Bass, 1980), 79–93.
Franklin, J.H. 'The Historian and Public Policy', in S. Vaughn (ed.), *The Vital Past: Writings on the Uses of History* (Athens: University of Georgia Press, 1985), 347–59.
Gillespie, C. *Negotiating Democracy: Politicians and Generals in Uruguay*. Cambridge: Cambridge University Press, 1991.
Grand Duke Alexander of Russia. *Once a Grand Duke*. London: Cassel, 1932.
Havel, V. 'Stories and Totalitarianism', *Index on Censorship* 17(3) (1988), 14–21.
Hegel, G.F. *Grundlinien der Philosophie des Rechts*. Berlin: Duncker & Humblot, 1833 [1820].
Heyden, T. 'The 10 Greatest Controversies of Winston Churchill's Career', *BBC News* (26 January 2015).
Hitchens, C. *The Trial of Henry Kissinger*. London: Verso, 2001.
Kant, I. 'Zum ewigen Frieden: Ein philosophischer Entwurf' (1795), in I. Kant, *gesammelte Schriften*, vol. 8. Berlin: Preußische Akademie der Wissenschaften, 1903.

———. 'Perpetual Peace: A Philosophical Sketch', in H. Reiss (ed.), *Kant: Political Writings* (Cambridge: Cambridge University Press, 1991), 93–130.

Kierkegaard, S. *Papers and Journals: A Selection*, A. Hannay (ed.). Harmondsworth: Penguin, 1996.

Lange, C.L. *Histoire de l'internationalisme*, vol. 1, *Jusqu'à la Paix de Westphalie, 1648*, Publications de l'Institut Nobel Norvégien, vol. 4; Christiania: Aschehoug, 1919.

Lentz, H.M. *Heads of States and Governments: A Worldwide Encyclopedia of over 2,300 Leaders, 1945 through 1992*. Jefferson, NC and London: McFarland, 1994.

Link, A. (ed.). *The Papers of Woodrow Wilson*, vol. 25, Aug–Nov 1912. Princeton: Princeton University Press, 1978.

Lyon, B. *Henri Pirenne: A Biographical and Intellectual Study*. Ghent: Story-Scientia, 1974.

Morris, B. 'Making History: Israeli President Shimon Peres Reflects on his Mentor, His Peace Partner, and whether the State of Israel Will Survive', *Tablet* (26 July 2010).

Moyn, S. *The Last Utopia: Human Rights in History*. Cambridge, MA and London: The Belknap Press of Harvard University Press, 2010.

Mukunda, G. 'Don't Trust Anyone over 70: Why Old Leaders Are Dangerous', *Foreign Policy* (27 February 2013).

Ndlovu-Gatsheni, S. *The Decolonial Mandela: Peace, Justice and the Politics of Life*. New York and Oxford: Berghahn, 2016.

Nehru, J. *Glimpses of World History, Being Further Letters to His Daughter, Written in Prison, and Containing a Rambling Account of History for Young People*. New Delhi: Oxford University Press, 1989 (originally 1934–35).

———. *The Discovery of India*. New Delhi: Indian Council for Cultural Relations, 1981 (originally 1946).

Nekrich, A. 'Perestroika in History: The First Stage', *Survey: A Journal of Soviet and East European Studies* 30(4) (1989), 22–43.

Nicholas, D. 'Zhou Enlai's Famous Saying Debunked', *History Today* (15 June 2011).

Nietzsche, F. *Also sprach Zarathustra – Ein Buch für Alle und Keinen*. Chemnitz: Ernst Schmeitzner, 1883.

Osbeck, L. and D. Robinson. 'Philosophical Problems of Wisdom', in R. Sternberg and J. Jordan (eds), *Handbook of Wisdom: Psychological Perspectives* (Cambridge: Cambridge University Press, 2005), 61–83.

Paget, R. (ed.). *Indonesia Accuses! Soekarno's Defence Oration in the Political Trial of 1930*. Kuala Lumpur: Oxford University Press, 1975.

Panikkar, K.M. 'As a Historian', in R. Zakaria (ed.), *A Study of Nehru*. Bombay: Times of India Press, 1959, 404–7.

Pivert, M. 'Problèmes du socialisme: quelques aspects théoriques des entretiens du Kremlin', *La Revue socialiste* 100 (1956), 282–93.

Plato. 'The Republic', book V, in *Plato in Twelve Volumes*, volumes 5–6. Cambridge, MA: Harvard University Press, and London: Heinemann, 1969.

Popper, K. *The Open Society and Its Enemies*, vol. 1, *The Spell of Plato*. London: Taylor & Francis, 2002 (originally 1945).

Quidde, L. *Caligula: Schriften über Militarismus und Pazifismus*, re-edition of the 34th edition of 1926. Frankfurt am Main: Syndikat, 1977.

Rempel, W. *Delusions of a Dictator: The Mind of Marcos as Revealed in His Secret Diaries*. Boston, MA: Little Brown & Co, 1993.

Renner, H. 'De oude handschriften uit Bohemen', in Z. Dittrich, B. Naarden and H. Renner (eds), *Knoeien met het verleden*. Utrecht and Antwerp: Het Spectrum, 1984, 75–87.

Roosevelt, T. *History as Literature and Other Essays*. New York: Cosimo, 2006 [1914].

Rürup, R. 'Ludwig Quidde', in H.-U. Wehler (ed.), *Deutsche Historiker*, vol. 3. Göttingen: Vandenhoeck and Ruprecht (1972), 124–47.

Schieder, T. 'The Role of Historical Consciousness in Political Action', *History and Theory*, 17(4) (1978), 1–18.
Schlegel, F. 'Fragmente', *Athenaeum* 1(2) (1798).
Schmidt-Hartmann, E. 'Forty Years of Historiography under Socialism in Czechoslovakia: Continuity and Change in Patterns of Thought', *Bohemia* 29(2) (1988), 300–24.
Sherlock, T. 'Politics and History under Gorbachev', *Problems of Communism* 37(3–4) (1988), 16–42.
Smith, D.M. 'Benedetto Croce: History and Politics', in W. Laqueur and G. Mosse (eds), *Historians in Politics* (London and Beverly Hills: Sage, 1974), 147–67.
Smith, S. 'The Story of Laurent Gbagbo', *London Review of Books* 33(10) (2011), 10–12.
Stalin, J. 'Some Questions Concerning the History of Bolshevism: Letter to the Editorial Board of the Magazine "Proletarskaya Revolutsia"', in J. Stalin, *Works*, vol. 13 (Foreign Languages Publishing House, 1954), 86–104.
———. 'Talk with the German Author Emil Ludwig (December 13, 1931)', in J. Stalin, *Works*, vol. 13. (Moscow: Foreign Languages Publishing House, 1954), 106–25.
Taleb, N.N. *The Black Swan: The Impact of the Highly Improbable*. New York: Random House, 2016 (originally 2007).
Tharoor, S. 'In Winston Churchill, Hollywood Rewards a Mass Murderer', *Washington Post* (10 March 2018).
Thünemann, H. and T. Sandkühler. 'Historia Magistra Vitae? The Banality of Easy Answers', *Public History Weekly: The International Blogjournal* (4 February, 4 March and 19 May 2016).
Todorov, T. 'The Evil that Men Do', *UNESCO Courier* (December 1999), 18–19.
Toland, J. *The Rising Sun: The Decline and Fall of the Japanese Empire, 1936–1945*. New York: Modern Library [Random House], 2003 (originally 1970).
Tønnesson, Ø. 'Controversies and Criticisms' (29 June 2000).
———. 'Mahatma Gandhi, the Missing Laureate', 2001.
———. 'Trends in Nobel Peace Prizes in the Twentieth Century', *Peace & Change* 26(4) (2001), 433–42.
———. 'Christian Lous Lange (Peace, 1921)', in O. Njølstad (ed.), *Norwegian Nobel Prize Laureates: From Bjørnson to Kydland* (Oslo: Universitetsforlaget, 2006), 83–117.
Toynbee, A. 'Jawaharlal Nehru', *Encounter* 33(2) (1964), 3–5.
Tuchmann, B. *The March of Folly: From Troy to Vietnam*. London: Abacus, 1985.
Weber, M. 'Politik als Beruf', in W. Mommsen and W. Schluchter (eds), *Wissenschaft als Beruf 1917/1919 / Politik als Beruf 1919*, Max Weber Gesamtausgabe, volume I/17 (Tübingen: Mohr & Siebeck, 1994), 35–88.
———. 'Politics as Vocation', in J. Dreijmanis (ed.), *Max Weber's Complete Writings on Academic and Political Vocations* (New York: Algora, 2008), 192–207.
Weststrate, N., M. Ferrari and M. Ardelt. 'The Many Faces of Wisdom: An Investigation of Cultural-Historical Wisdom Exemplars Reveals Practical, Philosophical, and Benevolent Prototypes', *Personality and Social Psychology Bulletin*, 42(5) (2016), 662–76.
Williams, E. *History of the People of Trinidad and Tobago*. New York: Praeger, 1962.
Wise, D. *The Politics of Lying: Government Deception, Secrecy, and Power*. New York: Random House, 1973.
Wolfe, B. 'Totalitarianism and History', *The Antioch Review* 13(2) (1953), 155–65.

CHAPTER 5

Historians with a Cause

Refugees' Memory and Historical Practices in Interwar Greece

Emilia Salvanou

Introduction

Historians always have a cause. Despite writing about the past, it is the present they are writing for and that defines the way the past is problematized.[1] Sometimes, though, historians delve into the study of the past for a more specific cause, seeking answers to major problems of their time. The interwar years were such a troubled period, during which the disruption of faith in the linear progress of humanity led to an intense preoccupation with the past, in the search for identity. Historians thus found a privileged field for intervention in the community.

As the end of the Great War approached, and immediately after the Armistice of 1918, Europe faced the largest population movement in its contemporary history. This migration was the result of the total reorganization of the world from an imperial to a national order, resulting in the transformation of inhabitants into citizens, refugees and minorities. Expatriation from the Ottoman Empire to Greece after the end of the Greek-Turkish War that followed World War I was part of this process of pursuing national homogenization for both countries. While such movements were protracted as a rational solution for the optimized function of the newly formed nation states, they were overall experienced traumatically.[2] Inclusion to the polity did not ensure the newcomers' social inclusion. On the contrary, issues of

Notes for this section begin on page 132.

exclusion and discrimination against newcomers emerged, evolving around cultural differences, economic and political antagonism and, bottom line, the lack of ties that would allow their inclusion in the national imaginary.[3] It was thus important for the refugees to make a space within the national imaginary.

This chapter is about the efforts undertaken by the refugees to create the space they needed. It aims to discuss the ways refugees from the Ottoman communities, and in particular from Thrace, shaped and negotiated their memories in the course of the following decades so as to be included in the national narrative. It argues that although negotiation of the past held a central role in accomplishing incorporation, a broader understanding of what such a negotiation entailed was imperative. Historical practices needed to be included alongside historical discourse. Furthermore, it claims that the limits between professional historians and intellectuals preoccupied with the practical past were feasible, giving the latter a leading role in the poetics of the new historical narratives.[4] On a broader level, this chapter contributes to the ongoing discussion of the role of historians within the academy and their role as citizens, by exploring the ways intellectuals participated in the nationalization of the past in the interwar period, when traumatic memories that emerged from the Great War had to be accommodated in already existing national narratives.[5]

The Past, Engaged Historians and the Practice of History

The Great War inflicted a significant trauma on its participants. It evolved to be much more widespread and inclusive and catastrophic than the war the Great Powers had planned in August 1914. The enormous number of its victims, the casualties it brought about and the massive sufferings exceeded all prior known experience, putting under question the validity of faith in a linear process of human progress. Existing regimes of knowledge regarding time were shaken, leaving space for the development of new regimes of historicity.

The past was not valid any more as a pool of experience. History could not point the way in a world that was totally different to how it was before the war: the old imperial order of Europe was destroyed, extensive population uprooting had taken place in the name of the new world, suffering was visible everywhere and the need to move on was imperative. The future needed to distance itself from the suffering, to construct a new world. The new hope was the machine. Its predictability could be used for planning economic growth and, as was hoped, social order. Social engineering promised a better future and relief from difficulties and pain. The past had no place in the new world. It was time to move forward, to heal, to progress.

However, the rapidly changing present provoked a resurgence of memory.[6] Time was not empty any more. It entailed the burden of history, past sufferings and injustices.[7] The present's duty towards the past was conceived as to protect it from oblivion and seek rectification for the injustices. Oblivion and memory proceeded hand in hand during the interwar years. Even if not all events of the past became part of the future's narratives, the past was still the pool from which identity drew its elements. Intellectuals moved between engaging in the project of planning the future and crafting narratives about the past that would make space for it in the present, saving memory from oblivion.

Likewise, intellectuals that were interested in the past – lay historians and some professional historians as well – participated in the task of making way for their societies towards the future destination they envisaged. But what would that future look like? Through the traumatic experience of the Great War and its aftermath, a new conception of the future emerged, and redefined the conception of the past. The future needed to be saved from an unbearable present, and the order of the past needed to be reconstructed. Historical narratives, especially those concerning the practical past, could not solely refer to war events and state history any more. It could not be only about battles and victories any more. The voices of the defeated, those who had no glorious narrative about the recent past to present, had to be saved, so as to find place in the future. Not all of the past events mattered. The past (its facts and its cancelled potentialities and expectations) mattered as far as it was meaningful for the present and the prospective future. The dominant discourse of historicism was turned upside down: not just what 'really happened' but the silenced and the cancelled were of importance. Intellectuals and amateur historians took on the moral obligation to preserve the voice of those who have been wronged, so the injustice could be rectified in the future.

Such a relation with the past cannot be limited to discursive history. It consists both of historical narratives and practices. Historical practice takes us further than the ideological, conceptual and narrative construction of historiographical texts and reveals the practical side that allowed such a construction. It is related to 'new materiality', which approaches the social and cultural phenomena through their material forms as well as their discursive ones. New materiality focuses on living matter. It perceives it as self-organizing and self-transformative, changing the way the social has traditionally been perceived and engaged. It proposes that the material world should be understood as an entity constructed and experienced through an interactive cultural process.[8] By focusing on the materiality of the interactions between agents and performances it leads to a broader understanding of history: it is not only the meaning and the representation of the past that is important, but the way it functions and creates spaces for becoming. Change, according to materiality, is caused by practice as a collective action, which presupposes agency and experience. In this context, agency is not merely a return to the theories of the agent's responsibility that were dominant before the linguistic turn in the theory of history. It rather is in accordance with theories of structuralism and refers to the subject's capacity to act according to its discursive and practical consciousness, both of which are culturally constructed, and cause change by re-signifying the signifier through repetition.[9]

Likewise, experience re-entered the field of theory of history in the realm of the post-linguistic turn. The quest for authenticity of experience and its conceptualization within the framework of epistemology and philosophy were on the front line of intellectual discourse of modernity.[10] During the interwar years, Walter Benjamin argued that experience is mediated and constructed through language and is therefore contextualized in culture. The question of experience was re-posed after World War II, when the need for memory called for testimonies, which function as bridges between personal experiences and official narratives. Experience was in this frame differentiated from language and offered understandings of the past that textuality obscured. Historical experience becomes a form of aesthetic experience, in the sense that it needs to be mediated by an object that enables resistance to the mediation of tradition and language.[11]

During the interwar period, intellectuals who functioned as agents of change, networks that facilitated the realization of the conceived projects and artifacts that functioned as carriers of memory became parts of an assemblage through which relations to the past were re-negotiated. While such assemblages were defined by power relations, through their heterogeneity and exteriority, they ensured stability of the produced identity.[12]

Historical Background

From the dawn of the twentieth century, there was increased population mobility in and around the Ottoman Empire. From the Balkans to Anatolia, the prospect of the Empire's collapse formed the conditions for ongoing wars between emerging nationalisms and a consequent movement of the populations as the rule of their territories changed. But such uprooting usually proved to be temporary, and the groups affected returned to their homelands when circumstances changed. The Ilinden uprising of 1903 was the starting point of a war adventure that affected all nationalisms of the region and lasted until the end of the Greek-Turkish war and the Lausanne

Treaty (1923), which determined the process of population exchange and the status of minorities. The Macedonian struggle, the Balkan wars, World War I and the following expenditure of the Greek Army at Asia Minor were the cardinal points of a period of clashes that lasted over a decade and reshaped the territorial organization of the Balkans and Anatolia. Favouring the prospect of national homogeneity and prosperity, massive uprooting of populations took place. Approaching and shortly after the end of the war, though, such uprooting became mandatory: its conditions were determined by treaties; it was regularized, and the population affected obtained the status of refugees and minorities. In the case of Greece, the key point for the uprooting of populations from the Ottoman Empire and their fleeting to Greece as refugees was the defeat of the Army in Anatolia in 1922 and the signing of the Lausanne Treaty. Ottoman subjects of orthodox religion followed the army's retreat in 1922, terrified of the prospect of revenge by the Kemalist troops, while the remaining orthodox communities were officially exchanged for the Muslims of Greece according to the terms of the Treaty.[13]

Refugees from the Ottoman Empire were far from being a homogenous group. They were divided by cultural, economic and social differences – differences that derived from the part of the Empire where they were settled, the networks they participated in and the way they had come in touch with the nationalization process during the last decades. Additionally, they conceptualized their collectivity according to their local communities rather than in a more abstract way, making the development of a symbolically constructed community difficult. Last, the way they had experienced expatriation in the different communities of Asia Minor and the Balkans differed so drastically that it defined their memory of the experience.[14]

Refugees from Thrace mostly belonged to the population groups that were exchanged due to the Lausanne Treaty. During the decade between the Balkan Wars and the end of World War I, Eastern Thrace had been occupied consecutively by the Bulgarians, the Allies, Greeks, French and the Ottomans, the Greeks again and lastly attributed to Turkey.[15] During this period, population movements and dislocations were constant but temporary. Different communities were moving back and forth according to the balance of political and military power in the region. Greece's defeat in its war against Turkey in 1922 and the signing of the Lausanne Treaty meant that the orthodox communities of Eastern Thrace had to move once again. The conditions of their dislocation were much less violent compared to those of other communities of the Ottoman Empire, since there was enough time and the opportunity to take along their belongings and seek refuge nearby their home communities, across the borders, hoping that this dislocation would once again be temporary. But this time the temporal movements of the previous period were turned into a permanent condition, and the status of refugee-hood acquired social and political connotations connected to the ways it should be accommodated by the receiving country.

Shortly after their settlement in Greece, refugees realized that although they had been granted citizenship they were actually excluded from the national imaginary; they were discriminated against and alienated.[16] The state did not take up the responsibility of including the newcomers to the national imaginary or to its narrative. Their story was absent from the school curriculum, and a cohesive narrative about what had happened to them was lacking.[17] Official narratives addressed only the military defeat in Anatolia and totally left out the refugees' experience.[18] Their sufferings and their past were not relevant for the official narrative; it was not part of the official historical event. Their arrival in Greece had transformed them into people without a past, people whose identity could be condensed to their present condition of refugee-hood.[19]

In this context, saving their past from oblivion was imperative for the refugees. Dealing with the past was operating on two levels: the first level was connected to the politics of memory and the need to make choices that carried forward the aim of their inclusion in the national context. The second level was connected to nostalgia and the historical consciousness that developed accordingly. The two levels functioned in parallel, not opposing but re-enforcing each other. The first one was focused on the present, the current situation the refugees were going through, with a temporal span connected to the subjects' lifetime. The second one was about hope and the horizon of expectations – about how the sufferings of the past would be vindicated. Both were equally important for coping with a traumatically destabilized present.

Politics of Memory and Historical Practices

In order to ameliorate the present, the refugees had to find a way to be included in the national imaginary: it was imperative they became part of the nation, escaping from the role of 'outsiders' that was imposed on them and at the same time avoiding assimilation. They had to replace such a representation with one that included them in the main historical narrative; not as collateral damage of the military defeat but as subjects who were carriers of their own past and memory. The best way to cause such a reversion, in the way the Asia Minor Catastrophe was conceptualized, was to make their subjectivities visible through renegotiating and nationalizing their past. It was thus a question of politics of memory.

Politics of memory do not refer solely to the object of the mnemonic narrative. It is not about the accuracy of past events. Politics of memory concern mainly the subjects who negotiate memory through the production of new historical knowledge and a new narrative.[20] With interlocutors of memory holding a central place in this process, communities of memory are formed so as to conform to the requirements of the new context. In the case of interwar refugees, such new communities took the shape of regionally defined refugee associations and were intermediated by intellectuals who originated from the Orthodox communities of the Ottoman Empire and served as interlocutors of memory.

Interlocutors of Memory

From the early twentieth century, the Greek state established an extended nationalization programme in the Ottoman Empire. Through a well-organized network of consultants, teachers and educated bourgeois, it aimed to diffuse the discourse of nationalism to the Greek Ottoman communities so as to be able to claim them as co-ethnic and eventually expand its territory and include them in the state. This programme entailed, among other practices, the foundation of an educational and societal nexus that allowed the literate bourgeois to move across the Ottoman communities and the Greek state, in the context of pursuing careers or university education.[21] Many of them had settled in Greece well before the massive expulsion of the refugees, serving in positions of high symbolic status, including deputies in the national parliament, professors at the University, high-ranking military officers, civil servants working at schools and clergymen.

Among them some were deeply interested in the past – amateur historians, who, resonating with the nationalizing process in their Ottoman homelands, pursued knowledge of local history. History was linked to the biography of the nation, and its knowledge was imperative for a stable national identity. Studying their homeland's past was a way to personalize national identity. History had become a field of intimacy and intellectual engagement.

After the refugees' settlement in Greece, studying the past acquired a new political orientation, and intellectuals became agents of political change. It was part of a project that was to be a bridge between the refugees and the state, in order to align them to the same historical trajectory. Of course, historians in Greece, and especially academic historians, were always engaged in a cause, history being part of the process of nation-building.[22] In this case, however, intellectuals intervened in a different way: instead of limiting themselves in public or professional debates, they did grass-roots work and aimed to cultivate a new historical consciousness. Additionally, they used their networks in order to obtain the much needed symbolic status for their work to have impact: their journals enjoyed the honourable recognition of prestigious national institutions such as the Academy of Athens or the Society for Greek Studies in Paris and received economic support from national funds. Their aim was to establish frameworks and practices that allowed the blossoming of historical studies and extensively renegotiated the past in order to reinvent it and align it with the national historical trajectory and include refugees in the national imaginary. But how would this project take on flesh and bones?

Regionalism and Refugee Associations

As already stated, intellectuals that undertook the role of interlocutors of memory were in their majority settled in Athens well before the refugee expulsion, pursuing high-status careers. In order to make the inclusion of refugees into the national imaginary possible, they undertook the initiative of establishing regional refugee associations. The goal was to promote the refugees' inclusion into the national imaginary as communities rather than as individuals. In this way, their local culture and memory would be included as well. Thus, a series of regionally defined associations was established during the interwar period.[23] Regional associations were not rare in Greece. It was, rather, the most common way to include regions in the national historiography, functioning as the intermediate spaces between regionalism and nationalism.

Nation-building in Greece was based on the essentialist assumption that Modern Greece was a direct resurrection of classical antiquity. Time was appropriated by historiography, which functioned as a biography of the nation and re-signified different parts of the past according to this assumption. Space, on the other hand, was appropriated through regionalism. New regions that were gradually acquired became part of the national imaginary, provided that they could present links to the narrative of the national time. Regional folklore, history and antiquities were re-signified and incorporated into the set of national symbols and places of memory.[24]

In the case of the refugees, the situation was further complicated by the fact that there was no region to nationally re-signify. The local communities that refugees conceptualized as homelands could not be aligned with the rest of the regions in the Greek national imaginary. Intellectuals had to work towards the invention of regions that would be re-signified as national and lost. The new communities that gradually took shape were materialized and performed through the participation in newly established regional associations. The regional division was established according to the ancient Greek regions of Anatolia, serving this way as a reminder of the connection between ancient history and the present and aptly underlining the Hellenicity of the refugees. Their management committees more or less consisted of the intellectuals that undertook the whole initiative. The up to then undifferentiated group of 'refugees' was regrouped according to regional categories that resonated with the Greek historic geography of Anatolia – a choice that a priori established a visible connection with the heritage of classical antiquity.[25] It was not sufficient, though, to regroup the refugees in an abstract manner. LaCapra argues that it is by 'converting absence into loss, one assumes that there was (or at least could be) some original unity, wholeness, security, or identity that others have ruined, polluted, or contaminated and thus made "us" lose'.[26] The invention of a lost region by the refugee intellectuals filled the gap of a missing referential context regarding their object of mourning (the absence they were experiencing). In other words, they attempted to produce a new historical consciousness – a way of understanding and referring to the past that would be conditioned to serve the intended future.[27]

In this context, intellectuals with Thracian origins founded the 'Thracian Centre' in 1926, an association that functioned as a framework for the blossoming of historical studies and engagement with the past. The association was founded by Filippos Manouilidis, an intellectual who originated from Eastern Thrace and who had already served as a deputy of the Greek Parliament. Besides Manouilidis, there were twenty-four more members in the first management committee, all of whom were high-status professionals (doctors, university professors etc.). A second association, the Association of Thracian Studies, was founded some years later (1933), with political support from Michail Kyrkos, a politician from Eastern Thrace who had served as a minister; Polydoras Papachristodoulou, a teacher from Eastern Thrace; and other politicians, doctors, architects, bank managers and so forth.

Historical Practices

The front-stage task that developed around the associations was to facilitate the emergence of communities of memory. The associations became a framework that functioned on a double level: on the one hand, through their discursive production, they transformed the refugees into a political community of memory; and on the other, they became centres around which communities of memory emerged. By meeting regularly, refugees had the chance to share their experiences and make them meaningful. In this way, they compensated the loss of their Ottoman communities and facilitated the transformation of personal and partial memories into a public shared narrative.[28] Through participation and the consequent emergence of an embodied subjectivity, new communities of memory with a regional reference took shape, and imagined geographies were transformed into a posteriori experienced spaces of belonging. The formation of a community of memory and its inclusion in the national imaginary were mutually reinforcing.

In this process, regular meetings with regard to the association were central for the shaping of the regional refugee communities. A number of initiatives, undertaken by the association, cultivated a sense of community. Obituaries, scholarships attributed to refugee pupils in economic need, grants to ensure the dowry of young ladies at the age of marriage and networks of scholars collecting materials and memories useful to construct a narrative of the past were all practices that strengthened the bonds among refugees originating from the same region and constructed the imagined community based on ethnic and regional origin.

In more detail, the above-mentioned practices were connected to a number of networks that were formed and that functioned under the supervision of the association's management board. The different tasks that were undertaken by these networks were important for creating shared experiences for the members. Tasks as different as organizing the annual ball of the association, establishing a help desk for members in need, identifying eligible members in different regions of Greece for various benefits, collecting material to document local culture in the Ottoman communities and publishing a journal were also part of the framework designed by the intellectuals in order to create spaces of shared experience and facilitate the emergence of networks. As a result, dense overlapping networks of refugees that perceived themselves as part of a regionally defined community emerged, substituting previous formations of co-belonging with a more manageable arrangement.

Practices, though, were not limited to the formation of communities. Past-ness was a defining element of their identities, as it was the perceived belonging to a region in the past that justified the community's existence. If the refugees were to be included in the national imaginary, they were in need of a cohesive narrative of their past that fell in line with the national historical narrative. Associations offered the framework for studies about the past to blossom. Their ideological organs were the journals that they published. In the case of the Thracian associations, two journals contributed to the process of renegotiating the past: the journal *Thrakika*, connected to the 'Thrakiko Kentro' (Thracian Centre), and the journal *Archeion Thrakikou Laografikou kai Glossikou Thisaurou* (*Archive of Thracian Folklore and*

Lingual Thesaurus), connected to 'Etairia Thrakikon Meleton' (Association of Thracian Studies). The journals as practices were important not only because of their content but because of the materiality of their functioning. Regardless of the end product, the practices required for publishing a journal form networks and contribute to the emergence of the subjectivities of the participants.

Through their pages, a narrative of the region's past that indicated its national character gradually appeared. Greekness was celebrated in the region and in its inhabitants. The region's Greekness was apparent from its monuments and relics of the past, from its inhabitants' participation in every fight the nation fought through the centuries and from their cultural practices that were re-signified as genuinely national. Even the Ottoman past was aligned with the national historical trajectory, mainly through the underscoring of the leading role of clergy and the importance of communal life for retaining national identity under the Ottoman Empire. Through a thorough rewriting of the region's history, archaeology, cultural life and geography, participating intellectuals reinvented a regionality that had various links with the national canon of historiography. In this context, even artefacts and objects of everyday life were excised from their usability and transformed into carriers of memory. In the mid 1960s such objects, collected and organized by local intellectuals and amateur historians, were transformed into 'exhibits' and formed the initial collection of a museum in Thrace. The past was gradually being historicized.

Memory, Nostalgia and Historical Consciousness

If politics of memory were focused on meliorating the refugees' present and foreseeable future, the discursive narrative that emerged through intellectuals' writings was linked to a new way of dealing with the past. 'Looking backwards' and creating modern nostalgias is related to wider shifts in historical consciousness.[29]

Expatriation inflicted a trauma on the refugees. The trauma was not only the dislocation itself. It was, rather, perceived as the destruction of the order of the past by modernity, due to nationalistic rivalries and wars. In other words, an important part of the trauma was the disruption of the communities the refugees lived in and, consequently, the end of their political and social identification as members of such communities. Expatriation entailed alongside their spatial dislocation the changing of the political and social context in which they lived. Furthermore, it was a rupture in time, a passage to a different regime of historicity, namely from pre-modernity to modernity.[30] The new order had not only devastated the present; it was threatening the past with oblivion. Therefore, saving the past in detail was crucial for retaining their threatened identity and was at the same time a way of resisting the total destruction that the present imposed. In this line of thinking, nostalgic undertones were attributed to the past, the salvation of which was a duty that would make future vindication possible.

When the past is approached in such a way, the narratives are co-formed by nostalgia. Nostalgia emerges in situations where disappointment with the present coincides with the realization that the past is definitively gone. At the basis of modern nostalgia is the difficulty to accept change in historical time; in other words, to accept linear, abstract time (instead of experienced time) as a measure of human life.[31] According to Shaw and Chase, in such conditions, nostalgia functions as an invented tradition and restores the disrupted community ties.[32] Thus, nostalgia is written in a future past, but invents, in the present, narratives of an anticipated future. In terms of handling traumatic experiences, nostalgia is relevant not to the experienced past but to its cancelled potentials. Furthermore, when temporal distance from the past is coupled with spatial distance, the emergence of restorative nostalgia attempts to alleviate the pain of the trauma. In such cases, restorative nostalgia combines 'cultural intimacy' with the need to make sense of the traumatic experience of the destruction of traditional ties and communities. It then creates 'invented traditions', which transcends the limits of pre-existing national and ethnic restrictions.[33]

Already from the first issues, the journals' orientation towards the practical past with the gaze towards a future that would rectify injustices of the present was clearly stated:

> In this journal shall be trusted everything that is connected, directly or indirectly, with the life and the appearance of Thrace – written or oral, history, monumental, linguistic, tradition, custom. Every aspect of the natural, national, social, patriotic, handicraft, art or any else life of the Thracians will be part of this periodical, reflecting in this way the past and the present of the Thracian intelligentsia. And all of this aiming to help a future scientist to use this rich material in order to write a general history of Thrace from its historical appearance until today.[34]

It was a new way of relating to the past. The present condition of uprooting, expatriation and refugee-hood – the present suffering – was not understood as an episode in the linear sequence of historical time towards progress but as a disruption of the continuity and a threat towards existence if oblivion occurred. In this sense, detailed engagement with the past exceeded the limits of politically negotiating the present – in other words, of aligning the narrative to the national canon. In addition to this dimension, such occupation revealed a deeper level of relation with historicity, a historical consciousness that urged for reversibility of time – the past would be rectified through future historical interest and the restoration of the region's contribution to the nation's cultural construction.

In the pages of the refugees' journals, the past was re-narrated in a way that was meaningful for the national narrative. Regional histories were constructed and symbols were re-signified in a national manner.[35] Such a practice promoted national inclusion. But it had a reverse function as well. By remembering the past as part of the national narrative, the refugees' fate becomes inscribed to the nation. The trauma of expatriation concerns therefore not only the refugees any more but becomes central and is perceived as a trauma inflicted upon the Greek nation. When re-signifying aspects of the past in a way that aligns it with the national time, the disruption that occurs with expatriation becomes a disruption in the continuity of the national time. Therefore, the painstaking collection of details about the past (details on material relics of the remote past, on the ecclesiastic history of the Byzantium and the Ottoman Empire, on the life within the Ottoman communities, on language and folk culture) – that is, the construction of a regional genealogy of national heroes and intellectuals, endued with sanctity and the emergence of nostalgia, is an aspect of the framework that facilitated the visibility and empowerment of the refugee's traumatized memory.[36]

Conclusion: Politicians, Intellectuals and Engaged Historians

By focusing on the case of Greece's interwar refugees from Ottoman Thrace, this chapter has traced the paths through which a refugee community renegotiated its practical past, gave shape to its memory, turned those memories into history and included it into the national narrative. The goal, however, was broader: to trace the ways a community with a traumatic past can deal with the trauma and transform itself into a new collective that does justice to its past while gazing towards its future. In this process, intellectuals, emotionally engaged with the project, held a central role, functioning as interlocutors of memory.

These intellectuals facilitated the emergence of the fragmented and often divided personal memories of the refugees and transformed them into a narrative anchored with the national narrative of Greek historiography. In this process, historical practices were central not only for the emergence of such a narrative but also and mainly for communicating with groups wider than those that produced it. Regional associations that were founded were part of such practices due to their functioning as reference points for the refugees, and they filled the gap that the dissolution of their home communities had left. With the practices that developed in their framework, communities of intimacy were formed; networks that connected refugees originating from the same mental geographical region and had settled in different areas of Greece developed; and a new narrative of a Greek Thracian identity emerged through the journals published and renegotiated the refugees' practical past.

In order for their past sufferings to be recognized and possibly rectified in the future, refugees had to find a way to communicate their memories beyond their community. They therefore organized their narrative, through the discursive contribution of the interlocutors, in alignment with the national narrative. They used the existing narrative form and filled it with content that made sense to their experience. In this way they not only created space for their co-patriots' inclusion into the national imaginary but also contributed to the formation of a new Greek historical consciousness. This alignment of refugee and national narrative into a new historical consciousness and the transforming of expatriation into a shared cultural memory was the core contribution of the intellectuals engaged with this project. Being mainly a political project, it became intertwined with the practical past so as to make sense of the lived traumatic experiences and negotiate memories and plan the future. The past was not cultivated for its own sake; neither was it neutral. It was, rather, a past that was still emotionally loaded, irrevocable and meaningful for the refugees' present. Such a project of total renegotiation did not concern only the intellectual elites; on the contrary, the intellectuals functioned as the cell at the centre of networks developed at different levels, ensuring a multivocal and multilayered memory emerged. This choice to form assemblages engaged with the planning of a common future is perhaps an indicator of the role engaged intellectuals can undertake in dealing with the challenges of their contemporaneity. In other words, it seems that engaged intellectuals can do justice to both the historical thinking and to the duties of citizenship by making the choice not to intervene in the challenges of contemporaneity in a 'narrow' political mode and provide short term solutions but instead by attempting to form new discursive frames for solutions to emerge and for change to be facilitated.

Emilia Salvanou teaches public history at the Hellenic Open University and Modern and Contemporary Greek History at the Aristotle University of Thessaloniki. She is also part of European research networks on topics related to memory, migration and refugee-hood, theory of history and politics of the past. She has published widely on issues of memory, migration and politics of the past. Her most recent book is *The Construction of Refugee Memory: The Past as History and Practice* (Athens: Nefeli 2018 – in Greek).

Notes

1. This chapter is part of a project undertaken under the Research Act Aristeia, with the title 'Greek Historiography in the Twentieth Century: Debates on Identity and Modernization', co-funded by Greece and the EU' (2012–2015).
2. Brubaker, 'Aftermaths of Empire and the Unmixing of Peoples: Historical and Comparative Perspectives', 189–218.
3. Hirschon, *Heirs of the Greek Catastrophe: The Social Life of Asia Minor Refugees in Pireus*.
4. On the notion of practical past, White, 'The Practical Past',10–19.
5. Berger and Lorenz, *Nationalizing the Past: Historians as Nation Builders in Modern Europe*.
6. Nora, 'The Reasons for the Current Upsurge in Memory'.
7. Benjamin, *Illuminations*, 253–64.
8. Joyce, *The Social in Question*; Gallant, 'Long Time Coming, Long Time Gone: The Past, Present and Future of Social History', 9–20; Carr, 'Narrative Explanation and its Malcontents', 19–30; Spiegel, 'Revising the Past/Revisiting the Present: How Change Happens in Historiography', 1–19.
9. Giddens, *The Constitution of Society: Outline of the Theory of Structuration*; Sahlins, *Islands of History*; William, 'The Concept(s) of Culture', 35–61.
10. Jay, *Songs of Experience: Modern American and European Variations on a Universal Theme*.
11. Domanska, 'Frank Ankersmit: From Narrative to Experience', 175–95.
12. Latour, *Reassembling the Social: An Introduction to Actor-Network-Theory*; Spiegel, *Practicing History: New Directions in Historical Writing after the Linguistic Turn*; Domanska, 'Beyond Anthropocentrism in Historical Studies', 118–130; DeLanda, *A New Philosophy of Society: Assemblage Theory and Social Complexity*.
13. On forced migration as an aspect of the unmaking of the Ottoman Empire: Loizos, 'Ottoman Half-Lives: Long-term Perspectives on Particular Forced Migrations', 237–63.
14. Such differences are evocatively described in the five-volume collection of refugees' testimonies *Exodos* published by the Centre of Asia Minor Studies in Athens, Greece (1980–2016). Most of the testimonies were collected during the period 1950–1975.
15. Vakalopoulos, *History of Northern Greece: Thrace*.
16. Giannuli, 'Greeks or "Strangers at Home": The Experiences of Ottoman Greek Refugees during their Exodus to Greece, 1922–1923', 271–87.
17. Koulouri, '"Catastroph", "Expenditure" and "War" at School: The Description, Presentation, Omissions and Extent of the Tragic Events in the History Textbooks'.
18. Gazi, '"Farewell Asia Minor": Writing and Telling the History of the Anatolia War (1919-2)'.
19. Malkki, 'Refugees and Exile: From "Refugee Studies" to the National Order of Things', 495–523, 518.
20. Huyssen, *Present Pasts: Urban Palimpsests and the Politics of Memory*, 11–29.
21. Lyberatos, *Economy, Politics and National Ideology: the Shaping of National Parties at Filipoupoli during the 19th Century*; Salvanou, 'Aspects of the Modernization Process of the Greek Orthodox Communities at the late Ottoman Empire: The Cases of Edirne and Rodosto'; Kechriotis, *The Greeks of Izmir at the End of the Empire a non-Muslim Ottoman Community between Autonomy and Patriotism*; Sideri, 'Associations as Carriers of the Greek National Ideology at the Late 19th and Early 20th Century'.
22. Karamanolakis, *The Construction of the Discipline of History and the Teaching of History at the University of Athens (1837–1932)*.
23. Warlas, 'The Construction of Refugee Memory', 161–67.
24. Liakos, 'The Construction of National Time: The Making of the Modern Greek Historical Imagination', 27–42 and Liakos, 'Historical Time and National Space in Modern Greece', 205–27; Peckham, *National Histories, Natural States: Nationalism and the Politics of Place*

in Greece and Peckham, 'Map Mania: Nationalism and the Politics of Place in Greece, 1870–1922', 77–95.

25. Kontogiannis, *Asia Minor Geography*.
26. LaCapra, *Writing History, Writing Trauma*, 48.
27. Rüsen, 'How to Make Sense of the Past – Salient Issues of Metahistory', 169–221.
28. Danforth and Van Boeschoten, *Children of the Greek Civil War: Refugees and the Politics of Memory*, 219 ff.
29. Rüsen, 'Historical Consciousness: Narrative Structure, Moral Function and Ontogenetic Development', 63–85; Seixas, 'What is Historical Consciousness', 11–22.
30. Hartog, *Régimes d'historicité: Présentisme et expérience du temps*.
31. Shaw and Chase, 'The Dimensions of Nostalgia', 1–17, 7.
32. Shaw and Chase, 'The Dimensions of Nostalgia'.
33. Boym, *The Future of Nostalgia*, 42–43.
34. Tsountas, Eleutheriadis and Kourtidis, 'Towards Thracians at Greece and Abroad and All the Greeks'.
35. Liakos, 'Hellenism and the Making of Modern Greece: Time, Space, Language', 201–36; Peckham, 'Map Mania'.
36. Chakrabarty, 'Remembered Villages: Representation of Hindu-Bengali Memories in the Aftermath of the Partition'.

Bibliography

Benjamin, W. *Illuminations* (edited and with an introduction by Hannah Arendt). New York: Schocken Books, 1968.
Berger, S. and C. Lorenz. *Nationalizing the Past: Historians as Nation Builders in Modern Europe*. London: Palgrave Macmillan, 2010.
Boym, S. *The Future of Nostalgia*. New York: Basic, 2001.
Brubaker, R. 'Aftermaths of Empire and the Unmixing of Peoples: Historical and Comparative Perspectives', *Ethnic and Racial Studies* 18(2) (1995), 189–218.
Carr, D. 'Narrative Explanation and its Malcontents', *History and Theory* 47(1) (2008), 19–30.
Chakrabarty, D. 'Remembered Villages: Representation of Hindu-Bengali Memories in the Aftermath of the Partition', *Economic and Political Weekly* 31(32) (1996).
Danforth L.M. and R. Van Boeschoten. *Children of the Greek Civil War: Refugees and the Politics of Memory*. Chicago: University of Chicago Press, 2012.
DeLanda, M. *A New Philosophy of Society: Assemblage Theory and Social Complexity*. London: Continuum, 2006.
Domanska, E. 'Frank Ankersmit: From Narrative to Experience', *Rethinking History* 13(2) (2009), 175–95.
———. 'Beyond Anthropocentrism in Historical Studies', *Historein* 10 (2010), 118–30.
Gallant, T. 'Long Time Coming, Long Time Gone: The Past, Present and Future of Social History', *Historein* 12 (2013), 9–20.
Gazi, E. '"Farewell Asia Minor": Writing and Telling the History of the Anatolia War (1919–2)', *The Second York University-University of Athens-Canadian Institute in Greece Workshop on the Mediterranean March 3–5*. Toronto, 2005.
Giannuli, D. 'Greeks or "Strangers at Home": The Experiences of Ottoman Greek Refugees during their Exodus to Greece, 1922–1923', *Journal of Modern Greek Studies* 13(2) (1995), 271–87.
Giddens, A. *The Constitution of Society: Outline of the Theory of Structuration*. Berkeley: University of California Press, 1984.

Hartog, F. *Régimes d'historicité: Présentisme et expérience du temps*. Paris: Le Seuil, 2003.
Hirschon, R. *Heirs of the Greek Catastrophe: The Social Life of Asia Minor Refugees in Pireus*. Oxford: Clarendon Press, 1989.
Huyssen, A. *Present Pasts: Urban Palimpsests and the Politics of Memory*. Stanford, CA: Stanford University Press, 2003.
Jay, M. *Songs of Experience: Modern American and European Variations on a Universal Theme*. Oakland: University of California Press, 2005.
Joyce, P. *The Social in Question*. London: Routledge, 2002.
Karamanolakis, V. *The Construction of the Discipline of History and the Teaching of History at the University of Athens (1837–1932)*. Athens: IAEN-INE/EIE [in Greek], 2006.
Kechriotis, V.C. *The Greeks of Izmir at the End of the Empire a non-Muslim Ottoman Community between Autonomy and Patriotism*, Leiden: Leiden University Press, 2005.
Kontogiannis, P. *Asia Minor Geography*. Athens: P.A. Petrakou [in Greek], 1921.
Koulouri, C. '"Catastroph", "Expenditure" and "War" at School: The Description, Presentation, Omissions and Extent of the Tragic Events in the History Textbooks', *To Vima* (1 September 2002).
LaCapra, D. *Writing History, Writing Trauma*. Baltimore, MD: Johns Hopkins University Press, 2001.
Latour, B. *Reassembling the Social: An Introduction to Actor-Network-Theory*. New York: Oxford University Press, 2005.
Liakos, A. 'The Construction of National Time: The Making of the Modern Greek Historical Imagination', in J. Revel and G. Levi (eds), *Political Uses of the Past: The Recent Mediterranean Experience* (London: Frank Cass, 2002), 27–42.
———. 'Historical Time and National Space in Modern Greece', in T. Hayashi and F. Hiroshi (eds), *Regions in Central and Eastern Europe: Past and Present* (Sapporo: Slavic-Eurasian Research Center, 2007), 205–27.
———. 'Hellenism and the Making of Modern Greece: Time, Space, Language', in K. Zacharia (ed.), *Hellenisms: Culture, Identity and Ethnicity* (Hampshire: Ashgate, 2008), 201–36.
Loizos, P. 'Ottoman Half-Lives: Long-term Perspectives on Particular Forced Migrations', *Journal of Refugee Studies* 12(3) (1999), 237–63.
Lyberatos, A. *Economy, Politics and National Ideology: The Shaping of National Parties at Filipoupoli during the 19th Century*. Crete University Publications [in Greek], 2009.
Malkki, L.H. 'Refugees and Exile: From "Refugee Studies" to the National Order of Things', *Annual Review of Anthropology* 24 (1995), 495–523.
Nora, P. 'The Reasons for the Current Upsurge in Memory', *Transit-Europäische Revue* 22 2002.
Peckham, R. 'Map Mania: Nationalism and the Politics of Place in Greece, 1870–1922', *Political Geography* 19(1) (2000), 77–95.
———. *National Histories, Natural States: Nationalism and the Politics of Place in Greece*. London: Tauris, 2001.
Rüsen, J. 'Historical Consciousness: Narrative Structure, Moral Function and Ontogenetic Development', in P.C. Seixas (ed.), *Theorizing Historical Consciousness* (Toronto: University of Toronto Press, 2006), 63–85.
———. 'How to Make Sense of the Past – Salient Issues of Metahistory', *TD: The Journal for Transdisciplinary Research in Southern Africa* 3(1) (2007), 169–221.
Sahlins, M. *Islands of History*. Chicago: University of Chicago Press, 1987.
Salvanou, E. 'Aspects of the Modernization Process of the Greek Orthodox Communities at the Late Ottoman Empire: The Cases of Edirne and Rodosto', unpublished PhD thesis, University of the Aegean [in Greek], 2006.

Seixas, P.C. 'What is Historical Consciousness', in R. Sandwell (ed.), *To the Past: History Education, Public Memory and Citizenship in Canada* (Toronto: Toronto University Press, 2006), 11–22.

Shaw, C. and M. Chase. 'The Dimensions of Nostalgia', in C. Shaw and M. Chase (eds), *The Imagined Past: History and Nostalgia* (Manchester: Manchester University Press, 1989), 1–17.

Sideri, M. 'Associations as Carriers of the Greek National Ideology at the Late 19th and Early 20th Century', unpublished PhD thesis, University of the Aegean [in Greek], 2003.

Spiegel, G.M. *Practicing History: New Directions in Historical Writing after the Linguistic Turn.* New York: Routledge, 2004.

———. 'Revising the Past/Revisiting the Present: How Change Happens in Historiography', *History and Theory* 46(4) (2007), 1–19.

Tsountas, C., D. Eleutheriadis and A. Kourtidis. 'Towards Thracians at Greece and Abroad and All the Greeks', *Thrakika* 1a–b [in Greek] (1928).

Vakalopoulos, K. *History of Northern Greece: Thrace.* Thessaloniki: Kyriakides [in Greek], 1996.

Warlas, M. 'The Construction of Refugee Memory', in Y. Tzedopoulos (ed.), *Beyond the Catastrophe.* Athens: IME, 2003, 161–67 [in Greek].

White, H. 'The Practical Past', *Historein* 10 (2010), 10–19.

William, Jr, S. 'The Concept(s) of Culture', in V.E. Bonnell and L. Hunt (eds), *Beyond the Cultural Turn* (Berkeley: University of California Press, 1999), 35–61.

CHAPTER 6

The Making of the Zhanguo Ce Clique

The Politicization of History Knowledge in Wartime China

Xin Fan

The practice of writing history has existed among China's educated elites since the beginning of the civilization. Yet, the emergence of the professional consciousness of modern historians is merely a recent development of the twentieth century. In this chapter, I first survey the general state of historical studies from the 1920s to the 1940s through the cases of Gu Jiegang 顾颉刚 (1893–1980), Lei Haizong 雷海宗 (1902–1962) as well as the scholarly group the Zhanguo Ce Clique 战国策派, a group of academic professionals who were active in the Sino-Japanese War of Resistance (1937–1945). By doing so, I examine the fluid process of the rise and transformation of this professional consciousness and argue that the professionalization process of historical studies played a significant role in shaping modern Chinese historians' identity: on the one hand, it created an amenable social condition that allowed academic professionals to pursue intellectual autonomy, to stay away from political influences and nationalistic concerns; on the other hand, as part of the modernization movement, it drew a closer relationship between state and intellectuals, which in turn made the incipient intellectual autonomy vulnerable to nationalist and totalitarian ideologies, especially during the time of the total war and the crisis of the nation.

Notes for this section begin on page 146.

Reconfiguration of Historical Studies

After the collapse of the Qing Empire in 1911, China experienced over a decade of political tumult. In the absence of a strong central government, however, the historical profession flourished in a period of intellectual freedom. In the meanwhile, professionalization as a major trend in the field of historical studies began to unfold. This process took place in various forms: the institutionalization of historical studies, introduction of state regulation and standardization of history teaching, reconfiguration of academic leadership and formation of collective identity among the new, highly trained academic professionals.

To be sure, the early Republican period was a time of change, during which Western-style colleges and universities superseded old-style Confucian academies, and the courses on sciences and modern languages began to dominate the new national curriculum.[1] This new system increasingly flourished in academic disciplines and was ingrained in modern institutions of scholarship and higher learning – i.e. colleges and universities.[2] With the shift of the focus of education, new, urban professional intellectuals (most of whom were university professors) supplanted the social role of rural gentry.[3] Major urban centres such as Shanghai and Beijing emerged as centres of professional historical scholarship, ensconcing the first superstars in the field by the late 1920s.[4]

The institutionalization of historical studies came with the price of state regulation and standardization. In the late 1920s, after the consolidation of power within the Nationalist Party, the fledgling Nanjing government issued orders to all schools. Regulations required schools to apply for accreditation from the Republican government before enrolling new students. Governmental mandates 'prescribed, at the same time, sets of financial, academic, and organizational criteria with which the various types of academic institutions were to be evaluated in their application for accreditation'. In rare but extreme instances, the government exercised the right to relocate and reorganize institutions.[5]

As a general trend, governmentally imposed standardization focused on secondary education. This was particularly true regarding historical teaching curricula – i.e. those introduced in 1923, 1929, 1932, 1936, 1940 and 1941. The Ministry of Education's 1929 national middle school history curriculum is perhaps the most representative one. It assigned history education the task of instilling a new generation of Chinese citizens with national spirit in the wake of the consolidation under the Nanjing government.[6]

Republican-era professionalization of historical studies created and consolidated academic leadership (or academic authority) within the field by reshuffling the power structure within China's academic system. This was no simple process of new ideas conquering the old. Rather, scholars intensively negotiated traditional practice alongside newly introduced foreign concepts (such as nationalism, liberalism and modernity) in historical studies.[7] In addition, a cadre of highly trained scholars came to surround new leadership. In turn, they developed a strong sense of group autonomy and expertise. Ultimately, they came to identify with one another as with the institutions upon which their profession depended. This collective identity illustrates an important facet of the nature of Chinese professionalization.

By the late 1920s and early 1930s, the rapid professionalization process gave rise to the consciousness for the pursuit of intellectual autonomy among professional historians. Like their fellow professional historians in Europe and the United States,[8] Chinese historians started to develop a strong belief in the autonomy of their academic discipline and attempted to prevent their scholarly research from external, political influences. For example, historians like Gu Jiegang claimed that the goal of their study was to pursue 'pure scholarship', with the dream of establishing an 'academic society' 学术社会 in China.[9] A 1920 graduate of Beijing University, Gu was part of the first generation of Chinese academic professionals. His leading role in the *Gushibian* 古史辨 (the debate on ancient history movement) profoundly impacted people's understanding of the ancient past. Gu argued that history should remain an objective, scientific pursuit of pure knowledge. By doing so, he argued, one should detach historical studies from contemporary politics.[10]

A brief anecdote from 25 March 1930 demonstrates Gu Jiegang's objective view of historical research.[11] On that day, a Beijing University colleague, Qian Xuetong 钱玄同 (1887–1939), repeated a conversation overheard in Beijing. During this exchange, person A asked person B, 'Why don't you like Gu Jiegang?' Person B answered:

> He once wrote an article saying, "from the academic point of view, it makes no difference whether you are the loyalist party or the Communist party" and, "the way we do research is the same under the rule of Chiang Kai-shek as under the rule of Zhang Zongchang".[12] [I presume] he will do the same thing under the yellow dragon flag.[13] This is why Lu Xun 鲁迅 (1881–1936) opposes him.[14]

Gu Jiegang admitted in his diary that he indeed wrote the first sentence. Although he did not write the second one, he may well have done it. He told himself, 'If the academy does not detach itself from politics, it will surely be unable to pursue truth.'

Gu Jiegang's story was just one example of how Chinese intellectuals pursued objective knowledge in the early Republican period. Cai Yuanpei 蔡元培 (1868–1940), chancellor of Peking University, and Hu Shi, a liberal professor on the campus, both had embraced the similar ideals.[15]

Politicization of Historical Writing in Wartime China

The pursuit of intellectual autonomy was a noble effort; however, in China, it was jeopardized by the changing political situation. Unlike West Europe and the United States, China during the early Republican period was still struggling in the shadow of Western and Japanese imperialism. The 're-unification' of China by the Nationalist Party in the late 1920s remained only in name in the rural areas in this country, and the momentum of the Northern Expedition provoked further aggression from Japan. From 1931 to 1937, the conflict between these two countries eventually broke into a full-fledged total war. As a weak and decentralized state, the Nationalist government suffered a huge loss of manpower and resources in the first few years of the war. By then, the Japanese army had already occupied most industrialized coastal area of China. The war also caused massive migration and suffering of Chinese citizens. As the war progressed, the Japanese daily bombings of the Chinese inland cities such as Chongqing and Kunming caused massive destruction and great casualties. Facing the disasters of the war, the boundary between state and society started to diminish.[16] No matter how objective the scholarly view was, now all the historians in China were facing the same question in the context of total war: could China and its culture survive this crisis?

With this question in mind, Chinese historians adopted history as a political tool and became convinced that it was their mission to preserve the Chinese nation through writing about China's past. Historians like Qian Mu 钱穆 (1895–1990) openly praised the spirit of the Chinese nation. Even the largely apolitical Gu Jiegang felt compelled to act. On 14 October 1932, Gu recounted a dream of having joined the Yiyong Army (Army of Resistance) and killed enemies (the Japanese) and Chinese traitors. He reflected feeling great satisfaction about it. This dream stirred in him a realization of the importance of the historian's craft. He realized that the responsibility of his research was to rouse China's national spirit and that was more important than physically killing enemies.[17] Gu subsequently joined other intellectuals and shifted his scholarship from the search for historical objectivity to reaffirmation of Chinese national identity through history.

I will use the historian Lei Haizong as an example to examine the impact of the changing political situation in China on the writing of history. Lei is an interesting case. If Gu Jiegang was the exemplar figure of the first generation of professional historians in China, Lei Haizong 雷海宗 (1902–1962) belonged to the second one.[18] He graduated from Tsinghua University, one of the elite higher education institutions in Republican China and then received the merit-based Boxer Indemnity Scholarship to study in the US. After receiving a PhD degree in history at the University of Chicago in 1926, he went back to China and taught at several national universities, including National Central University and Wuhan University. In the 1930s, he returned to his mother school Tsinghua University and soon became chairperson of the history department and professor of history.

As a product of the modern higher education system, both in China and in the United States, Lei Haizong maintained a high professional standard in his works in the early 1930s. He was most outspoken about the weakness of the Chinese culture. According to Lei Haizong, China underwent a gradual decline after the collapse of the Han Empire as its culture lost its militaristic spirits. His comparative approach and grand view of history made him a very popular teacher. As a chairperson of the history department, he was concerned about curriculum developments and the job placement of history graduates.

The war became a decisive moment in the development of Lei Haizong's world view. As a student of his recalled, at the peak of the Japanese invasion, 'all of us [scholars and students at Tsinghua University] were constantly haunted by the presence of the spearhead of the Japanese Kwantung [Guandong] Army merely 200 kilometres from Peiping [Beijing].'[19] In the context of the war, Lei switched his position and started to underscore the hopes of Chinese culture.[20] Although Chinese culture faced a moment of danger, hope remained. He passionately proclaimed that Chinese culture was a miracle in human history because it was the only one that had had two cycles of cultural development, and because it had had two cycles before it might well have a third cycle soon. For him, cultures were like living organisms; some like annual plants: after their flowers flourished, they died. China was more like a perennial: the flowers opened this year; next year they would open again.[21] Lei's passionate view of Chinese history struck a powerful chord in his students and general readers, who desperately sought to save the nation.

Years ago, Ping-Ti Ho, a student of Lei, remembered his time studying with Lei Haizong and felt the greatest benefit that he got from his teacher was to appreciate the deepness of his historical thoughts. He considered Lei a truly patriotic historian who

> could not hesitate to lay out the various weaknesses in the traditional culture in order to search for explanations of the thousand-year accumulation of weak conditions [in China] – why such a grand Chinese world had repeatedly been fully or partially conquered by "barbarian" peoples, and in the modern age was being bullied by the West and Japan as well.[22]

With his deep concern about the future of China, Lei Haizong politicalized history in service of the Chinese state. Some other scholars also shared his vision. With some loosely shared similar political and academic aspirations, Lei and these scholars were considered to be active members of the 'Zhanguo Ce Clique'. Their political aspirations were all centred on how to preserve the Chinese nation within a gloomy world order. The key figures in this group were Lin Tongji 林同济, a political scientist, Chen Quan 陈铨, a playwright and literary critic, and Lei Haizong, a historian.²³ Like Lei, these professors had all earned foreign doctoral degrees and gained positions at prominent Chinese universities.²⁴ The group began the journal *Zhanguo ce banyue kan* in April 1940, though it closed in July 1941 due to financial troubles. They continued to organize the 'Zhanguo Supplement' 战国副刊 in *Dagong bao* 大公报 (*L' Impartial*), an influential paper in Chongqing. The 'Zhanguo Supplement' appeared from December 1941 to July 1942.²⁵ The most active figure, who organized many group events, was Lin Tongji.²⁶ Chen admired German philosophy and literature and was therefore more active in philosophical and literary debates. Lei Haizong's work, meanwhile, offered a historiographical foundation for the ideas shared by the group.

Yet, as a school of intellectual thought, the Zhanguo Ce group represented an intellectual trend that politicized China's ancient past (i.e. Zhanguo, Warring States Period) to make sense of the contemporary world order. It contains two striking features: first, a cyclical view of time; second, a China-centred view of space.

For the first point, Lei Haizong and his friends compared the contemporaneous world with the Warring States Period in ancient China. The Warring States Period (战国时代), also known as the Era of Warring States, or the Warring Kingdoms period, covers the period from either 476 BC or 453 BC to the reunification of China under the Qin Dynasty in 221 BC. It is considered to be the second part of the Eastern Zhou Dynasty, following the Spring and Autumn Period. The name Warring States Period was derived from the *Record of the Warring States*, a work compiled early in the Han Dynasty. The date for the beginning of the Warring States Period is disputed. While it is frequently cited as 475 BC (following the Spring and Autumn Period), 403 BC, the date of the tripartite Partition of Jin (a powerful feudal kingdom), is also considered as the beginning of the period. This period represents two critical changes in Chinese history. First, China transformed from a feudal state to a centralized power. Second, the transition was marked by most ruthless total warfare. According to traditional Chinese historical sources, major battles in this period could sometimes kill a quarter of a million people.

Scholars commonly believe that the era is marked by the chaos of political orders and the totality of the war. It was an age linking the previous age of feudal and aristocratic society to a militarized, totalized and unified Qin empire.²⁷ The analogy between contemporary politics and China's ancient past shaped the historiographical foundation of the Zhanguo Ce group's belief system.[28]

The interplay between time, space and peoples was central to their conception of history, which was the historiographical foundation for the Zhanguo thought.[29] Zhanguo Ce scholars gave up national history as a temporal and spatial framework and presented and adopted culture as a basic unit to understand world history. Influenced by Oswald Spengler (1880–1936), they believed culture was like a living organism, with all cultures following the same cycle of life: birth, growth, decadence and demise. Based on this conception, these scholars argued that history could be adopted as a guide to make sense of contemporary politics.[30] Using the Warring States period in Chinese history as an analogy, they emphasized, first, the link between cultural reconstruction and national power; second, the necessity of war, the will to power and hero worship; third, the supremacy of the nation state.

True, the concern for the total war and foreign aggression dominated Zhanguo Ce scholars' thinking. Lin Tongji concluded that there were three trends in the current state of international politics. First, war had become the centre of life. Lin argued that each era had its own gravity. The Warring States era had been shaped by war, the major event of that era, which became 'the standard for all the major activities in society'. Beliefs, enterprises and social reforms would all but become auxiliary to the goal of war.[31] Second, war would be all-inclusive. Lin predicted that like the ancient Warring States era, the current war would become total. If every aspect of social life is hinged on the state of the war, democracy, as a result, must submit to the goal and purpose of war. Lin implied that a strong leader like Shang Yang 商鞅 (395–338 BC) would serve better for the wartime victory than a group of specialists sitting around a table and following a democratic process of debate.[32] The massive annihilation of war was the third characteristic of the coming Warring States era. Lin spoke of two types of warfare: one with the purpose of victory; the other seeking annihilation. From the Spring and Autumn Periods to the Warring States Period, China transformed from pursuing victory to annihilating enemies. Lin argued that world warfare experienced a similar transition in the 1930s/1940s. The increased cruelty of annihilation that accompanied total war would, he held, bring about a world empire.[33]

The gloomy perception of world politics turned a world historical focus back into a China-centred focus, which compelled Lei Haizong and his Zhanguo Ce friends to cry out for a strong leadership in the chaotic age, making possible the survival of Chinese culture. They sought to revive the militarism that had been historically lost. Lei Haizong argued that China should work military education into its curricula, thereby reviving the militia system.³⁴ This could only be achieved, however, through stable and absolute leadership of Chiang Kai-shek, the generalissimo from the Nationalist Party.

In the context of the national crisis, Lei Haizong put aside the concerns of morality and adopted a purely utilitarian view of international politics to ensure the survival of the Chinese nation. Observing the history of total war, he asserted that the diplomacy in the Warring States must be merciless in its method and relentless in its purpose. If someone lived during the Warring States following the diplomacy of rituality and morality like those in the Spring and Autumn Period in China, they might lose their sovereignty and even face the downfall of the nation. He further argued that the result of the Warring States, for all nations, would be the unification of the entire cultural zone: India, China, Greece and Rome all followed the same principle, and this applied to the major powers in Euro-America as well. For him, the most merciless and relentless country would usually be the one that achieved final success.³⁵ This strong utilitarianism and support of Chiang Kai-shek drew further barbs from their contemporaries and students alike.³⁶ CCP intellectuals severely criticized Zhanguo scholars, labelling them Fascists.

History Writing in Wartime Politics

The political situation in 1940s China was extremely delicate. After the first round of fighting, Japan took control of major industrial zones before shifting focus to the Pacific War. This gave a little time for all kinds of political forces in China to reshuffle. The Nationalist government retreated to Chongqing, attempting to consolidate its power there. Nationalist officials relied upon propaganda to boost popular support for the government. They wished to accomplish this through taking control of historical, civic and geographical education.³⁷ In the latter processes, the rhetoric of Zhanguo Ce scholars proved to be particularly useful in the implementation of their goals.

The Chinese communists, in contrast, settled in Yan'an with ambitions to gain a larger sphere of influence in national politics. They promised to follow the leadership of the Nationalist government in the name of the united front against foreign invaders and presented themselves as a democratic force. Yet, in Yan'an a fierce ideological battle emerged in the early 1940s. This infighting allowed Mao Zedong to tighten the reins on literature and political thought within the Communist movement. Be that as it may, before audiences of the nation, the communist propagandists continued the rhetoric of democracy, attempting to foil Nationalist attempts to consolidate power in Chongqing. Intellectuals sought to demonstrate that despite having accepted Nationalist rule the Chinese Communist Party (CCP) remained an important democratic force in the resistance movement. The CCP thus relied upon such democratic rhetoric to maintain an independent status along with the Nationalists.[38]

The Zhanguo Ce scholars' cries for strong centralized government were especially harmful to the CCP, as the latter remained by and large an independent force. Fearful of losing its independent status, the CCP propaganda machine launched caustic attacks on Lei Haizong and his friends. The Zhanguo Ce scholars were anti-democratic, for they supported violent and aggressive domestic and international politics, as CCP party intellectuals claimed. For example, the party propagandist Hanfu disparaged Zhanguo Ce *scholars'* cyclic view of time in history. He countered that history is a progressive movement in which human society increasingly moves forward. Although there might be some small setbacks in its development, history never repeats itself. In accordance with this view, He accused Zhanguo Ce scholars of having drawn only superficial analogies between the Warring States period and the contemporary world, thereby neglecting the fundamental difference: the role of justice. In contrast to feudal warfare's goal of annexation, participants in World War II included semi-colonial China pursuing liberation, liberal capitalist nations such as the United Kingdom and United States fighting fascist aggression and socialist states such as the Soviet Union seeking to defend the motherland. The modern example thus featured a democratic coalition opposing the injustices of fascism.[39] He maintained that these scholars' pursuit of power suggested that what they believed held democracy as obsolete, seeking instead to: consolidate the government, centralize the military, control the economy, create a national religion and control the will of the people.[40] In contrast, according to Hanfu, the CCP saw no conflict in respecting individuals while developing national power. As such, democracy was a necessary stage for a feudal society developing into a capitalist society. It was thus an efficient tool with which a government could concentrate power.[41] He proclaimed that an overemphasis on autocratic power would be harmful to China, as well as to all the anti-Fascist nations and peoples. Hanfu focused on the issue of justice. As such, he argued that, in appropriating knowledge from the ancient Chinese Warring States, Zhanguo Ce scholars neglected the role of moral values in war. Instead, he claimed that justice played a fundamental role in wartime, offering a foundation for coalitions among the nations. Denial of the significance of justice in modern warfare could only help enemies. Therefore, combining the above arguments, Hanfu concluded that the nature of the Zhanguo Ce group was fascist. As such, it was harmful to the war effort.

Hanfu's article offers but one example of CCP criticism of Zhanguo Ce. Active CCP propagandists and intellectuals, including Hu Sheng 胡绳 (1918–2000), also wrote extensively on the group.[42] Newspapers and journals in Chongqing and Yan'an printed these articles.[43] After the founding of the People's Republic of China, a history with the Zhanguo Ce marred the political files of former participants; many continued to be attacked in political campaigns in the following decades.[44]

Conclusion

The professionalization process that took place in historical writing during the Republican period in China had transformed the relationship between individual historians, society and state. Following the trend of professionalization, historians in the 1920s started to pursue intellectual autonomy as detaching politics from historical studies.[45] However, this situation changed dramatically after the outbreak of the War of Resistance. The total war diminished the boundary between state and society and forced Chinese historians to rethink the nature of scholarly research. Therefore, some historians idealized China's past, highlighting its uniqueness in a world-historical context, and gave up the independent status of academic professionals.

The above narrative is certainly a simplistic view of the loss of intellectual autonomy among historians in China. However, it more broadly hints at the complicated relationship between the professionalization and modernity in a wider historical context. After all, as scholars believe today, the Zhanguo Ce ideal represented a variation of modernity, the one that 'combined military and civil virtues, guaranteed national security and enabled the country to stand against foreign aggression'.[46] Therefore, despite their strong commitment to professional standards, new Chinese professional historians were vulnerable to another aspect of modernity: the intensified demands placed upon scholars by nationalism and totalitarian ideologies. Transcending the Chinese context, one may raise the question: if modernity was a globally circulated idea during the twentieth century, then would it be too ambitious to suggest that the story about Chinese historians' failure to pursue intellectual autonomy is actually less foreign to the experiences of their Western counterparts? If this is the case, the story of Chinese historians' wartime experiences also has world-historical significance.

Xin Fan is Assistant Professor of East Asian History at the State University of New York at Fredonia. As a historian of twentieth-century China, he is strongly interested in historical theories, world history and global history. He was a recipient of the Volkswagen Foundation/Andrew Mellon Foundation postdoctoral fellowship in humanities, and he will serve as book review editor of the new journal *China and Asia: A Journal in Historical Studies*. His book manuscript on world history in China is currently under review. He is also the second editor of the conference volume *Receptions of Greek and Roman Antiquity in East Asia* (Brill, 2018).

Notes

An earlier version of this chapter appears in *Berliner China-Hefte/Chinese History and Society* 43 (2013): 64–76, entitled 'The Lost Intellectual Autonomy: State, Society, and Historical Writing in Republican China'. I would like to thank Professor Mechthild Leutner for her permission to authorize the publication of this revised version. In this version, the global context for the intellectual change in China is further emphasized.

1. Yeh, *The Alienated Academy: Culture and Politics in Republican China*, 3.
2. Wang, *Fu Ssu-nien: A Life in Chinese History and Politics*.
3. Hon and Culp argue that Chinese intellectuals could pursue four possible academic paths in the Republican period: academic institutions, education, publishing circles and government sector. As Hon and Culp have illustrated, only blurry boundaries existed between these circles. Hon and Culp, 'Introduction', 5.
4. Hu Shi 胡适 (1891–1962) held a professorship at Beijing University, and he is commonly considered as a leading liberal scholar of the Republican period. Gu Jiegang, one of the key characters in this research, taught at Beijing University and Yenching University. Chen Yinque 陈寅恪 (1890–1969), known as an erudite sinologist in China today, held a professorship at Tsinghua University.
5. Yeh, *Alienated Academy*, 172–73.
6. Jiaoyubu zhongxiaoxue kecheng biaozhun qicao weiyuan hui 教育部中小学课程标准起草委员 [Ministry of Education Committee on Drafting Elementary and High School Curricula] (ed.), 'Zanxing kecheng biaozhun' 暂行课程标准 [Provisional Curriculum Standards], 2: 25–26. Gu Jiegang and Lei Haizong participated in drafting the curriculum. Also, Shi Guirong 史桂荣, '1929 nian zhongxue lishi zanxing kecheng biaozhun yanjiu 1929', 14. Gu Jiegang and Lei Haizong participated in drafting the curriculum.
7. Yeh, *The Alienated Academy*, 28.
8. For the relationship between professionalization and the rise of academic objectivism in the American context, see Novick, *That Noble Dream: The 'Objectivity Question' and the American Historical Profession*, especially 47–60.
9. See Wang Fan-sen, '"Zhuyi Chongbai" yu jindai Zhongguo xueshu shehui de mingyun – yi Chen yinke wei li'主义崇拜"与近代中国学术社会的命运 – 以陈寅恪为例 ['The 'Blind Belief in Isms' and the Fate of Modern Chinese Academic Society; Chen Yinke as an Example'], 463–88.
10. Scholars tend to portray Gu as a 'reluctant' nationalist of the Republican period. Laurence Schneider's biographical study of his early life situates his innovative historical thinking in the context of the rise of nationalism in twentieth-century China. Schneider, *Ku Chieh-kang and China's New History*; Duara, *Rescuing History from the Nation: Questioning Narratives of Modern China*, 42–44. The recent publication of Gu's voluminous diaries and reading notes allow scholars a new opportunity to introduce an increasingly nuanced reading of his views of nationalism. His deeply held belief that academics commit themselves to objective knowledge

complicates efforts to analyse his nationalistic stance in historical research. Fan, 'Gu Jiegang and the Creation of Chinese Historical Geography', 193–218.

11. Gu Jiegang, *Gu Jiegang riji*顾颉刚日记 [*Gu Jiegang's Diary*], (25 March 1930).

12. The loyalist party refers to the group that were still supportive of the past Qing regime; Zhang Zongchang 张宗昌 (1881–1932) was a local warlord who controlled the Shandong area in the 1920s.

13. The yellow dragon flag refers to the Qing government's national flag.

14. Gu Jiegang and Lu Xun disliked one another. The latter once provoked a student movement in an attempt to expel the former from Guangzhou.

15. For Cai Yuanpei's role in the May Fourth Movement, see Chow, *The May Fourth Movement Intellectual Revolution in Modern China*.

16. For the recent discussion on the impact of Japanese airborne bombings on people's lives, see Mitter, *Forgotten Ally: China's World War II, 1937–1945*, 176–78, and ff.

17. Gu Jiegang, *Gu Jiegang riji*, 2: 698.

18. In China today, he is often remembered as being among the first generation of professional world historians. In the meanwhile, he was also renowned for his bold attempts to bridge Chinese and world history, and he is honoured for having promoted a 'macroscopic view in history'. A Hong Kong historian, Xu Guansan许冠三, argues that Lei is one of the leading scholars in modern Chinese historiography. Michael Godley is the only scholar to have focused on Lei Haizong in English. Prasenjit Duara has also briefly mentioned Lei in his discussion of modern Chinese historiography. Xu Guansan 许冠三, *Xinshixue jiushi nian* 新史学九十年 [*New Historiography of the Last Ninety Years*]; Godley, 'Politics from History: Lei Haizong and the Zhanguo Ce Clique', 95–122; Duara, *Rescuing History*, 40–42.

19. He Bingdi 何炳棣 [Ping-ti Ho], *Dushi yueshi bashinian*读史阅世八十年 [*Eighty Years of Studying History and Experiencing the World*], 150.

20. Godley, 'Politics from History', 100.

21. Lei Haizong, *Bolun shixue ji* 伯伦史学集 [*A Collection of Lei Haizong's Historiographical Works*], 257.

22. Lianda refers to *Xinan Lianda* 西南联大 [Southwest United University]. Bingdi, *Dushi yueshi*, 119–20.

23. Lei Haizong was the senior member of this group. He Lin, a philosopher, was a key figure in the group. Wen Rumin 温儒敏 and Ding Xiaoping 丁晓萍, *Shidai zhi bo——Zhanguo ce pai wenhua lunzhu jiyao* 时代之波 – 战国策派文化论著辑要 [*Tide of the Times: A Selection of the Main Cultural Works from the Zhanguo ce Clique*].

24. Lin Tongji received a BA from the University of Michigan and an MA and PhD from the University of California. In the 1940s, he served as a dean while chairing the Yunnan University Department of Political Science. Chen Quan received an MA from Oberlin College and a PhD from the University of Kiel in Germany (1933). He taught English and German at Lianhe University in the early 1940s, then English at the Nationalist Party school in 1943.

25. Authors included He Lin 贺麟 (1902–1992), He Yongji 何永佶 (1902–?), Guo Daixi 郭岱西, Shen Congwen 沈从文 (1902–1988), Tao Yunkui 陶云逵 (1904–1944), and Liang Zongdai 梁宗岱 (1903–1983). A total of only seventeen scholars published in both journals. Godley, 'Politics from History', 95.

26. Lin Tongji and Lei Haizong had a close relationship. Both graduated from Chongde high school 崇德中学 in Beijing and attended Tsinghua University. They then pursued doctoral degrees in the United States.

27. Lei Haizong, *Bolun shixue ji*, 145

28. Lin Tongji 林同济, 'Zhanguo shidai de chongyan' 战国时代的重演 ['A Repetition of the Warring States Period'], 103–9.

29. Lei Haizong, *Bolun shixue ji*, 136

30. Fung, *The Intellectual Foundations of Chinese Modernity: Cultural and Political Thought in the Republican Era*, 126.

31. Lin Tongji, 'Zhanguo shidai de chongyan', 104.

32. Shang Yang was a minister in the Qin kingdom. He introduced radical reforms in military and government centralization. As such, he is considered to have laid the foundation that allowed the Qin to unify China in 221 BC. He represents the legalist tradition, which prioritized law over moral values as the foundation of a political system.

33. Lin Tongji, 'Zhanguo shidai de chongyan', 105

34. Lei Haizong, 'Jianguo—zaiwang de disanzhou wenhua' 建国 – 在望的第三周文化 ['Founding the Nation: The Third Period (of Chinese Culture) in Sight'], 189.

35. Lei Haizong, 'Waijiao: Chunqiu yu zhanguo' 外交: 春秋与战国 ['Diplomacy: Spring and Autumn (Period) and Warring States (Period)'], 183.

36. He Zhaowu, a leftist student at Lianhe University, also criticized the lack of humanism in Zhaoguo Ce scholars' writing. He Bingdi, *Dushi yueshi*, 65.

37. Chan, 'Contending Memories of the Nation: History Education in Wartime China, 1937–1945', 177ff.

38. Yang Kuisong 杨奎松, *'Zhongjian didai' de geming—Zhongguo gemin de celue zai guoji beijing xia de yanbian* 中间地带"的革命 – 中国革命的策略在国际背景下的演变 [*Revolution in the "Middle Zone": Evolution of the Chinese Revolutionary Strategy in International Context*].

39. During the war, the CCP promised to give up anti-capitalist goals in order to form a United Front with the Nationalist Party. Hanfu 汉夫 [pseud.], '"Zhanguo" pai de Faxisi zhuyi shizhi' 战国派的法西斯主义实质 ['The True Fascist Nature of the "Zhanguo" Clique'], 1.

40. Hanfu, '"Zhanguo"', 2.

41. Ibid.

42. Sheng Sheng 胡绳, 'Lun fan lixing zhuyi de niliu' 论反理性主义的逆流 ['On the Counter-trend of Anti-rationalism'] and 'Shi shengren haishi pianzi—Lun weixinlun zai shiji shenghuo zhong de biaoxian' 是圣人还是骗子 – 论唯心论在实际生活中的表现 ['Are they Saints or Swindlers: On the Implications of Idealism in Daily Life], 21–34.

43. Jiefang ribao 解放日报, '"Minzu wenxue" yu Faxisi miulun' 民族文学与法西斯谬论 ['"National Literature" and the Fallacy of Fascism'], 40–41.

44. Following the establishment of the PRC, Lin Tongji shifted his research focus from political science to English literature, a less politically sensitive field. He still received substantial criticism in subsequent political campaigns in the People's Republic of China.

45. Politics is a term that contains multiple layers of meaning. In this chapter, politics is more rigidly defined as the exercises of power through the state apparatus.

46. Fung, *Intellectual Foundations*, 126.

Bibliography

Chan, W. 'Contending Memories of the Nation: History Education in Wartime China, 1937–1945', in T. Hon and R. Culp (eds), *The Politics of Historical Production in Late Qing and Republican China* (Leiden: Brill, 2007), 169–210.

Chow, Tse-Tsung. *The May Fourth Movement Intellectual Revolution in Modern China*. Cambridge: Harvard University Press, 1960.

Duara, P. *Rescuing History from the Nation: Questioning Narratives of Modern China*. Chicago: The University of Chicago Press, 1995.

Fan, X. 'Gu Jiegang and the Creation of Chinese Historical Geography', *The Chinese Historical Review* 17(2) (2010), 193–218.

Fung, E. *The Intellectual Foundations of Chinese Modernity: Cultural and Political Thought in the Republican Era*. Cambridge University Press, 2010.

Godley, M. 'Politics from History: Lei Haizong and the Zhanguo Ce Clique', *Papers on Far Eastern History* 40 (1998), 95–122.

汉夫 Hanfu [pseud.]. '"Zhanguo" pai de Faxisi zhuyi shizhi' 战国派的法西斯主义实质, in Zhong Limeng 钟离蒙 and Yang Fenglin 杨凤麟(eds), *Zhongguo xiandai zhexue shi ziliao huibian (disan ji disan ce)* (Shenyang: Liaoning daxue zhexuexi, 1982), 1.

何炳棣 He, Bingdi. *Dushi yueshi bashinian* 读史阅世八十年. Guilin: Guangxi shifan daxue chubanshe, 2005.

Hon, T. and R. Culp. 'Introduction', in T. Hon and R. Culp (eds), *The Politics of Historical Production in Late Qing and Republican China* (Leiden: Brill, 2007), 5.

胡绳 Hu, Sheng. 'Lun fan lixing zhuyi de niliu' 论反理性主义的逆流 and 'Shi shengren haishi pianzi – Lun weixinlun zai shiji shenghuo zhong de biaoxian' 是圣人还是骗子 – 论唯心论在实际生活中的表现, in Zhong Limeng 钟离蒙 and Yang Fenglin 杨凤麟 (eds), *Zhongguo xiandai zhexue shi ziliao huibian (disan ji disan ce)* (Shenyang: Liaoning daxue zhexuexi, 1982), 21–34.

教育部中小学课程标准起草委员会 Jiaoyubu zhongxiaoxue kecheng biaozhun qicao weiyuan hui 'Zanxing kecheng biaozhun' 暂行课程标准, in *Zhongxiaoxue kecheng zanxing biaozhun* 中小学课程暂行标准 [Temporary Standards for Middle and Primary School] (Shanghai: Qingyun tushu gongsi, 1930), 25–26.

解放日报 *Jiefang ribao*. '"Minzu wenxue" yu Faxisi miulun' 民族文学与法西斯谬, in Zhong Limeng 钟离蒙 and Yang Fenglin 杨凤麟(eds), *Zhongguo xiandai zhexue shi ziliao huibian (disan ji disan ce)* (Shenyang: Liaoning daxue zhexuexi, 1982), 40–41.

顾颉刚 Gu, Jiegang. *Gu Jiegang riji* 顾颉刚日记. Taipei: Lianjing, 2007.

Lei, Haizong. 'Jianguo – zaiwang de disanzhou wenhua' 建国 – 在望的第三周文化, in Zhong Limeng 钟离蒙 and Yang Fenglin 杨凤麟 (eds), *Zhongguo xiandai zhexue shi ziliao huibian (disan ji disan ce)* [*Collection of Materials for the History of Modern Chinese Philosophy (3rd vol., series 3): Critiques of the Fascism of the Zhanguo ce Clique*] (Shenyang: Liaoning daxue zhexuexi, 1982), 189.

———. 'Waijiao: Chunqiu yu zhanguo' 外交: 春秋与战国, in Zhong Limeng 钟离蒙 and Yang Fenglin 杨凤麟 (eds), *Zhongguo xiandai zhexue shi ziliao huibian (disan ji disan ce)* (Shenyang: Liaoning daxue zhexuexi, 1982), 183.

———. *Bolun shixue ji* 伯伦史学集. Beijing: Zhonghua shuju, 2002.

林同济 Lin, Tongji. 'Zhanguo shidai de chongyan' 战国时代的重演, in Zhong Limeng 钟离蒙 and Yang Fenglin 杨凤麟 (eds), *Zhongguo xiandai zhexue shi ziliao huibian (disan ji disan ce): Zhanguo ce pai Faxisi zhuyi pipan* 中国现代哲学史资料汇编(第三集第三册): 战国策派法西斯主义批判 (Shenyang: Liaoning daxue zhexuexi, 1982), 103–9.

Mitter, R. *Forgotten Ally, China's World War II, 1937–1945*. Boston, MA: Houghton Mifflin Harcourt, 2013.

Novick, P. *That Noble Dream: The 'Objectivity Question' and the American Historical Profession*. Cambridge: Cambridge University Press, 1988.

Schneider, L. *Ku Chieh-kang and China's New History*. Berkeley: University of California Press, 1971.

史桂荣 Shi, Guirong. '1929 nian zhongxue lishi zanxing kecheng biaozhun yanjiu 1929'年中学历史暂行课程标准研究, MA thesis, Yangzhou University, 2007.

Wang, F. *Fu Ssu-nien: A Life in Chinese History and Politics*. New York: Cambridge University Press, 2006.

Wang, Fan-sen. '"Zhuyi Chongbai" yu jindai Zhongguo xueshu shehui de mingyun – yi Chen yinke wei li'主义崇拜'与近代中国学术社会的命运 – 以陈寅恪为例, in *Zhongguo jindai sixiang yu xueshu de xipu* 中国近代思想与学术的系 [*A Genealogy of Modern Chinese Thought and Scholarship*] (Taipei: Lianjing, 2003), 463–88.

温儒敏 Wen, Rumin and 丁晓萍 Ding, Xiaoping (eds). *Shidai zhi bo – Zhanguo ce pai wenhua lunzhu jiyao* 时代之波 – 战国策派文化论著辑要. Beijing: Zhonguo guangbo dianshi chubanshe, 1995.

徐冠三 Xu, Guansan. *Xinshixue jiushi nian* 新史学九十年. Hong Kong: Chinese University Press, 1986.

杨奎松 Yang, Kuisong. *'Zhongjian didai' de geming – Zhongguo gemin de celue zai guoji beijing xia de yanbian* 中间地带"的革命 – 中国革命的策略在国际背景下的演变. Taiyuan: Shanxi renmin chubanshe, 2010.

Yeh, Wen-hsin. *The Alienated Academy: Culture and Politics in Republican China, 1919–1937*. Cambridge: Harvard University Press, 1990.

CHAPTER 7

The Historicization of World War II in Greece after the Civil War

Looking Back on the Public Debate over a Lecture by British Historian C.M. Woodhouse

MANOS AVGERIDIS

Introduction

In Greece, the experience of World War II was followed almost immediately by the civil war of 1946 to 1949.[1] The latter ended with the defeat of the left and the exile or imprisonment of most of those who had actually taken up arms against the Axis. The earlier period of guerilla warfare against the Axis occupation was re-codified in the concept of the 'national resistance'.[2] The politics of memory prevalent in Greece in the civil war's aftermath attempted to obscure significant parts of the country's history during the turbulent 1940s and focused mainly on assigning civil and criminal blame on the communists. This public discourse was closely associated with an internalization of the new realities of the Cold War, the priorities of rebuilding state and economy and the traumatic experience and legacies of the recent past.[3] Already within a decade after the end of the Greek Civil War, however, re-evaluation and restoration of this relatively silenced memory began. This process had various agents, means and products. To some extent it crossed a number of political and ideological separations, shaping the historical perceptions of Greek society and – after the catalyst provided by the rise and fall of the military dictatorship of 1967 to

Notes for this section begin on page 160.

1974 – finally leading to the official recognition of the left-wing resistance in 1982.

In outlining the course of this process, I wish to highlight three key observations on historical production concerning the 1940s in Greece: first, this production has always been closely connected with contemporary politics; the 1940s are one of the strongest sites of memory and reference in the Greek public sphere. Explicitly or implicitly, in debates on the present or future of the Greek state, or in struggles over the identity of Greek society, the war-torn history of the 1940s has been present in the country's political discourse at all times since the events themselves.[4] The meanings of this history have varied according to the contemporary stakes.[5]

Second, during much of the postwar era, this production was conducted outside the bounds of academic research, instead taking the many paths of public history: memory testimonies, public debates in the press, hybrid forms of political historiography, literary and artistic representations and various performative practices and memorial strategies.

Third, this production has been spread out among several geographic centres and originates not only in Greece but also in the East-bloc republics that resettled the approximately 100,000 exiles of the Greek Communist Party (KKE) and other political refugees from the civil war; in the countries that were involved in Greece during the war, such as Great Britain, Germany and the United States; and, finally, in certain countries that became host and home to a number of Greek students and scholars in the postwar period, such as France.

Any attempt to periodize this historical production will be subject to debate; however, periodization is necessary for studying the production over the long term.[6] I shall distinguish three main periods[7], keeping in mind, however, that different aspects of society move according to different temporalities and remembering also that a study of historical culture should be interested not only in *ruptures* but also – perhaps mainly – in *continuities*, in the strands that connect this culture diachronically and create common understandings through time. The first period can be defined from the end of World War II until the fall of the military dictatorship in Greece (1974), when professional historical research is relatively absent and the actors themselves in that past play an important role in shaping its history. What one can distinguish is the attempt to choose, narrate and give visibility to the facts that form a recent but still largely uncharted and oppressed past.[8] The second period starts from the fall of the junta and the transition to democracy, which marks a new era, not only for Greek society but also for Greek historiography.[9] Finally, the end of the 1980s coincided with the collapse of the Communist regimes and the definitive end of the bipolar cold war world. In relation to this crucial event and the fundamental change that it brought regarding the view of the world from then on, 1989 was also a fateful year for the Greek political scene and society.[10]

This chapter focuses on the first of these periods. I will deliver some thoughts on the paradigmatic thinking of the British historian Christopher Montague Woodhouse as presented in a lecture he delivered in Munich in 1957; and on the ensuing debate in the pages of the Greek press. In highlighting Woodhouse's lecture[11] and its reception, the intent here is to explore the forms of engagement: the requirements then prevailing with regard to the objectivity and impartiality of historians and the ways in which political and ideological engagement during the war was transformed into engagement with the history of the war. We shall pose three questions: 1) what is the role of politics and the international constellation in the historical perception of the participants? 2) *who has the right to talk about the history of the war?* 3) and what of the demand for recognition of the national resistance in Greece? All three questions refer in multiple ways to a central, if not dominant notion in the debate: that of historical truth.[12]

The Historian

British public discussion on the history of the war often referred to the Greek case and also interacted with the simultaneous discussion in Greece.[13] By the end of the 1950s, London houses had published more than thirty books written by veterans of the British secret military missions and former war correspondents.[14] Many of these made for big news in Greece, entering public debate through translations of extended extracts in the press, articles and reviews, and even full Greek-language editions. Among the best-known publications was *Greek Entanglement* by the former commander of the Special Operations Executive (SOE),[15] Brigadier Eddie Myers, in 1955; and, earlier, *Apple of Discord* by the subcommander Colonel C.M. Woodhouse, in 1948.[16]

Besides being a military officer, Christopher Montague Woodhouse (1917–2001) was also a professional historian, with studies in Classics at Winchester College and New College, Oxford. His contribution to Greek historiography was rich. Widely known as 'Monty' in Great Britain and 'Chris' in Greece, Woodhouse was also a diplomat, businessman and politician. He held several governmental and state positions during the postwar period. He was recognized as an expert on Greek and Middle East issues, and he entered Parliament twice, in 1959 and 1970, standing as a Conservative. Many of his books were translated into Greek, including works not only on World War II but also on the Greek Enlightenment, the Revolution of 1821 and the formation of the Greek state.

The Lecture

In November 1957, Woodhouse, as historian and general director of the Royal Institute of Foreign Affairs of Great Britain, gave a lecture in Munich at the Institute of Contemporary History (Institut für Zeitgeschichte) under the title, 'On the History of Resistance in Greece' (*Zur Geschichte der Resistance in Griechenland*). The lecture was published the next year in the journal of the institute, *Contemporary History Quarterly* (*Vierteljahrshefte für Zeitgeschichte*).[17] The place and the environment chosen for this lecture had various connotations, leading to persistent and often ironic comments from Greek veterans.

Woodhouse's lecture began by considering British historical production on the guerilla movements against the Axis in Greece and throughout Europe. Generally, British writers had focused on the British role and commitment to such movements. Woodhouse favoured re-evaluating this part of the history, with the intent of seeing its 'true' dimensions within the war's larger contexts, and arguing that until then it had been either overstated or ignored. This would require professional historians to take the field back from the amateurs. They had been absent, according to Woodhouse, because of the proximity in time and the internal controversies of the British state apparatus. The latter had made it difficult to access a wide range of diplomatic documents and other archives of the period.

Woodhouse then cited some data for the study of the Greek case with regard to the main resistance groups, the most important military achievements, and the internal conflicts of the Greek resistance. Within this framework, he gave special attention to the deliberations and role of the British mission. Contrary to his initial protestations, his manner of narrating this history had a markedly personal tone; beyond a few abstract references to British diplomatic archives, he barely referred to any sources in justifying his arguments.

One of Woodhouse's main conclusions was that the contribution of the Greek resistance in the military struggle against the Nazis was very small, a 'little more than a pustule', as he put it; a phrase that caused many outraged reactions in the Greek press.[18] Woodhouse argued, however, that the resistance was *politically* important in forming the postwar situation in Greece and that this had been underestimated. The British activity in Greece during the war, as well as the military intervention in Athens starting in 1944, was crucial, in his view, for blocking the communist National

Liberation Front (EAM) from taking power, thus allowing Greece to remain in the 'free world', with all that this entailed for the next phase of European history.

The Debate

A five-part Greek-language translation of Woodhouse's lecture was published from 2 to 7 November 1958 in the daily *Eleftheria*. The newspaper, though it was close to the then fragmented political space of the centre, provided angry headlines and subheads like 'Woodhouse distorts historical truth: A purulent lecture in Munich' and 'Systematic anti-Hellenic propaganda'. The translation was by the paper's correspondent in Bonn, the journalist and jurist Vassos Mathiopoulos, and was accompanied by his extended criticism.[19] By the end of the year, *Eleftheria* had published six additional pieces responding to Woodhouse, and the debate had spread to other Greek newspapers.[20] Most of these came from veteran officers and members of guerilla groups who had gone into politics and written books about the history of the resistance movement and their experience during the Axis occupation.[21] Woodhouse replied to the criticisms via an interview given at BBC Radio (25 November 1958) and an interview with *Eleftheria* some months later (17 May 1959).

It is useful to study the media of the time, such as the daily press, and not only because of the information they provide. As Tessa Morris-Suzuki points out:

> But as the media of historical expression multiply, so they increasingly interact with one another … In this context there is much to be gained from exploring the ways in which a variety of popular media of historical expression coexist and relate to one another … I am particularly interested in the subtle ways in which popular media, by their silences as much by what they present, shape our imaginative landscape of the past. Popular culture tends repeatedly to return to certain events and images, making particular parts of history familiar and vivid, while rendering others distant or unknown. To understand how these imagined landscapes are created, reinforced or transformed, we need to look both at the political and at the aesthetic economy of mass media.[22]

Morris-Suzuki focuses mainly on newer media (such as television, graphic novels and the internet) and the forms of historical expression that they can interactively create. In our case, the way that the daily press is structured is significant for at least two reasons: first, it allows the publication of long texts in instalments, from historical articles and tributes to entire novels, theatrical texts or historical studies. Second, the publication of readers' letters creates, in many cases, a relatively open and in any case public forum of discussion inside its pages.

The Politics or Who Wants Whom to Remember What, and Why?

In his lecture and article, Woodhouse was actually participating in a recently started British debate about British strategy during the war and its effects in the present.[23] As an advocate of the strategy of supporting guerilla movements while also seeking to control these, he was defending it against military and political analysts, such as the historian Liddell Hart, who were arguing that the strategy had turned against the British Empire by fostering the rise of anti-colonial movements; also, that it was amoral, giving the new generations false messages.[24] Woodhouse names several examples in his lecture, such as Malaysia, Kenya and, most importantly, Cyprus. Tensions were high in Cyprus at that time, and Woodhouse was involved directly as the general director of the Institute of Foreign Affairs and as a sought-after expert on Greek issues. His narrative aimed to find a balance between the Cold War and the British Empire's policy towards its colonies as two realities of the international situation. Woodhouse's view was that a 'serious and reliable scientific research' on the history of the Greek resistance, 'faithful to truth', would prove that the British policy had a positive outcome in preventing the integration of Greece in the Soviet bloc. Moreover, he underlined the differences between the Greek and the Cypriot (EOKA) resistance movements, refuting rumours that any EOKA guerillas, and especially the leader, Georgios Grivas, had participated in the earlier Greek resistance or had a history of cooperation with the British in Greece.[25]

The Cyprus issue was also central to the responses. The responses to Woodhouse allow us to distinguish two main trends. The first argument was that the British mission had offered too much tolerance and support to the communists during the war, leading to their dominance among resistance forces and, as a result, to the later outbreak of civil war. The second held that British strategy undermined the nationwide character of the resistance to occupation and thus led to the later national division. In 1958, these two 'schools of thought' seemed to be united, however, in their common opposition to ongoing British policy in Cyprus, and both related Woodhouse's lecture to the Cypriot situation. As even Woodhouse observed:

> If something unites the Greeks in the moment it is their conflict with Great Britain and Turkey on the Cyprus Issue, just like the Arabic world will be united due to the existence of Israel. Under the surface, the political condition of Greece today is more uncertain than ever.[26]

Thus, the historical perception of the war in Greece shows an evident and intense antipathy to Britain. In this narrative, the British take the position of the 'Other', often even more so than the 'internal enemy'. This interpretation, which is variously prevalent during the 1960s, is at the same time of interest to me insofar as it serves as a unifying element among the different perspectives on the history of the war.

The responses to Woodhouse also allow us to see the formation of a new national resistance genealogy. The fighters of Cyprus appear as successors to the fighters of the anti-Axis national resistance, and the tradition of resistance is seen as reaching all the way back to the revolutionaries of 1821. So frequently do the responses to Woodhouse associate the heroism of the Greek independence fighters of the 1820s with the national resistance during the Axis occupation *and* the ongoing anti-colonial struggle in Cyprus that, finally, even Woodhouse seems to adopt at least part of the trope, comparing the 1820s revolutionaries with the Greek guerillas: 'These first guerillas made on me the same impression that the Klephts of 1821 would have made. They were not afraid of adventure and they had faith in the Struggle.'[27]

Who Owns Historical Truth?

The second issue arising from this debate has to do with the questions of who owns 'historical truth' and who deserves to speak on its behalf. For Woodhouse, these are the monopoly of professional 'historians and serious scholars'. According to him, up until the time of his lecture the history of the Greek resistance had been a field for a series of testimonials and memoirs and otherwise, 'mainly, for movie producers, literature authors and artists, but not for professional historians'. This, for Woodhouse, meant that the historical truth had yet to be explored: 'I know very well that it is really difficult for anyone who has taken part in the historical events to judge with the same objectivity as a historian would judge.'[28]

By this standard, the author rejected even his own work, saying that his 1948 book, *Apple of Discord*, was not a reliable historical study, because the numbers it gave, especially regarding the losses among German troops, were exaggerated:

> I realized later that these numbers that were written under the tension of the battle ... it is not possible to be true, they are exaggerated. But when these numbers are written and lists are made, it is very difficult to be corrected and so they are reproduced. In 1955, for example, these numbers were used in Myer's book. But, even more important is that the British government itself used this data, in the 6th volume of the "Grand Strategy", part of the official British military history.[29]

Woodhouse's respondents disagreed. According to the Greek historian Rena Stavridou-Patrikiou, in postwar Greece historians surrounded by common trust were both the institutional authors and the witnesses of the events.[30] At a first glance, Woodhouse was both. However, the respondents questioned both of these statuses. His critics did not recognize Woodhouse as a historian, because he was involved with politics and used history as a means for promoting his country's interests. His reliability as a witness was also questioned: first because he himself had disclaimed it. Second, some of the responses questioned his reliability as a witness by questioning his bravery in battle. A 'cowardly fighter' could not be a credible witness. Thus historical truth exists in the bravery of heroes and the blood of the martyrs. History 'has been written by the blood of the Greek fighters and sealed by the emptiness of the destroyed villages', and not by any Woodhouse, 'with his alchemical numbers and his unacceptable claims'.[31]

The Demand for Recognition

The responses to Woodhouse make a repeating motif of the blood of the dead, still crying for justice. In this context, history appears as debt, a moral duty to the dead. The demand that the resistance receive recognition was addressed in two directions. The history of the resistance was looking for its place in Greek national history, on the one hand, and in the history of World War II, on the other. Recognition, as the following anonymous letter points out, would be an inevitable act of justice, redemption and liberation:

> In any case, Mr. Woodhouse and his compatriots should know that … whether they want it or not, one day the national resistance of Greece will be recognized as one of the decisive factors in the Allies' victory. This will happen for sure because this chapter that is called national resistance is necessary in order for history to be written and people to live freely.[32]

In this case, the agency is vested in veterans of the partisan struggle, a varicoloured memory community whose members now belonged to different parts of the political centre and had participated in the non-communist part of the resistance – remaining clean, in a way, from the stigma of the civil war but maintaining a strong identity as members of the *Resistance* and a commitment to its history. They published books, wrote articles and participated in or created events throughout the postwar and pre-dictatorship period, based on the emergence of the history of 'resistance' and the need for its recognition in Greece and abroad.

Conclusion

The case of Woodhouse is an eloquent but also rather extreme example of the complexity to which the profession of historians is heir. He personifies at least three attributes that seem to be contradictory regarding the prevailing requirements of this profession and that mix temporalities: he had lived the experience of the historical event, being a witness and an active subject with a crucial role in the way that things turned out; he was a politician with permanent relations to the British special intelligence services and an acting expert in foreign affairs, especially with regard to Greece and the Middle East; and he was a professional historian, teaching in British universities, giving lectures and publishing historical studies, mainly on contemporary Greek history.

How could Woodhouse's obvious political and ideological engagement coexist with history as a craft and the credibility that it required? His method of maintaining this credibility was precisely in his often repeated distinction between History as science (with its training, method, documentation, scientific ways of establishing causality and adherence to truth) against other forms of dealing with the past. However, this raises what Ankersmit called the 'double bind of historical objectivity'. The frequent display of 'objectivity' and 'impartiality' eventually brings the subject (the historian) to the foreground, in effect self-defeating the argument.[33]

Woodhouse, the historian, was not the only one using the historiographical tools of the time in the effort to give validity to his own narrative. Most of the participants in this debate also used documentation and cited excerpts and documents beyond their personal experience in claiming an aggregate interpretation of the historical events. Their objections did not refer to specific aspects but to the big narrative of the war. They laid claim to the 'true history' of the war. This claim shows an important trend of the historical production on World War II, especially during the 1960s, and needs further study as a field. The heirs of the civil war (or the proxy war, as it was for Britain), whether inside or (mainly) outside academic history, attempted to construct reliable narratives with historical tools but without historical questions, making the distinction between a historical and a practical past seem even blurrier than it is anyway, even in the eyes of today's scholars.

Manos Avgeridis is a research associate at the Faculty of History and Archaeology of the University of Athens, and member of the Board of Directors of the Contemporary Social History Archives (ASKI). He has worked in research projects and published on the history and historiography of World War II, the history of the Greek Left and the history of displacement. His recent publications include 'Debating the Greek 1940s: Histories and Memories of a Conflicting Past since the End of the Second World War' (*Historein*, 16(1–2), 8–46, 2017) and 'Metapolitefsi: Greece at the Crossroads of Two Centuries' (Themelio, 2015, co-edited with Effi Gazi and Kostis Kornetis, in Greek).

Notes

1. This chapter is part of the Research Act Aristeia, by the title 'Greek Historiography in the 20th century: Debates on Identity and Modernization', co-founded by Greece and the EU (2012–2015).

2. National Resistance (Ethniki Antistasi) as a concept was rarely used during the Axis occupation. After the war, however, it became a main analytical term for describing the recent past – probably entering the language as a transfer of the French *Résistance Nationale* – and was used by the competing ideologies of the time with greater or lesser abstraction or specificity. A thorough biography of the concept in Greece has yet to be written.

3. For the postwar situation in Greece, see Mazower, *After the War Was Over: Reconstructing the State, Family and the Law in Greece, 1943–1960*; See, also, Mazower, 'The Cold War and the Appropriation of Memory: Greece after Liberation', 212–32.

4. To remember the remark of Fernando Sánchez Marcos: 'history is the arena in which the present and future identity of the community is debated,' see Sánchez Marcos, 'Historical Culture', http://www.culturahistorica.es/historical_culture.html.

5. For this reason, a Greek scholar has recently described the 1940s decade as 'a war without end'. See Paschaloudi, *Enas polemos horis telos*.

6. Some brief overviews of the historiography on the 1940s decade have already been written. See, indicatively, Papastratis, 'I istoriographia tis dekaetias 1940–1950' ['Historiography of the Decade 1940–1950'], 183–87; Liakos, '*Antartes* kai *Symmorites* sta akadimaika amfitheatra' ['*Guerillas* and *Bandits* in the Academic Theaters'], 25–36; Marantzidis and Antoniou, 'The Axis Occupation and Civil War: Changing Trends in Greek Historiography: 1941–2002', 223–31.

7. For a more extensive examination of the developments in these periods, see Avgeridis, 'Debating the Greek 1940s: Histories and Memories of a Conflicting Past since the End of the Second World War', *Historein* 16 (1–2), 9–46.

8. A visibility in the way that Joan Scott has masterfully put it. See Scott, 'The Evidence of Experience', 773–97.

9. See Liakos, 'Modern Greek Historiography (1974–2000): The Era of Transition from Dictatorship to Democracy', 351–78.

10. See Vangelis Karamanolakis's chapter in this volume.

11. In fact, it is the Greek translation of the edited version of Woodhouse's lecture, originally published in German in April 1958.

12. Theoretically, the chapter is in large part grounded in two distinctions about the ways in which societies and individuals deal with their past. The first, originally made by Michael Oakeshott, differentiates between the concepts of the historical and practical past as developed by Hayden White, see White, 'The Practical Past', 17. The second distinction, made by Jörn Rüsen, refers to the differences between the concepts of memory and historical consciousness; see Rüsen, 'How to Make Sense of the Past – Salient Issues of Metahistory', 172. These distinctions are not meant to set up completely separate categories. They are not absolute but pragmatic systems of understanding and usually coexist in every historical expression.

13. Additionally, the fact that a number of British scholars who studied Greek history, anthropology and literature during the postwar years, such as Woodhouse, Douglas Dakin, John Campbell, Nicholas Hammond, Elizabeth Baker, Philip Sherrard and others, had been involved with the Greek events during World War II is an interesting issue that needs further study.

14. Fleischer and Bowman, *Greece in the 1940s: A Bibliographic Companion*.

15. For the history of the SOE's creation, see Foot, *SOE in France* and Stafford, *Britain and European Resistance, 1940–1945: A Survey of the Special Operations Executive, with*

Documents. For the presence and activity of SOE in Greece, see Clogg, *Anglo-Greek Attitudes: Studies in History*.

16. See Woodhouse, *Apple of Discord* and E.C.W. Myers, *Greek Entanglement*.
17. Woodhouse, 'Zur Geschichte der Resistance in Griechenland', 138–50.
18. 'O Woodhouse diastrefei tin istoriki alitheia' ['Woodhouse Distorts the Historical Truth'], 4.
19. See Mathiopoulos, 'A Letter on Woodhouse's Lecture', 4.
20. Other than *Eleftheria*, there were responses at least to the newspapers *Vima*, *Makedonia* and *Avgi*.
21. More specifically some of the responders were: Giorgos Petrakogiorgis, former leader of a Cretan guerilla group later elected to Parliament with the Liberal Party; Christos Zalokostas, former member of a royalist group in Peloponnese and one of the first to publish a book about the Occupation years (*To hroniko tis sklavias* [*The Chronicle of the Slavery*], 1946); Stylianos Choutas, a veteran leader of a local guerilla group of Epirus belonging to the National Democratic Hellenic League (EDES), later elected to Parliament first with the National Party and then with the Liberal Party; and Komninos Pyromaglou, former EDES subcommander and author of the books *Ethniki Antistasis* (*National Resistance*), 1948, and *O Doureios Ippos: Politiki kai ethniki krisis kata tin Katohin* [*The Trojan Horse: Political and National Crisis during the Occupation*] (1956–1958), later Member of Parliament cooperating with the Unified Democratic Left (EDA).
22. Morris-Suzuki, *The Past within Us: Media, Memory and History*, 16–17.
23. In reference to the heading of this section, see Burke, 'History as Social Memory', 108.
24. Liddell Hart, *Defence of the West*, 53–57. See also, Stafford, *Britain and European Resistance*, 4–5.
25. Grivas was the founder and leader of the far-right paramilitary 'Organization X'.
26. 'O Woodhouse diastrefei tin istoriki alitheia', 4.
27. 'O Woodhouse amvlinei idi tin epithesin tou enantion tis Ellinikis Antistaseos' ['Woodhouse already Mitigates his Attack against the Greek Resistance'], 1, 5.
28. 'O Woodhouse amvlinei'.
29. 'O Woodhouse diastrefei tin istoriki alitheia', 4.
30. Stavridou-Patrikiou, 'O fovos tis Istorias' ['The Fear of History'], 70–76.
31. Dimitriadis, 'O k. Woodhouse diastrevlonei tin istoriki alitheia: Oi Aggloi kai i Elliniki Antistasis' ['Mr. Woodhouse Misrepresents the Historical Truth: English and the Greek Resistance'], 1, 5.
32. Anonymous reader, 'I Elliniki Antistasis' ['The Greek Resistance'], 4.
33. Ankersmit, 'The Ethics of History: From the Double Binds of (Moral) Meaning to Experience', 86–87.

Bibliography

Ankersmit, F.R. 'The Ethics of History: From the Double Binds of (Moral) Meaning to Experience', *History and Theory* (Theme Issue: Historians and Ethics) 43(4) (2004), 84–102.
Anonymous reader. 'I Elliniki Antistasis', *Eleftheria* (2 December 1958).
Burke, P. 'History as Social Memory', in T. Butler (ed.), *Memory: History, Culture and the Mind* (New York: Blackwell, 1989), 97–113.
Clogg, R. *Anglo-Greek Attitudes: Studies in History*. London: Palgrave Macmillan, 2000.
Dimitriadis, D. 'O k. Woodhouse diastrevlonei tin istoriki alitheia: Oi Aggloi kai i Elliniki Antistasis', *Eleftheria* (20 November 1958).

Fleischer, H. and S.B. Bowman. *Greece in the 1940s: A Bibliographic Companion*. Hanover, NH: University Press of New England, 1981.

Foot, M.R.D. *SOE in France*. London: Her Majesty's Stationery Office, 1966.

Liakos, A. '*Antartes* kai *Symmorites* sta akadimaika amfitheatra', in H. Fleischer (ed.), *I Ellada '36–'49: Apo ti Diktatoria ston Emfylio: Tomes kai syneheies* [*Greece 1936–1949: From Dictatorship to Civil War: Ruptures and Continuities*] (Athens: Kastaniotis, 2003), 25–36.

———. 'Modern Greek Historiography (1974–2000): The Era of Transition from Dictatorship to Democracy', in U. Brunnbauer (ed.), *(Re)Writing History: Historiography in Southeast Europe after Socialism* (Münster: LIT Verlag), 2004, 351–78.

Liddell Hart, B. *Defence of the West*. London: Cassell, 1950.

Marantzidis, N. and G. Antoniou. 'The Axis Occupation and Civil War: Changing Trends in Greek Historiography: 1941–2002', *Journal of Peace Research* 41(2) (2004), 223–31.

Mathiopoulos, V. 'A Letter on Woodhouse's Lecture', *Eleftheria* (7 November 1958).

Mazower, M. 'The Cold War and the Appropriation of Memory: Greece after Liberation', in I. Deak, J.T. Gross and T. Judt (eds), *The Politics of Retribution in Europe* (Princeton: Princeton University Press, 2000), 212–32.

Mazower, M. (ed.). *After the War Was Over: Reconstructing the State, Family and the Law in Greece, 1943–1960*. Princeton: Princeton University Press, 2000.

Morris-Suzuki, T. *The Past within Us: Media, Memory and History*. London: Verso Books, 2005.

Myers, E.C.W. *Greek Entanglement*. London: Rupert Hart Davis, 1955.

'O Woodhouse amvlinei idi tin epithesin tou enantion tis Ellinikis Antistaseos', *Eleftheria* (28 November 1958).

'O Woodhouse diastrefei tin istoriki alitheia', *Eleftheria* (6 November 1958).

Papastratis, P. 'I istoriographia tis dekaetias 1940–1950', *Synchrona Themata* 35–36–37 (1988), 183–87.

Paschaloudi, E. *Enas polemos horis telos*. Thessaloniki: Epikentro publications, 2010.

Pyromaglou, K. *Ethniki Antistasis*. Athens, 1948.

———. *O Doureios Ippos: Politiki kai ethniki krisis kata tin Katohin*. Athens, 1956–1958.

Rüsen, J. 'How to Make Sense of the Past – Salient Issues of Metahistory', *TD: The Journal for Transdisciplinary Research in Southern Africa* 3(1) (2007), 169–21.

Sánchez Marcos, F. 'Historical Culture', *culturahistorica.es*. Retrieved 15 November 2018 from http://www.culturahistorica.es/historical_culture.html.

Scott, J.W. 'The Evidence of Experience', *Critical Inquiry* 17(4), 773–97.

Stafford, D. *Britain and European Resistance, 1940–1945: A Survey of the Special Operations Executive, with Documents*. London: Macmillan, 1980.

Stavridou-Patrikiou, R. 'O fovos tis Istorias', in Etaireia Spoudon Neoellinikou Politismou kai Genikis Paideias, *1949–1967: I ekriktiki eikosaetia* [*1949–1967: The Explosive 20 Years*]. (Athens, 2000), 67–77.

White, H. 'The Practical Past', *Historein* 10 (2010), 10–19.

Woodhouse, C.M. *Apple of Discord*. London: Hutchinson, 1948.

———. 'Zur Geschichte der Resistance in Griechenland', *Vierteljahrshefte für Zeitgeschichte* 6(2) (1958), 138–50.

CHAPTER 8

Historians as Dissidents

Intellectual 'Eros' in Action

NINA WITOSZEK

Intellectuals as Gravediggers of Civilization?

The beginning of the twenty-first century has witnessed a re-evaluation of the civilizational role of intellectuals in world history. There has been a crop of alarmist studies – from Andre Glucksmann *Dostoïevski à Mahattan* (2002), Richard Wolin's *The Seduction of Unreason* (2004) to Mark Lilla's *The Reckless Mind* (2004) – showing the ways in which the 'priviligentsia' has been the chief choreographer of the decline of Western civilization. This complicity has been embarrassingly long and persistent. European anti-Semitism was fuelled not just by vulgar rumours but by the deliberate propaganda of intellectual elites. Hitler came to power not solely on the wave of the democratic support of an enthusiastic mob but because of the silence of the German educated 'unpolitical man' who failed to oppose the Nazi thugs.[1] In the 1980s, sixteen sour members of the Serbian Academy of Sciences and Arts – a number of respectable historians among them – decided to compile a dossier of Serbian national fears that would legitimize their compatriots' revolt against the ostensible anti-Serb conspiracy. Their memorandum was full of hate-breeding myths that fuelled the Balkan genocide.[2] The Rwandan atrocities were carefully planned by the intellectuals that passed through the universities of Paris and Butara and who rallied against the enemy via Radio/Television Libre des Mille Collines.[3] Peru's

---

Notes for this section begin on page 180.

Shining Path – the most vicious guerilla movement in the world of its time – was headed and founded by professors and mainly staffed by students.

These intellectual engineers of hatred were all cases of 'engaged intellectuals' – something that puts a corrective both on the theme of our volume and on the dilemmas facing historians and anthropologists today. Some of these dilemmas had been earlier illuminated by a number of masterful studies, from Hannah Arendt's *The Origins of Totalitarianism* (1951), Czesław Miłosz's *The Captive Mind* (1954), Edward Shils' *Intellectuals and the Powers* (1958; 1972), to Robert Conquest's *Reflections on a Ravaged Century* (1999). But while the evermore inventive ways in which intellectuals romanced the tyrants and legitimized revolutionary bloodshed are now well documented, what is less studied are the values and mechanisms through which intellectual elites resisted the Empire and promoted a humanist agenda. Are there any cases of 'historians as engaged intellectuals' who exemplify thought and action that provide both a bulwark against the totalitarian temptation and actively influence the course of a democratic transition?

In what follows I wish to draw attention to the role of historians in the emergence of one of the most unique – and successful – anti-authoritarian upheavals in the twentieth century: the Polish Solidarność (Solidarity) movement of 1980–81. I wish to argue four theses. Firstly, the historians who were the chief architects of the Polish revolution – Jacek Kuroń, Adam Michnik, Karol Modzelewski and Bronisław Geremek – succeeded not so much in organizing a political movement as in creating a 'parallel polis' that existed side by side with the communist state. Secondly, they not just thought, theorized and argued; they acted as well. I argue that without their preparatory groundwork, the scope of workers' protest would have been much more transient and particularistic and would have hardly gained the proportions of a massive moral revolution. Thirdly, their worldview – which I tentatively call an 'oppositional humanism' – was based *not* on revolutionary ideas of a new beginning but on preserving historical continuities from the past to the present (including a dialogue with the communist apparatchiks). Finally, oppositional humanism in action has been a problematic – if not hazardous – project: it points to the creative potential and the limitations of its underlying dialogic and cosmopolitan modus. This is especially evident in the dissidents' confrontation with *la volonté general*, which construed a collective identity that tolerated no difference and no dialogue.

The 'Eros' of Dissent

Plato, the classical expert on tyranny, illuminates the aphrodisiac component in all intellectual engagement. In *The Symposium* he argues that the psychological forces that draw certain men to despotic acts of power and other men to commit selfless acts of good are one in the same. That force is love; eros. To be human is to be a striving creature – one who does not live simply for bread alone but is driven to expand and sometimes elevate his needs and in this way transcend the here and now. 'All men are pregnant in respect to both body and soul,' and many cannot rest until some potential they sense within is made actual and they can 'beget in the beautiful'.[4] Those who have such desiring souls become thinkers or poets who concern themselves with 'the right ordering of cities and households' – that is, with politics in the highest sense. There is thus a Socratic moral Eros connected with action for the public good.

But Plato adds a qualification to his ideas on positive intellectual engagement. There are some who become slaves to their eros. In Plato's *Republic*, Socrates describes the tyrannical soul as one in which the madness of love – 'love has from old been called a tyrant,' after all – drives all moderation out and sets itself up as ruler, turning the soul itself into 'a tyranny established by love'.[5] Many of these tyrannical souls enter public life not as rulers but as teachers and writers – what today we would call intellectuals. These men can be most dangerous, Plato continues, for they are 'sunburned by ideas'.[6] This Socratic perspective throws interesting light on the modality of intellectual engagement. On the one hand there are historians who, like Eric Hobsbawm, have been 'intellectuals sunburned by ideas'. For all his brilliance, Hobsbawm defended the Stalinist genocide and was unable to imagine that a party capable of slaughtering millions of people was never going to create a radiant tomorrow.[7] On the other hand, there are those 'desiring souls' that wish to contribute to a better and kinder humanity.

In what follows I wish to discuss the ways in which an extraordinary 'historian imagination' shaped the period that began in Poland in 1976 and concluded with the dismantling of the Soviet Empire in 1989. In some ways these two decades can be called 'The second European Renaissance': a stage for human rebirth; a rediscovery of human agency and dignity; a rebellion against the communist religion and dogma. But first and foremost, it was the time when a small *res publica litterarum* – a group of Eastern European thinkers and writers – succeeded in laying the foundations of liberation from Soviet bondage. Let us have a glimpse of this risorgimento through a prism of an outside historian who became seduced by the 'eros' of its architects.

On 18 August 1980, the fifth day of the Gdańsk shipyard strike against the communist regime that gave birth to Solidarność, a young Oxford student of history, named Timothy Garton Ash, flew from Germany to Poland, curious to see what was happening in the neighbourhood. Originally set on studying the German resistance of Hitler in Berlin, he ended up exploring the resistance to communism in Eastern Europe.⁸ As a historian, he could not but be intrigued by a paradoxical revolution unfolding in front of his eyes – an upheaval that was both cosmopolitan and nationalist, religious and secular, right wing and left wing, conservative and progressive, fixated on the workers and trade unions and yet featuring a new type of alluring oppositional intelligentsia. I can only imagine what went through his head when he saw a crowd in Victory Square in Warsaw interrupting an anti-communist sermon with a rhythmic chant: 'We want God, we want God, we want God in the family circle, we want God in books, in schools, we want God in government orders, we want God, we want God, we want God.' And I can understand his puzzlement when he listened to the dissident historian Adam Michnik, who, 'stylishly dishevelled as ever' and smoking forty cigarettes an hour, told him that the role of intellectuals is crystal clear: 'they should be like the Roman geese who warn the Romans against Barbarians at the gate.'⁹ For Michnik, communism was a continuation of an earlier Oriental despotism that was a frighteningly decivilizing force – and it had to be counterbalanced by a 'recivilizing mission' (i.e. via non-violence and dialogue). To Ash, everything about Michnik was exotic: his kamikaze courage, his phenomenal memory, his weakness for intelligent women, his 'hungry, sensuous enjoyment of every moment' combined with a hint of desperation – even the slight stammer that Michnik turned into a 'devastating rhetorical effect, like a brilliantly articulate submachine gun'.¹⁰

Ash's two books on the Polish upheaval, *The Polish Revolution: Solidarity* (1984) and *The Uses of Adversity* (1990), clearly evoke his ambition to capture history in the making – but they are more than that. They are testimony to a process of seduction – of being slowly entranced by the eros of intellectuals who engaged in building a parallel democratic society in a police state. In this project, private flats, factories and churches replaced communist schools, universities, concert halls and art galleries. Most importantly, historians – Michnik, Jacek Kuroń, Karol Modzelewski, Jerzy Jedlicki – functioned as agents of cultural innovation both in terms of thought and action. The project started from a comprehensive revision of the official version of national history. To this effect, they reactivated the tradition of an underground 'Flying university', used in Poland both under the partitions (1791–1818) and during the Nazi occupation (1939–1945). Like their predecessors, the dissidents created their own independent publishers and mobilized the most influential emigration journals (see Paris *Kultura*) to their cause. Lectures and seminars were moved to private flats. As a young novice in this movement, I can still remember the thrill and shock we felt at hearing the unvarnished version of the national 'romantic-heroic past': from the anatomies of the Ribbentrop-Molotov pact, to iconoclastic revelations about how Poland contributed to its own destruction by nationalist rivalries. What was perhaps most fascinating to the young generation at the time were dissident historians' emphasis on a new model of resistance against the Soviet empire. It was not about the armed struggle. In fact, it was not about any struggle at all. It was about the project of living 'as if'. Acting and thinking *as if* we were part of the free, democratic world. The essence of this project has been captured by Kurt Vonnegut, who said: 'We are what we pretend to be so we better pretend well.'[11] As I shall show, the pretence led to an emergence of the world of learning and culture independent of the oppressive state.

Strikingly, apart from scattered remarks in Ash's enchanted essays, Jeffrey Goldfarb's chapter on Eastern European opposition in *Civility and Subversion* (1998) and Barbara Falk's informative *The Dilemmas of Dissidence in East Central Europe* (2003), there are the few comprehensive studies that have analysed the moral and cultural origins of the collapse of the former Soviet empire.[12] The intellectuals' role has been either eclipsed, or criticized, or found to be downright embarrassing.[13] In the influential anatomies of Solidarność, Western scholars such as Alain Touraine, Roman Laba and Lawrence Goodwyn argue that the Polish upheaval was largely propelled by pre-war socialism and the workers' tradition of occupational strike.[14] David Ost goes as far as to accuse the Polish oppositional intelligentsia of losing touch with the people.[15] With a few exceptions – such as Andrzej Friszke's and Dariusz Gawin's studies of the intellectual opposition (e.g. Friszke 2011; Gawin 2013) – even Polish thinkers have been more enthusiastic about unmasking the intellectual heroes of Solidarność rather than rhapsodizing about their role in co-creating the workers' movement.[16] The founding fathers of Solidarność (such as Michnik, Kuroń or Frasyniuk) have been accused of mismanaging Solidarity and bungling the democratic transition.[17] Moreover, Andrzej Wajda's iconic film about the origins of Solidarity, *Wałęsa, Man of Hope* (2013), refers to the intellectuals' role in an ironic and dismissive way. It is as if neither the public opinion nor the intellectuals themselves have been able to acknowledge a positive role of the true architects of the revolution, as if the majority was more comfortable about the standard procedure of unmasking the intelligentsia's double agendas and the rule of cynical reason, or indeed reducing noble actions to the work of Freudian libido.[18]

There are obvious cognitive errors in this hermeneutics of suspicion and willed self-flagellation. Firstly, the emphasis on the workers' revolution and religious symbols ignores the original, extraordinary pluralist – even cosmopolitan – dimension of Solidarność, a facet which was hardly the workers' imaginative act of transcendence of their paricularist interests. Secondly, occluding the role of intellectuals leads to a situation where we cannot fully explain the staying power of the Solidarność revolution – its initial 16-month-long 'carnival' – and its culmination in the first democratic government in Eastern Europe in April 1989. Nor can we illuminate fully the reasons for Poland's peaceful transition to democracy: the lack of witch-hunts, no rise of extreme ethnic hatred and relatively weak nationalist sentiment in the early 1990s. I wish to contend that without the intellectual eros – and certainly without a sustained imaginative effort of engaged historians – Solidarność would have been yet another workers' strike about the prices of meat or, at best, a purely nationalist-religious movement presided for a while by the Catholic Pope. The *sine qua non* basis of post-communist democracy – the civic and pluralist component – was in place in 1989 thanks to the sustained, hard – and often perilous – work of small groups of people, who 'wished to beget in the beautiful'.

'The Players'

Though the idea of transcending class and ethnic distinctions and building a national front against the authoritarian rulers was germinating in the minds of committed intellectuals and writers since the first Polish partition in 1772, its first proper theoretical and practical implementation did not occur before the 1970s.[19] In October 1976, after a series of workers' strikes followed by brutal communist repression, a small circle of historians, lawyers and political activists gathered in a Warsaw apartment and issued the *Appeal to Society*, which demanded broad financial, medical and legal help for the oppressed workers and their families. The group called itself the Workers' Defence Committee (KOR): a clever rhetorical ploy that the communist authorities preached but did not practice. The Security Police called them 'The Players'.

The Players' altruistic initiative was unprecedented in the history of Poland, where intellectuals usually give the people what the intellectuals want. But not this time. The Players, including three leading historians, Adam Michnik, Jacek Kuroń and Antoni Macierewicz, went far beyond empty declarations of Solidarność or informed analysis of the situation. They embarked on publishing an information broadsheet that recorded all cases of state repression against the workers in a workers' state. They went to the defeated cities, sat through the trials, knocked on people's doors, gave out money and collected names and addresses of victims of state repression. Predictably, these were not particularly uplifting transactions; rather they were the shortest way of getting to know the taste of arrests, beatings and long prison sentences.[20] But KOR did not wallow in martyrdom; rather it proposed a new type of opposition that mixed altruism with carnival. They were a buoyant, heterogeneous team, bringing together socialists,

Catholics, Jews, Poles, and even Masons.[21] From the founding day of KOR, the lives of its members was punctuated by rituals of hate – threats, beatings and jail sentences – and rituals of love – the magic of friendship, euphoric bacchanalia after fooling the police and long, inspired chats. This perhaps proves that intellectuals are like cream: they are at their best when whipped.

The scattered comments and musings accrue to a picture. The action takes place in Kuroń's flat, where 24 hours a day people camp, work, argue, sleep and eat. When one walks through the yard in the evening, one hears the incessant *taktaktak* of typewriters. The phone never stops ringing. There is a constant stream of students, journalists, possible collaborators, security police issuing threats and people offering money. Many of the callers are madmen and looneys: a woman who claims her sex life has been ruined by the security police and Scotland Yard and demands that KOR provides her with a flat; a man who claims that he has been poisoned by the Special Units and needs an immediate medical check-up; a gentleman who introduces himself as a representative of the clandestine underground government of Lithuania, Latvia, Ukraine and Poland. As Kuroń put it, they were the 'distorted mirror of the disease we were all suffering from'.[22]

KOR's communal *modus vivendi* was regulated by a set of fragile, democratic principles. There were no more or less important members, although to many people's fury, Kuroń was often confused as the press spokesman of KOR. The force of strong, often intractable personalities was the reason why, when an important decision was to be made, the members preferred not to vote in order to avoid splitting the unsavoury division into a minority and majority; they just kept arguing and hammering out the problems until everybody agreed. Though Kuroń describes it as a 'school of democracy', this was less a democratic than Socratic way of tackling problems – one that created havoc and splits but also, paradoxically, forced the Players to develop and refine a 'dialogic imagination'.

What deserves attention in this context is the Players' extraordinary rise from a small group of concerned intellectuals and workers' spokesmen to an almost mythical organization that – in the public consciousness – was perceived as an all-powerful 'sect' specializing in missions impossible. Within a year, KOR established a virtual 'republic of friendship' that included a wide national and international network of collaborators and patrons, its own independent publishing houses, a Flying University, its own legal experts and even its own foreign policy – disseminated by Voice of America, the BBC, Radio Free Europe and the émigré publications. KOR's publishers and journals – such as *NOWA*, *Aneks* and *Krytyka* – promoted the uncensored version of Polish and European history and circulated translations and discussions at the cutting edge of contemporary Western thought. *Robotnik* ('The Worker') – an independent broadsheet circulated in factories and shipyards – was a hotline to the proletariat. The Flying University and its sister institution, Towarzystwo Kursow Naukowych ('The Society of Scholarly Courses'), were the intellectual shock troops that circulated the best analytical achievements of independent thought. The alliance with the Student Solidarność Committees ensured a constant influx of young activists. Support of international writers, such as Günter Grass, Heinrich Böll or Saul Bellow, gave KOR the status of a *cause celèbre*.

Rarely in human history has a group – which originally counted 14, then 34, and finally a few hundred intellectuals – succeeded in implementing a positive, empowering moral vision of such magnitude; one can only think of the American Founding Fathers or the French Encyclopaedists – but the former did not act in concert and the latter were taking no dramatic personal risks. The Players' actions had two immediate effects: firstly, they led to amnesty for the imprisoned workers in July 1977; secondly, they lifted the unimaginable solitude and fragility of the individual in the Polish state. Nobody who was arrested or beaten by the police felt forsaken and at the mercy of communist thugs any longer. A person's name would be recorded, their fate would be followed by the independent and international media, and their trial (if there was a trial) would be monitored by KOR's lawyers and followers. Everybody in opposition – and beyond – knew Kuroń's home phone number by heart: 39 39 64. This was the number one called to report every arrest and act of repression.[23]

The barrier isolating the Poles from each other – and from the outside world – was broken. Poland was no longer a grey *terra incognita* filled with communist misery but the locus of an anti-totalitarian struggle. And even if people shook their heads, they heard KOR's message of the importance of human rights and social Solidarność every day. It was repeated *ad infinitum* by Radio Free Europe and Voice of America, which were listened to in every home, and in this way the message gradually leaked into the collective unconscious. What I am arguing here is that before Solidarność there was a 'collective Zola' writing appeals and documenting every case of beating, blackmail or abduction and speaking and acting out Solidarność before the actual emergence of Solidarność. The KOR's imperative of building an inter-class alliance based on the principle of social solidarity was hammered most persuasively in *Robotnik*, whose 100,000 illegal copies spread the idea of workers' rights and peaceful strategy of resistance in factories and shipyards.

By engaging in a social solidarity crusade, the Players certainly challenged the Aristotelian claim that in a despotic city friendship and Solidarność could not thrive because all social relations are based not upon positive ideals such as justice or virtue but upon negative doctrines such as the power of fear.[24] In the communist state, this reclaimed connection with the fellow brothers – and with the outside world – became a powerful weapon against fear.

Historical Imagination at Work

In the months preceding the Solidarność revolution in August of 1980, the landscape of the Polish opposition hardly presented a harmonious or unified picture. On the contrary: there were continuous splits and pronounced tensions between the cosmopolitan KOR and the more radical wings of dissent, including groups representing a traditional, religious-patriotic sentiment that was boosted by the 1980 visit of the Polish Pope.[25] These tensions were of a complex nature. The Players had started their project at the time where individual courage and challenging taboos were not particularly admired; rather they were treated as a sign of the lack of adaptive skills and practical sense. Furthermore, their tireless petitions, signature hunting and bold brinkmanship were unpopular in many intellectual circles, if only because they exerted a moral blackmail on all people whose conscience was clean (i.e. unused). Many felt uneasy about KOR's message, which went beyond the usual litany of easy accusations and jeremiads directed at the communist regime. KOR's acts of kamikaze courage, their erudition and imagination, were as much admired as they were envied and scorned by lesser souls and minds.

This does not mean that the Players were staging a 'dictatorship of virtue'. On the contrary, the police records of surveilled KOR meetings reveal that its members often doubted their right to put people's lives at risk and discussed the necessity of understanding those who collaborated with the system.[26] One reason may have been that, ultimately, they were dependent on them: on officials who would make a kind gesture in prison or those would allow them to earn a living. But, as a participant observer in the 1976–1980 upheaval, I recorded that to many ordinary Poles, KOR was 'psychiatric opposition' – a group that *must have had* ulterior motives behind their surface benevolence. Nobody in their right mind would risk so much with so many horrors in return. The question is: did the fact that there were so many engaged historians among the KOR's leaders and sympathizers have any impact on the design and trajectory of the Polish revolution?

There are at least three features of the Players' mindset and their programme of action that indicate that a study of history lessons was a vital ingredient in the Players' vision of an open society. The first sprang from the fact that the Players' two most influential and internationally known leaders and thinkers – Adam Michnik and Jacek Kuroń – represented the postwar generation known as 'Komandosi': the *spiritus movens* of the uprising against the communist regime in March 1968.[27] As historians, former socialists and legendary 1968 rebels, Kuroń and Michnik were intent on creating a social movement that would not depart from - but build on - national history in a way that was unique when seen against rebellious convulsions elsewhere in the world. Komandosi demanded freedom, but – unlike in the West – it was not the freedom to destroy but freedom to reclaim national culture and history, to reactivate stories that were part of the 'confiscated national memory'.[28] It is important to emphasize that this reclamation of the linkage with the past was not an antiquarian or idealizing exercise. On the contrary, as in Hannah Arendt's argument about the treasure of revolution that hides in the past, it was underpinned by a strong conviction that the communist deletion and distortion of national history made human identity fragile, experience precarious and expectations confused. It was the critical rereading of the national past that guaranteed what Arendt called the 'deadly impact of new thoughts'.[29]

In redesigning the contours of the narrative of an anti-authoritarian struggle, Michnik and Kuroń engaged in 'history lessons' anatomizing all sublime failures and spectacular disasters that characterized past Polish hecatombs. Their vision was a prophylactic against yet another folly. They assaulted national illusions and comforting stories. They studied the Polish underground state during the Nazi occupation from 1939 to 1944 – the biggest project of clandestine education in Europe. They promised no utopias, apart from creating a democratic, open society.

The second intriguing feature that Michnik, Kuroń and Jan Józef Lipski (literary historian) brought to KOR was a distrust of revolution.[30] By their reflexive demanding a strategy of exit out of communism, the Players acted consciously as a moral community that proposed less a revolution and more an original paideia. Kuroń stubbornly repeated: 'Do you want to fight tyranny? Then read! Read as much as you can. Talk, write, look for people like you. Demand books from abroad [and] lend them out. And buy the criminal codex and try not to break it.'[31]

It is difficult, if not impossible, to describe their ideological-religious allegiances. Although Michnik, Kuroń and Lipski were agnostics, their writings clearly draw on – and reimagine – the original Christian caritas; the tradition of Polish democratic Romanticism; early socialist thinkers; the humanist legacies of Camus, Chiaromonte, Bonhoeffer, Hannah Arendt and Leszek Kolakowski; and the visions of the two greatest bards of oppositional humanism, Czesław Miłosz and Zbigniew Herbert. KOR's often quoted motto came from Herbert's famous poem, *The Message of Mr. Cogito*: 'You were saved not in order to live/you have little time you must give testimony.'[32]

The third, and perhaps most original, dimension of Kuroń and Michnik's writings was a strong 'dialogic' orientation in their conception of the parallel polis. Already in 1976, in an interview for *La Repubblica*, Michnik emphasized that the opposition had to act on the premise that sometime in the future the communists would be the opposition's partners rather than enemies to be exterminated as soon as the dissidents win.[33] Similarly, his classical book *The Church and the Left*, was a historical study highlighting the meeting points between the classical socialist ideology and original Christianity. Both emphasized the ideas of equality, social compassion, peace and brotherhood, and hence both had to evolve from being adversaries to becoming partners in the struggle for democracy. A principle of historical continuity with the past, and a dialogue with the communist – and the Catholic – 'church' was thus part and parcel of Michnik's idea of the future free and independent democracy.

In short, the ethical foundation of KOR was a difficult *historical wisdom* – one that cannot be reduced to a secular-left ideology or to a sectarian, romantic mindset. As I have argued, a strong Christian ingredient and the redefinition of friendship as an instrument of politics gave the Players' Weltanschauung a pre-modern touch. The ethics of *caritas* and the invocation of the old code of honour gestured towards the Renaissance rather than the modern world view. So did the discourse of human dignity that lay the foundations of the Solidarność revolution. The interest in the concrete human being rather than, say, class or universal humanity echoed sixteenth century humanism rather than the values of the Enlightenment. The dislike of patriotic exhibitionism and reluctance to invoke the mantra of the 'Motherland' was a departure from romantic obsessions and a reactivation of Erasmian cosmopolitanism. Ditto the appeal to the 'habits of the heart' as the corrective to abstract rationality.[34]

In short, there are many elements that bring KOR close to the Renaissance *res publica litterarum* – that group of scientists, thinkers and aficionados of antique literature who knew and corresponded with one another and were united by the concrete tasks of promotion of European citizenship, religious reform and struggle against fanaticism through the invocation of the wisdom of antiquity. And, I wish to argue, just as the friendship of – and argument between – Erasmus and Luther, Pico and Ficino, Leonardo and Machiavelli contributed to a momentous change in European sensibility, so the intellectual legacy of the Players created the basis for a historical breakthrough in 1980.

At the risk of simplifying a complex moral vision, I roughly distinguish eight pillars of KOR's agenda:

1) the Aristotelian–Arendtian conception of politics as a public struggle for values and interests carried through peaceful means;
2) the programme of social solidarity and self-organization designed by Kuroń in his *Thoughts on the Program of Action* (1977);
3) the reorientation of the oppositional struggle from the one directed *against* the authority to the one focused on creating the independent public sphere elaborated in Michnik's programme of the *New Evolutionism* (1976);
4) the creative reworking of the values of original Christianity as the ethical platform of action codified by Kuroń in the influential essay 'A Christian without God' (1975);
5) the ethics of dialogue theorized by Michnik in *The Church and the Left* (1979);
6) the code of honour, exhumed by Michnik in his prison book *Z dziejów honoru w Polsce* (*From the History of Honour in Poland*, 1976);
7) the imperative of speaking truth to power (Havel 1977); and
8) the demand for self-education.

Intellectuals as the Enemies of the People

From my slightly biased perspective of participant observer, many elements of the 'revised' story of the Players – the parts I lived through as a participant in the events of the time – invite a potential Hollywood film based on Kurosawa called *The Magnificent 14*. The film is about a group of determined daring-dos arriving in towns whose inhabitants are afraid of their own shadow. It goes on to tell about resourceful ways in which the magnificent fourteen mobilize a broad network of collaborators that will finally engineer a peaceful protest against the communist gangsters. But, this being Poland, the finale of KOR's epic is, predictably, not a happy ending. At the moment of their greatest triumph – in the Gdańsk shipyards during Solidarność upheavals – the Players were not feted and extolled, their suffering was not acknowledged and rewarded and their writings were not studied and analysed.

In 1981, at the end of the sixteen months of freedom under Solidarność, the attacks on KOR were coming from all fronts: the Communist Party, Solidarity's rank and file, even from the best and brightest of the intelligentsia. This was a historical anticlimax. One of the clever communist ploys – the argument that KOR was a bunch of radical 'Jewish' intellectuals and unsavoury cosmopolitans who schemed to take over power on the workers' backs – was found persuasive by many. What was perhaps most disturbing was that the former beneficiaries of KOR – the workers from

Radom – so easily forgot the Players' past largesse and their extraordinary rescue operations. Indeed, there was quite a wrangle about mentioning Solidarność's debt to KOR in the report of the first Solidarity Congress. Even leading Polish intellectuals, who had previously never bothered to rise from their armchairs, took to unmasking the 'heroic amateurs' of resistance. Michnik writes: 'I remember a meeting in the KIK (The Club of the Catholic Intelligentsia), at which [they] talked about the strikes in the shipyards. They spoke about KOR with such ironic superiority that I couldn't bear it and left slamming the door... For those who had just been released from prison this irony was painful and deplorable.'[35]

To add insult to injury, some Western scholars, mainly of Marxist persuasion, published sociological studies that demonstrated that KOR played little or no role in the creation of Solidarność, or that they 'betrayed the revolution' by being too critical of the masses and their problems.[36] Without underestimating the role of the workers, this reductionism leads to a misunderstanding of the complex sources of Solidarność's success; implicitly, it implies that the dissidents would have been more successful if – in the difficult years of transition – they stopped criticizing Polish ethnocentrism, bigotry and anti-Semitism. Surely, it was *not* the case of the revolution devouring its own children. It was the classical case of patricide. The begetters of Solidarność found themselves either reduced to a bunch of impotent windbags or travestied to what the Polish security police always insisted they had been: an omnipotent Jewish mafia conspiring to overturn the state, destroy Solidarność's Catholic soul and take over power. The secret police that had bugged their meetings and used to beat the hell out of the Players must have been rubbing their hands with glee.

There were many political and psychological reasons for this brutal 'character assassination' of the chieftains of the Polish of opposition. Firstly, a number of the leaders of KOR – including Adam Michnik, Seweryn Blumsztajn or Jan Lityński – were Poles of Jewish extraction, with a socialist past added to their dossier. There is no doubt that, in the conditions of uncertainty and impending Soviet invasion, the communist propaganda's image of KOR as the 'Judeo-masonic' sect manipulating the masses and leading them astray was found half-convincing by many. As in every revolution, the atmosphere of mistrust and suspicion was further intensified by ubiquitous agents. 'The situation during Solidarność was such,' Kuroń writes, 'that if the true news was spread that the government laid a golden egg, people would say: firstly, not golden; secondly not an egg; and thirdly, it didn't lay it but stole it.'[37] Ironically, the former defenders of Polish workers were very much perceived in similar terms: firstly, not the defenders but Freemasons; secondly, not of workers but of their own interests; and thirdly, on whose payroll were they?

Tadeusz Mazowiecki, Solidarność's main advisor, believed the Players should not enter the movement's structures, not just because they were the communists' *bête noir* but because they 'had an overdeveloped instinct of group interest'.[38] He touched the nerve of the problem. To many outside observers, KOR was first of all a tight and powerful group of friends 'who did the impossible' – a liability rather than an achievement in the crooked context of the revolution under siege. KOR's leaders' extraordinary erudition and strong personalities were misunderstood as signs of 'haughtiness', an 'attitude of disdain towards the silent majority'.[39] Ironically, this perception prevailed, in spite of Michnik's and Kuroń's obsession with not becoming 'the possessed from Dostoevsky's novel.' They were both acutely aware of the hazards linked to 'the road which transforms a movement of the democratic opposition into a religious sect or a gang of bandits – the fate of the triumphant Jacobins, Bolsheviks or the bearded partisans of Fidel Castro'.[40]

But even with all these qualifications, the charges of KOR's alleged elitism or membership in a superior 'Warsaw salon' are not only unjust; they are outrageous. For it is only in sheer ill will that one chooses to forget that the predicament of the Players had little to do with any salons; big chunks of their lives were spent behind bars, in rather unedifying conditions, or in the factories, where they were sent to labour as punishment for 'disturbing the peace'. For many, prison was an education in physical, often humiliating work like scrubbing toilets or doing laundry. It was also a stage of close encounter with the common criminals and dregs of society, where they learned how to negotiate with them and gain their respect. Kuroń wrote to his wife Gaja:

> [After all this time] I experience prison to the umpteenth power. Not by sympathizing with the "professionals of crime" but by trying to feel myself into their way of seeing the world, their lives and pasts. In these lives there had been no room for friendship, love, or human feelings. And then, suddenly, I discover a human being in this sump – his dreams and longings – and the landscape becomes even darker.[41]

To sum up: the public demotion of the Players and their role in the making of Solidarność was undoubtedly a comprehensive envy towards a group that stole the monopoly on martyrdom from the Church, the monopoly on compassionate socialism from the socialists and the monopoly on patriotism and courage from the 'true Poles'. There is, however, one more thread that seems to be particularly suggestive. The Players challenged the 'natural order of things' with their cultivation of dialogue. They made a go at a balancing act, trying to avoid the pitfalls of dogma and fundamentalism. They wanted to practice *both* politics *and* friendship. They were *both* patriots *and* cosmopolitans. They were *both* compassionate Christians *and* secular socialists. As 'liberal-conservative-socialists',[42] they fought *both* for socialism *and* capitalism with a human face. Even their attitude towards the hateful communist rulers was characterized by tolerance, as one of the former members observed.[43] In short, already then and there the Players were perfect citizens in a utopia of 'dialogic democracy' as imagined by Anthony Giddens and professors of multicultural studies. And here, precisely, lies the problem.

Solidarność and Social Cooperation

In his thought-provoking study of human cooperation, *Together*, Richard Sennett argues that the twentieth century 'perverted cooperation in the name of solidarity'.[44] The regimes that spoke in the name of unity were tyrannies, where the idea of solidarity often invited command and manipulation from the top. According to Sennett – very much as for Hannah Arendt – the concept of solidarity has a potential to exert a fatal attraction. It often appears in an 'us-against-them' form that figures in exclusionary-fundamentalist or ethnocentric social movements, including those that call for a return 'to family values'. Thus solidarity – which has been the Left's traditional response to the evils of capitalism – has a deceptively positive ring, but it often effectively sustains and reinforces a Manichean outlook. Sennett juxtaposes this exclusionary type of solidarity with cooperation, which is more about transcending a particularistic mindset, if it is to be effective. This is one of the reasons why cooperation has 'rarely figured as a strategy for resistance'.[45]

Though Sennett makes a valid and helpful analytical distinction between solidarity and cooperation, he is wrong about the scarcity of cooperative effort as a strategy of resistance. If we look closer at the fifteen years between 1976 and 1989, we see massive cooperation as a vital and highly effective part of the Players' project – in fact, a modus operandi that yielded a massive anti-totalitarian movement. As I have argued elsewhere, KOR lived with difference and engineered a 'dialogic revolution'.[46] Ironically – but perhaps aptly in Sennett's terms – this revolution was called Solidarność: a movement that was as impressive as ultimately detrimental to the idea of social ooperation. As the initial, cosmopolitan initiative became embraced by broad masses, cooperation did not increase; it devolved into solidarity in Sennett's sense. In fact, we can talk about two stages of the Eastern European revolution. The first one was a broad cooperative effort ignited by the cosmopolitan intellectuals: one that transcended class, ethnic and national divisions. It oiled the machinery of getting things done; it was inclusive and pluralist in its outlook. As it transformed – symbolically and literally – into *Solidarity* – problems started occurring. Gradually, Solidarność acquired the tribal *us-versus-them* mien, increasingly linked to the aggression towards those who were 'different'. At the end of its carnival of freedom, one influential (national-religious) wing of the Polish revolution attempted to impose on the rest what Aristotle called a 'repressive unity'.[47] If their efforts did not succeed, and if the KOR's project ended in a Round Table Agreement between the opposition and the communists in April 1989, it is only because the cooperative spirit was kept alive by Kuroń, Michnik and their colleagues, who remained influential, if controversial, advisors of Solidarność.

It is considerably thanks to their efforts that the Round Table Agreement – signed by the Solidarity leadership with the members of the Communist Party in the spring of 1989 – was the start of the first democratic government in Soviet-dominated Eastern Europe. In Michnik's eyes, the agreement was the crowning achievement of KOR's dialogic politics. The ethos of compromise – marshalled by the Players as part of their strategy to build a bulwark against another authoritarian temptation – seemed to have won. But for Michnik, the basis of this dialogue went beyond the readiness to find a pragmatic consensus; it invoked the Christian principle of 'charity before justice'. His motto was 'Yes to amnesty, no to amnesia'.[48] While settling accounts with the communist generals and apparatchiks, he made a spectacle of forgiving his former oppressors. Persecuting them, he insisted, would mean that 'these people will never grow up ... that, being the victims of my fanaticism, they'll be locked in the ghetto of the damned in which there's no point to become better'.[49] This sounds persuasive, as always with Michnik. But whatever brilliant justification he conjures, his rapport with the post-communists had an underlying pragmatic foundation. The former apparatchiks were also *both-and-people* – though of a different sort – now eager to modernize and join Europe, unlike the Solidarność's Catholic-nationalist hinterland. There was a bitter irony about this anticlimax. While the communists blossomed, and were 'Europeanizing' in the transition to democracy, the working masses – bearing the brunt of economic hardships – found good reasons to cultivate a sense of entrenchment and xenophobia.

To sum up: although the Polish dissident historians did not necessarily prove to be the most astute politicians, there is little doubt their ethical work and cultural innovation played a significant part in peaceful transition to democracy in 1989. The fact that post-communist Poland was free from violent episodes, the resurgence of anti-Russian sentiment, ideological witch-hunts and anti-Semitic extremism is largely thanks to KOR's moral ideal, which launched a fusion of cosmopolitanism and cooperation. This ideal – although more often an irritant than an inspiration to the broad masses – was nevertheless a guiding signpost in a period of 'muddling through' the democratic transformation.

But the fate of KOR is also instructive as an emblem of the dubious role of engaged intellectuals in social upheavals. Indeed, there is something allegorical about the way in which a group of friends in a communist country put to test the best ideas of modern dialogic democracy – and revealed their often problematic nature. One is, of course, tempted to inquire into the question of the Players as 'power-players'; to unmask the ways in which friendship became contaminated by politics and dialogue compromised by ulterior motives. I wish, rather tendentiously, to propose another way of revaluating KOR's legacy – one which is particularly pertinent at a time when we are both rethinking central values of Western civilization and the idea of an anti-authoritarian opposition. One is the archetypal story of 'virtue unrewarded'; of Plato's 'desiring souls who yearn to beget in the beautiful' and are hated for just that reason. The other is the ancient, and yet novel, conception of the Players' resistance. As I have argued, what made KOR unique as the European group of dissidents advocating social emancipation was a world view that embraced not the spirit of the classical nationalist struggle but the spirit of the modern cosmopolis. At the same time, however, it reached back to the pre-modern values neglected by the Enlightenment: the importance of religion and of the 'habits of the heart' – the centrepiece of human dignity and honour.

Most importantly in the context of this volume, the legacy of oppositional humanism draws attention to the cultural roots – and the constructive role of engaged historians – in the anti-authoritarian struggle. Jeffrey Goldfarb has discussed the unique mixture of civility and subversion advanced in the dissidents' vision.[50] What he has not attended to, however, is the fundamental problem attached to this 'civilizing mission'; the problem springing from a general aversion to the humanist project. Today, rebuffed by the masses, often mocked by the academy, and overlooked by Western philosophers, oppositional humanism seems to have been relegated to a heroic but antiquarian – if dubious – episode in the history of European civilization. The fate of the dialogic *rinascimento* in East-Central Europe points clearly to the terrible beauty of humanist ideas – desirable but resisted, often unacknowledged and hardly ever rewarded. The twentieth century expired among declarations of humanism alongside wars and crises that unleashed suppressed repositories of violence and revealed weaknesses at the heart of the West's intellectual life. Today one returns again to the concepts of Renaissance thought – such as 'dignity', 'conscience', even 'spirit' – but one is hardly aware of the difficult wisdom and frightening costs of humanism in action – the humanism that is not about being a winner but a moral pest, an often belittled and derided advocate of humanity's ethical advancement.

The East Central European Renaissance is a testimony to the inhumanity of the humanist ethos. The cruel imperative inherent in this ethos has been best captured in Zbigniew Herbert's summons, which was often quoted by the members of KOR:

> you were saved not in order to live
> you have little time you must give testimony ...[51]

And yet, for all the ironic bitterness of Herbert's poem, the ultimate message of the Players' achievement is that of hope. Its crunch has been captured by Margaret Mead, who is supposed to have said: 'Never doubt that a small group of thoughtful, committed citizens can change the world; indeed, it's the only thing that ever has.'[52]

Nina Witoszek is a research professor and the director of the Arne Naess Programme on Global Justice and the Environment at Oslo University, Norway. She has specialized in the comparative history of cultures, Scandinavian studies, history of Eastern Europe and environmental history. Her latest publications include *The Origins of Anti-Authoritarianism* (Routledge, 2018) and *Sustainable Modernity: The Nordic Model and Beyond* (Routledge, 2018).

Notes

Parts of this chapter have been previously published in Nina Witoszek, *The Origins of Anti-authoritarianism* (London: Routledge, 2018).

1. Stern, *The Politics of Cultural Despair*.
2. Anzulovic, *Heavenly Serbia*.
3. Chege, 'Africa's Murderous Professors', 32–40.
4. Plato, *The Symposium*, 17.
5. Plato, *Republic*, 27.
6. Plato, *Republic*, 31.
7. Hobsbawm's intellectual project as the case of perverted eros was very much on display in the famous BBC interview with Michael Ignatieff, where Hobsbawm openly confirmed that, for him, the radiant tomorrow in the USSR justified the loss of 20 million lives. Quoted in Conquest, *Reflections on a Ravaged Century*.
8. Ash, *The Polish Revolution: Solidarity*.
9. Private conversation at the conference 'The 30th Anniversary of KOR', Victoria Hotel, Warsaw, 23 September 2006.
10. Ash, *Polish Revolution*, 122–23.
11. See http://www.goodreads.com/quotes/13719-we-are-what-we-pretend-to-be-so-we-must, accessed 9 May 2014.
12. Since the time this chapter has gone to print the author of this chapter has tried to fill the gap by writing *The Origins of Anti-authoritarianism* (London: Routledge, 2018).

13. Goldfarb, *Civility and Subversion: The Intellectual in Democratic Society*; Falk, *The Dilemmas of Dissidence in East Central Europe*; Szulecki, 'The "Dissidents" as a Synecdoche and Western Construct: A Fresh Look on the Democratic Opposition in Central Europe'.

14. Touraine et al., *Solidarity: The Analysis of the Social Movement 1980–81*; Laba, *The Roots of Solidarity: A Political Sociology of the Polish Working Class Democratization*; Goodwyn, *Breaking the Barrier: The Rise of Solidarity in Poland*.

15. Ost, *The Defeat of Solidarity*.

16. Friszke, *Czas KOR-u* [*The Time of KOR*]; Gawin, *Wielki Zwrot: Ewolucja Lewicy i idei społeczeństwa obywatelskiego* [*The Great Turn: The Evolution of the Left and the Idea of Civil Society*].

17. For example, Bielik-Robson, 'Obrona Kołtuna?' ['The Defense of the Babbit?']; Ziemkiewicz, *Michnikowszczyzna* [Michniksland].

18. In a book on the 1968 generation of future anti-authoritarian rebels, Lidia Burska talks about the 68ers' 'extraordinary reluctance, even antipathy to one's own idealistic and resonant past. They look at their youth as if it was lived by somebody else'. See Burska, *Awangarda i inne Złudzenia: O pokoleniu 68 w Polsce* [*The Avant-garde and Other Illusions: On the 68 Generation in Poland*], 9.

19. Witoszek, *The Origins of Anti-Totalitarianism*.

20. Many members of the opposition lost their jobs and careers, experienced radical social isolation and, in some cases, toyed with suicidal ideas. Jacek Kuroń's ability to make a living was dependent on his wife Gaya, who worked as a psychologist, and on his more 'politically correct' friends, who would allow him to publish his crime fiction and essays under a pseudonym. If there was a method in the Players' madness, it worked mainly thanks to the power of friendship.

21. The Masons in KOR included prof. Edward Lipiński, Jan Kielanowski, Jan Szczypiorski, Ludwik Cohn and prof. Jan Józef Lipski.

22. Kuroń, *Gwiezdny czas*, 45.

23. KOR's 'republic of friendship' was a bohemian community sharing things, money and food (and occasionally ladies); a 'warm circle' that provided a sense of security and an awareness that 'you can risk everything because there will always be people who love you, who will help you and who will be with you to the end'. Blumsztajn, 'Rocznica KOR-u'.

24. Porter and Tomaselli, *The Dialectics of Friendship*; King and Devere, *The Challenge to Friendship in Modernity*, 52.

25. Gawin, *Wielki Zwrot*, 344–45; Friszke, *Czas KOR-u*, 439–58.

26. Friszke, *Czas KOR-u*, 13.

27. Friszke, *Anatomia Buntu: Kuroń, Modzelewski i komandosi* [*The Anatomy of Rebellion: Kuroń, Modzelewski and Komandosi*].

28. Witoszek, *The Origins*.

29. Adam Michnik, private conversation, October 2004.

30. As one of the members of the Komandosi, Barbara Toruńczyk argued: 'We had a reflexive attitude to the revolution, war and destruction – this is what made us different from the revolt in the West. I remember the discussions in Michnik's club pondering whether communism was to be blamed for the gulags. And the majority decided that since the communists built the gulags, sentenced innocent people and broke their lives, then all those who identify with the ideals of communism, face the moral burden of the gulags … It was very hard to accept the idea that we had to renounce revolution … But we saw ourselves as a link between generations. Our school readings were Camus and Conrad … And like Conrad's heroes, he also knew that we had to face challenges'. See Toruńczyk, 'Pokolenie marca: Rozmowa Cezarego Michalskiego i Barbary Toruńczyk'.

31. Friszke, *Czas KOR-u*, 70–71.

32. Herbert. 'The Envoy of Mr Cogito', trans. John and Bogdana Carpenters, a poem registered by the Polish Academic Information Center at the State University of New York,

Buffalo. Retrieved 9 May 2014 from http://redfrog.norconnect.no/~poems/poets/herbert.html.

33. *La Repubblica* 16 November 1976, 'Adam Michnik: Teczka osobista' ('Adam Michnik: Personal Files'), Warszawa, KARTA III/18.

34. Lipski, *KOR*, 70.

35. Żakowski et al., *Między panem a plebanem* [*Between Lords and Parish Priests*], 299.

36. Touraine et al., *Solidarity*; Laba, *Roots*; Goodwyn, *Breaking the Barrier*; Ost, *The Defeat*.

37. Kuroń, *Polityka i odpowiedzialność*, 201.

38. Jankowska, *Rozmowa z Tadeuszem Mazowieckim: Portrety niedokończone: Rozmowy z twórcami Solidarności 1980-1981* [Interview with Tadeusz Mazowiecki: Unfinished Portraits: Conversations with the Creators of Solidarity 1980–81], 151.

39. Zuzowski, *Political Dissent and Opposition in Poland: The Workers' Defense Committee 'KOR'*, 73.

40. The tension between the temptation to think in terms of *la nation c'est moi* and the imperative of humility is especially evident in Michnik's writing. Once he dumbfounded us with half-ironic statements such as 'For five minutes God put me in charge of the Poles' honour'. Then he redeemed himself with brilliant polemical essays exposing dissidents' vanity. See especially Michnik, 'Ticks and Angels', 178–185. See also Michnik, 'Rzecz o Jacku: Wolność, sprawiedliwość i miłosierdzie' ['On Jacek Kuroń: Freedom, Justice and Charity'], 57.

41. Admittedly, Kuroń and Michnik tried to make the best out of their dungeon misery. The sojourn in prison allowed Michnik to read the *Collected Works of Marx and Lenin* and become a winner of the all-Poland competition on the history of Leninism – something that was a source of great discomfort to the party secretaries. Furthermore, prison trained him 'how to oppose degradation and debasement, how to be brave, patient and not turn his traumas into bitterness and hatred'. Personal communication, Warszawa, Summer 2003.

42. The designation 'liberal-conservative-socialist' has been proposed by Leszek Kołakowski as an epitome of his – and KOR's – ideological stance (see Kołakowski, 'How to be a Conservative-Liberal-Socialist?', 225.

43. Jankowska, *Rozmowa*, 305.

44. Sennett, *Together: The Rituals, Pleasures, and Politics of Cooperation*.

45. Sennett, *Together*, 279.

46. Witoszek, *The Origins*.

47. Sennett, *Together*, 4.

48. Michnik's slogan was originally launched in his *Gazeta Wyborcza* and widely discussed in the Polish media in the ensuing debates on settling accounts with the former communist elites. See Michnik, *Letters from Freedom: Post-Cold War Realities and Perspectives*, 324.

49. Quoted by Jacek Żakowski et al., *Między panem*, 96.

50. Goldfarb, *Civility and Subversion*.

51. Zbigniew Herbert, 'The Envoy of Mr. Cogito'.

52. M. Mead. Retrieved 9 May 2014 from http://www.brainyquote.com/quotes/quotes/m/margaretme100502.html.

Bibliography

Anzulovic, B. *Heavenly Serbia*. New York: NYU Press, 1999.
Ash, T.G. *The Polish Revolution: Solidarity*. New York: Scribner, 1984.
Bielik-Robson, A. 'Obrona kołtuna?' *Krytyka polityczna* 1(1) (2002).
Blumsztajn, S. 'Rocznica KOR-u', *Gazeta Wyborcza* (20 September 2006).

Burska, L. *Awangarda i inne Złudzenia: O pokoleniu 68 w Polsce*. Warszawa: Wydawnictwo Słowo, 2013.
Chege, M. 'Africa's Murderous Professors', *The National Interest* 46 (1996), 32–40.
Conquest, R. *Reflections on a Ravaged Century*. New York: W.W. Norton, 1999.
Falk, B. *The Dilemmas of Dissidence in East Central Europe*. Budapest: Central European University Press, 2003.
Friszke, A. *Anatomia Buntu: Kuroń, Modzelewski i komandosi*. Kraków: Znak, 2010.
———. *Czas KOR-u*, Kraków: Instytut Akademii Nauk, 2011.
Gawin, D. *Wielki Zwrot: Ewolucja Lewicy i idei społeczeństwa obywatelskiego*. Kraków: Znak, 2013.
Glucksmann, A. *Dostoïevski à Manhattan*, Paris: Robert Lafont. 2001.
Goldfarb, J.C. *Civility and Subversion: The Intellectual in Democratic Society*. Cambridge: Cambridge University Press, 1998.
Goodwyn, L. *Breaking the Barrier: The Rise of Solidarity in Poland*. Oxford: Oxford University Press, 1991.
Herbert, Z. 'The Envoy of Mr. Cogito'. Retrieved 3 December 2018 from https://www.poetryfoundation.org/poems/48501/the-envoy-of-mr-cogito.
Jankowska, J. *Rozmowa z Tadeuszem Mazowieckim: Portrety niedokończone: Rozmowy z twórcami Solidarność 1980–1981*. Warszawa: Biblioteka Wiezi, 2003.
King P. and H. Devere. *The Challenge to Friendship in Modernity*. London: Frank Cass, 2000.
Kołakowski, L. 'How to be a Conservative-Liberal-Socialist?' in L. Kołakowski, *Modernity on Endless Trial*. Chicago: Chicago University Press, 1990.
Kuroń, J. *Polityka i odpowiedzialność*. London: Aneks (Samizdat), 1984.
———. *Gwiezdny czas*. London: Aneks, 1991.
Laba, R. *The Roots of Solidarity: A Political Sociology of the Polish Working Class Democratization*. Princeton: Princeton University Press, 1991.
Lilla, M. *The Reckless Mind: Intellectuals and Politics*. New York: New York Review of Books, 2016 [2004].
Lipski, J.J. *KOR*. Warszawa: Wydawnictwo CDN (Samizdat), 1983.
Michnik, A. 'Ticks and Angels', *Survey* 25(1) (1980), 178–85.
———. 'Rzecz o Jacku: wolność, sprawiedliwość i miłosierdzie', *Zeszyty literackie* (special issue) (1986).
———. *Letters from Freedom: Post-Cold War Realities and Perspectives*, I. Grudzinka-Gross (ed.). Berkeley: University of California Press, 1998.
Miłosz, Cz. *The Captive Mind*. New York: Vintage, 1990 [1954].
Ost, D. *The Defeat of Solidarity*. Ithaca, NY: Cornell University Press, 2004.
Plato. *The Symposium*. Cambridge: Cambridge University Press, 1980.
———. *Republic*. Oxford: Oxford University Press, 1984.
Porter, R. and S. Tomaselli. *The Dialectics of Friendship*. London: Routledge, 1994.
Sennett, R. *Together: The Rituals, Pleasures, and Politics of Cooperation*. New Haven, CT: Yale University Press, 2012.
Stern, F. *The Politics of Cultural Despair*. Berkeley: University of California Press, 1961.
Szulecki, K. 'The "Dissidents" as a Synecdoche and Western Construct: A Fresh Look on the Democratic Opposition in Central Europe', PhD dissertation, Constance University, 2011.
Toruńczyk, B. 'Pokolenie marca: Rozmowa Cezarego Michalskiego i Barbary Toruńczyk', *Europa* (8 March 2008).
Touraine, A., et al. *Solidarity: The Analysis of the Social Movement 1980–81*. Cambridge: Cambridge University Press, 1983.
Witoszek, N. *The Origins of Anti-Totalitarianism*. London: Routledge, 2018.

Wollin, R. *The Seduction of Unreason: The Intellectual Romance with Fascism from Nietzsche to Postmodernism*. Princeton University Press, 2014.
Żakowski et al., *Między panem a plebanem*. Kraków: Znak, 1995.
Ziemkiewicz, R.A. *Michnikowszczyzna*. Warszawa: Red Horse, 2006.
Zuzowski, R. *Political Dissent and Opposition in Poland: The Workers' Defense Committee 'KOR'*. Westport, CT: Praeger, 1994.

CHAPTER 9

The *Social Movement History* as a Social Movement in and of Itself

MICHIHIRO OKAMOTO

An Attempt to Publish Social Movement History

From 1972 to 1985, young academics in Japan studying modern and contemporary history published an innovative and groundbreaking journal entitled *Social Movement History* (*SMH*).[1] As the title suggests, it examined social movement history from the perspective of those people who experienced the Japanese student movement. The new perspectives brought into historical studies had an intimate connection with the scholars' formative student lives. As will be shown, *SMH*, first published in 1972 after two years of preparation, was greatly influenced by the movements of the late 1960s.

Publishing *SMH* was a kind of social movement in itself because it was an attempt to criticize conventional academics through the founding of a new research group with fresh principles. *SMH* had no sponsoring publishers, no professional editors and the copies were sold by its members to secure funds for the next issues, although it must be said, some sympathizing editors and booksellers supported the group to maintain the journal. As was often the case in the student struggles during the late 1960s, the *Social Movement History* group made much of the principles of voluntary association; having no regulatory rules, no fixed leaders, no restrictions for membership and initially kept no records. This was reflected in the journal's approach to social movement history. *SMH* made much of the autonomous aspects of social movements. It also adopted the 'history from

---

Notes for this section begin on page 198.

below' approach by taking up the *sociabilité* and *mentalité* of ordinary people as a component of social history. The Annales school heavily influenced the *SMH* members and some of its works were subsequently translated by them. These innovative approaches distinguished the *SMH* members as historians. This helped them ironically to receive credit in the academic world that they had criticized. They gradually established themselves as insiders in academia. Some of them – or rather, say, many of them – are currently playing leading roles in the studies of European modern and contemporary history in Japan.[2] In this chapter, I would like to analyse how the experiences of historians and the conditions surrounding them influenced their own historical treatises, by referring to the book *History as Memory, Memory as History* (2013), which collects the essays of the former members of the *SMH* group and discusses their facticity as historians. As the title suggests, the book refers to the past from two points of view, namely memory and history. It is an attempt by historians to write history about their past depending on their memory.[3] At the same time, it includes review essays on the roles and achievements of *SMH* by historians of later generations. The book created a stir among Japanese historians immediately after its publication because the readers could find revealing autobiographical essays by leading historians. The question became why they presently assume leading roles in the discipline of history. Is it because they are still working on social movement history? The answer is no. On the contrary, it is rather because many of them turned away from it, especially after the ceasing of *SMH*, and made innovative works that made a profound contribution to the development of Japanese historiography.

The purpose of this chapter is not simply to criticize their conversion nor praise their achievements, because the experiences of historians and the conditions surrounding them clearly influence their works. However, historians cannot experience the past. They are only experiencing the present as Hayden White puts it.[4] If the present determines the past as history like E.H. Carr argued,[5] what determines historians' works more is the present condition surrounding them rather than the past experiences in their individual memory. Why? Because what conditions they were in is now significant in considering their historical works. However, concentrating too much on the conditions is likely to be too deterministic, as the given conditions do not necessarily result in the same thoughts and behaviours. This is so with the historians who joined *SMH*. Their trajectories and standpoints as historians are diverse as will be introduced in this chapter. There are clear differences in how they memorialize their past experiences and how they think about the present conditions. To explain this, the chapter will consider the conditions of postwar Japan pertaining to historical studies and the experiences of a group of historians depending on their studies and memory.[6]

From World War II to the Zenkyoto Movement

As was usual in many defeated countries, anti-government feeling grew in post-World War II Japan. The immediate postwar period in Japan was an age of successive social movements. Movements inspired by the Allied Forces' policy to introduce democracy had wide appeal at first. But they soon had to face the reactionary policies taken by the Supreme Commander for the Allied Powers, whose aim was to involve Japan in the Cold War as a loyal partner of the USA. Anti-reactionary politics became a common vehicle to save imported democratic values. The Korean War aroused a strong and visceral anti-war sentiment. Furthermore, the San Francisco Peace Treaty generated strong opposition because it excluded the USSR and mainland China. All this led to a united front against the revision of the Japan-US Security Treaty in 1960, which can be viewed as the greatest mass movement ever seen in Japan. In May and June, more than one hundred thousand workers, students, citizens and the 'so-called' silent majority surrounded the Diet Building almost every day to protest against the steam-rolling of the new treaty's ratification.[7] The student movement under the leadership of the National League of All Student Unions (*Zengakuren*) played a great role in this movement.

The labour movement was also active. The General Council of Trade Unions (GCTU), which was originally established to counteract the pro-Japanese Communist Party (JCP) labour movement under the aegis of the GHQ, became increasingly militant and adopted a leftist position together with the reunited Japanese Socialist Party (JSP). After the conclusion of the San Francisco Peace Treaty, the GCTU-JSP coalition increasingly occupied the leading position in the democratic camp in place of the disunited JCP, which was losing influence for several local, national and international historical reasons including its violent tactics in the early 1950s, the events in 1956, the secret report of the 20th congress of the USSR Communist Party and the USSR's violent military interferences in East European satellite countries. However, the influence of Marxism was still great among the students engaged in politics although the influence of the JSP and the GCTU was larger among the public at large. In this way, New Left thought remained of paramount concern among the younger generation.

Despite differences of opinion among the participants, the movement of 1960 against the Japan-US Security Treaty was a united front for democracy. Compared with the movement of 1960, the movement in the late 1960s expressed a different world view although it also included the opposition against the revision of the Japan-US Security Treaty scheduled in 1970.

The 1960s was the age when the new youth cultures sprung up across the planet. Young males with long hair, young females with miniskirts, and free love were fashionable symbols of the new generation. Freedom was the emblematic word of the day as Joan Baez sang her heart out. The eagerness for unfettered freedom inspired youths not only in the cultural sphere but also in politics. They joined movements for democracy, equality and peace, which culminated in the May–June events in France in 1968. In these circumstances, in Japan there also occurred a huge movement with long strikes and the occupation of university campuses called the Zenkyoto movement.

The Zenkyoto movement began at two of the main Japanese universities, Nihon University and the University of Tokyo in 1968. Nihon University – Nichidai – is a private institution, having the largest number of students with more than forty thousands. It was notorious for prioritizing economic profits and producing a standardized form of education. It did not have a strong student movement history, but the protest against the embezzlement of a large amount of money by managing executives spread among 'ordinary' students spontaneously. Meanwhile, the University of Tokyo – Todai – is the biggest of the national public universities and is often criticized for its elitist and privileged position. It has a long history of student protests, and its leaders played a central role in the national student movement. Having started as the protest against the penalty imposed on the postgraduate medical students, who insisted on the improvement of their status, the Todai Struggle spread when the police force entered the campus with the approval of the university president to exclude and remove the protesting students. It aroused the ire of 'ordinary' students because police were banned from university campuses to protect academic freedom in the postwar period.

The Zenkyoto movement soon spread to other Japanese universities and mobilized large numbers of students. It developed new characteristics compared with hitherto formations. First, the main tactic was the occupation of university campuses. Second, in addition to political demands such as stopping the Vietnam War and the abolition of the Japan-US Security Treaty, the movement also requested the total reform of universities. Third, it was a spontaneous, autonomous movement based on voluntary association: with no permanent organization, no regulations or professional leaders. To sum up, it was an unprecedented movement – an event – with a new direction.

In addition, what should be noticed here is that the Zenkyoto movement contested not only the conservative political regime but also the progressive and modernist thought that had underpinned the Japanese postwar democratic movement. This out-and-out contestation against the establishment, including its criticizers, had the potential to renew the whole society. However, such inchoate radicalism had weaknesses at the same time. Although Zenkyoto attracted huge sympathy initially, it could not sustain its influence among sympathizers for long. The more radical Zenkyoto became, the more it lost support. And the more it lost support, the more radical its slogans and tactics. As students began to retire from the movement through ennui and disillusionment with the protracted struggle, the few who remained became more and more professionally politicized. Some founded the extreme leftist groups. The tragic collapse of the Red Army group with fratricide among themselves and the gunfight with the police at Mt. Asama villa in 1972 was its disastrous outcome. Despite the efforts to keep the heritage of the movement, the influence of the Zenkyoto movement faded in the 1970s. Conservatism insinuated itself in all domains of society. Universities were no exception. Student movements declined and so did labour movements. The numbers of strikes diminished year by year and big strikes were less frequent. This was the milieu in which the *SMH* was issued.[8]

Marxist Tendencies in Early Post-World War Japanese Historiography

As is indicated above, many of the contributors to *History as Memory, Memory as History* are connected in one way or another to the student movements of the 1950s and 1960s. In addition to the experiences during their student days, the condition of humanities and social sciences in postwar Japan was another factor that influenced their later activities as historians. Scholars in democratized universities, liberated from the surveillance of the pre-war totalitarian state, competed with each other to incorporate new ideas, especially those from abroad. In this situation, modernist and progressive ways of thinking had a clear influence on the humanities and social sciences. Masao Maruyama, a political scientist, and Hisao Otsuka, an economic historian, both professors at the University of Tokyo, were representatives of this trend. Maruyama analysed authoritarian states and their infrastructural logics through comparative studies between the Emperor-centred authoritarian regime and Nazism based on modern politics,[9] and Otsuka argued for liberating Japan from the burden of non-modernity via Max Weber's theses regarding the development of capitalism.[10]

Historical studies were no exception. *Kokoku-shikan* (emperor-centred historiography) was criticized by the postwar historians. Rekishigaku Kenkyukai (The Historical Science Society of Japan), founded in 1932, albeit under severe surveillance of the totalitarian state because of its pro-Marxist tendency, gained influence together with Shigakukai (The Historical Society of Japan), the most authoritative organization based on the Historical Department of the University of Tokyo. Both associations made the scientific and empirical approach the fundamental principle, but there were some differences between them. The Marxism-influenced Rekishigaku Kenkyukai was politically minded compared with the Shigakukai, which aspired to more lofty academic goals.[11]

Compared with economics, politics and history, the influence of other disciplines remained largely insignificant. Sociology was not yet fully fledged as an empirical discipline. Folklore was often criticized for its traditionalism, especially as it was perceived to underpin the pre-war national regime. Anthropology, due to having only a limited number of independent departments at Japanese universities, had only a minor impact during the time when everything modern was valorized.

Although the influence of progressivism – that is to say, emulating the modern European model – was especially strong in postwar Japan, the rise of Asia's presence with the independence from colonial rule played no less an important role in learning, specifically in history. Some pro-Marxist historians took Asian perspectives into consideration. Two of them, Senroku Uehara and Bokuro Eguchi, should be mentioned here. Uehara, who had started his early career as a historian researching medieval Germany, considered the problem of Weltanschauung in his later life. His conclusion was to grant primary importance to actualities present in non-European worlds in order to construct a more 'general', non-Occident-centric view of world history.[12] Eguchi, one of his majors being the Russian Revolution and who was a fellow traveller with Marxism throughout his life, took up the problem of imperialism from a critical standpoint. Eguchi's understanding of imperialism was unique in that he analysed it not only systemically and structurally but also from the activities of actual peoples in colonized regimes. He thought that the relationship between imperialism and ethnicity was crucial for interpreting imperialism.[13]

The Older Members of the *Social Movement History* Group

History as Memory, Memory as History consists of three chapters, 'History in Memory', 'Probing Age', and 'Historical Perspectives'. The first two chapters are collected autobiographies or rather, it would be better to say, a kind of prosopography of a group of historians depending on their memories. The four contributors to chapter 1 were born from 1931 to 1938 and experienced the period when the once prevalent influence of orthodox Marxism was on the wane because of the aforementioned events. Akira Kiyasu, the eldest of them, once an 'emperor boy' as he recollects, became interested in the thought and movement against the postwar regime as was usual of his generation but always held reservations pertaining to some modernist tendencies. As a result, he inherited the arguments of Uehara and Eguchi.[14] From this standpoint he took up the *sociabilité* and *mentalité* of 'peripheral' people, often regarded as backward-looking, and wrote a book on revolutionary syndicalism in France. The round table talk by the members on the book was the main article of the first issue of *SMH*.[15] Although Kiyasu greatly influenced *SMH* group members, he nevertheless was affected by discussions with the younger members as he recollects in an essay in chapter 1. From this impetus he wrote *Saint Monday in Paris* and other stimulating works on French social movement history.[16]

Kiyasu's approach was shared with the members of *SMH* – Haruyasu Kato, Atsushi Kitahara, and Wakio Fujimoto, born in 1936, 1937 and 1938 respectively – who experienced the movement in 1960 as students. Kato, the eldest of them, had studied first French Literature, of which J.P. Sartre and Albert Camus were most influential, and moved later to the history department to learn the history of French socialism. As the long intellectual autobiography in chapter 1 illustrates, he was interested in the currents of New Left thought prevalent in Europe at that time. But at the same time he also extended his interest to the lives of colonized people and movements, criticizing the thought that had idealized the European social movements as a prototype. This derives from his experience of having opposed the JCP movement, whose authority depended on a dogmatic reading of the lessons of its European counterparts, especially those of the Russian Revolution.[17]

Lenin's argument that the lesson of the Russian Revolution was the presence of a strong, centralized advance party was the modus operandi of communist parties since the establishment of the Communist International. Kitahara, after having joined the movement against the JCP, centralized leadership with Kato in his student days and began to make the relationship between party and movement his main subject. As an assistant scholar of European history in the Department of History, the Todai Struggle was a fresh event or aspect of social movement history. That is to say, it was possible that the movement could have originated from an autonomous source rather than organized leadership. The concern for this possibility is shown in his essay in chapter 1 and other works on the Italian modern social movement and thought.[18]

Different from the three contributors above, Fujimoto was a postgraduate student of the Department of International Relations, which had two historians studying the Russian Revolution – the above-mentioned Bokuro Eguchi and Masanori Kikuchi – who published *The Stalin Age as History*, the first scholarly book in Japan on the Great Purge based on empirical research.[19] Fujimoto studied the Russian Revolution under Kikuchi's tutorship from a critical viewpoint against the Bolshevik leadership but resisted to submit his thesis, as he was an organizer of the boycott movement during the Zenkyoto movement. Not only Fujimoto but also the contributors of the next chapter contested the academic establishment and probed new ways to study and write, rejecting the idea to write theses for degrees and articles in authorized academic journals, which was the usual practice for young scholars to secure academic promotion. This is why *SMH* was published voluntarily as Fujimoto testifies.[20]

In relation to Kato, Kitahara and Fujimoto, it is necessary here to introduce another important person, Hisashi Nagao, a distinguished theoretical leader of the movement who paid attention to the real aspects of the Russian Revolution and the Soviet Regime in his student days. He was also distinguished as a young scholar and published *The History of the Russian Revolution* in his early thirties. However, he began to have grave doubts about studying European history in the academic world and instead became interested in the problems of ethnicity and traditional ordinary lives. He contributed two manifesto-like essays professing a move away from the study of European history.[21] Regrettably, he died early in 2013 prior to the publishing of *Memory as History* and so did not have the chance to contribute to it.

The Graduate Generation

The seven contributors to chapter 2, born from 1941 to 1947, belong to the generation that was involved for the most part in the Zenkyoto movement as postgraduate or graduate students, except Seiji Kimura, who was already an assistant scholar from 1968 and was studying abroad during the high times of the struggle. But before mentioning each individual in detail, the situation surrounding them should be highlighted.

As Kato put it, interest in New Left thought spread immediately after its formation.[22] The works of Perry Anderson and E.P. Thompson in *The New Left Review* were translated into Japanese.[23] But most influential among Japanese historians was E.J. Hobsbawm. His early works such as *Labouring Men*, *The Age of Dual Revolution*, *The Primitive Rebels* and *The Bandits* were translated to critical acclaim.[24] The method adopted in *The Primitive Rebels* and *The Bandits* was especially stimulating and apt to the study of social movement because it took up peripheral people who had been hitherto largely ignored. In this sense, Hobsbawm's oeuvre significantly influenced Japanese historians who were looking for new perspectives for social movement history. It is worth reminding ourselves, on the other hand, that E.P. Thompson's *The Making of English Working Class* was not translated until the 2000s.[25]

The attempts of Hobsbawm and Thompson shared much with the innovative approach that was introduced by Georges Lefebvre and George

Rudé on the study of the French Revolution, in the sense that they wrote 'history from below'.[26] In relation to this, it is necessary to mention Michio Shibata, who had a great influence on the members of *SMH* as a professor in the European History department of the University of Tokyo. Shibata, born in 1926, wrote first an analysis of the French monarchy from a social and economic perspective.[27] But his main concern was the French Revolution itself. So he wrote *Babeuf's Conspiracy* using the sources he read during his stay in France, referring to Lefebvre, Rudé and others.[28] It was a new type of historical work written by Japanese European historians in that it was an attempt to do positivistic research akin to that of 'native' historians.

The 1970s, the period when the Zenkyoto movement was fading away, was a time of rapid economic development in Japan. This assisted studying abroad. Historians, especially the younger generation, competed to visit archives to investigate primary sources. So did many of the contributors to chapter 2 as they recollect in their essays. They could thus distinguish themselves from the theory-inclined traditional studies of European history. Masatoshi Sagara wrote innovative essays on the French possibilists in *SMH* by using the police records collated during his stay in France. His papers were excellent in that they were not only very positivistic but also quite unique in their style, with few footnotes and full of colloquial expressions. And they dealt with the collective life of the people that supported the unity of the movement.[29] Why historians should use academic style when they describe the lives, struggles and expectations of ordinary people was one of his main problematics as he suggests in his memoir.[30]

The concern with the *sociabilité* and *mentalité* of ordinary people was shared by Kenichi Kinoshita, who wrote the leading article in the first number of *SMH* on the Paris Commune.[31] Marx regarded the Paris Commune as the event in which the prototype of dictatorship of the proletariat was manifested. His thought was inherited by Lenin, who saw in it the eventual possibility of the dying out of the state. These theoretical positions had been the canon of the leftist movement, but Kinoshita instead emphasized the autonomous gathering of the people who supported the Paris Commune. According to him, this conviction derived from his witnessing the Zenkyoto movement, especially Nichidai Zenkyoto, which spread autonomously and quickly gained sympathy among apolitical students.[32]

A sympathizer but not one actively engaged in the movement was the position taken by Seiji Kimura, whose major was German history. Kimura was interested in the new ideas born from the movement although he was not in Japan during the time of the Todai Struggle. According to his recollections, he joined almost all of the *SMH* research meetings after his return to Japan. This encouraged him to write a book on the German Revolution from the viewpoints of ordinary soldiers based on the testimonies he read in

Germany.³³ Hideyuki Yamamoto, also a historian of German history, notices the ambiguity he realized in his experience. He calls it the 'Boomerang' phenomenon – that is, the double role the same person plays. The role of the *SMH* member had switched: those who once criticized the echelons of academia themselves became authority figures. Regarding this concern and focusing on ordinary people's behaviour, he wrote a book on the Nazi regime, depicting how and why the supporters of the SPD had turned into the ardent followers of Nazis.³⁴

The approach 'history from below' embraced by the members of *SMH* led to a collaborative effort to translate works of social history promoted by Hiroyuki Ninomiya, an intimate younger friend of Shibata, who, as a historian studying French social-economic history, was interested in the Annales school's works, especially those of Marc Bloch.³⁵ Also Norihiko Fukui, whose first research project was on the anarchist movement during the era of the First International, was influenced by the social history approach during his stay in France. He translated many works based on such an approach and wrote introductory works after returning to Japan.³⁶ In later years he went further to write several well-balanced works on the theory of history.³⁷ In the intellectual autobiography in *History as Memory, Memory as History*, he admits that his conversion to a generalist of historiography derived in part from understanding the limits of studying foreign history during a sojourn in France.³⁸

The trajectories of the members of *SMH* were diverse. Kazuhiko Kondo started his career as a historian by writing essays on the food riots in England, referring to E.P. Thompson's notion of 'moral economy'.³⁹ However, he was critical of leaving out the traditional socio-economic approach, because he gained a formative understanding of Marxism and Weberian ideas during his student years. He wrote many excellent works that deserved high academic accolade, and this in part sanctioned his professorship in the European history department of the University of Tokyo as a successor of Shibata – that is to say he went 'from outsider to insider', according to Kimura, who also became professor at the same institution. Utilizing his authority among academics, Kondo promoted several projects – one of which was a series of monographs on modern and contemporary European history, which he edited with Fukui.⁴⁰ Kondo states that these studies paved the way for new historical research that combined innovative approaches.⁴¹

The experience of the last contributor to chapter 2, Minoru Tanigawa, differs from the others in that he belonged to the University of Kyoto, where the Zenkyoto movement was started by a few students and was more radical. After he joined the Zenkyoto movement, Tanigawa participated in the *SMH* group but sometimes criticized its mainstream outlook. As the subtitle of his essay suggests, he welcomed the transition from a social movement history to social history.⁴² With this in mind, he founded the Society of Modern Society Research with Masatoshi Miich, who wrote an excellent monograph on the history of disease later.⁴³ Together with younger historians, Tanigawa discovered new paths for historical research. This made him introduce Pierre Nora's concept of *Les Lieux de Mémoire* when he became professor of the University of Kyoto.⁴⁴

The Post-Zenkyoto Movement Generation

The contributors of chapter 3 had no direct experience of the Zenkyoto movement because they were born from 1948 to 1965. The exception was Norie Ishii, who joined it at Tokyo University's Komaba campus for general education. He studied the USSR regime after the 1917 Revolution, focusing on the origins of the 'party-state constitution'. But his intention was not only to criticize the USSR regime but to explain why its ideology disseminated rapidly across the planet. He regarded the USSR as a civilization that had a major cultural influence on the twentieth century.⁴⁵ In his paper in chapter 3, he explains how the burden of the Russian Revolution influenced Japanese historiography after the war. Though founded on Rankean positivism, the ideological implications were latent in Japanese historiography even after the war. However, he casts doubt about the tendency that prefers history without any intellectual perspective and concludes that history cannot leave out politics if it wants to problematize itself.⁴⁶

The other contributors did not join the Zenkyoto movement directly. However, Masahide Ishizuka and Kiyoshi Hara, born in 1949 and 1953, belong to the generation to which the influence of the movement was considerable. Ishizuka's career is unique because he graduated from a night university as a student worker. Ishizuka established himself as a self-made scholar and wrote a short book on Blanqui and Weitling.⁴⁷ He joined *SMH* for a short while after writing it but disagreed with its academic direction and started to organize a research group for other postgraduate students. Admitting that he was influenced by *SMH*, he insists on the importance of the common knowledge of history held by ordinary people, which could be called historiosophy.⁴⁸ Kiyoshi Hara was a high school student during the Zenkyoto events. After graduating from a local high school, he entered Tokyo Foreign Language University where he studied under Kato, a visiting lecturer then. After graduation, he strengthened his interest in minority groups, which made him choose multilingualism as his subject. Hara writes that his interest in the ethnographical and anthropological approach prepared him for his role as a proponent of cultural history in Japan.⁴⁹

The last four contributors, Naoki Odanaka, Takahiko Hasegawa and Tetsuya Yamane, born in 1963, 1963 and 1965, and Ryuichi Narita, in 1951, are historians who pen excellent monographs on specific subjects. Yet they have also made the theory of history an important topic and wrote distinguished works on it. This is why they were chosen as the contributors to discuss the meanings of *SMH* and its members' works. Odanaka is a historian of French economics influenced by Tadami Chizuka, an intimate friend of Shibata and Ninomiya.[50] Odanaka points out that the *SMH* group could not invert the development of historiography, because social movement history on which they relied was originated by New Left historians like E.P. Thompson. Social history to which some of the members turned was also the method that had first been introduced by Ninomiya and others who belonged to the earlier generation. In this sense, the members of SMH are followers of former generations. Odanaka argues that they returned to the earlier approaches eventually.[51] Likewise Hasegawa, a student of Kondo at the University of Tokyo, an expert for the New Left historians, points out the similarity between the approaches of New Left thinkers and the *SMH* group. However, Hasegawa finds in these approaches, adopted by the *SMH*, a trend that is becoming important in historiography, which is the resuscitation of agency.[52] Yamane, a student of Kimura, who applied E.P. Thompson's approach to the study of food riots in Germany,[53] summarized the transformation of historical research after the war. He claims that the younger generation can learn much from the fact that the concern about the present was an underlying trend in Japanese historiography and a main concern of *SMH*.[54]

Narita, who wrote many distinguished historiographies on contemporary Japanese history that made much of the view from the periphery, concludes chapter 3 by insisting that the role of *SMH* was significant in that it attempted to build the method for studying social movement history that was lost in the 1970s and 1980s in Japanese history research. This was because many of the historiographical works in Japan were firmly embedded within academia and as such relied on naive positivistic research to the detriment of other tentative approaches. Narita argues that *SMH* played an integral role in Japanese historical studies, with its overall significance still worthy of reconsideration today.[55]

SMH Historians as Engaged Intellectuals

In this chapter I introduced an aspect of historical studies in postwar Japan by focusing on historians who first joined *SMH* and produced a variety of works on European modern and contemporary history in later years.

After they had experienced an era of political student struggle, they began their early careers as historians by making social movement history their main subject and publishing *SMH*. As they established themselves as professional historians, they turned to a variety of new topics influenced by new 'trends' from abroad. In this process, 'movements' faded out from their works although a few continued to make the history of movements their chief subject and did not lose their concern for contemporary politics as is mentioned in the essays in *History as Memory, Memory as History*. Some of them still today join movements, such as for the abolition of nuclear reactor plants, and oppose reactionary policies, like the strengthening of governmental control on history education.

The trajectories of the historians that joined *SMH* are diverse. This in part stems from the agreement among them when *SMH* was started. 'Associate together for the same purpose but respect each other's individual thought and behaviour' was the principle of the student movements in the late 1960s that inspired the publication of *SMH*. In the preface to *History as Memory, Memory as History*, I wrote that

> The differences of the members might be explained in terms of the differences of the generations, their political thought and attitude to historical studies. However, such differences made the discussion among them more viable and fertile. The principles of free and voluntary association assisted it further. Such diversity provided the energy to make its activities more significant.[56]

To conclude, experience is the matrix of historians' works. What they experienced and how they keep it in mind often decides what they write. However, memory changes as time passes. And so does the history written by them. *SMH* represents an attempt to criticize conventional history during an age when the memory of the movements was fresh in the collective mind. As was introduced in this chapter, the historians who once joined *SMH* accumulated experiences as time went by and, inspired by these new experiences, extended their research fields and introduced 'new ways' into the discipline. Their works now extend across all domains of historical studies including social, cultural, anthropological, linguistic and global.[57] Their contributions on historiography have been significant, and the historians of the younger generations are greatly influenced by them – that is to say, by those who have authority in the discipline. Those who once were engaged in the movements that criticized the institutionalized discipline have become established historians.

Does it mean that they are not politically engaged anymore? What we can say is 'Yes' and 'No'. On the one hand, in a sense they are engaged, especially with regard to the specific problems in historiography as professional intellectuals. On the other hand, the answer is negative because there is no actual connection with the movement theoretically or practically speaking. I am not sure which answer we should take. As I put it at the start of the chapter, what determines the works of historians pertains to the present conditions surrounding them. Such work should be evaluated not only in terms of how innovative it appears but also the criticisms and questions it raises vis-à-vis the present condition. A decreased interest in social movement history in Japan in some ways reflects the present state of affairs – that is to say, 'society with fewer movements than before'. Historians have to consider in what conditions they were and are, then and now. It is their responsibility as engaged intellectuals.

Michihiro Okamoto is Emeritus Professor of Toyo University in Japan. He studied English social movement history, specifically the Chartist movement, at first, and wrote several articles on it. He translated Dorothy Thomson's *The Chartists* into Japanese with Hideo Koga and played an important role in publishing the journal *Shakai Undo-shi* (*Social Movement History*). He has also published several books and articles on the theory of history, beginning with *History in the Borderless Age* (Kindai Bungeisha, 1993). His recent books are *Making History Open: What is There beyond Deconstruction* (Ochanomizu Shobo, 2013) and *Past and Histories: Far from Nationality and Modernity* (Ochanomizu Shobo, 2018). He also co-edited *History as Memory, Memory as History: Social Movement History 1970–1985* (Ochanomizu Shobo, 2013) and *Shooting History: Linguistic Turn, Cultural History, Public History & National History* (Ochanomizu Shobo, 2015).

Notes

1. Most of the books and articles introduced in this chapter are written in Japanese only and have Japanese titles, which have been translated into English for readers' convenience. With regard to translated works, the original titles are referred to, but in the case of an anthology the titles are those of Japanese versions. *Social Movement History* (SMH), no. 1–10, 1972–1985, Tokyo: Society for the Study of Social Movement History.

2. The first articles published in *SMH* by the historians who will be mentioned in this chapter are the following: Kinoshita, 'People's Movement on the Eve of the Paris Commune', 1 (1972); Kimura, 'The Situations in the Age of Fascism', 1 (1972); Kitahara, 'Fascism and the Communist Party: Italia in the 1920s', 2 (1973); Kondo, 'People's Movement on the Eve of the Industrial Revolution: Manchester, 1757–1758', 2 (1973) and 4 (1974); Kiyasu, 'Comments on the Review of Revolutionary Syndicalism', 2 (1973); Yamamoto, 'Anton Pannekoek and the SPD in Bremen', 3 (1973); Fujimoto, 'On Brest-Litowsk Peace Treaty: Armistice', 3 (1973); Tanigawa, 'The Position of Allmanisme in Terms of the Interpretation of Syndicalism', 3 (1973); Fukui, 'History of Anarchist Groups of the First International', 4 (1974) and 5 (1975); Okamoto, 'Chartism after 1848: From Democratic Conference to the 1851 New Program', 4 (1974); Kato, 'On the Methods of Social Movement History', 6 (1977); Ishii, 'Making of the Party-State Constitution in Revolutionary Russia', 9 (1981). This

list will help the readers understand what topics of the European social movement history they were initially interested in.

3. The idea of this attempt is similar to Munslow, *Authoring the Past: Writing and Rethinking History*.

4. Domanska, 'Interview with Hayden White', 35.

5. Carr, *What is History*.

6. Many books have been written on postwar Japan in English and Japanese. The recommendable books recently written in English, of which translated versions have a good reputation among Japanese readers is Dower, *Embracing Defeat: Japan in the Wake of World War II*.

7. A female student in the history department of the University of Tokyo, a colleague of the contributors to chapter 1, Kato and Kitahara, was killed during the confrontation with the police on 15 June.

8. Oguma, *1968*. Oguma also analysed the ways of thinking that were particular to postwar Japan, focusing on the relationship between postwar democracy and nationalism. See Oguma, *Democracy and Patriotism: Nationalism and Publicness in Postwar Japan*.

9. Maruyama, *Thought and Behaviour in Modern Japanese Politics*.

10. Otsuka liked to use the word 'modernization' as his book's title. Otsuka, *Historical Starting Point of Modernization*; Otsuka, *Human Foundation of Modernization*.

11. Nagahara, *Historiography in the 20th Century Japan*; Suda, *Until a Breakdown of the Icon: The History of Popular Movements in Postwar Historiography*; Narita, *Modern and Contemporary Japanese History and Historiography: Past under Rewriting*.

12. Uehara, *The New Making of World View*.

13. Eguchi, *Imperialism and Ethnicity*.

14. Kiyasu, 'Ankle against Hammer: From Postwar Historiography to Popular Movement History'; Kiyasu, *A Story of a Boy around the Shadow of the Emperor: An Autobiography during and Post War Japan*.

15. Kiyasu, *Revolutionary Syndicalism*; Kiyasu et al., 'On Revolutionary Syndicalism'.

16. Kiyasu, *Saint Monday in Paris*.

17. Kato, '"Long 1960s": My Experience of the Turning Period of Historical Consciousness and World Knowledge'.

18. Kitahara, 'On the Period of Starting the Bulletin'; Kitahara, *Study on Contemporary History of Italia*.

19. Kikuchi, *Stalin Age as History*.

20. Fujimoto, 'The Foundation of "*SHM*"'.

21. Nagao, *History of the Russian Revolution*; 'The Problem of Ethnicity in Japan'; Nagao, 'Closing Japan'.

22. Kato, '"Long 1960s"'.

23. Thompson, *New Left*.

24. Hobsbawn, *Labouring Men*; Hobsbawn, *The Age of Revolution*; Hobsbawn, *The Primitive Rebels*; Hobsbawn, *The Bandits*.

25. Thompson, *The Making of English Working Classes*.

26. Lefebvre, *Les paysans du Nord pendant la Révolution française*; Lefebvre, *Études sur la révolution française*; Rudé, *The Crowds in the French Revolution*.

27. Shibata, *On the Absolute Monarchy of France*.

28. Shibata, *Babeuf's Conspiracy*; Shibata translated Lefebvre's *Les paysans du Nord* (1958) and *Quatre-vingt-neuf* (1975).

29. Sagara, 'French Socialist Movement in 1890s'; Sagara, 'For the Method of Social Movement History'.

30. Sagara, 'Probing in the Darkness'.

31. Kinoshita, 'People's Movement on the Eve of the Paris Commune'.

32. Kinoshita, 'Let it Be: The 1960s and "*SMH*"'.

33. Kimura, 'From Outsider to Insider'; Kimura, *Soldiers' Revolution: Germany in 1918*.

34. Yamamoto, 'History in the Age of Everything Turned Back on Ourselves'; Yamamoto, *Memory of Nazism*.

35. Ninomiya, who majored in medieval history, played a great role in introducing the main Annales works with Koichi Kabayama, professor of the University of Tokyo. Many members of *SMH*, such as Nirihiko Fukui, Masatoshi Sagara, Kenichi Kinoshita and Minoru Tanigawa, helped with his work. Ninomiya, Kabayama and Fukui, *Selected Essays of Annales School*.

36. Delon, *Le temps des prisons*; Loux, *Le jeune enfant et son corps dans la medicine traditionelle*; Braudel, *Une leçon d'histoire*; Perrot, *Les femmes dans l'histoire de la France contemporaine*; Ariès, *Images de l'homme devant la mort*; Duby, *Amour et sexualité en Occident*; Fukui, *A Social History of Time and Customs*. Fukui also translated the works of Michel Foucault, Pierre Bourdieu and Roger Chartier as anthologies.

37. Fukui, *Introduction to the Study of History*.

38. Fukui, 'Self-portrait of a Historian Written on the Fragments of Memory'.

39. Kondo, 'People's Movement on the Eve of the Industrial Revolution' (1973 and 1974).

40. Kondo, *Moral of the People*; Kimura, 'From Outsider to Insider'.

41. Kondo, '"*SMH* Group as 1970s' Phenomenon"'.

42. Tanigawa, 'Remaining Shadow of the Zenkyoto Movement and Historians: From Social Movement History to Social History'.

43. Miichi, *Cholera in World History*. Miichi, born in 1946, was originally a student of Chushichi Tsuzuki, who published *H.M. Hyndmann and the British Socialism* (1961), which was one of the first works written in English by a Japanese historian.

44. Nora, *Les Lieux de Mémoire*.

45. Ishii, *The USSR as Civilization*.

46. Ishii, 'Historiosophy of the Age of Soviet-Russia and "*SMH*"'.

47. Ishizuka, *Rebels and Revolution: Note on Blanqui & Weitling*. This was written under the influence of Chikara Rachi, who wrote an intellectual biography of the 'opponents' of Marx, including Weitling. Rachi was critical of Marx-centred intellectual history. He developed his critical viewpoint to historiography further and wrote an interesting book on the March Revolution in 1848 by using a variety of leaflets, posters and bills distributed among the people. Rachi, *Marx and Portraits of His Opponents*; Rachi, *The Orgy on the Riverside of the Blue Danube: Vienna in 1848*.

48. Ishizuka, 'The Home Range That Fructifies Historiosophy'.

49. Hara, 'My "*SMH*" Experience'.

50. Tadami Chizuka's major was French socio-economic history and the French Revolution. His voluminous book on the theory of history, which he left as his life's work, honestly reflects the problems a theory-inclined positivist historian like him faced in his later life when the social history and linguistic turn became prevalent. Chizuka, *General Theory of Historiography*.

51. Odanaka, 'Rehabilitation of "*SMH*"'.

52. Hasegawa, '"*SMH*" and New Left Historiography'.

53. Yamane, *Bread and People: Moral Economy in Nineteenth-century Prussia*.

54. Yamane, 'Considering the "Question to History": The Method and the Present Condition of Historical Studies'.

55. Narita, '"Lost 1980s" in the Study of Japanese History'.

56. Okamoto, 'Preface', ii.

57. The historians introduced in this chapter translated many works on European modern and contemporary history. There is not enough space to list them all precisely, so only the authors, the titles, the translators and published years are introduced here. *Collected Works*

of Rosa Luxemburg, 4 vols. (Kiyasu et al., 1962–63); Selected Works of Blanqui, 2 vols. (Kato, 1967); P.O. Lissagaray, L'histoire de la Commune de 1871 (Kiyasu and Osabe, 1968–9); Collected Works of Trotsky, 2nd ed., 6 vols. (Fujimoto et al., 1969); K. Korsch, Schriften zur Sozialisierung (Kimura and Yamamoto, 1971); G. Lefranc, Le syndicalisme en France (Tanigawa, 1974), B. Lazitch and M.M. Drachkovitch, Lenin and the Comintern, vol.1 (Fujimoto et al., 1977); D. Thompson, The Chartists (Okamoto and Hideo Koga, 1988); A. de Tocqueville, Souvenirs (Kiyasu, 1988); R.A. Medvedev, The October Revolution (Ishii, 1989); D. Peukert, Volksgenossen und Gemeinschaftsfremde (Kimura and Yamamoto, 1991); Nove, An Economic History of the U.S.S.R., 1917–1991 (Ishii et al., 1992); M. Vovelle, La révolution contre l'église (Tanigawa et al., 1992); L. Chevalier, Classes laborieuses et classes dangereuses à Paris, pendant la première moitié du XIXe siècle (Kiyasu and Sagara, 1993); P. Burke, New Perspectives on Historical Writing (Tanigawa et al., 1996); M. Nadaud, Mémoires de Leonard: ancien garçon maçon (Kiyasu, 1997); A. Guttman, Games & Empires (Tanigawa, 1997); M. Raeff, Comprendre l'ancien régime russe (Ishii, 2001); N. Werth, La Russie en révolution (Ishii et al., 2004); W. Doyle, The ancien regime (Fukui, 2004); K. Jenkins, Re-thinking History, (Okamoto, 2005); J.-L. Menetra, Journal de ma vie (Kiyasu, 2006); A. Porter, European Imperialism, 1860–1914 (Fukui, 2006); S. Hoffmann, Civil Society, 1750–1914 (Yamamoto, 2009); O. Zimmer, Nationalism in Europe, 1890–1940 (Fukui, 2009). In addition, Kondo translated the works of E.P. Thompson and Peter Burke; Okamoto those of Hayden White and Peter Burke in journals. The above list clearly shows the extensive knowledge and wide array of interests of the SMH members. Although their first works of translation concentrated on the works of the opponents of mainstream Marxism-Leninism, history of institutionalized movements and memoirs of militants, they gradually moved to works of 'history from below', lives of ordinary people, and social history. In addition, several general works on modern and contemporary history and historiography have been penned recently.

Bibliography

Ariès, P. Images de l'homme devant la mort. Tokyo: Japan Editors School, 1990.
Braudel, F. Une leçon d'histoire, trans. N. Fukui. Tokyo: Shinyosha, 1987.
Carr, E.H. What is History. London: Macmillan, 1961.
Chizuka, T. General Theory of Historiography. Tokyo: Tokyo University Press, 2011.
Chushichi, T. (ed.). H.M. Hyndmann and the British Socialism. Oxford: Oxford University Press, 1961.
Deyon, P. Le temps des prisons, trans. N. Fukui and M. Matsumoto. Tokyo: Shinhyoron, 1982.
Domanska, E. 'Interview with Hayden White', in E. Domanska (ed.), Encounters: Philosophy of History after Postmodernism. Charlottesville/London: University Press of Virginia, 1998.
Dower, J.W. Embracing Defeat: Japan in the Wake of World War II. New York: W.W. Norton, 1999.
Duby, G. Amour et sexualité en Occident, trans. N. Fukui and M. Matsumoto. Tokyo: Shinyosha, 1993.
Eguchi, B. Imperialism and Ethnicity. Tokyo: Tokyo University Press, 1954.
Fujimoto, W. 'On Brest-Litowsk Peace Treaty: Armistice', Social Movement History 3 (1973), 26–46.
———. 'The Foundation of "SHM"', in A. Kiyasu, A. Kitahara, M. Okamoto and M. Tanigawa (eds), History as Memory, Memory as History: Social Movement History, 1970–1985 (Tokyo: Ochanomizu Shobo, 2013), 84–97.
Fukui, N. 'History of Anarchist Groups of the First International', Social Movement History 4 (1974), 59–92.

———. 'History of Anarchist Groups of the First International', *Social Movement History* 5 (1975), 66–92.

———. *A Social History of Time and Customs*. Tokyo: Shinyosha, 1986.

———. 'Self-portrait of a Historian Written on the Fragments of Memory', in A. Kiyasu, A. Kitahara, M. Okamoto and M. Tanigawa (eds), *History as Memory, Memory as History: Social Movement History, 1970–1985* (Tokyo: Ochanomizu Shobo, 2013), 157–75.

———. *Introduction to the Study of History*. Tokyo: Iwanami Shoten, 2006.

Hara, K. 'My "*SMH*" Experience', in A. Kiyasu, A. Kitahara, M. Okamoto and M. Tanigawa (eds), *History as Memory, Memory as History: Social Movement History, 1970–1985* (Tokyo: Ochanomizu Shobo, 2013), 253–60.

Hasegawa, T. '"*SMH*" and New Left Historiography', in A. Kiyasu, A. Kitahara, M. Okamoto and M. Tanigawa (eds), *History as Memory, Memory as History: Social Movement History, 1970–1985* (Tokyo: Ochanomizu Shobo, 2013), 274–85.

Hobsbawn, E.J. *Labouring Men*, trans. M. Suzuki and Y. Nagai. Kyoto: Minerva Shobo, 1968.

———. *The Age of Revolution*, trans. E. Yasukawa and H. Mizuta. Tokyo: Iwanami Shoten, 1968.

———. *The Primitive Rebels*, trans. T. Aoki. Tokyo: Chuo Koronsha, 1971.

———. *The Bandits*, trans. S. Saito. Tokyo: Misuzu Shobo, 1972.

Ishii, N. 'Making of the Party-State Constitution in Revolutionary Russia', *Social Movement History* 9 (1981), 21–39.

———. *The USSR as Civilization*. Tokyo: Yamakawa Shuppansha, 1995.

———. 'Historiosophy of the Age of Soviet-Russia and "*SMH*"', in A. Kiyasu, A. Kitahara, M. Okamoto and M. Tanigawa (eds), *History as Memory, Memory as History: Social Movement History, 1970–1985* (Tokyo: Ochanomizu Shobo, 2013), 215–45.

Ishizuka, M. *Rebels and Revolution: Note on Blanqui & Weitling*. Tokyo: Izara Shobo, 1975.

———. 'The Home Range that Fructifies Historiosophy', in A. Kiyasu, A. Kitahara, M. Okamoto and M. Tanigawa (eds), *History as Memory, Memory as History: Social Movement History, 1970–1985* (Tokyo: Ochanomizu Shobo, 2013), 246–52.

Kato, H. 'On the Methods of Social Movement History', *Social Movement History* 6 (1977), 56–62.

———. '"Long 1960s": My Experience of the Turning Period of Historical Consciousness and World Knowledge', in A. Kiyasu, A. Kitahara, M. Okamoto and M. Tanigawa (eds), *History as Memory, Memory as History: Social Movement History, 1970–1985* (Tokyo: Ochanomizu Shobo, 2013), 37–67.

Kikuchi, M. *Stalin Age as History*. Tokyo: Morita Shoten, 1966.

Kimura, S. 'The Situations in the Age of Fascism', *Social Movement History* 1 (1972), 18–23.

———. *Soldiers' Revolution: Germany in 1918*. Tokyo: Tokyo University Press, 1988.

———. 'From Outsider to Insider', in A. Kiyasu, A. Kitahara, M. Okamoto and M. Tanigawa (eds), *History as Memory, Memory as History: Social Movement History, 1970–1985* (Tokyo: Ochanomizu Shobo, 2013), 101–13.

Kinoshita, K. 'People's Movement on the Eve of the Paris Commune', *Social Movement History* 1 (1972), 1–17.

———. 'Let it Be: The 1960s and "*SMH*"', in A. Kiyasu, A. Kitahara, M. Okamoto and M. Tanigawa (eds), *History as Memory, Memory as History: Social Movement History, 1970–1985* (Tokyo: Ochanomizu Shobo, 2013), 147–56.

Kitahara, A. 'Fascism and the Communist Party: Italia in the 1920s', *Social Movement History* 2 (1973), 1–20.

———. *Study on Contemporary History of Italia*. Tokyo: Iwanami Shoten, 2002.

———. 'On the Period of Starting the Bulletin', in A. Kiyasu, A. Kitahara, M. Okamoto and M. Tanigawa (eds), *History as Memory, Memory as History: Social Movement History, 1970–1985* (Tokyo: Ochanomizu Shobo, 2013), 68–83.

Kiyasu, A. *Revolutionary Syndicalism*. Tokyo: Gogatsusha, 1971.
———. *Saint Monday in Paris*. Tokyo: Heibonsha, 1982.
———. 'Comments on the Review of Revolutionary Syndicalism', *Social Movement History* 2 (1973), 87–99.
———. *A Story of a Boy around the Shadow of the Emperor: An Autobiography during and Post War Japan*. Tokyo: Tosui Shobo, 2003.
———. 'Ankle against Hammer: From Postwar Historiography to Popular Movement History', in A. Kiyasu, A. Kitahara, M. Okamoto and M. Tanigawa (eds), *History as Memory, Memory as History: Social Movement History, 1970–1985* (Tokyo: Ochanomizu Shobo, 2013), 5–36.
Kiyasu, A. et al. 'On Revolutionary Syndicalism', *Social Movement History* 1 (1972), 24–32.
Kiyasu, A., A. Kitahara, M. Okamoto and M. Tanigawa (eds). *History as Memory, Memory as History: 'Social Movement History' 1970–1985*. Tokyo: Ochanomizu Shobo, 2013.
Kondo, K. 'People's Movement on the Eve of the Industrial Revolution: Manchester, 1757–1758', *Social Movement History* 3 (1973), 38–62 and 4 (1974), 125–70.
———. 'People's Movement on the Eve of the Industrial Revolution', *Social Movement History* 2 (1973), 38–62 and 4 (1974), 125–70.
———. *Moral of the People*. Tokyo: Yamakawa Shuppansha, 1993.
———. '"*SMH* Group as 1970s' Phenomenon"', in A. Kiyasu, A. Kitahara, M. Okamoto and M. Tanigawa (eds), *History as Memory, Memory as History: Social Movement History, 1970–1985* (Tokyo: Ochanomizu Shobo, 2013), 170–82.
Lefebvre, G. *Les paysans du Nord*, trans. M. Shibata. Tokyo: Miraisha, 1958.
———. *Les paysans du Nord pendant la Révolution française*. Bari: Laterza, 1959.
———. *Études sur la révolution française*. Paris: Presses universitaires de France, 1963.
———. *Quatre-vingt-neuf*, trans. M. Shibata. Tokyo: Miraisha, 1975.
Loux, F. *Le jeune enfant et son corps dans la medicine traditionelle*, trans. N. Fukui. Tokyo: Shinhyoron, 1983.
Maruyama, M. *Thought and Behaviour in Modern Japanese Politics*. Tokyo: Miraisha, 1955–56.
Miichi, M. *Cholera in World History*. Tokyo: Kodansha, 1998.
Munslow, A. (ed.). *Authoring the Past: Writing and Rethinking History*. London/New York: Routledge, 2013.
Nagahara, K. *Historiography in the 20th Century Japan*. Tokyo: Yoshikawa Kobunkan, 2003.
Nagao, H. *History of the Russian Revolution*. Tokyo: Shakaishisosha, 1968.
———. 'The Problem of Ethnicity in Japan', *Social Movement History* 5 (1975), 43–65.
———. 'Closing Japan', *Social Movement History* 7 (1978), 70–82.
Narita, R. *Modern and Contemporary Japanese History and Historiography: Past under Rewriting*. Tokyo: Chuokoron Shinsha, 2012.
———. '"Lost 1980s" in the Study of Japanese History', in A. Kiyasu, A. Kitahara, M. Okamoto and M. Tanigawa (eds), *History as Memory, Memory as History: Social Movement History, 1970–1985* (Tokyo: Ochanomizu Shobo, 2013), 299–313.
Ninomiya, N., K. Kabayama and N. Fukui (eds). *Selected Essays of Annales School*, 4 volumes., Tokyo: Shinhyoronsha, 1982–1985.
Nora, P. *Les Lieux de Mémoire*, 4 volumes. Tokyo: Iwanami Shoten, 2002–2003.
Odanaka, N. 'Rehabilitation of "*SMH*"', in A. Kiyasu, A. Kitahara, M. Okamoto and M. Tanigawa (eds), *History as Memory, Memory as History: Social Movement History, 1970–1985* (Tokyo: Ochanomizu Shobo, 2013), 261–73.
Oguma, E. *Democracy and Patriotism: Nationalism and Publicness in Postwar Japan*. Tokyo: Shinyosha, 2002.
———. *1968*. Tokyo: Shinyosha, 2009.
Okamoto, M. 'Chartism after 1848: From Democratic Conference to the 1851 New Program', *Social Movement History* 4 (1974), 171–208.

———. 'After Editing', in A. Kiyasu, A. Kitahara, M. Okamoto and M. Tanigawa (eds), *History as Memory, Memory as History: Social Movement History, 1970–1985* (Tokyo: Ochanomizu Shobo, 2013), 315–22.

Otsuka. H. *Historical Starting Point of Modernization*. Tokyo: Gakusei Shobo, 1948.

———. *Human Foundation of Modernization*. Tokyo: Chikuma Shobo, 1968.

Perrot, M. *Les femmes dans l'histoire de la France contemporaine*, trans. N. Fukui and H. Kaneko. Tokyo: Japan Editors School, 1989.

Rachi, C. *Marx and Portraits of His Opponents*. Tokyo: Heibonsha, 1971.

———. *The Orgy on the Riverside of the Blue Danube: Vienna in 1848*. Tokyo: Heibonsha, 1975.

Rudé, G. *The Crowds in the French Revolution*. Oxford: Oxford Press, 1959.

Sagara, M. 'French Socialist Movement in 1890s', *Social Movement History* 4 (1974), 1–57.

———. 'For the Method of Social Movement History', *Social Movement History* 6 (1977), 72–92.

———. 'Probing in the Darkness', in A. Kiyasu, A. Kitahara, M. Okamoto and M. Tanigawa (eds), *History as Memory, Memory as History: Social Movement History, 1970–1985* (Tokyo: Ochanomizu Shobo, 2013), 133–46.

Shibata, M. *On the Absolute Monarchy of France*. Tokyo: Ochanomizu Shobo, 1960.

———. *Babeuf's Conspiracy*. Tokyo: Iwanami Shoten, 1968.

Suda, T. *Until a Breakdown of the Icon: The History of Popular Movements in Postwar Historiography*. Tokyo: Aoki Shoten, 2008.

Tanigawa, M. 'The Position of Allmanisme in Terms of the Interpretation of Syndicalism', *Social Movement History* 3 (1973), 123–47.

———. 'Remaining Shadow of the Zenkyoto Movement and Historians: From Social Movement History to Social History', in A. Kiyasu, A. Kitahara, M. Okamoto and M. Tanigawa (eds), *History as Memory, Memory as History: Social Movement History, 1970–1985* (Tokyo: Ochanomizu Shobo, 2013), 183–211.

Thompson, E.P. (ed.). *New Left*, trans. K. Fukada et al. Tokyo: Iwanami Shoten, 1963.

Thompson, E.P. *The Making of English Working Classes*, trans. K. Haga and H. Ichihashi. Tokyo: Seikyusha, 2003.

Uehara, S. *The New Making of World View*. Tokyo: Sobunsha, 1955.

Yamamoto, H. 'Anton Pannekoek and the SPD in Bremen', *Social Movement History* 3 (1973), 1–25.

———. *Memory of Nazism*. Tokyo: Yamakawa Shuppansha, 1998.

———. 'History in the Age of Everything Turned Back on Ourselves', in A. Kiyasu, A. Kitahara, M. Okamoto and M. Tanigawa (eds), *History as Memory, Memory as History: Social Movement History, 1970–1985* (Tokyo: Ochanomizu Shobo, 2013), 114–32.

Yamane, T. *Bread and People: Moral Economy in Nineteenth-century Prussia*. Tokyo: Yamakawa Shuppansha, 2003.

———. 'Considering the "Question to History": The Method and the Present Condition of Historical Studies', in A. Kiyasu, A. Kitahara, M. Okamoto and M. Tanigawa (eds), *History as Memory, Memory as History: Social Movement History, 1970–1985* (Tokyo: Ochanomizu Shobo, 2013), 286–97.

CHAPTER 10

Professional Historical Writing and Human Rights Engagement in the Twenty-First Century
Innovative Approaches and Their Dilemmas

Nina Schneider

This chapter addresses a broad and complex question that has preoccupied me for some years now: how can engaged historians best contribute to both high quality research and the advancement of human rights? Is it possible to reconcile historical professionalism (a term that in itself requires a definition) with a genuine engagement with human rights? If not, are there particular situations or conditions that make it possible to reconcile these two objectives?

In order to clarify what is meant by 'engagement', this chapter starts by offering three defining characteristics of an 'engaged historian'. The subsequent section discusses a very specific kind of engagement, by introducing a new and rapidly growing field of studies called the 'historical accountability and dialogue' network, situated between history, memory and human rights studies. The historian Klaus Neumann convened a constitutive conference focusing on this area in February 2012 in Melbourne, but it is more commonly associated with Elazar Barkan's (2009) call to historians to actively engage in processes of historical justice through contributing to a new 'shared narrative' about a violent past that transcends the traditional conflict lines (discussed further later).[1] Neumann, Barkan and others working in the area of human rights and memory studies are

---

Notes for this section begin on page 216.

currently building up a new network of engaged scholars, 'Dialogues on Historical Justice and Memory' (formerly the Historical Justice and Memory Network), which is delineated at the end of the second section together with the resources it offers to academics specializing in this field. While Barkan's peace-building goals are noble and worthwhile, the practical and theoretical challenges to this approach loom large. The last section uses the example of post-authoritarian Brazil to illustrate a historian's dilemma in writing about contentious cases and poses a series of questions: is it possible to adhere to the highest standards of historical scholarship while simultaneously supporting human rights values and practices? Must historians choose between prioritizing historical professionalism over human rights? What if they are visionaries aiming to move beyond the mere technical craft of a historian?

Three Meanings of Engagement

In this chapter I focus on three defining characteristics of the 'engaged' historian: sensitivity towards contemporary and future challenges; a research agenda; and the historian's capacity to self-critically revisit his/her own assumptions. Firstly, an 'engaged' historian requires sensitivity towards contemporary issues and those of the immediate future. Engaged historians are tasked with investigating and making intelligible the defining characteristics, developments and key problems of their own era; a daunting challenge, given that historians are simultaneously living in this era and thus lack the luxury of hindsight. The second defining feature of engagement, the research agenda, relates to a historian's personal and, more importantly, social motivation for his/her research topic (and hence his/her approach). Engagement, as I understand it, means adopting a motif or assuming a societal role that moves *beyond* the mere technical production of knowledge (and personal career goals), to serve a larger purpose or vision, thus justifying the choice of research topic vis-à-vis society as a whole.

While engaged historical writing goes beyond a technocratic, empirically impeccable craft, it is nonetheless distinct from ideologically or politically biased history (an accusation often levelled by its critics).[2] Many scholars have criticized the highly problematic notion of 'scientific' historical writing and yet relativistic postmodernist thought continues to invoke the dichotomy between 'scientific' and 'engaged' or 'political' historical writing, both explicitly and implicitly.[3] Attacks by postmodern 'relativists' may thus have revived this neat distinction; an idea that many historians formerly perceived as simplistic. Ultimately, this second defining characteristic of engagement relates to the founding values of historical writing. To counter the claims of 'scientific' historians on the one hand (alleging political bias) and 'postmodern' relativists (facts are irrelevant, all is invented and equally valid) on the other,[4] this chapter seeks to find a middle ground between ideological history and engaged historical writing that remains rooted in historical facts. As will become clear, however, the main challenge to engaged historical writing lies not in debates about facticity.

Although the malleable concept of 'human rights' is problematic in itself and has been frequently misused, the way that human rights are codified in declarations and decrees may offer useful guidelines for engaged historical writing, precisely because it facilitates impartial engagement, as human dignity transcends political, ideological, religious and national boundaries. This resonates with Jörn Rüsen's suggestion that, ultimately, historical judgment should be based on the concept of 'human dignity', and with the code of ethics for historians developed by Antoon de Baets, outlined in his *Responsible History*.[5] Yet my suggestion to posit human rights as the benchmark of historical judgment stems from more than a mere defensive stance against 'scientific' historical writings and clear dichotomies between 'scientific' and 'non-scientific' writing. I am aware that these pseudoscientific constructs are themselves a defensive reaction against relativistic postmodernists, who have attacked the very foundations of *history* as a discipline (a defence that, in principle, I endorse). However, I believe that adopting human rights as a basis offers a potential means of professionalizing the discipline by contributing to the production of historical knowledge itself. By conceptualizing 'knowledge' as constructed and necessarily 'political', it deconstructs notions of a 'technocratic', 'scientific' and apparently neutral discourse of events (arguments previously raised by Michel Foucault and numerous postcolonial theorists, including Edward Said and Gayatri Spivak). Claiming to produce 'apolitical', 'scientific' writing is, paradoxically, 'unscientific' because it overlooks the fact that the categories and concepts used are themselves constructed and unstable over time. Professional historical writing in the twenty-first century, therefore, needs to take this dimension of knowledge production into account.

Lastly, the dichotomy between 'scientific knowledge' and political experience is discredited by the examples of some of the brightest intellectuals and scholars from whose personal experience knowledge and innovative methods have emanated. The historian Georg G. Iggers is a case in point: his experience of exile from Nazi-Germany contributed to his pioneering critique of historicism.[6] In sum, I move beyond simply invoking standards of human rights to defy pseudoscientific claims and argue that even a basic principle for historical judgment such as this can contribute to knowledge (rather than invoking human rights solely on the basis of moral and ethical claims).

Besides sensitivity to contemporary concerns and a research agenda that extends beyond technocratic production of knowledge, a third defining characteristic of historians' intellectual engagement is their ability to critically revisit their own assumptions in the light of contemporary developments (self-reflexivity); a self-correcting capacity or process that prioritizes an altruistic cause rather than historians' egos or careers in a highly competitive academic environment. This aspect will be discussed further in the final part of this chapter because although it may appear obvious it can still confuse historians in the actual process of writing.

Barkan's Appeal and a New Researcher Network

Human Rights have formed a key subject of historical enquiry in the new millennium, spawning a wealth of recent studies.[7] One such pioneering study that both described and sought to explain the new global trend towards redressing the past was Elazar Barkan's *The Guilt of Nations* (2000), which is briefly outlined in the following section together with the key ideas developed in a subsequent article.[8] In trying to account for the recent wave of writing seeking to redress a violent past (a practice that he terms 'restitution'), Barkan notes two phenomena: an increasing human rights mobilization, on one hand, which began with the first wave of campaigns for minority rights between the 1950s and 1970s in the United States and later continued with the human rights claims of indigenous groups; and a new perspective that sees history and historical identity as 'constructed' or 'negotiated', on the other hand.[9] In Barkan's view, both these trends contributed to history assuming a new, more centre-stage role because it hence came to be seen 'as a formative political force', and as 'malleable', while the trend towards redressing the violent past served precisely to demonstrate that the process of renegotiating history was taking place.[10]

> Our histories shape our identities. This truism is particularly applicable in the postmodern and post-Cold War world, where an increasing number of groups and nations recognize the malleable nature of history and, on the basis of perceived historical rights, negotiate their own political space.[11]

According to Barkan, history in contemporary times – the postmodern and Cold War era – is increasingly (ab)used as a means of policymaking, and hence the process of engagement assumes greater urgency. Despite numerous contradictions in terms of developments in human rights, he observes that the world 'increasingly subscribes to a shared political culture, which pays greater attention to history as a formative political force'.[12]

Barkan even makes the audacious claim that this trend towards redressing the past has replaced realpolitik as the primary focus of international relations.[13] The Kosovo intervention in the 1990s, he argues, gave rise to a new moral era in human rights, and hence a world in which compliance with human rights was elevated to a kind of 'moral expectation' that opened up space for self-criticism, whereas formerly countries accused each other and whitewashed their own past.[14]

Barkan's bold theses invite many questions. For example, is the contemporary era actually characterized by an increased 'negotiation' of history or has history always been negotiated? Is the difference simply that the constructivist turn has better equipped us to detect, theorize and define such processes? Is a new global human rights *morality* really replacing realpolitik or are various moral claims, in particular those based on human rights, simply the ideal vehicle to disguise powerful political and economic interests (as has been the case in the past)? Or, to consider a concrete example that challenges Barkan's theory, was it not the case that the Federal Republic of Germany created the largest reparations programme in world history (Foundation Entschädigung, Versöhnung und Zukunft, EVZ) in order to permanently protect German multinational companies (mainly operating in the United States) from future criminal charges, thus safeguarding German exports – the powerhouse of the German (and arguably European) economy? And, can it be argued that even phenomena cited as explanations for the new global trend towards redress – pro-rights movements and a new understanding of 'fashioned' history – actually *explain* the changes or do they merely *describe* developments?

However, two points are key for addressing our overarching question of whether historians can reconcile high-quality historical writing and practical human rights advocacy.[15] Firstly, Barkan seeks to analyse his own era and identify its most salient societal concerns (in tandem with the first defining characteristic of engagement outlined previously). Undoubtedly, human rights violations remain a major global concern.[16] Most importantly, though, Barkan extended his ideas in an article published in the *American Historical Review* in 2009, which directly appeals to historians to engage in conflict resolution and reads like a historical manifesto. As this article arguably forms the basis of the Historical Dialogue network, it is worth revisiting some of its core arguments. The piece introduces a special issue on 'Truth and Reconciliation in History'.[17]

Barkan appeals to historians to abandon their ivory towers and 'employ their scholarship ... in a way that enables them to act as advocates in the cause of reconciliation'.[18] The proclaimed short-term goal is to 'delegitimize the nationalist (and often hateful) historical myths that feed ethnic and national xenophobia and conflict'.[19] By adopting the role of 'midwife', historians (both as scholars and historical activists) can be instrumental in giving birth to 'a narrative on which the [antagonistic] stakeholders can agree'.[20] The term 'shared narrative' is central to Barkan's argument, and he defines it as follows:

> a historical narrative that intertwines and brings closer the perspectives of two or more national histories that are in direct conflict. It is unlikely to be linear or monovocal and will most likely have distinct registers. There may be meta-agreement and a variety of interpretations about the local and the specifics, or the other way around. The aim of a shared narrative is to erase the dichotomies along national lines.[21]

Altogether it remains unclear exactly what is meant by the term – some kind of common set of narratives, perhaps? What it does *not* mean, however, is the necessity of forging a *single* 'compromise' narrative. The term is thus misleading because it should, if nothing else, refer to 'shared narratives' in the plural form. In Barkan's view these attempts at 'historical reconciliation' – multiparty conferences, historical commissions and workshops directed towards 'shared narrative(s)', including physical encounters with antagonist groups – form a third means of redress alongside prosecutions and truth commissions, one with the capacity to investigate the root causes of conflict and 'long-term memories of group animosity'.[22]

The Historical Dialogue and Accountability network's 2013 conference call for papers illustrates that Barkan's ideas directly translated into a definition of the new field.[23] Thus, Historical Dialogue and Accountability is 'a growing field of advocacy and scholarship' that '[supports post-conflict countries'] efforts … [to] come to terms with their pasts', that 'contests nationalist myths' and provides 'analysis of past violence'.[24] Methodologically, it aims to conduct 'empirical research' by analysing, in particular, how history is being misused while simultaneously seeking 'to acknowledge the victims' and 'enhance public discussion'. The network's website provides a wealth of information about the most recent scholarship, encompassing literature and experts in the field, events of interest to scholars and practitioners and organizations and related sites.[25]

Significantly, Barkan still holds on to 'rigorous' historical scholarship, acknowledging that this may constitute a problem: 'The challenge for historians is to write these narratives while maintaining the highest professional standards.'[26] This echoes the key question posed by this chapter: is it practically possible to write historical narratives that contribute to conflict resolution and support human rights on which antagonistic groups can agree? While Barkan's ideas are audacious, visionary and noble, some aspects remain vague and theoretical, possibly even naive. Moving beyond general theory to consider the concrete, empirical case of post-authoritarian Brazil helps to problematize this claim.

A Historian's Practical Dilemma: How to Write about Post-authoritarian Brazil?

To comprehend the dilemma, it is necessary to briefly revisit the Brazilian dictatorship and consider how Brazil has attempted to deal with its authoritarian past. On 31 March 1964, sectors of the Brazilian armed forces launched a coup against the democratically elected President João Goulart (Jango). The coup had manifold causes; in a nutshell, Brazil was in the midst of economic, fiscal and political crisis at the time, and powerful, mainly upper and middle class, interest groups opposed Jango's plans, particularly land reform.[27] The coup led to a dictatorship lasting twenty-one years that systematically committed human rights violations. The first official report from 2007 records 474 Brazilians as killed or disappeared.[28] It is estimated that a further 50,000 were imprisoned, 20,000 tortured, 10,000 exiled and several thousand purged.[29] These figures have only been slightly revised by Brazil's first official truth commission, the so-called Commissão Nacional de Verdade (National Truth Commission, hereafter CNV). The majority of victims were very young (between 16 and 25 years old) and from white, urban middle-class backgrounds. Violent repression generally involved selective targeting of organized political opposition groups, primarily those involved in the armed struggle.[30]

Brazil is still trying to come to terms with the legacy of its military past and has followed an unusual trajectory compared to its post-authoritarian Latin American neighbours, who instated truth commissions and punished perpetrators relatively quickly, albeit not without resistance.[31] Most scholars agree that the main obstacle for Brazil's reckoning process has been the 1979 Amnesty Law that grants impunity to human rights perpetrators and that has been neither revoked nor reinterpreted since the country's return to democracy.[32] More than just a judicial obstacle, the amnesty set the dominant cultural framework by emphasizing Brazil's need for 'reconciliation' (a highly problematic term because, as in most other post-authoritarian Latin American cases, it effectively became a euphemism for impunity or lack of accountability measures).[33]

While Brazil failed to punish torturers (although São Paulo state attorneys have recently filed criminal charges in a process that is still ongoing), the state nonetheless launched a two-step reparations programme (1995/2002), and several official truth-seeking initiatives including the Comissão Especial sobre Mortos e Desaparecidos Políticos (Special Commission on the Killed [or Dead] and Disappeared Political Activists), ratified in 1995, and the recent National Truth Commission (2012–2014). From 2006 onwards, the state introduced several further official memory initiatives commemorating the victims of the military regime.[34] However, neither the military nor the judiciary was reformed, and all the aforementioned accountability measures resulted from the decade-long struggle by the victims' families.[35]

Although between 2012 and 2014 Brazil experienced a moment of heightened attention towards the dictatorship, its reckoning process has been characterized by frictions. An in-depth analysis is beyond the scope of this chapter, but what matters is that this tension can only be understood in relation to the broader historical context.[36] For decades families fought tirelessly against a state indifferent or even hostile to their claims, and although eventually a truth commission was installed (twenty-seven years after formal democratization!), the conflicts have not abated. On the contrary, it is precisely this decade-long frustration that makes collaboration with the so-called Comissão Nacional de Verdade (CNV) – and historians' engagement with it – difficult. Among the most controversial aspects are the human rights community's criticism of the government's lack of political will, along with the denial of a voice to the victims and the lack of transparency. However, the issue that has attracted most condemnation is the refusal to reinterpret the 1979 Amnesty Law and punish former perpetrators.

What is important for our purposes is that this antagonistic setting, involving multiple layers of conflict, can be compared to a *minefield* in two ways: first, regarding power relations between the antagonists in the present; but second, in terms of the wider historical context (the dominant narrative mode that prioritizes reconciliation rather than a break with the past, a narrative initially engineered by the dictatorship and continued by the amnesty framework). This second dimension relates to a narrative mode that dates from authoritarian times because the amnesty discourse reproduces the logic of the repressive regime.

Keeping these minefields in mind, we must now consider what role historians can play through historical dialogue in the specific case of Brazil. What does 'engagement' mean in this context? In August 2012, I conducted twenty-four interviews with several key individuals involved in the process of memory and the work of both the national and local truth commissions which testified to the existence of major conflicts (The Brazilian Truth Commission has a historically unique structure; besides a National Truth Commission, dozens of local truth commissions emerged all over Brazil.).[37] While many state agents generally favoured a change yet opted for a more strategic and circumscribed version of the commission (for example, deferred punishment), victims demanded a radical break with the repressive past.

This posed a dilemma concerning how to write about a conflict setting such as this. Speaking to victims gave me access to sensitive information; it emerged that many had been denied a voice and even humiliated by the very state officials who apparently supported accountability measures.[38]

More than just a personal dilemma,[39] this raised methodological questions about academic engagement more generally: who can speak for the survivors? Is it viable to even ask them to aspire to 'shared narratives'? Realistically, what role can we, as researchers, play in the reckoning processes: how should/can/must we write about a violent past (if it is a minefield)? However, my main concern here is not the role of 'evidence' or 'facts' or the ethical problem that we are afraid to criticize victims' accounts. Rather, I am concerned with having to adopt a particular stance and choose a single narrative against which to measure (or set in opposition to) our own historical writing. We are writing in a non-neutral discursive field, not a power vacuum, and thus need to decide whether to deconstruct a larger historical narrative (in my case, the amnesty framework, a narrative initiated by the generals, who would now be feeling triumphant) or a more recent narrative focusing on the power struggles in post-millennium Brazil.

I had two decisions to make. First, in relation to my comment on the CNV, I could criticize the commission and (in alliance with human rights advocates and the victims' families) call for a rupture with the past. However, this narrative might have undesired consequences and even weaken human rights. Since the CNV has been attacked by its many opponents – including the armed forces, the foreign ministry (Itamaraty), sectors of the generally conservative privately owned daily media and nostalgic supporters of the regime – it seemed unhelpful to criticize the CNV, because at least it symbolized some kind of accountability initiative. Alternatively, I could examine and justify the CNV's moderate approach for strategic reasons.

The historical background to the social relations of my subject was vital. The discursive field had a past, and I could correct, denounce or rectify (authoritarian) narratives through my work. In light of the decade-long official denial of systematic human rights crimes and the reconciliation framework imposed by the amnesty, I felt that an 'engaged' historian should diverge from the narrative of compromise and choose to acknowledge the broader historical context and victims' struggle instead. At that point and, importantly, without violating historical methods or manipulating facts, I could have exercised my 'narrative power' to support the victims' cause and engage in the public discourse by deconstructing the authoritarian fallout, but to do so would have been precisely the opposite kind of engagement to that which Barkan suggested. It would have involved the historical work of 'deconstructing' previous, historically incorrect, and unjust narratives, but it would not have constituted active engagement in creating a 'shared narrative'. Was my work therefore contributing less to 'conflict resolution'? Would it not be better for the sake of human rights to prioritize the downfall of the 'reconciliation' framework created by the 1979 Amnesty Law?

Eventually, I published an article in which I rationalized and described the various perspectives but questioned whether I had truly 'engaged' with human rights.[40] Inevitably, historians have to make clear historical judgments, which creates a potential dilemma; historians are tasked with 'assessing' historical events as well as facts, even if many do not admit this openly, hiding behind a facade of 'scientific' historical writing. My knowledge of the historical context of the struggle meant that I had to decide which version to support: the moderate state's or the victims' (actors); the gradual process or the call for rupture (story), respectively. Yet, if historians take sides, can they still be effective analysts? Should an 'engaged' historian write about the recent violent past at all, as Barkan and the evolving field of dialogue and accountability propose; and, if so, what does this mean for the craft of historical writing? Secondly, *how* should 'engaged' historians write about it, assess their judgments, and in which narrative form? Form is more than just a matter of aesthetics; it involves a decision about which discursive narrative to *write against*. There is a danger in setting oneself so much 'against' a problematic version that the victims' perspective will dominate.[41] What is crucial is that instead of being linked to historical facticity, the main problem is the narrative that the historian writes *against* or his/her key narrative reference point (measured against a weak human rights background, the CNV seemed like a blessing, but against international human rights law it became a mere window-dressing initiative).

Choosing a Narrative in a Minefield

In Brazil, as in other post-conflict settings, multiple political memory struggles are operating, and it is not clear which narrative will ultimately strengthen human rights.[42] It is therefore valid to ask whether triumphalist narratives or sceptical accounts are more effective in furthering human rights. The issue remains of what criteria success is measured against and, depending on these criteria, different argumentations may be regarded as factually correct or appropriate.[43] It also depends on the audience: to whom is the message being addressed and whose narrative is it juxtaposed against (what I referred to previously as multilayered memory struggles)? Here, again, it is necessary to consider the question of what 'engagement' means: what are the consequences of a particular narrative? In turn, and by way of conclusion, even though in theory human rights laws and principles appear to provide a useful guideline for historical writing (one that offers political and social engagement while preventing ideological or party political overtones), in the actual practice of writing they do not resolve the historian's dilemma; while historians are trained to check the facts, they also have to choose a narrative, a perspective and an addressee. Self-reflexive historians may therefore question whether the narrative they produce genuinely supports human rights.

In the case of post-authoritarian Brazil, I was unable to state with certainty what 'engagement' really meant. The problem lay not in having to choose between historically accurate facts and human rights advocacy (in the sense of manipulating facts), but in selecting a narrative form or reference point. What kind of narrative would ultimately strengthen human rights? In terms of striking a balance between historical professionalism and human rights advocacy, I broadly concur with Barkan; professional historians cannot prioritize human rights advocacy over scholarly excellence (in terms of robust fact-checking), but professional writing also means making narrative choices and ultimately prioritizing a particular perspective, and historians do not receive training in how to do this. Based on the same empirical evidence, I could have written several technically sound histories.

Given the conceptual and practical-methodological problems of contributing to conflict resolution and historical dialogue, it will be intriguing to see how this new courageous and visionary school of historians evolves, as the project is still in its infancy.[44] One way to address the questions outlined here is to first develop more precise theories and concepts ('shared narrative', for one) and secondly to examine empirical studies already authored by historians engaged in the field of conflict resolution.[45] Researching events that occurred in the past (the development of the steam engine, for example) certainly yields fewer problems. The question thus remains: can professional historians play an *active* role rather than merely an analyst's role, deconstructing false historical narratives and myths?[46]

Nina Schneider is Senior Research Fellow at the Käte Hamburger Kolleg/Centre for Global Cooperation Research (KHK/GCR21) at the University of Duisburg-Essen, Germany. She was Visiting Scholar at Columbia University's Institute for the Study of Human Rights (ISHR, 2012), Marie-Curie Fellow at the *Zukunftskolleg*, at the University of Konstanz (2013–2015), Visiting Scholar at the National University of Brasília (UNB, 2015) and Senior Research Fellow at the Global South Studies Center (GSSC) at the University of Cologne (2015–2018). She is the author of *Brazilian Propaganda: Legitimizing an Authoritarian Regime* (University Press of Florida, 2014); 'Between Promise and Skepticism: the "Global South" and our Role as Engaged Intellectuals', *The Global South* 11(2) (2017), 18–38; and (with R. Atencio) 'Reckoning with Dictatorship in Brazil: The Double-Edged Role of Cultural-Artistic Production', *Latin American Perspectives* 43(5) (2016), 12–28 (Honorary Mention for the Best Article of 2016, Latin American Studies Association's Brazil Section).

Notes

1. Klaus Neumann (Swinburne University of Technology) has published extensively on German memories of the Nazi past and recently edited a special issue entitled 'Historians and the Yearning for Historical Justice', *Rethinking History: The Journal of Theory and Practice* 18(1) (2014), 145–63. From 2010 to 2013, Neumann served as convener of the Historical Justice and Memory Research Network, which has since evolved into the Dialogues on Historical Justice and Memory.

2. Ernst Schulin coined the term '[h]errschaftsgesteuerte Geschichtsideologie', a form of manipulating historical facts for political convenience in violation of the rule of historical facticity. Clearly, this does not fall under my definition of 'engagement', which aspires to currently available objective knowledge (even though the author is aware that the term 'objective' remains problematic). Schulin, '"Ich hoffe immer noch, daß gestern besser wird" – Bemerkungen zu einem von Jörn Rüsen gewählten Motto', 6.

3. See, for example, Lorenz, 'Drawing the Line: "Scientific" History between Myth-Making and Myth-Breaking', 35–56.

4. The author is aware that 'postmodernism' is a heterogeneous school of thought and thus uses the term in a simplified way, referring mainly to its relativist wing, due to limitations of space.

5. See also the rights and duties emerging from the Universal Declaration of Human Rights in De Baets, 'The Impact of the Universal Declaration of Human Rights on the Study of History', 20–43. The question that remains, however, is how does De Baets' Code translate into a tangible way of writing about post-conflict settings? While it represents a concrete solution to a challenging problem, the Code still seems abstract and theoretical as the remainder of the chapter seeks to show.

6. For Georg G. Iggers' critique of German historicism, see Iggers, *Deutsche Geschichtswissenschaft: Eine Kritik der traditionellen Geschichtsauffassung von Herder bis zur Gegenwart*. For his and his wife's joint autobiography, consult W. and G. Iggers, *Zwei Seiten der Geschichte: Lebensbericht aus unruhigen Zeiten*.

7. See, for example, Hunt, *Inventing Human Rights: A History*; Moyn, *The Last Utopia: Human Rights in History* and S.-L. Hoffmann (ed.), *Human Rights in the Twentieth Century*.

8. Barkan, *The Guilt of Nations: Restitution and Negotiating Historical Injustices*, xi, xvii, xi.
9. Barkan, *Guilt of Nations*, xxi–xxii.
10. Barkan, *Guilt of Nations*, x.
11. Barkan, *Guilt of Nations*, x.
12. Barkan, *Guilt of Nations*, x.
13. Barkan, *Guilt of Nations*, xvi, xi–xii.
14. Barkan, *Guilt of Nations*, xi–xii, xvi.
15. While an elaborated critique of *The Guilt of Nations* is beyond the scope of this chapter, the book received mostly positive reviews. Michael Ignatieff calls it a 'well-researched and discriminating study'; Ignatieff, 'Blood Money', *The New York Times* http://www.nytimes.com/books/00/09/10/reviews/000910.10igna.html (accessed 10 May 2012) from. In Ken Betsalel's view the 'thoughtful book' skilfully addresses 'complex and difficult questions'; Betsalel, 'Book Reviews: The Guilt of Nations: Restitution and Negotiating Historical Injustices', *Human Rights Quarterly*, 820–36. Simon Reich concludes that its stories are 'compelling' and it is 'worth reading', even if the 'stories' are dispersed and vary in depth; Reich, 'Global Injustice', *World Today*, 27. A more in-depth German language review praises the 'fascinating questions' raised by the book, but questions whether a shared German-Jewish narrative may ever be possible, Goschler, 'Elazar Barkan: The Guilt of Nations', http://www.sehepunkte.de/2002/09/3423.html (accessed 10 May 2011).

16. Referring to a 2010 report by the United Nations Development Programme (UNDP), Antoon de Baets reveals that while over the last forty years democracy increased worldwide there was no decrease in human rights violations. De Baets, 'Does Inhumanity breed Humanity? Investigation of a Paradox', 451–465, 464.

17. Barkan, 'AHR Forum: Truth and Reconciliation in History. Introduction: Historians and Historical Reconciliation', 899–913. In the three subsequent articles historians describe their efforts and the challenges they faced in contributing to 'shared narratives' that transcend 'national and ethnic divides'.

18. Barkan, 'AHR Forum', 900.

19. Barkan, 'AHR Forum', 900.

20. Barkan, 'AHR Forum', 903.

21. Barkan, 'AHR Forum', 908.

22. Barkan, 'AHR Forum', 903. In 2004, Barkan co-founded the Institute for Historical Justice and Reconciliation (IHJR, Salzburg, Austria), which aims to bring together opponents to write a post-conflict history that all sides can agree on. Barkan, 'History on the Line. Engaging History: Managing Conflict and Reconciliation', 229–36. Later Barkan initiated the Alliance for Historical Dialogue and Accountability network, allowing a dozen fellows to receive training and develop projects in the field of historical dialogue, http://hrcolumbia.org/ahda/about (accessed 5 December 2013).

23. The first constitutive conference was convened by Klaus Neumann in Melbourne in February 2012; the second and third annual conferences were hosted by Columbia's Institute for the Study of Human Rights (ISHR) in December 2012 and 2013, respectively.

24. http://www.hrcolumbia.org/ahda/conference (accessed 5 December 2013).

25. Some of the most useful resources are the registers of experts working in specific regions and on different topics but in the same country. The network also produces a newsletter and has an ongoing call for working papers, see http://historicaldialogues.org/ (accessed 20 December 2013).

26. Barkan, 'AHR Forum', 903.

27. The literature on the coup is extensive; for a classic and authoritative English account of both the coup and the regime, see Moreira Alves, *State and Opposition in Military Brazil*; for a recent historiographical debate of the Brazilian regime in Portuguese, consult Fico, *Além do golpe*.

28. Secretaria Especial dos Direitos Humanos (SEDH; Special Ministry of Human Rights), *Direito à memória e à verdade*, 32–33.

29. Pereira, *Political (In)justice: Authoritarianism and the Rule of Law in Brazil, Chile, and Argentina*, 68.

30. De Abreu, 'Os anos de chumbo: memória da guerrilha', 14–32.

31. It is difficult to describe Brazil's unusual reckoning process in non-derogatory terms. As an alternative, Paulo Abrão and Marcelo D. Torelly suggest the term 'delayed' – 'delayed transitional justice'. Abrão and Torelly, 'The Reparations Program as the Lynchpin of Transitional Justice in Brazil', 482.

32. Numerous scholars have argued in a similar vein, for example, Abrão and Torelly, 'The Reparations Program', 444.

33. For a historical overview of the 1979 Amnesty and impunity, consult Schneider, 'Impunity in Post-Authoritarian Brazil: The Supreme Court's Recent Verdict on the Amnesty Law', 39–54; for its cultural framing, see Schneider and Atencio, 'Reckoning with Dictatorship in Brazil: The Double-Edged Role of Culture', 12–28. Many scholars have criticized the concept of 'reconciliation' in Latin America, see, for example, Roht-Arriaza, 'The New Landscape of Transitional Justice', 12.

34. Schneider, 'Breaking the "Silence" of the Military Regime: New Politics of Memory in Brazil?', 198–212.

35. See SEDH, 'Direito', 32–33, or MacDowell Santos, Teles and Teles (eds), *Desarquivando a ditadura: memória e justiça no Brasil*, 472–95.

36. The numerous and ongoing problems between the CNV, local commissions and survivors have been a recurrent topic at major Latin American Studies Conferences, including the Latin American Studies Association (LASA) conferences in 2013 and 2014. Meanwhile, Brazil has suffered a major human rights backlash with the victory of extreme right-wing candidate and regime nostalgic Jair M. Bolsonaro in November 2018. This chapter has been written prior to this event. For further details about the key antagonists involved in the Brazilian struggle for memory, truth and justice in the English language, consult Schneider, '"Too Little too Late" or "Premature"? The Brazilian Truth Commission and the Question of "Best Timing"', 149–62, and N. Schneider 'Waiting for a Meaningful Apology: Has the Brazilian State Apologised for Authoritarian Repression?', 1–6.

37. Schneider, '"Too Little too Late"', 158. Although there is no authoritative list, commissioners of the São Paulo state local truth commission speak of approximately one hundred such local committees.

38. At the first encounter between civil-society human rights and victims' families' representatives (most of whom later formed local truth commissions) and commissioners of the CNV on 29 July 2012 in Brasília, I personally witnessed how survivors were rudely interrupted when they exceeded their allotted five minutes' speaking time, often precisely when they were recounting how they (or friends) had been tortured.

39. My body and brain revolted in a literal sense; I felt confused and no longer wanted to assume the role of an academic analyst but simply narrate their stories as they were; as a human being rather than an analyst.

40. While I am a curious scholar willing to test new methods, in writing about post-authoritarian Brazil from an engaged historian's perspective (neither a moralist's, nor a compassionate human being's, nor a political commentator's perspective), I felt that I was unsuccessful. Schneider, '"Too Little too Late"'.

41. Antoon de Baets has termed this exclusively victim-centred approach the 'lachrymose conception of history' in *Responsible History*, 2. This danger can be generalized to all narratives; writing 'too much against' a certain version, regardless of who an author sides with.

42. Baets points out that historians are involved in different kinds of conflicts; 'high intensity conflicts' associated with 'assassins of memory' (those who block it) and 'low intensity conflicts' related to those who feel misrepresented by the historian or for some reason regard his/her objectivity-seeking historical account as 'uncomfortable'. Baets, *Responsible History*, 197–98. What I call a twofold minefield – related to the past narrative justifying the regime and that of 'reconciliation' and present conflicts, respectively – seems to correlate with his distinction.

43. Baets problematizes the measurement of success in human rights terms by asking the question 'What do I measure the human rights situation against?' See Baets, 'Does Inhumanity', 462–63.

44. Barkan, 'History on the Line', 229.

45. Scholars have recently paid attention to historians' contribution to historical and truth commissions, for example, Barkan's former PhD student A.M. Karn's 'Depolarizing the Past: the Role of Historical Commissions in Conflict Mediation and Reconciliation', 31–50.

46. This question was also raised by Nina Witoszek (University of Oslo) in her keynote address 'Historians as Dissidents: or Intellectual Eros in Action', on 19 September 2013 at the conference 'Historians as Engaged Intellectuals: Historical Writing and Social Criticism' in Bochum, Germany.

Bibliography

Abrão, P. and M.D. Torelly. 'The Reparations Program as the Lynchpin of Transitional Justice in Brazil', in F. Reátegui (ed.), *Transitional Justice: Handbook for Latin America* (Brasília and New York: Brazilian Amnesty Commission and International Center for Transitional Justice, 2011), 443–85.

Barkan, E. *The Guilt of Nations: Restitution and Negotiating Historical Injustices*. New York and London: W.W. Norton & Company, 2000.

———. 'History on the Line. Engaging History: Managing Conflict and Reconciliation', *History Workshop Journal* 59(1) (2005), 229–36.

———. 'AHR Forum: Truth and Reconciliation in History. Introduction: Historians and Historical Reconciliation', *American Historical Review* 114(4) (2009), 899–913.

Betsalel, K. 'Book Reviews: The Guilt of Nations: Restitution and Negotiating Historical Injustices', *Human Rights Quarterly* 25 (2003), 820–36.

De Abreu, A.A. 'Os anos de chumbo: memória da guerrilha', in M. de Morães Ferreira (ed.), *Entre-vistas: abordagens e usos da história oral* (Rio de Janeiro: Editora Fundação Getúlio Vargas, 1994), 14–32.

De Baets, A. *Responsible History*. Oxford: Berghahn, 2009.

———. 'The Impact of the Universal Declaration of Human Rights on the Study of History', *History and Theory* 48(1) (2009), 20–43.

———. 'Does Inhumanity Breed Humanity? Investigation of a Paradox', *History and Theory* 51(3) (2012), 451–65.

Fico, C. *Além do golpe*. São Paulo: Record, 2004.

Goschler, C. 'Elazar Barkan: The Guilt of Nations', *Sehepunkte* 2(9) (2002).

Hoffmann, S.-L. (ed.). *Human Rights in the Twentieth Century*. New York Cambridge University Press, 2011.

Hunt, L. *Inventing Human Rights: A History*. New York: W.W. Norton & Company, 2007.

Iggers, G. *Deutsche Geschichtswissenschaft: Eine Kritik der traditionellen Geschichtsauffassung von Herder bis zur Gegenwart*. Munich: DTV, 1976.

Iggers, W. and G. Iggers. *Zwei Seiten der Geschichte: Lebensbericht aus unruhigen Zeiten*. Göttingen: Vandenhoeck and Ruprecht, 2002.

Ignatieff, M. 'Blood Money', *The New York Times* (10 September 2000).

Jaeger, F., H.W. Blanke and T. Sandkühler (eds). *Dimensionen der Historik: Geschichtstheorie, Wissenschaftsgeschichte und Geschichtskultur heute. Jörn Rüsen zum 60. Geburtstag*. Cologne: Böhlau, 1998.

Karn, A.M. 'Depolarizing the Past: The Role of Historical Commissions in Conflict Mediation and Reconciliation', *The Journal of International Affairs* 60(1) (2006), 31–50.

Lorenz, C. 'Drawing the Line: "Scientific History" between Myth-Making and Myth-Breaking', in S. Berger, L. Eriksonas and A. Mycock (eds), *Narrating the Nation: Representations in History, Media and the Arts* (Oxford: Berghahn, 2008), 35–56.

MacDowell Santos, C., È. Teles and J. de Almeida Teles (eds). *Desarquivando a ditadura: memória e justiça no Brasil*. São Paulo: Aderaldo & Rothschild, 2009.

Moreira Alves, M.H. *State and Opposition in Military Brazil*. Austin: University of Texas Press, 1985.

Moyn, S. *The Last Utopia: Human Rights in History*. London and Boston, MA: Harvard University Press, 2010.

Neumann, K. 'Historians and the Yearning for Historical Justice', *Rethinking History: The Journal of Theory and Practice* 18(1) (2014), 145–63.

Pereira, A.W. *Political (In)justice: Authoritarianism and the Rule of Law in Brazil, Chile, and Argentina*. Pittsburgh: University of Pittsburgh Press, 2005.

Reich, S. 'Global Injustice', *World Today* 56(12) (2000), 27.

Roht-Arriaza, N. 'The New Landscape of Transitional Justice', in N. Roht-Arriaza and J. Mariezcurrena (eds), *Transitional Justice in the Twenty-First Century: Beyond Truth versus Justice* (Cambridge: Cambridge University Press, 2006), 1–12.

Secretaria Especial dos Direitos Humanos (SEDH; Special Ministry of Human Rights), Comissão Especial Sobre Mortos e Desaparecidos Políticos (Special Commission for the Dead and Disappeared for Political Reasons), *Direito à memória e à verdade*. Brasilia: SEDH, 2007.

Schneider, N. 'Impunity in Post-Authoritarian Brazil: The Supreme Court's Recent Verdict on the Amnesty Law", *European Review of Latin American and Caribbean Studies* 90 (2011), 39–54.

———. 'Breaking the "Silence" of the Military Regime: New Politics of Memory in Brazil?', *Bulletin of Latin American Research* 30(2) (2011), 198–212.

———. '"Too Little too Late" or "Premature"? The Brazilian Truth Commission and the Question of "Best Timing"', *Journal of Iberian and Latin-American Research* 19(1) (2013), 149–62.

———. 'Waiting for a Meaningful Apology: Has the Brazilian State Apologised for Authoritarian Repression?' *Journal of Human Rights* 13(1) (2014), 1–6.

Schneider, N. and R.J. Atencio. 'Reckoning with Dictatorship in Brazil: The Double-Edged Role of Culture', *Latin American Perspectives* 43(5) (2015), 12–28.

Schulin, E. '"Ich hoffe immer noch, daß gestern besser wird" – Bemerkungen zu einem von Jörn Rüsen gewählten Motto', in H.-W. Blanke, F. Jaeger and T. Sandkühler (eds), *Dimensionen der Historik: Geschichtstheorie, Wissenschaftsgeschichte und Geschichtskultur heute. Jörn Rüsen zum 60. Geburtstag* (Cologne: Böhlau, 1998), 6.

CHAPTER 11

Using the Past

The Brazilian Cinema between Censorship and Representation

Meize Regina de Lucena Lucas

This article examines film censorship in Brazil during the civil-military dictatorship between 1964 and 1985. Three main aspects will be highlighted: first, the role of censorship in dictatorial regimes; second, the historical, social and political background that legitimizes censorship actions; and, finally, the control of historical representations in movies.

What is recognized by society as history forms the basis of human action practices, according to the significance and meanings that are produced by them.[1] Historical culture with its concepts, narratives and images shapes societies and therefore spreads out in various media, such as movies.[2] Moviemakers are attracted by the very power of images (and history), which mobilizes their creativity. However, history has always been a battlefield of interpretations. Consequently, one of the characteristics of dictatorships is the attempt to control the past and its representations. For instance, schools are one of the first places suffering from the state's action through the control over textbooks, curricula and teaching methods. Moreover, the state urges control of the historical content, concepts and ideas represented in films to fit in with the concept of its authoritarian rule. Before the Brazilian coup d'état of 1964, a large number of commercial movie theatres existed in the country, along with multiple film festivals, film clubs (which continuously increased, especially in universities) and cinematheques, mainly in São Paulo and Rio de Janeiro. TV was a different matter, since it massively entered

---

Notes for this section begin on page 234.

Brazilian homes and, for the first time, integrated the immense national territory through its images. Film productions, especially documentaries, were expanding since the introduction of cheaper and easier-to-handle equipment and due to state financing through the INC (National Cinema Institute) and Embrafilme (Brazilian Movie Company). Both were created by the federal government in 1966 and 1969. The INC was responsible for an increase of so-called 'cultural' productions (mainly documentaries and movies with historical contents or about Brazilian art), whereas Embrafilme backed the production and distribution of commercial films. The domestic production itself and the existence of a large network for movie circulation led to a strengthening and perfecting of governmental image control. This was a period of reshaping the censorial operation structure, which followed the bureaucratic modernization of the state.[3]

Reading the censorship proceedings, one can observe that the representation of the distant or near past was an ever-present concern in the censors' reports. Film-makers, other intellectuals and academics have extensively referred to history in order to reflect on and discuss the country.

Not only were movies, magazines, newspapers, books and theatre plays under tight control but also those who produced them:

> It is important to realise that when the aim is to control the past, the censor actually attaches importance to both professional and non-professional producers of history and to interpretations of the past in either written, spoken or visual form. Indeed, the report shows that popular history is as much a target of censorship as academic history, and probably even more so. Therefore, a flexible definition of the term "historian" is certainly necessary.[4]

Censorship action was combined with the control, surveillance and often imprisonment of Brazilian intellectuals, including film-makers, who largely came from political movements that had been established in universities.

The criterion used to guide the choice of processes to be analysed was the centrality of themes incorporated by the historiography when developing the narrative and cinematic storylines. Foreign movies and national documentaries stood out because censorship focused on historical contents, their representations and also on the ideas and concepts that were present in cinematic narratives.

Brazil: A Country with a Censorship Culture?

On 1 April 1964, a coup d'état carried out by sectors of the Armed Forces with the support of a significant part of the civil society as well as financial groups, industrialists, large landowners and sectors of the Catholic Church implemented a civil-military dictatorship in Brazil that lasted until 1985.

To remain in power, dictatorships traditionally resort to two instances of power: violence and culture. For the first of these instances, a common enemy must be created who has to be watched and fought (which implies that the different opposition groups lose their singularity) and who furthermore mobilizes the fears and dread present in the people's imagination. The second power instance, culture, creates discourses and symbols of unity and cohesion as counterpoints to potential disintegrating elements. As a result, both produce role models for ordinary life meant to provide the cement needed to affirm, support and consolidate the state. We can infer from this part that experienced and felt everyday life is forged both by the legitimation of power and the alliances of the ongoing political project.[5]

But this proposition has the forbidden as its counterpart: contents, images and words are suppressed and prevented from circulating through censorial action. By cutting out, classifying, ordering and prioritizing, censorship expresses the discourse of order.

In the case of Brazil, contrary to what one might imagine, censorship predates dictatorship by many years. Since the early days of the Republic, proclaimed in 1889, censorship was a police matter and remained so during the following years. The urbanization of large cities in the early twentieth century, in particular of the federal capital Rio de Janeiro, also transformed the type of entertainment and space occupancy. Imposing order to these spaces was one of the government's priorities: 'it will be the responsibility of the police to deal with the smoothness of business transactions and the morality of artistic spectacles'.[6] Thereby the censorial act was seen as an administrative function, and this continued to be the case for decades.

In the specific case of the cinema, which had been a target of police censorship and the Catholic Church since very early on, the Brazilian government had established the nationalization of film censorship services already in 1932. Certificates were issued by the Ministry of Education and Public Health through a censorship commission composed of a police chief, a judge of minors, the director of the National Museum, a teacher appointed by the Ministry and an educator.[7] It was stipulated by decree that cinema should have the function of educating society.

The goals of this cinematic production were present not only in laws but also in state policies,[8] whose control was a police matter. In its first article, the law decree no. 8.462 of 26 December 1945 created the Federal Department of Public Security and Services of Public Entertainment Censorship, which reported directly to the chief of police.

The political and moral character of censorship laws continued to prevail during the following decades. Therefore, the censorial model developed in Brazil cannot be considered without having the time frame in mind in which a Catholic and repressive police perspective determined and legitimized censorial actions.

At the same time, the specificity of censorship during the dictatorship should not be left out of sight. The parameters for releasing, prohibiting, classifying and cutting scenes, as well as selecting the employees who worked as censors, were still the same as prior to the 1964 coup. In 1966, however, the government decided to centralize censorship in the capital Brasilia. Subsequently, university training became mandatory for working for the Censorship Department, and thus the government started administering training courses. In 1972 the DCDP (Censorship Division for Public Entertainment) was created, and it was subordinated to the Federal Police Department of the Ministry of Justice.

In this study, two observations are outstanding: the first concerns the expansion of censorship over the years, its association with police actions and especially its modernization during the dictatorship.[9] The second point concerns the thinking that guided state actions. In this context, it is essential to analyse the 'National Security Doctrine'[10] and the performance of the War College 'ESG', established in 1949 with American and French technical assistance, which was intended to 'receive and theorize the "National Security Doctrine", and provide the necessary doctrinal and ideological contents to arrive in power in 1964, and remain there'. Target audiences of the War College were, apart from the military, civilians, especially liberal professionals, businessmen, judges, trade unionists, university professors and leaders of public agencies. They took part in the courses that aimed at training high-level people to occupy posts related to managing and planning national security.[11]

Individuals who occupied strategic positions or had proposed important projects adopted by the state were trained at the ESG College or worked in it, such as some presidents of the Republic and heads of the National Information Service.[12] Two of the research objects of these ideological leaders are crucial to understand censorship: the writings on moral and civic responsibility and the concept of internal war. Civilian action worked and was propagated through different channels such as schools, the media and role models. It defended the institutions that, according to military doctrine, were the basis of the native country, such as family, school, justice, churches and the Armed Forces.[13] With regards to war, the concept of an internal, total and permanent war applied in the case of Brazil, since the defence of the system after 1964 implied disregard for laws, the creation of arbitrary laws, the use of force and the adoption of constant vigilance.

Censorship was a coordinated action between government departments and civil society sectors; it was based on the thinking that sustained the state's ideological framework.

The Works of Censorship

In Brazil, every movie was censured, regardless of whether it was of domestic or foreign origin and no matter for which circuit it was intended: commercial cinemas, film clubs, embassies or television channels. This explains the extent of the documentary background on movie censorship: over thirty-five thousand processes were registered. The censors' assessment of each film led to the issuance of a display stamp specifically for cinema movies and a different one for TV productions. In the case of domestic films, a third stamp was necessary for exportation and display abroad.

Censorship controlled the exhibition of ethnic, socio-economic and religious conflicts. Recurring themes and figures on which a more intensive prevention tended to focus were the appearance of clerics and manifestations of afro-Brazilian beliefs, private relations between whites and blacks and hierarchy breaks between bosses and workers or between rich and poor.

The complexity of censorship can also be understood in other aspects that will be analysed in the following: the importance of history and its cinematographic representation. With regards to this historical question, we must consider a specificity of those years, which is the heyday of the 'National Security Doctrine' and its enforcement in different power spheres.

Among the concerns that guided the work of the censors, there was one nuisance due to its nature: films with a historical approach. Two kinds of films can be highlighted in this context: those that showed a historical context and plot and those that referred to events consolidated by historiography.

To understand how censors developed their actions necessarily involves the propagation of the 'National Security Doctrine' principles, which introduced a new vocabulary in politics and the military.

Traditionally, war was conceived as a form of external aggression between states, initiated by the declaration of belligerence from one country to another and that, by its nature, was limited: it would be called classical or conventional warfare.[14] But then modern times brought subversion into the country through new kinds of war: *insurrectionary war*, an internal conflict in which an armed part of the population seeks the deposition of a government, and *revolutionary war*, a (usually internal) conflict stimulated or aided from abroad and usually inspired by an ideology that seeks to conquer power by progressively controlling the nation.

One of the main or *the* main weapons in the latter was a psychosocial strategy. On one side, the communists were, according to the 'ESG', trying to undermine the ideas of authority and national unity; on the other side, the War College proclaimed the use of all means and all social institutions (family, school, church, trade unions and media) to fight this internal enemy as valid. Thus, communism, rather than an ideology in books and texts of

Marxist bias, was, according to the 'National Security Doctrine', rooted in the behaviour of the individuals, making them unprepared for perpetuating social institutions and maintaining social roles.

Parallel to these conceptions, censorship controlled any representation of such social institutions rigidly. But what about films based on historical facts and those that must be shown?

Burn! (dir. Gillo Pontecorvo, 1969) tells the story of an English mercenary who is sent to a Portuguese colony in the Caribbean with the intention of provoking a rebellion among the slaves to enforce English economy. *Sacco and Vanzetti* (dir. Giuliano Montaldo, 1971) focuses on the true story of the trial of two Italian immigrants who were accused of murder in the United States in 1920. The motivation for their prosecution and conviction, which led to their execution in 1927, was based on the fact that they were foreigners and anarchists, which was opposed by American conservatism. The outcome of the trial provoked numerous counter-reactions because evidence confirmed the men's innocence.

In February 1971, the movie *Burn!* was evaluated, as usual, by three censors, each judging it differently: approval, interdiction and approval with referral to higher authorities. This last position was frequent, especially in cases of plots that focused on situations of war, guerillas, social conflicts, strikes or trade unions. The story of a dominated and underdeveloped population passing from Portuguese to English rule, where a native leads a revolt, raised two types of argument: the qualities of the film that had 'invaluable merits' and the possibility that the film may invoke a parallel with the Brazilian situation. Domination by another country and underdevelopment were words coming from the vocabulary of social sciences that became current in the press and in political jargon and critiques in the 1960s and 1970s. One of the censors recalled in an accurate and well-reasoned film analysis that another movie of the director Gillo Pontecorvo, *The Battle of Algiers* (*La battaglia di Algeri*, 1966), had already been restricted, in September 1968, for supposedly suggesting 'crime practices against the National Security'.[15] The film was banned from public but was used in several military police courses run by the National Police Academy and the Elite Officer School.[16] In the process of the confiscation of the film, seized for review, a letter was sent to the delegate Oresto Mannarin, head of the Censorship Group of the Regional Office of Guanabara, in which the author repeats arguments and introduces new elements to evaluate the film. The cinematic techniques used in the film were considered to be a problem, since they allowed a better psychosocial domination:

> The film quality and remarkable performance of the actors, the plain language and its revolutionary spirit provide an easy content to be explored in the already happening indoctrination of the less informed. The perfect soundtrack,

colorful and well-crafted images are part of psychodynamic color techniques which strengthen the argument.[17]

This is an important aspect because the censors deemed well-played films with a naturalistic language more damaging than those who resorted to allegories and parables, as the former would be more easily understood. This was the case of *Land in Anguish* (*Terra em transe*, 1967) by the Brazilian director Glauber Rocha. In a fictional Eldorado, the director depicts the different political tendencies in the country through metaphors that make use of different movie characters. The allegorical tone, language and plot supposedly alienated the public and hence were appealing to minors.

A few months later, *Burn!* was put on the list of prohibitions. Two out of three censors voted against its release; it was finally released on 9 December 1979 thanks to a unanimous vote of the Supreme Censorship Council.[18]

The fact that the plot referred to the colonial period, i.e. to the past, indicates that the so-called historical films constitute a specific problem. In this case, we have a romanticized work. The historical element is crucial to the development of the plot because the rebellion is related to a particular situation that can be located in time and space, i.e. slave colonies during the industrialization.

How about in the case of movies based on true events, such as the case of *Sacco and Vanzetti*? The report of 25 October 1972, signed by two censors, defined its age rating to be over eighteen years, without cuts due to scenes of violence, and pointed out the film's positive message 'to the extent that it aims at the union of peoples and freedom without borders'. It continued stating that the movie dealt with 'irrefutable historical facts' and therefore should be released, despite showing a degrading phase of the American justice system.

After its seizure in 1973, the film was submitted to three censors, who decided that the maintenance of the certificate should be granted. The arguments were that the time difference and the political context (the film was set in the American period of the 1920s), as well as the fact that the United States had perfected its system of justice and that there was no mention of Marxist references, justified the movie's release.

> It causes revolt only because of the blatant injustice in the process ... which can extend to others of the same nature, but never draws a parallel between that situation and our country, living under a regime guided by the ideals of social justice. There are no Marxist preachings, the existing ones are much more in the spirit of anarchism and radicalism ... It's an invaluable film as a practical law class, however, very dangerous due to the spirit of revolt it provokes in the viewer against the U.S. American justice organs. Still the fact has to be considered that the reported facts took place more than thirty years ago, and that there are no connotations referring to the Brazilian reality ...[19]

The reports received top consideration, but the final decision was taken in the opposite direction: the film was banned until 1979 despite the veracity of facts, as pointed out by the censors. It is necessary, however, to raise a hypothesis about its interdiction. At a time when authority figures with their systems and institutions were placed above citizens, for being responsible for the protection of the latter, it would have been horrible to allow the exposure of their flaws and especially their deliberate mistakes. And returning to what was stated in the beginning of this topic: the 'National Security Doctrine' allegedly focused on creating an undivided and mainly homogeneous nation. The case of Sacco and Vanzetti was a story that belonged to its time and space (the United States of the 1920s) but also constituted a reflection on the intolerance towards strangers.

History/Stories of Present Times

New political movements also caused preoccupation and were targeted. The film *The Working Class Goes to Heaven* (*La classe operaia va in paradiso*, 1971) by director Elio Petri focuses on the story of a blue collar worker who questions his values throughout the film and those of the Italian society of the 1970s. The production was meant to be banned but was finally released with cuts for an audience over eighteen years. The film's classification was justified by saying that an 'irregular family life contributes in the given context to the making of bad decisions' – which were, in that case, supporting a strike and workers' movement. Thus, the characters' revolt, the 'break of hierarchy' and sudden indiscipline are related to 'communism', to 'professional students' and the status of being a separated man who has a relationship with a single mother.[20] The worker's evaluation describes his political and moral profile as inseparable.

At the same time, the complexity of *The Working Class Goes to Heaven* seemed to open up the possibility of a dubious interpretation. One of the censors even considered the message ambiguous because the main character himself cannot settle on a clear political position and shows many transformations throughout the film. There is also the figure of the 'professional student', who maintains a tense relationship with the workers.[21] Is it good or bad to show this? It was decided not to show *The Working Class Goes to Heaven*.

Missing (1982), directed by Constantin Costa Gavras, tells the story of the father and wife of a young US American who disappeared during the Chilean dictatorship. The film was assessed by seven censors (usually there were three censors), who were concerned about two aspects: the establishment of a possible parallel with Brazil and what to do with existing references in the dialogues referring to Brazilian torturers. This film was also released with cuts for an audience over eighteen years, as the censors had to recognize that the Chilean coup d'état had had wide press coverage and would soon be commonly known about.

The lack of temporal distance had not led historians to research the topic, so the censors decided the references to Brazil would be considered mere 'assumptions'. However, they were cut out.[22]

The censorship report reveals not only a major concern about the images in circulation but about the sophistication in using the categories of film analysis and with regards to historical issues shown in the respective movies.

Possible analogies or homologies between Brazil and other societies were closely observed, which highlights how governmental control over the past was central to maintaining social unity. For Brazilian film-makers, directing their cameras at the past or the countryside – a territory that differed from the modernity and urbanity of the great centres – was a way to cause a fissure or a tear in the image of a homogeneous, cohesive society that was united by the same principles and ideals.[23]

Brazil on the Big Screen

Film productions that dealt with national historical and cultural themes were incentivized by considerable state financings. However, even these productions were not free of cuts and interdictions, regardless of whether they were fictions or documentaries.

In the following, I will focus on documentary films because they expressed a certain concept of history, and in the 1960s a new national documentary cinema emerged that proposed a political and aesthetical view based on the country's reality. The existence of lighter, cheaper and easier-to-handle equipment, as well as the use of synchronous sound, made it possible to see landscapes and places and hear people who were absent from the national cinema.

What also defined the choice for documentary films was the existence of a cinematic language through which the film-makers tried to subvert the logic of movie genres, such as documentary/fiction or drama/comedy, for example. As a fact, from the 1960s, the barriers between fiction and documentaries were thoroughly researched, tested in the national cinema, analysed and subsequently removed.

A third element also influences the choice to concentrate on the censorship of documentaries: the repression of one documentary production immediately in the first hours after the coup d'état. This fact rejects the idea that fictional productions were more controlled due to their greater range. In my opinion, the question should centre around the specific control objectives for different cinematographic productions. By doing this, the analysis of censorial action during the dictatorship should maintain its distance to the past, in order to understand how some of its mechanisms were established.

The 1946 Constitution, paradoxically established after the end of the New State (1937–1945), continued to be the main legislation for censorial action until 1988, when censorship was abolished. In the following years, a series of laws was included in order to adjust to the new guidelines given by the government. However, the laws of 1946 continued to be the basis of censorial action as can be inferred from the reports and justifications to be found in the publication *Federal Censorship* (1971), a collection of laws, law decrees and decrees and regulations related to this activity.

Along with legal changes, the censors' actions improved, with reports that started to show a better textual quality. The texts became more complex, often long, showing details about the filmography of some directors and adopting a specific vocabulary used in film theory and criticism. Many censors elaborated documents that presented film arguments and reviews in reference to the film industry and Brazil's (or even the world's) social and historical situation.

National films could receive three different classifications, each valid for five years: display in the cinema, on television and free for exportation. Furthermore, there was the possibility of requesting a classification review of a film after its original classification; this was usually requested by the respective director or producer.

In the case of national cinema, at that time, the role of censorship went beyond banning, liberating, classifying or cutting scenes. From the mid 1950s, film culture passed through profound changes guided by the idea that the film industry should have a political function. Its aesthetics were meant to be totally different from that of the Americans and even Europeans. Cinema was to have new aesthetics and be based on the ethic that a person (and reality) not shown on screen had an image and voice, and the director was supposed to clearly state his point of view with regards to society. His choice of what to film and how to do it defined his political position.

Consequently, the moviemaker who positioned his camera in front of the world was forging a way of looking, thinking, questioning and representing the country. He integrated the plot into society by the act of shooting and transforming the elements captured by the camera into sensitive data. Therefore, censoring was an action directed at the country's intellectual domain.

The film-makers considered their time through their films. And these films, in return, constituted material for reflection on references such as the *Revista Civilização Brasileira* and the *Revista Brasiliense* for Brazilian thinkers. Sociologists who were well known among Brazilians, like Octavio Ianni and Roberto Schwarz, discussed the domestic film production. Their pages were occupied by texts of men related to cinema business, such as Gustavo Dahl, Jean-Claude Bernardet and Alex Viany, three film critics and film-makers.[24]

> Every group of intellectuals also organizes itself around a common ideological or cultural sensitivity and more diffuse affinities, but also around determinants that form the basis of a will and taste for socializing. These sociability structures are difficult to grasp, but they cannot be ignored or underestimated by the historian.

The state's concern regarding the power of images can be evaluated by examining a special case, which had a strong impact. On 1 April 1964, the date of the coup d'état, the army campaigned against a movie about the life story of the rural leader João Pedro Teixeira, murdered in the rural area of Paraíba State in 1962. The film was directed by the young Eduardo Coutinho and produced by the Popular Culture Center of the National Students' Union (UNE CPC), who intended to change the country through theatrical, filmic and literary productions.

Local farmers took part in the shooting, and many of them were active in the movement of the Peasant Leagues, and also Maria Elizabeth Teixeira, the widow of João Pedro Teixeira, participated. The army persecuted the film crew and the peasants, who acted in their real life roles. This military campaign was a success: some persons were arrested and even spent years in jail in the capital of Pernambuco State, Recife. Part of the equipment and filmed material was seized; another part was hidden by the local residents and farmers. The production was never concluded.[25] In its early days, the repressive force was showing its power and reach.

Thomaz Farkas and the New Documentary Cinema

The young director Geraldo Sarno's film *Viramundo*, together with three other titles, was part of Thomaz Farkas' filming project *Brasil verdade* and represents stereotypical social realities: football and 'cangaço' (outlaws who fought for social justice during the nineteenth and beginning of the twentieth century), as well as a reality that not even Brazilians themselves knew well, like daily life in the slums around the preparation for carnival parades, and the phenomenon of migration to São Paulo. Three other documentaries of this project - *The Soccer Underground* (*Subterrâneos do futebol*, 1965), by

Maurice Capovilla; *Cangaço memories* (*Memórias do cangaço*, 1965), by Paulo Gil Soares; and *Our Samba School* (*Nossa escola de samba*, 1965), by Manuel Horacio Gimenez - were initially shown separately, and then combined in one feature film titled *The Truth about Brazil* (*Brasil verdade*, 1968).

These were the first Brazilian films of 16 mm and with synchronous sound, light and modern equipment that formed the technical basis of direct cinema in Europe, Canada and the United States. Through them, for the first time, poor migrants, slum dwellers, football fans and former outlaws (*cangaçeiros*) were seen and heard in their dwellings. This ethical and aesthetic element, as well as the quality, was responsible for the positive impact these movies had on the audience at the time. They are, still today, milestones in the national cinematography. Like every movie shown in the country, they had to pass through the sieve of censorship. All censorship certificates were valid for five years and necessary for showing the movies in the country and obtaining exportation rights. The censorship processes were incomplete, however, as were many dictatorship files, so the film trajectory through the censor offices cannot be identified. But this fact does not prevent reflection on the censorial action.[26]

Viramundo discusses the migration of impoverished peasants to large urban centres and the problems they face working in the still booming construction industries and in factories. *Cangaço memories* questions the image of the outlaw, who is represented in studies as a violent and anarchic person: the film shows the contrast between a policeman, who has chased and killed bandits and later becomes a powerful landowner, and a former outlaw, a poor man who remains in his helpless condition.

According to the censorship certificate no. 5412/77 of 13 December 1977, both movies show

> distorted concepts about the culture of our country, which compromise the socio-political area, when resources used by the community are exploited, and the population suffers from the neglect imposed by the responsible authorities. The exposure of degrading scenes, dialogues and situations that only reinforces the unfair image of an underdeveloped country aggravated by the selected characters who, in some cases, are undernourished and due to environmental conditions must express a low cultural level.[27]

The report concludes with 'denying release' for the exportation of the film because it contradicted the interests of the country: article 37 of decree 20.493/46 was applied, which guarantees the protection of national security through the veto of movies.

The modernizing and modern face of Brazil was questioned by a past that was present. And the poor man – peasant, outlaw, bricklayer, worker – without a history became an annoying presence, voice and image. The rural and underdeveloped backwardness 'insisted' on coming back and was then shocked by the images of an urban, industrialized and progressive country as it was propagated by the state. The voices and images that appeared for the first time on screen still broke the national order and unity by permitting the 'stimulation of revolting feelings and passions that had, before, been unperceived by the peasants (as shown through protest dialogues)'.

Later, they would be released. It is, however, essential to understand with the help of the documents what the government's and censorship's concerns were at the time and what kind of disputes were going on. The film-makers Geraldo Sarno, Maurice Capovilla, Paulo Gil Soares and Manuel Horacio Gimenez, as well as the producer Thomaz Farkas, continued to shoot films during the following years. They even managed, although facing great difficulties, to open new work opportunities in important university research centres, such as the IEB (Institute of Brazilian Studies), part of the USP (University of São Paulo).

Farkas, who at the end of 1968 began teaching at the Arts and Communications School of the São Paulo University (ECA-USP), wrote a 1972 doctoral thesis 'Method of Documentary Cinema', a reflection on the place of the documentary film in understanding Brazilian problems. This thesis, however, was only defended in 1977.

He had the same fate as many teachers during the dictatorship: he was arrested and expelled from university. His dismissal, justified by the fact that he had left office for being imprisoned, was prevented by the solidarity of his colleagues, who took turns administering his classes. These events fall within the framework of the political persecutions conducted at Brazilian universities, which as a primary target were the teaching staff, activists, sympathizers of the left and those opposed to the traditional order reigning in the university environment.[28]

The fighting around the use of history mobilized the government to control not only school practices – as can be learned by analysing the censorship processes – but to fight for the 'right use' of history in other areas. Still, intellectuals, including historians, sociologists, philosophers and film-makers, as depicted in this study, identified – in image representations and inquiries to an established historical knowledge – the possibility of using film and cinema as a privileged place for questioning and disputes.

The distant or near past, domestic or foreign history, the national hero or indistinct mass, they all have been carefully designed by film-makers and also observed by censors, who sought to suppress statements or words that could cause cracks in the image of unity and harmony as propagated by the state.[29]

Meize Regina de Lucena Lucas is Associate Professor of History at Ceará Federal University in Brazil. She has published on the history and historiography of cinema, the cultural history of reading and patterns of relationship between texts and images. Her most recent research focuses on the analysis of censorship procedures during the Brazilian civil-military dictatorship (1964–1985). Her publications include 'Dizer é poder - escritos sobre censura e comportamento no Brasil autoritário: 1964–1985' (Imprensa Universitária da Universidade Federal do Ceará (UFC), 2017, in collaboration with Ana Rita Fonteles and Jailson Pereira), 'Por uma escrita da história do cinema' (UFC, 2016) and *Caravana Farkas: itinerários do documentário brasileiro* (Annablume, 2012).

Notes

1. Rüsen, *Razão histórica – teoria da história: os fundamentos da ciência histórica*.
2. According to Simon Schama (*Landscape and Memory*, 1995), the landscape is a product of the mind to the extent that man produces representations that guide his perception of nature. They are formed by layers of memories and a bedding of rocks. 'Reality' and its representations combine meanings and significations of nature, from pictures elaborated by painters, photographers and writers. The latter are those who 'paint with words'.
3. Stephanou, *O procedimento racional e técnico da censura federal brasileira como órgão público – um processo de modernização burocrática e seus impedimentos (1964–1988)*.
4. Baets, 'The Organisation of Oblivion: Persecuted and Censored Historians in Africa, Asia and Latin America', 18th International Congress of Historical Sciences, Montreal, 1995, 2.
5. Eco, *Construir o inimigo – e outros escritos ocasionais*; Baczko, 'A imaginação social', 296–331; Patto Sá Motta, *Em guarda contra o perigo vermelho*.
6. Kushnir, *Cães de guarda – jornalistas e censores, do AI-5 à Constituição*, 86; this feature remained, since the processes of film censorship are composed of the censors' reports and the bureaucratic documentation of movies, like proofs of import duty and tax payments.
7. Decree no. 21.240 of 24 April 1932.
8. The first policies aimed at protecting and stimulating the Brazilian film production targeted non-fiction movies. One should also remember the creation of the INCE (National Educational Film Institute) in 1936. Throughout thirty years, the institute conducted over four hundred films between short and medium-length films.
9. Stephanou, *Procedimento Racional*.
10. This Doctrine represented a theory and reflection that started out reviewing the concept of a 'national defence'. It was based on the grounds of the traditional concept of protecting the country's borders in the event of an external attack. At the end of the 1950s, a shift of the enemy figure took place due to the bipolarization of the world caused by the so-called 'Cold War'. The government started to worry about the 'enemy within', 'internal agitation forces' and 'internal subversion' – that is, groups and individuals who were believed to be aligned to international communism and completely opposed to democratic countries. This context given, the exercise of state power during the dictatorship was characterized by a growing and absolute control in the name of the maintenance of national security. The underlying principles were formulated at the ESG (Superior School of War) in attunement with the national safety guidelines drawn up by the United States of America.

11. Borges, 'A Doutrina de Segurança Militar e os governos militares', 13–42, 17; Moreira Alves, *Estado e oposição no Brasil (1964–1984)*.

12. Presidents: Humberto Castelo Branco (1964–1967; Study Director of the ESG), Emílio Garrastazu Médici (1969–1974; President of the SNI – National Information Service), João Baptista de Oliveira Figueiredo (1979–1985; President of the SNI). General Golbery do Couto e Silva was one of the first ideological leaders of the regime; he worked for the ESG, invented the SNI and had strategical posts during the military rule, e.g. as the Chief Minister of the Civil House of the Presidents Ernesto Geisel (1974–1979) and João Figueiredo.

13. According to José Murilo de Carvalho, an 'interesting and not yet fully examined aspect is the religious affiliation of the military forces. The old imperial army was entirely Catholic. The positivist influence radically changed this situation in the period from the last decade of the Empire until about the third decade of the Republic, when almost all of the officials leaving the Military Schools of "Praia Vermelha" and "Realengo" were materialists. Then there was a reaction proceeding back to Catholicism, which already dominated at the end of the 1930s'; Carvalho, *Forças armadas e política no Brasil*, 201.

14. Alves, *Estado*.

15. Fund of Public Entertainment Censorship, National Archives, Regional Coordination of National Archives in the Federal District. Box 566.

16. The use of banned films in courses was frequent. The commander of the Command School and General Head of Army Staff requested on 14 February 1975, besides the *Battle of Algiers*, the movies *Z*, *Sacco and Vanzetti*, *Red Harvest*, *Che Guevara*, *Green Berets* and *The French Connection*. Pontecorvo's film was only released in 1981, for an audience over eighteen years.

17. Fund of Public Entertainment Censorship, National Archives, Regional Coordination of National Archives in the Federal District. Box 96.

18. Decree no. 83.973, of 13 September 1979.

19. Fund of Public Entertainment Censorship, National Archives, Regional Coordination of National Archives in the Federal District. Box 407.

20. Fund of Public Entertainment Censorship, National Archives, Regional Coordination of National Archives in the Federal District. Box 508.

21. The student movement was a major focus of state repression and control.

22. Censorship Division of Public Entertainment Fund, National Archives, Regional Coordination of National Archives in the Federal District. Series 'prior censorship'. Subseries: 'film programming'. Box 68.

23. Didi-Huberman, *Images malgré tout*.

24. Sirinelli, 'Os intelectuais', 231–70, 248.

25. In 1981, Eduardo Coutinho resumed the film shooting that lasted two more years. In 1984 *Goat marked for death* (*Cabra marcado para morrer*) was released, which tells the story of the shooting start and interruption of a film with the same name, in 1964. Starting from that point in time, the movie traces its original participants and rebuilds their lives during the years of dictatorship. It centres around the figure of Elizabeth Teixeira, whose family broke up due to the coup d'état.

26. De Baets, 'The Dictator's Secret Archives: Rationales for Their Creation, Destruction, and Disclosure', 181–96.

27. Fund of Public Entertainment Censorship, National Archives, Regional Coordination of National Archives in the Federal District. Box 167.

28. Patto Sá Motta, *As universidades e o regime militar*.

29. Abuses of history are frequently dangerous. They are common under dictatorships and in periods of gross human rights violations; De Baets, 'The Abuse of History: Demarcations, Definitions and Historical Perspectives', 159–73.

Bibliography

Baczko, B. 'A imaginação social', in Edmund Leach et al. (eds), *Anthropos-Homem* (Lisboa: Imprensa Nacional/Casa da Moeda, 1985), 296–331.

Borges, N. 'A Doutrina de Segurança Militar e os governos militares', in J. Delgado Ferreira, and L. de Almeida Neves (eds), *O tempo da ditadura – regime militar e movimentos sociais em fins do século XX* (Rio de Janeiro: Civilização Brasileira, 2012), 13–42.

De Carvalho, J.M. *Forças armadas e política no Brasil*. Rio de Janeiro: Jorge Zahar Ed, 2005.

De Baets, A. 'The Organisation of Oblivion: Persecuted and Censored Historians in Africa, Asia and Latin America', in 18th International Congress of Historical Sciences (Montreal, 1995), p. 2.

———. 'The Dictator's Secret Archives: Rationales for Their Creation, Destruction, and Disclosure', in A. MacDonald and A.H. Huussen (ed.), *Scholarly Environments: Centres of Learning and Institutional Contexts 1600–1960* (Groningen Studies in Cultural Change, vol. 7) (Louvain: Peeters, 2004), 181–96.

———. 'The Abuse of History: Demarcations, Definitions and Historical Perspectives', in H. William Hoen and M.G. Kemperink (eds), *Vision in Text and Image: The Cultural Turn in the Study of Arts* (Leuven: Peeters, 2008), 159–73.

Didi-Huberman, G. *Images malgré tout*. Paris: Les Éditions de Minuit, 2003.

Eco, U. *Construir o inimigo – e outros escritos ocasionais*. Lisboa: Gradiva, 2011.

Kushnir, B. *Cães de guarda – jornalistas e censores, do AI-5 à Constituição*. São Paulo: Boitempo, 2004.

Moreira Alves, M.H. *Estado e oposição no Brasil (1964–1984)*. Petrópolis: Vozes, 1987.

Patto Sá Motta, R. *Em guarda contra o perigo vermelho*. São Paulo: Perspectiva/Fapesp, 2002.

———. *As universidades e o regime military*. Rio de Janeiro: Jorje Zahar, 2014.

Rüsen, J. *Razão histórica – teoria da história: os fundamentos da ciência histórica*. Brasília: Editora da Universidade de Brasília, 2010.

Schama, S. *Landscape and Memory*. New York: Harper Perennial, 1995.

Sirinelli, J.-F. 'Os intelectuais', in R. Rémond (ed.), *Por uma história política* (Rio de Janeiro: FGV, 2003), 231–70.

Stephanou, A.A. *O procedimento racional e técnico da censura federal brasileira como órgão público – um processo de modernização burocrática e seus impedimentos (1964–1988)*. Porto Alegre: Pontifícia Universidade Católica do Rio Grande do Sul, 2004.

CHAPTER 12

Historians and the Trauma of the Past

The Destruction of Security Files on Citizens in Greece, 1989

Vangelis Karamanolakis

Since the 1970s, but mainly at the sunset of the Cold War, many countries experienced a period of transition from authoritarian to more democratic forms of government.[1] In the context of those transitions – associated with the particularity of each country, its history and its political and social conditions – these societies had to confront their authoritarian past and, often, even the evidence of this past, which were connected with collective traumas and with situations that determined the life and memory of a large part of their citizens. There were a large number of documents created to record citizens' activities and beliefs, to intimidate and force them into conforming and collaborating. Actually, most of these archives[2] were produced by the police and intelligence services, through labyrinthine procedures that were closely connected to the state authority; they were fully or partially preserved and were part of the 'heritage' of the regimes removed through violent or peaceful transitions. And though the countries of the Eastern bloc – and especially East Germany – feature most in the relevant literature, this phenomenon can be observed in various cases, such as Greece and in Latin American countries such as Argentina and Uruguay. At the centre of the public discussion regarding these archives were issues concerning the uses and interpretations of the documents and their content, their destruction, their rescue and the redefinition of their value and use, either in the context of confronting new enemies or in judicial proceedings for the crimes that

Notes for this section begin on page 247.

had been committed. The central question in the following chapter, which has Greece as its field of reference, concerns the ways in which historians are involved in these discussions: what is the role of historians when a society confronts its traumatic and sometimes 'unwanted' past? How does their professional involvement with the past provide them with a special role? What are the limits to their intervention and engagement in public life? Can they help to heal the traumatic moments of the past that often divide societies? Can they act like physicians of memory, as Paul Ricoeur has written?[3]

In Greece in July 1989, a coalition government between the main foes of the postwar period, the left and the right, came to power, emerging from a significant rearrangement of the political landscape in the aftermath of the fall of the communist bloc, and also against the backdrop of the financial scandals of Andreas Papandreou's previous socialist government. This coalition introduced a bill to parliament on 'lifting the effects of the civil war'. According to the provisions of the bill, what happened during the period from the withdrawal of the occupation troops from Greece until 1949 was no longer officially considered as a communist revolt against the state but as a civil war. People who had fought against the communists would be equated with their opponents. Moreover, convictions for participating in the civil war on the side of the communists would be annulled.

It should be noted that the Greek Civil War resulted in the biggest war-related bloodshed in twentieth-century Greece. According to the most modest estimates, it left behind some 70,000 dead, on both sides, many more than the number killed in combat during World War II. In addition, thousands of refugees fled to communist countries as soon as the civil war ended.[4] The civil war did not end with the cessation of hostilities, and not just from the aspect of the issue of the political refugees in the Eastern bloc, who had to remain there for the foreseeable future. Through a number of legislative arrangements, the government maintained the state of emergency in many respects, elevating anti-communism to a dominant element of political legitimacy. Those considered to be on the side of the defeated remained hidden in silence; they could not mourn their dead, claim the honour of their family or take pride in their bravery and in the hardships suffered by them during the war. Commemorative ceremonies referred to the victors. Thousands of left-wing citizens found themselves in prison or in exile, also because of their activities during the resistance.[5] Members and supporters of left-wing parties had to deal with defeat, silence and accusations of national treason levelled by officials and diffused through a massive anti-communist campaign that involved all state bodies and institutions.[6] Up to the fall of the military junta in 1974, millions of citizens had been forced to repudiate their political beliefs in written statements; those who were not persecuted, imprisoned, deported or deprived of their right to employment.

The end of the dictatorship in 1974 triggered a chain reaction of political changes. The abolition of the monarchy and the legalization of the Communist Party of Greece (KKE) were accompanied by a gradual weakening of the right, which was blamed for the dictatorial regime, whereas the demand for change and modernization of Greek society was linked with the left, particularly with a new socialist party, Andreas Papandreou's PASOK, which first came to power in 1981.[7]

Nevertheless, the repercussions of the civil war and the legal and institutional discrimination of the defeated were still evident in many respects. In 1989, the coalition government decided not only to eliminate all 'effects' of the civil war but also to remove all evidence of that traumatic past. To this end, it decreed the destruction of citizens' files that were kept mainly at police headquarters but also in local police stations. Those files contained detailed information about the personal lives, religious beliefs, families, working environment and social lives of those under surveillance.[8] The authorities used to have a network of informers across the country to monitor individual citizens and collect, store and update information on them. The police files had not been studied or catalogued: in 1989 there were an estimated 17 million individual dossiers kept in police stations across the country. This dizzying figure – for a country with a population of a little less than ten million – may be explained by the fact that it included the files of citizens who had died. There were also citizens with more than one file because they were under surveillance in more than one place.

This was not the first time that the destruction of the records had been proposed. As prime minister, Papandreou had made it an issue in 1984, in the context of the abolition of all measures relating to the civil war. Five years later, the decision to incinerate the police files sparked an important debate among politicians and journalists about the desirability and advisability of preserving these types of documents.[9] At the political level, the main voice in favour of keeping them was PASOK, which, despite its previous position, accused the right of attempting to destroy, with the consensus of the left, the evidence of its criminal policies in the past. Another group that strongly resisted the destruction plans was a group of left-wing politicians, mostly veteran civil war combatants, who went to court demanding their personal file, over which they claimed exclusive rights, as it was material that had to do with their personal life.

But the most militant reaction came from a group of historians, who demanded that the files be kept for reasons associated with their professional capacity. For the first time, a large number of professional historians and archivists were united in protest, publishing articles, collecting signatures, organizing public events and even taking court action.[10] Their basic argument was that destroying the files would amount to the loss of a very important historical source that could provide unique insights into postwar Greek society.

The reactions of the historians generated publicity in newspapers and magazines, as the press was keenly interested in history and in the past.[11] In the *metapolitefsi*, as the period following the end of the junta is known, history had come to focus on numerous public debates on the identity of Greek society.[12] Questions regarding the cause of the junta, on why Greece followed a different path from that taken by Europe or what needed to be done to avoid another junta needed a historical answer.

Many studies published immediately after the fall of the dictatorship attempted to provide answers to these questions. The majority turned to earlier historical periods or were macrohistorical approaches that started with the creation of the Greek state (1830) and usually ended in the interwar period. They mainly focused on the evolution of Greek society and especially the political system and the phenomena that characterized it (patronage, clientelism) in the last two centuries. Concepts such as dependence, reproduction, modernization; questions such as the Greek state's position in the global capitalist system; and the relation between the metropolis (Western Europe) and the periphery (Greece) dominated this debate. Interestingly, most of these studies were undertaken by authors who were not historians in the traditional sense. They were scientists from related social sciences (historical sociology, economics and political science) who had studied abroad, were exiled on political grounds or had gone into self-exile before 1974.

The renewal of historical studies occurred mainly in the 1980s and was instigated by a number of historians who, during the dictatorship, found themselves living outside Greece, mostly for political reasons. Their historical apparatus, their contact with the ideas circulating abroad and their work enabled them to embed Greek history in the international context. Upon their return home, where they were joined by younger colleagues who had been radicalized during the dictatorship, they were absorbed by the third-level education system, and they assumed important positions in the new institutional framework.[13] From the late 1970s, new history departments were established in the main Greek cities, which helped to spread historical research and teaching at university level throughout the country. History became more independent from archaeology and philology and drew ideas from sociology and political science. At the same time, a series of historical institutions and professional positions, archives, museums and research centres appeared, mainly during the 1980s. These new institutions turned to the study of social and economic history for the first time and acted as a counterweight to older ones – the Academy of Athens and older universities – that served the prevalent nationalistic and anti-communist academic historiography aimed mainly at defending 'national issues'. This is not to say that they took the upper hand or that there were no conservative institutions or individuals perpetuating older notions. But the key tone was set by this particular group of historians, who gradually gained leadership in the 1980s, setting the agenda of historical publications due to their institutional role as well as their appeal to a wider public.

An increased interest in history was also reflected in the formation of a number of associations and societies by young or independent historians. One of the most important of these societies has been the Etaireia Meletis Neou Ellinismou (Society for the Study of Modern Hellenism), founded in 1971. Its journal, *Mnemon*, has published numerous papers by the advocates of this 'new history', a term coined by the historians themselves. 'New history' found its most forceful medium in the journal *Ta Istorika*, first published in 1983 by the country's most prominent Greek historians, Spyros Asdrachas, Philippos Iliou and Vassilis Panagiotopoulos, all of whom had lived and worked in France for several years.

The central aim of this new history was to differentiate itself not only from the prevalent academic historiography but also from the previous left-wing one, which had been written to mirror KKE politics and ideology. They opposed what Iliou, one of the most emblematic figures of 'new history' and a prominent member of the Greek left, called *the ideological use of history* by the right and the left.

The main priority of this historiographical trend, if indeed one could speak of a trend, was to liberate history from myths and ideological uses, whose rejection was associated with a wider issue regarding the quest for historical truth: the formation of a reliable 'academic history'. As was reflected in the texts of the main representatives of this trend, academic history had to be documented in a way that was objective and as a result progressive, since history was by definition liberating: changing society presupposed changing its relations with the past.

In an atmosphere of political optimism, the aim was to rewrite history by posing new questions, and modernizing approaches. The reinstatement of historical truth became a major stake of the period, particularly for the left, which endorsed the reference to and the study of the past with a view to finding out the truth as a key component of its own (the left's) identity. 'New history' was attributed the role of an emancipating intellectual force. Breaking with the dominant image of the historical past was seen as a precondition for the emancipation of citizens, a sine qua non for a changing society. The pursuit was the 'scientific' discovery of a past that had been muted or falsified for the sake of political expediencies, a past that should be seen under a new light in order to justify policies, establish genealogies, remedy injustices and heal wounds. In fact, this 'scientific' perception would also serve a political agenda, different from the one that had prevailed but equally political: the modernization of Greek society.

In the late 1970s and the 1980s, a new period emerged as a research field for this new academic historiography: the years from 1940 to 1944, which became known as the national resistance during the German occupation. Up to that point, the resistance, which had been predominantly associated with the left, was excluded from official historiography. In the same year, 1978, the first two history conferences on the occupation and resistance took place, not in Greece but in Washington and London. In parallel, the first doctoral theses on the resistance period were completed; written abroad during the time of the dictatorship and primarily based on British and US archives, they focused on the period because they sought primarily to understand the role of foreign powers and to study the differences between the left and right in the context of the active political involvement of these young historians. In 1982, the socialist PASOK government officially recognized the national resistance, which allowed the resistance fighters – mainly left-wing citizens – to enter the pantheon of national heroes. A new national narrative was formed, which projected the heroic, unifying and socially liberating nature of the resistance as its key element.[14]

Although the 1940–1944 period was integrated in official history, the civil war that followed (1946–1949) would remain outside the scope of academic interest, until the mid 1990s at least. It remained a very difficult period for Greek society to discuss, as its wounds remained open and the memory of it was divided. The issue of the 'communist insurrection' was still considered taboo, with attempts to discuss the civil war triggering reactions from conservative parts of society. On the other hand, the choice to elevate the resistance, but not the civil war, in the collective memory reflected the recognition of the left as a patriotic force and, also, the rejection of the use of violence for political ends and the acceptance of the legal and parliamentary system. Historians specifically avoided the civil war period, invoking as a key problem – apart from the lack of any institution dedicated to the period – their inability to treat it fairly and objectively, referring to the classified character of most files from that period as well as their own personal and political engagement. In 1980, Iliou was the first historian to publish archival documents of the KKE on the civil war, in a daring initiative that was not picked up by his colleagues.[15]

The threat of burning the security files, however, put things in a different perspective. Even if the systematic study of the civil war had yet to begin, the preservation of relevant historical evidence and its transformation into historical sources were absolutely necessary. The destruction of millions of documents was considered a nightmare scenario by historians; they based their arguments on the concept of 'sources' – in this case the reliable, documented knowledge of the past. Their academic affinities, the commonly accepted rules on how to generate history, had become commonplace, part of their own habitus, which they felt compelled to defend. The historians recognized the fears of citizens that publishing the files might cause pain, disputes and possibly reignite civil war rivalries. They also understood that if the files were preserved there would always be the possibility that they might be used by the state against citizens in the future. As an answer to all these fears, the historians proposed the strict observation of academic methodology and the transformation of these files into archival sources. They also suggested prohibiting access for a number of years before the documents could be declassified and, possibly, processed by professional historians.

Responding to the public's concerns that these files contained biased and false information, they said that even falsifications are facts themselves and proof of certain realities. The argument against the validity of the documents was for some historians a shallow justification and was seen as an 'intolerably positivistic one'.[16] For some of the historians and intellectuals of the left, in fact, the problem was deeply political.[17] The right-wing party in the coalition sought the destruction of the files in order to conceal their questionable deeds and to shift the blame for the persecution of the left. As the files revealed, this policy was in force over a long period, was spread throughout the political system and was associated with the concept of *ethnikofrosini* (nationalism), which excluded a large part of Greek society from the public sphere, namely those on the left of the political spectrum. On the other hand, the decision of the left-wing component in the coalition to agree to this symbolic act was associated with a 'new left' as it had emerged from the collapse of the communist regimes in 1989. This left supported the need for national reconciliation and cooperation by tearing up an important page of its history – its attempt to take power through force of arms.

But what did the historians propose? They argued that reconciliation would occur through adopting a critical stance based on the knowledge of what happened in the past. Historians were against oblivion. As another significant Greek historian, George Dertilis, mentioned in a letter in *To Vima* newspaper: 'History, as collective memory and self-awareness, needs shame and guilt.' As regards the question of how societies can overcome their traumatic past, historians argued along the lines of what Frank Ankersmit later called 'the pain of Prometheus'.[18] Overcoming trauma is possible only by gaining constant knowledge in a never-ending process where the study of the past constantly provides new information. We circle around trauma in an attempt to understand it. However painful, the past must be investigated if it is to be understood. The goal is, after we have mourned, to accept it and then form a more integrated identity based on its acceptance. The aim is to incorporate the common past in the collective history, to include even those moments that a large part of society may wish to forget and to accommodate even the most traumatic moments. The past was considered to be a vast archive, constantly yielding new material. In this sense, the files were a privileged field, representing a massive, unique archive of recorded testimony that would help answer questions forever.

Despite the loud protestations of historians in the public realm, the Greek government and parliament showed themselves to be indifferent to, or even in favour of, destroying the files. The right-left coalition government's decision to destroy them was clearly part of a strategy to showcase what was an unprecedented political alliance, and it was not met with any significant opposition, with the exception of the historians. Although the historians' arguments circulated widely in the press and were even raised during parliamentary sessions, there was no change. The only concession made was to keep a limited number (around 2,000) of these files concerning well-known individuals (politicians and activists) on the grounds that they were of 'special historical interest'. The criteria for choosing these particular files were never explicated and they remain inaccessible: neither the documents nor the catalogue covering them are available to researchers. The government decided that these files would become accessible after twenty years, only to announce, in 2009, an extension of another twenty years.[19] Finally, in 2016 the newly elected government of SYRIZA granted access to this material.

Unlike in cases such as the former East Germany, there was no widespread demand to unmask those who spied on others.[20] Arguably, fifteen years after the fall of the junta and given the important changes that had taken place the files amounted to an embarrassing reminder of a past that could now be forgotten on the political, and even personal, level. Government leaders, supposedly representing public opinion, decided to write off this aspect of the past. The statement of Konstantinos Mitsotakis, the leader of the right-wing New Democracy party, which participated in the coalition government, is telling: 'There are pages in history that nobody wants to read. Everyone would skip over them. Everyone wishes that they didn't exist' (30 September 1989). Expressing a similar position, Public Order Minister Ioannis Kefalogiannis remarked: 'Nobody cares anymore for this political past' (27 September 1989).

Throwing the files into the pyre destroyed historical traces, took the blame off the persecutors and released the victims from the anxiety over what their files might contain. According to those who advocated burning them, preserving the files might become an impediment; it could destabilize the identity of those called to move forward into a new era by reminding them of a conflictual past. The desire to know the past was superseded by fears over the implications of this knowledge and perhaps reflected fatigue in a society eager to turn a page. The concerns and fears that the files might be used again in the future if circumstances changed were grounded in historical experience. Indeed, one of the most widely circulated claims was that the most important data had already been transferred to databases, using the new technology of personal computers. Politicians, on behalf of society and symbolically representing both sides in the civil war, preferred amnesia, a complete deletion of the past, in theory at least, over knowledge, which is based on choice about what to forget and what to remember. This past was a wasteland; it could not function either in terms of correction or fiction. The destruction of the files amounted to nothing less than the denial of the past. At the critical moment of renegotiating this traumatic past vis-à-vis contemporary reality, society chose to destroy the evidence, seen as an undesirable reminder, preferring to dispense with it through silence.

The files were incinerated in spectacular bonfires throughout the country on the same day. These symbolical rituals laid bare the limits historians had as a community to intervene in the public realm. The fate of the files betrayed also the limits of the chimera of professional historians as it had evolved in the initial post-dictatorship period: the idea that professional historians can deploy the authority of their knowledge in political and social life to help their contemporaries understand the 'right' past or to free themselves from its myths using a new history that would prevail in institutions such as archives and research centres. A history whose utmost political stake consisted precisely in illustrating its academic nature and emphasizing its impartiality and the processing of sources, in contrast to the nationalistic historiography of the past on the one hand or a kind of public history constantly rewritten by the press on the other. History was there to evaluate the past with its own toolkit and methodology. An event organized by the two most important historical Greek journals at the time, *Mnemon* and *Ta Historica*, at which eight historians from various generations and political persuasions spoke is indicative. In their speeches, as well as in the rest of the articles that appeared in the same period, there was a general consensus: what had happened was largely seen as a defeat in the struggle for a renewal of the perception of history and the work of historians in Greece. It was an absolute refutation of what historians had been attempting to do for the previous twenty years. From another point of view, the fate of the files was not necessarily a cause for pessimism. Historians, as Antonis Liakos argued, could always continue their work by using alternative sources such as oral testimonies.[21] Clashing with those in political power was expected. Historians should be pioneers; they had to offer an alternative voice: the academic voice. According to Spyros Asdrachas, even if they had not managed to persuade society, they had to insist on their opinions in order to change the way things were.[22]

What were, then, in general, the ethics and the limits of historians' public interventions? Could they be located somewhere 'above' the fields of conflict? Could historians be the ones who would deliver justice? Or could they end up being part of the conflict, since preserving the files would also mean preserving all those documents that showed the practices of one side, the right. Historians declared the need for catharsis, asserting the need to preserve memory and the treatment of documents as historical sources, and to disregard, to a large extent, the implications of this for the lives of victims and perpetrators. The justice that history attempted to deliver derived from the idea of a past that was absent or distant, of a past that was no longer changeable. The 'time of history', as Berber Bevernage writes, is an irreversible time that stresses the already absent or distant character of what happened in the past.[23] But for the majority of those citizens who had lived under persecution and surveillance, all that had happened was present; the past was present, ready to return. For a certain part of Greek society, for an older generation, the destruction was a liberation from the guilt about what they had done, while others felt liberated from the fear that in the future they could be persecuted again based on evidence contained in the files. Let us recall what Hayden White has said.[24] If historians, through the preservation of these files, wished to enforce even more the image of the historical past they constructed, citizens chose the destruction of this material wishing to detach it from their practical past, a past that could help them cope with their everyday life in the present and in the future, without being afraid of what might be revealed from the past.

In June 2013, the parliamentary spokesman of New Democracy, the biggest party in the coalition government of the period, justified the sudden decision to shut in the coalition government of the period the national public broadcaster ERT, arguing, among others, that its channels propagated only the left-wing view about the Greek Civil War. Such a statement – coming at a time when the far right is on the rise, a time of crisis, of collapsing prospects for people, polarization, the re-emergence of the right-left divide – brings the debate back to the 1940s, demonstrating once again the complex relations societies entertain with traumatic moments of their past and how trauma can be reproduced in different ways in the context of new sociopolitical confrontations. And, of course, it raises again the issue of the role of historians and the limits of their intervention in these processes, the boundaries of their jurisdiction and their engagement in public life.

Vangelis Karamanolakis is Assistant Professor in Theory of History and History of Historiography at the Department of History and Archaeology (National and Kapodistrian University of Athens) and Director of the University Historical Archive. He is, also, Secretary of the Society's Board of Directors of the Contemporary Social History Archives. He is the author of *The Formation of Historic Science and History Teaching at the University of Athens, 1837–1932* (Athens 2006, in Greek) and *The University of Athens and its History, 1837–1937* (in collaboration with K. Gavroglou and Ch. Barkoula, Irakleion 2014, in Greek). He has edited a number of collective volumes on Greek historiography, postwar history and the legacies of World War II. His new book *Unwanted Past: The Destruction of the Citizens' Personal Records in Greece (1989)* will be released soon.

Notes

1. This chapter is part of an Aristeia research programme entitled 'Greek Historiography in the 20th Century: Debates on Identity and Modernization', which is cofunded by Greece and the EU (2012–2015).

2. The notion of the archive is crucial, as it is connected to the notion of materiality, the substrate of the documents that it includes and also the information that it encloses, as well as the knowledge and the power that it provides to the one who has responsibility for it and the right to access it. In other words, it is important to see the archive as *place* and as *law*, according to Derrida, and the limits of the interpretative competence that its guards and managers have. See Derrida, *Archive Fever: A Freudian Impression*.

3. Ricoeur, *Memory, History, Forgetting*.

4. Margaritis, *History of the Greek Civil War*, 50–51. See among others Close, *The Origins of the Greek Civil War*.

5. Regarding the political prisoners, see Voglis, *Becoming a Subject: Political Prisoners during the Greek Civil War*.

6. For the postwar situation in Greece, see Mazower (ed.), *After the War was Over: Reconstructing the State, Family and the Law in Greece, 1943–1960*.

7. For contemporary Greek political history, see indicatively Clogg, *A Concise History of Greece*.

8. For the control and monitoring measures of left citizens in Greece, see *Alivizatos, Les institutions politiques de la Grèce à travers les crises, 1922–74*.

9. The Greek case, as far as I can tell, was the first public debate of its kind in Europe in the 1980s. The debates on the security records in the former Eastern European people's republics – records that had been maintained by the secret police of the communist regimes — started some months later. On December 1989, Stasi offices throughout East Germany were occupied by citizens in protest at the agency's activities.

10. In August and September 1989, the Greek press hosted dozens of articles by historians, where they, individually or collectively, expressed their disagreement with the destruction of the files. See also Asdrachas et al., *Contemporary Archives, Files and Historical Research*; and among others Iliou, *The Files*.

11. In July 1977, *Ta Nea*, one of the most popular Greek newspapers, published a series of interviews with historians entitled 'Our History: Do You Need to Rewrite it?'

12. For contemporary Greek historiography, see Kitroeff, 'Continuity and Change in Contemporary Greek Historiography', 143–72; Liakos, *'Modern Greek Historiography (1974–2000): The Era of Tradition from Dictatorship to Democracy', 351–78.*

13. The case of Nicos Svoronos, one of the most important Greek historians of the twentieth century, is evidential. In 1955, Svoronos, who lived in self-exile in Paris for political reasons, lost his Greek citizenship because of a history book considered leftist by Greek officials. In 1977, immediately after the end of the junta, the School of Philosophy of the University of Athens bestowed the title of emeritus professor on Svoronos, who during the 1980s assumed some high-level management positions in the tertiary education system. Among them, he became a member of the organizing committee of the newly established University of Crete.

14. For memory and historiography of the time, see Mazower, 'The Cold War and the Appropriation of Memory: Greece after Liberation', 212–32.

15. Iliou was the founder in 1992 of the Contemporary Social History Archives (Aski). The KKE's archives made up a large part of the archive (1945–1968). See www.askiweb.eu.

16. See, among others, the contribution of V. Panagiotopoulos, in Asdrachas et al., *Contemporary Archives.*

17. Besides Iliou's articles (1989), see also the article by A. Elefantis, one of the best-known Greek intellectuals of the left: 'Giati kaikan oi fakeloi' ['Why Were the Files Burned?'], 4–6.

18. Ankersmit, *Sublime Historical Experience.*

19. See M. Couroucli and V. Karamanolakis, 'Renegotiations of Twentieth-Century History: Access to "Sensitive" Government Records and Archives in Greece', 136, where there is reference to the wider issue of archival accessibility in Greece.

20. Three years after the adoption of a law allowing citizens to view their personal files from the Stasi archives in the united Germany, there were already over 2.7 million applications. See Miller, *Narratives of Guilt and Compliance in Unified Germany: Stasi Informers and their Impact on Society*, 8–9.

21. The formation of the first association of Greek archivists some months later, on the grounds that there was a need for measures for the conservation of the archives, is evidential.

22. See the contributions of V. Panagiotopoulos, A. Liakos and S. Asdrachas in Asdrachas et al., *Contemporary Archives.*

23. Bevernage, *History, Memory, and State-Sponsored Violence: Time and Justice*; and especially for police files see McAdams, 'Transitional Justice: The Issue That Won't Go Away', 304–12.

24. White, 'The Practical Past', 10–19.

Bibliography

Alivizatos, N. *Les institutions politiques de la Grece à travers les crises, 1922–74.* Paris: Librairie Generate de Droit et de Jurisprudence, 1979.

Ankersmit, F. *Sublime Historical Experience.* Stanford, CA: Stanford University Press, 2005.

Asdrachas, S. et al. *Contemporary Archives, Files and Historical Research.* Athens: Etaireia Meletis Neou Ellinismou (in Greek), 1991.

Bevernage, B. *History, Memory, and State-Sponsored Violence: Time and Justice.* London: Routledge, 2012.

Clogg, R. *A Concise History of Greece*, 3rd ed. Cambridge: Cambridge University Press, 2013.

Close, D.H. *The Origins of the Greek Civil War.* London: Routledge, 1995.

Couroucli, M. and V. Karamanolakis. 'Renegotiations of Twentieth-Century History: Access to "Sensitive" Government Records and Archives in Greece', *Zeithistorische Forschungen/Studies in Contemporary History* 10(1) (2013), 131–39.

Derrida, J. *Archive Fever: A Freudian Impression*. Chicago and London: University of Chicago Press, 1998.

Elefantis, A. 'Giati kaikan oi fakeloi', *O Politis* 111 (1989), 4–6.

Iliou, P. *The Files* (in Greek). Athens: Themelio, 1989.

Kitroeff, A. 'Continuity and Change in Contemporary Greek Historiography', in M. Blinkhorn and T.M. Veremis (eds), *Modern Greece: Nationalism & Nationality* (Athens: ELIAMEP, 1990), 143–72.

Liakos, A. 'Modern Greek Historiography (1974–2000): The Era of Tradition from Dictatorship to Democracy', in U. Brunnbauer (ed.), *(Re)Writing History: Historiography in Southeast Europe after Socialism* (Münster: Lit Verlag, 2004), 351–78.

Margaritis, G. *History of the Greek Civil War*, vol. 1. Athens: Bibliorama, 2001.

Mazower, M. 'The Cold War and the Appropriation of Memory: Greece after Liberation', in I. Deák, J.T. Gross and T. Judt (eds), *The Politics of Retribution in Europe* (Princeton: Princeton University Press, 2000), 212–32.

Mazower, M. (ed.). *After the War was Over: Reconstructing the State, Family and the Law in Greece, 1943–1960* (Princeton: Princeton University Press), 2000.

McAdams, A.J. 'Transitional Justice: The Issue That Won't Go Away', *International Journal of Transitional Justice* 5(2) (2011), 304–12.

Miller, B. *Narratives of Guilt and Compliance in Unified Germany: Stasi Informers and their Impact on Society*. London and New York: Routledge Chapman & Hall, 1999.

Ricoeur, P. *Memory, History, Forgetting*. Chicago: University of Chicago Press, 2004.

Voglis, P. *Becoming a Subject: Political Prisoners during the Greek Civil War*. New York: Berghahn, 2002.

White, H. 'The Practical Past', *Historein* 10 (2010), 10–19.

CHAPTER 13

Historians and/in the New Media

Effi Gazi

If an engaged intellectual is someone who is constantly curious about the world and its politics and positively eager to intervene and make a contribution and an impact in her field or area of expertise, it goes without saying that the digital and the new media domains are critical areas for the involvement of historians.[1]

History is moving fast beyond the 'written word'. Information and communications technology (ICT), multimedia installations and digitization projects provide new formats for researching, reflecting, presenting, exhibiting and performing the past. The 'digital turn' necessitates a revision of the public roles of historians and a reassessment of their involvement with the wider social, cultural and political domain internationally. Our relation to and with the digital networking world of the internet is a critical factor in the transformation of history and historical consciousness nowadays.[2] Without succumbing to technological determinism, it is necessary to examine the changes in the roles of history and historians within the new media ecologies, taking into account the internal properties of new technologies, their social and cultural as well as cognitive and epistemological implications.

In this context, archival preservation, historical narratives and performances beyond the written text and the history/memory nexus are challenging themes related to the wider areas of the politics of history and the public roles of historians. Prominent historians and theorists have intervened either in scholarly journals, website domains or online forums in order to address key issues regarding the new media ecologies. My chapter will discuss certain themes and topics raised in these interventions in an attempt to offer an

---

Notes for this section begin on page 258.

overview of the major issues concerning historians and/in the new media, in preserving, narrating, performing and remembering the past. The final part of the chapter will focus on some reflections concerning how historians can move in the new media ecologies as well as how they can act as important navigators towards a critical engagement with the past within the new media domain. The chapter touches on the possible consequences of these changes to scholarly communities, to academic and non-academic communications ecosystems, on the digital versus print issue concerning publications and on multimodal historical narratives (such as multimedia, visual, sound components).

Preservation

The past decade or so has seen a tremendous alteration in processes of *preservation and archiving* in digital media. This represents a third milestone in history in transcoding and archiving past evidence into a new medium. First, there was the post-Renaissance transcription of manuscript culture in print, which started in the late fifteenth century and climaxed in the eighteenth and nineteenth centuries. This was followed by the transcription of print and image culture in film (photography, cinema, microfilm, microfiche) throughout the late nineteenth and twentieth centuries and, more recently, the ongoing transcription of archival content into digital format and the creation of digital archives. As Gregory Paschalidis points out, 'every one of these moments of transcription … or remediation … involves a sweeping process of cultural rewiring; a total rearrangement of mnemonic resources … as well as new and different cultural politics'.[3]

If cultural repercussions are overwhelming, what are the implications of new processes for the discipline of history? More than a decade ago, the late Roy Rosenzweig claimed that 'the future gurus of historical research methodology may be the computer scientists at Google who have figured out how to search an equivalent of a 100 mile-high pile of pages in half a second'.[4] This was perhaps an eccentric argument once upon a time. As digitization explodes, however, it no longer sounds that strange. Computing, cinema, television, music, video, telephones, communication – different areas of social life are being affected in a myriad of ways by digital techniques that are replacing older analogue forms. Technologically mediated experience has, of course, had a long history, especially throughout the twentieth century.[5] Yet, digitization is now such an overwhelming phenomenon that it calls for further exploration within the frame of social and cultural practices. The plethora of digitization projects in recent decades has initiated a new 'system' for preserving the past and has incorporated a variety of new technologies into 'the ancient practice of history'. It seems that an entire paradigm shift is taking place as older preservation systems are being gradually replaced by new ones. For years, historians have been used to looking for sources, material, evidence – and, perhaps, constantly complaining about their scarcity as Rosenzweig succinctly pointed out.[6] What happens now? Do we have more or less? What about the 'information overload' that digital techniques of preservation have caused? Are we moving towards a 'complete historical record' or is this just another illusion of techno-optimists? The life expectancy of digital material is currently being questioned while its fragility is being pointed out. Yet, no matter how short-lived it might eventually prove to be, the 'information overload' is a constant phenomenon of our historical and mnemonic culture.[7]

What might be the epistemological, cultural or even political implications of this abundance? Certain historians and scholars in the humanities and social sciences regard these issues as 'technical' ones. They think they are not related to the core concerns of history. Yet, they are. Digital archives and material, and digital information in general, pose complex theoretical questions. Who saves and what, who preserves historical material, who uploads it in the web? Who is interested in it and what do individuals and collectivities do with it? Blurring the boundaries between scholarly and public/popular images of the past is an important consequence of digital preservation. Audiences are being redefined constantly, requiring us to rethink the social and cultural uses of the past. Also, who preserves historical data nowadays? In the course of modernity, we have been used to the 'archive', to the official collection of material normally linked to the concerns of national states and their politics. A variety of agents, private and public, individual and collective, have now entered the field of preservation – especially digital preservation. Photographs, correspondence, videos and films are uploaded every single moment and become immediately accessible, particularly to internet users. This paradigm shift in archiving is indicative of the multiplicity of factors involved in the preservation of the past.[8] Techno-optimists applaud 'the democratization of history' and the end of 'hierarchical controls' while techno-pessimists lament the loss of concrete historical narratives. Although binary oppositions of this sort tend to be reductive and simplistic, the public responsibility of preserving the past is a complex social and political issue.

Narratives and Performances

Digital textuality, on the other hand, has more similarities to the 'patchwork quilt', the mosaic, the pastiche and the collage, as Paul Arthur claims, rather than the 'embroidery' we have been used to in mainstream historiography.[9]

In a similar vein, Ann Rigney discusses how the 'stand-alone monograph' written by the individual historian is challenged in the new media ecology, while the 'book' is no longer the exclusive model for theoretical reflection on narrativity or on historical knowledge.[10] This is indeed a challenging issue. Firstly, on the narration front, the authority of the single narrator is being questioned. The openness of online texts invites us to think along the lines of interactivity, participation and multiplicity. Fragmentary story forms resist linearity and perhaps a narrowly defined homogeneity.[11] Moving from the individual plot to the universe of interactivity, one has to rethink the processes of immersivity and experientiality, as Rigney suggests, and perhaps reapproach the social production of historical narratives in terms of their circulation and transformation across different genres and media. For instance, contemporary research in psychology has pointed to the fact that visual-spatial processing is different in technologically constructed 'immersive' and 'non-immersive environments'. As a result, immersive environments may require different image encoding and transformation strategies as they evoke 'real-life experiences'. In a non-immersive environment, individuals utilize scene-based frames of reference whereas immersive environments encourage viewer-centred frames of reference and equivalent strategies of encoding. It goes without saying that 'experience' is defined in quite different terms in different contexts.[12]

Despite the reservations of historians for the need to assess contemporary media ecologies and technologies, certain contributions and public interventions raise very important issues. Roger Chartier, for instance, points out the different formats of objects in the written world (letters, posters, newspapers etc.) that define categories of texts and uses of words, while he also underlines the surfacing of digital databases as new forms of textuality. The 'databization' of textualities challenges, in Chartier's view, traditional cognitive operations and imposes new modalities based on relational argumentation rather than a deductive, linear one.[13] More importantly, historians have to take into account the issues of property and authorship digital texts, libraries, blogs and sites involve. Although open access and mobile texts offer tremendous new opportunities for information and even knowledge deepening, textual overabundance and textual overload should not be misinterpreted. Indeed, there is growing tension between electronic communities of shareware and e-publishing and processes of restricted access. The historian Robert Darnton has defined Google Book Search as a 'monopoly of a new kind' and has been involved in the Digital Public Library of America, an open access project, arguing for the necessity to safeguard knowledge as a public good. Ever since the British Library sold off print collections of American newspapers after microfilming them, Darnton insists that the short lives of microfilms and digital collections should make us cautious of the potential dangers of 'great book massacres'. He also pointed out that the 'microfilm fever' of that first phase resulted in a great cultural loss, by not just getting rid of paper but also by disbinding books, splitting their spines etc.[14]

The History/Memory Nexus

Memory challenges history in a variety of ways in the new media ecologies. Within the digital media domain, projected memories appear less fixed and monolithic than traditionally defined 'history'. Memory studies have recently developed in very interesting directions in their exploration of memory, digitization and media. One of them is the 'participatory' nature of contemporary memory, especially within the domain of grief, trauma, loss and its blurring of the concepts of public/private and production/consumption. The social networking of memory allows for its variations, particularly in the digital domain. It also entails 'empathy at a distance' by linking experiences, images, representations in the 'globital memory field', as Anna Reading has defined it.[15] 'Globalization' and 'digitization', in this respect, reshape memory discourses and practices as they develop among 'hypersocial', networked individuals. Constant remediations enable processes of transcoding which affect both collective and individual identities. 'Crowdsourcing', that is the production of historical narratives 'from below' by a variety of contributors (not necessarily specialists), results in collaborative online history projects that promote 'combined expertise' at the expense of 'scholarly expertise' and that also challenge 'authorship', at least as the latter was defined in the age of the 'historical monograph'. If central institutions and organized groups, such as the communities of professional historians, were central in the formation of history and memory in the past, different individuals and collectivities take control now while the boundaries between 'producers' and 'consumers' are blurred.[16]

Memory-making tools have spread far and wide. Yet, do we need 'perfect memory' or is it a questionable gift? Viktor Mayer-Schönberger has discussed extensively the political repercussions of the 'digital inability to forget' and its impact on 'digital discrimination'.[17] Consciously or not, we keep storing data and disclosing information: biometric information, electronic IDs, information about our preferences, actions, opinions, habits and memories in a variety of formats on the internet. For millennia, we have been struggling to preserve memory and the past. It has been part of our education as historians and citizens to treasure the past. Now, the balance has shifted as data is continually stored. Mayer-Schönberger claims that we are threatened by 'perfect memory'. This is a challenging and thorny issue.

Are we perhaps the 'victims' of digital memory, which attacks privacy and empowers surveillance technologies in a 'digital panopticon'? The discrimination against 'information privacy' challenges, I think, our conceptualizations of memory and preservation in the age of 'digital citizenship'. We need, perhaps, to re-examine the frames of 'information privacy' without becoming engaged, on the other hand, in technophobic dystopias. This is a challenging intellectual and political enterprise; yet we have to undertake it. Historians, in particular, can develop important public roles by offering insights on the uses of past data and on the necessity both to remember but also to forget.

The historians – and theorists – I have mentioned so far have intervened in an ongoing scholarly and public debate on the implications and repercussions of new media for historical knowledge and for the past in general. Their involvement primarily addresses the theme of the public and political roles of historians in the digital age, as well as relevant issues concerning researching, writing but also *sharing* history. In this context, it is perhaps more constructive not to think along the lines of a 'success story' of history and digitization or of a linear and progressive narrative. We could, rather, imagine the digital era as a *process itself* through which we are trying to navigate ourselves. This is a crucial debate about the future of history, and its primary scope should be how to bring the discipline forward.

Navigation

How can we navigate ourselves – as historians, as intellectuals and as citizens – in the digital era? Firstly, more than simply 'borrowing' or even constructively appropriating concepts and knowledge from other disciplines, historians can make a significant contribution by investigating mass culture, popular culture, mass media and technologically mediated experience in previous eras. As George Lipsitz points out, 'time, history, and memory become qualitatively different concepts in a world where electronic mass communication is possible'.[18] In this sense, the relationship between history, technology and mass communication in various epochs and contexts is of particular interest, both in order to better conceptualize the historically bound nature of many contemporary phenomena and the changing nature of historical thinking – and acting. Secondly, it is important to reflect on history in the digital domain without succumbing to Manichaean dichotomies or binary oppositions. Challenging ideas and concepts are constantly being developed in this direction. The concepts of 'transduction' and 'trans-materiality' are important points of departure for a reappraisal of the digital world, particularly for historians and humanists. In a recent article, the historian William

Turkel begins with the example of a medical historian who, each time he visited an archive, smelled rather than read letters because he was particularly interested in paper sprayed with vinegar in order to prevent the spread of cholera. By tracing documents sprayed with vinegar, the historian was able to track the course of an eighteenth-century epidemic.[19] Quite a few historians would lament the loss of scents and smells, and as a consequence of crucial historical evidence, through digitization. However, Turkel analyses the various ways contemporary machines can digitize Volatile Organic Components (VOCs) and produce scent analysis, proceeding in this way in the materialization of different formats and modalities. The author defines this process in terms of *transduction* and *trans-materiality* – that is, as *a conversion of energy from one form to another*. It is, I think, a provocative theme, which calls for further investigation. The new possibilities of *materialization in different formats* might allow us to overcome the losses of the material traces of the past in digitization. Not only scents but also other crucial evidence, such as stains or the chemical composition of paper, might be saved. Both historical evidence but also historical experience might gain new perspectives. Imagine digital books, for instance, enhanced with scents or different sensory modalities such as taste.

Finally, the critical and reflective ways the new economies of social memory and the interplay of history/memory/technology contribute to the re-examination of major given assumptions in history are important. This is an issue of primary importance for the changing public roles of the historians in an age of 'transitional turmoil'. Stefan Tanaka argues that the current digital media revolution should remind us that our present-day conceptions of history did not arise until the late eighteenth century, when people began writing about the past in linear chronological time. In this context, history became a foundational technology for stabilizing modernity.[20] Tanaka engages in a constructive 'dialogue' with Andreas Huyssen, who has argued that contemporary temporal boundaries have weakened the relative stability of the past and the present and have contributed to the rise of an 'eternal present'.[21] By offering a more nuanced approach to the relationship of history and time, Tanaka turns to a history of the concept of time itself and points to the ways time became linear over the course of history. In this vein, he argues that the 'danger of an "eternal present" threatens this form of historical thinking … linking the past to linear chronological narratives … not necessarily to history, broadly conceived'.[22]

There are many points of departure and many points of entry in the 'wonderland' of new media and digital technologies. In this field, historians can develop new roles and practices that can contribute to new forms of both historical and civic knowledge. It is evident that there has been a breakdown in the disciplinary identity of academic history. This phenomenon, however, does not equate necessarily with the replacement of critical historical thinking by 'commodified pasts'. On the contrary, it primarily invites us to a reassessment of the complex skills required in order to develop 'digital historical literacy'. More than just 'teaching history' today, it might be important and urgent for historians to enable history students and all those interested in history to become active and critical *users* of historical information.[23] The vast opportunities for the circulation of historical information in recent decades is most welcome; yet, this phenomenon does not exclude contradictions, inconsistencies, silences, gaps, misinformation, even manipulation. Digital historical literacy requires explorations outside the 'epistemology of the analogue' – i.e. an epistemology that relies on the 'stability' and 'presence' of sources, data, evidence etc.[24] It involves a multiplicity of processes, including, first, a critical reflection on major binary oppositions such as the presence/absence of data or the subject/object of scholarly research or the fixity of categories such as 'time' and 'space', 'body' and 'mind'. Second, it involves an exploration of the varieties and complexities of digital literacy, which includes information assessment, visual learning, emotional and affective involvement and learning. In this context, it is of particular interest for historians to take into account the fact that a crucial cognitive effect of the digital era is that instead of knowing 'by memory', it might be more important to know where to find the information. Also, 'transactive memory' as well as 'external memory' – that is, the storing of information that entire groups of people can share and use – might not necessarily belong to the realm of science fiction but to relatively close cognitive realities.[25]

Professional historians might not be *the* experts of the past, but they are, perhaps, sensitive and skilled organizers and thinkers who can guide themselves and others through the corridors of history in the new media, by offering perspectives, codes and criteria. In this case, historians may be able to help others to distinguish between 'usable' and 'disposable' pasts and engage in the processes of 'productive remembering' and 'creative forgetting'.

Effi Gazi is Associate Professor of History at the Department of Social and Educational Policy, University of the Peloponnese (Greece). She has taught at the Universities of Thessaly (GR), Athens (GR), Crete (GR) and Brown (USA). She was Research Fellow at Birkbeck College, London and at the Institut für Griechische und Lateinische Philologie, Free University, Berlin. She has published on the history and theory of historiography, public history, intellectual and cultural history as well as on the history of nationalism and the history of modern politics and religion. Her recent publications include *Metapolitefsi: Greece at the Crossroads of Two Centuries* (co-edited with Kostis

Kornetis and Manos Avgeridis, Athens 2015, in Greek), 'The English, the French and the Senegalese: Nation, Race and Empires in Greece during World War I', in Efi Avdela et al. (eds), *Racial Theories in Greece, 19th – 20th c.* (Heraklion 2017, in Greek) and 'Greek Historiography in the 20th Century: Opening a Research Agenda', *Historein* 16 (1–2) (2017) (editor).

Notes

1. Research for this chapter was conducted within the framework of the research act Aristeia I 'Greek Historiography in the 20th Century: Debates on Identity and Modernization', co-financed by Greece and the European Union (2012–2015).
2. Poster, 'Manifesto for a History of the Media', 39–49.
3. Paschalidis, 'Towards Cultural Hypermnesia: Cultural Memory in the Age of Digital Heritage', 179–81, academia.edu, last accessed 10 February 2014.
4. Rosenzweig, 'Scarcity or Abundance: Preserving the Past in a Digital Era', 735–62.
5. With regard to the relation between older visual media and history, see especially Sobchack, *The Persistence of History: Cinema, Television and the Modern Event*.
6. Rosenzweig, 'Scarcity or Abundance'.
7. Rosenzweig, 'Scarcity or Abundance'.
8. For an analysis of this process, see especially Kansteiner, 'Alternate Worlds and Invented Communities: History and Historical Consciousness in the Age of Interactive Media', 131–48. See also, Morris-Suzuki, *The Past Within Us: Media, Memory, History*.
9. Arthur, 'Digital Fabric, Narrative Threads: Patchwork Designs on History', 106–20.
10. Rigney, 'When the Monograph is no Longer the Medium: Historical Narrative in the Online Age', 100–17.
11. Rigney, 'Monograph'.
12. For an overview of contemporary research and literature on the topic of 'immersivity', see Kozhevnikov and Dhond, 'Understanding Immersivity: Image Generation and Transformation Processes in 3D Immersive Environments', 1–10.
13. Chartier, 'Languages, Books, and Reading from the Printed Word to the Digital Text', 133–52.
14. Darnton, 'The Great Book Massacre', 16–19.
15. Reading, 'Memory and Digital Media: Six Dynamics of the Globital Memory Field', 241–52; Reading, 'Globital Time: Time in the Digital Globalised Age', 143–62 and the volume by Garde-Hansen, Hoskins and Reading, *Save as… Digital Memories*.
16. Kansteiner, 'Alternate Worlds and Invented Communities'.
17. Mayer-Schönberger, *Delete: The Virtue of Forgetting in the Digital Age*.
18. Lipsitz, '"This Ain't No Side Show": Historians and Media Studies', 147–61.
19. Turkel, 'Intervention. Hacking History: From Analogue to Digital and Back Again', 287–96.
20. Tanaka, 'Pasts in a Digital Age'.
21. See especially Huyssen, 'Present Pasts: Media, Politics, Amnesia', 21–38 and by the same author *Present Pasts: Urban Palimpsests and the Politics of Memory*.
22. Tanaka, 'Pasts in a Digital Age'.
23. On 'active users of history', see Arthur, 'Exhibiting History: The Digital Future', 33–50.

24. For the 'epistemology of the analogue' in historical studies, see Poster, 'History in the Digital Domain', 17–32. See also, Poster, 'Culture and New Media: A Historical View', 134–40.

25. On the particularities of digital literacy, Eshet, Y., 'Digital Literacy: A Conceptual Framework for Survival Skills in the Digital Era', 93–106, www.openu.ac.il, last accessed 24 April 2014.

Bibliography

Arthur, P.L. 'Exhibiting History: The Digital Future', *reCollections: Journal of the National Museum of Australia* 3(1) (2008), 33–50.

———. 'Digital Fabric, Narrative Threads: Patchwork Designs on History', *Interdisciplinary Humanities* 25(2) (2008), 106–20.

Chartier, R. 'Languages, Books, and Reading from the Printed Word to the Digital Text', *Critical Inquiry* 31(1) (2004), 133–52.

Darnton, R. 'The Great Book Massacre', *The New York Review of Books* 26(4) (2001), 16–19.

Eshet, Y. 'Digital Literacy: A Conceptual Framework for Survival Skills in the Digital Era', *Journal of Educational Multimedia and Hypermedia* 13(1) (2004), 93–106. Retrieved 24 April 2014 from www.openu.ac.il.

Huyssen, A. 'Present Pasts: Media, Politics, Amnesia', *Public Culture* 12(1) (2000), 21–38.

———. *Present Pasts: Urban Palimpsests and the Politics of Memory*. Stanford, CA: Stanford University Press, 2003.

Garde-Hansen, J., A. Hoskins and A. Reading (eds). *Save As … Digital Memories*. Basingstoke and New York: Palgrave Macmillan, 2009.

Kansteiner, W. 'Alternate Worlds and Invented Communities: History and Historical Consciousness in the Age of Interactive Media', in K. Jenkins, S. Morgan and A. Munslow (eds), *Manifestos for History* (London: Routledge, 2007), 131–48.

Kozhevnikov, M. and R.P. Dhond. 'Understanding Immersivity: Image Generation and Transformation Processes in 3D Immersive Environments', *Frontiers in Psychology* 3(284) (2012), 1–10.

Lipsitz, G. '"This Ain't No Side Show": Historians and Media Studies', *Critical Studies in Mass Communication* 5(2) (1988), 147–61.

Mayer-Schönberger, V. *Delete: The Virtue of Forgetting in the Digital Age*. Princeton and Oxford: Princeton University Press, 2009.

Morris-Suzuki, T. *The Past Within Us: Media, Memory, History*. London: Verso, 2005.

Paschalidis, G. 'Towards Cultural Hypermnesia: Cultural Memory in the Age of Digital Heritage', in M. Tsipopoulou (ed.), *Digital Heritage in the New Knowledge Environment: Shared Spaces and Open Paths to Cultural Content* (Athens: Hellenic Ministry of Culture, 2008), 179–81. Retrieved 10 February 2014 from academia.edu.

Poster, M. 'History in the Digital Domain', *Historein* 4 (2003–2004), 17–32.

———. 'Culture and New Media: A Historical View', in L.A. Lievrouw and S. Livingstone (ed.), *The Handbook of New Media: Student Edition* (London: Sage, 2006), 134–40.

———. 'Manifesto for a History of the Media', in K. Jenkins, S. Morgan, A. Munslow (eds), *Manifestos for History* (London: Routledge, 2007), 39–49.

Reading, A. 'Memory and Digital Media: Six Dynamics of the Globital Memory Field', in M. Neiger, O. Meyers and E. Zandberg (eds), *On Media Memory: Collective Memory in a New Media Age* (Basingstoke and New York: Palgrave Macmillan, 2011), 241–52.

———. 'Globital Time: Time in the Digital Globalised Age', in E. Keightley (ed.), *Time, Media and Modernity* (Basingstoke and New York: Palgrave Macmillan, 2012), 143–62.

Rigney, A. 'When the Monograph is no Longer the Medium: Historical Narrative in the Online Age', *History and Theory* 49(4) (2010), 100–17.

Rosenzweig, R. 'Scarcity or Abundance: Preserving the Past in a Digital Era', *The American Historical Review* 108(3) (2003), 735–62.

Sobchack, V. (ed.). *The Persistence of History: Cinema, Television and the Modern Event*. London: Routledge, 1995.

Tanaka, S. 'Pasts in a Digital Age', in J. Dougherty and K. Nawrotzki (eds), *Writing History in the Digital Age* (University of Michigan Press, 2013). Retrieved 9 December 2013 from http://writinghistory.trincoll.edu/.

Turkel, W.J. 'Intervention. Hacking History: From Analogue to Digital and Back Again', *Rethinking History* 15(2) (2011), 287–96.

CHAPTER 14

Street History

Coming to Terms with the Past in Occupy Movements

Antonis Liakos

The aim of this chapter is to explore how history is experienced and how we make sense of the past beyond academic boulevards or the plateaus of public history. One of the fallacies that impedes the understanding of these non-academic ways of perceiving the past is the concept of 'lay history', which puts into contrast two ways of conceiving the past.[1] But it is misleading to think that historical thinking inside or outside the historical community is coherent and uniform. Relations to the past, the concept of the past itself, are culturally constructed and hardly conform to a general pattern. Nevertheless, the discipline of historiography has been based on a canon of thinking the past, codified by historicism in nineteenth-century Europe, which substituted older and different ways of conceiving the past.[2] The central concept of the new discipline was defined by distance and detachment. In its premises was, first, the disconnection of the knowing self from the object of knowledge and, second, the distinction of the present from the past as well as the attribution to the present the role of the observatory of the past. The past turns into the historical past when it is estranged from the present and when its familiarity has vanished. Generations of students of history learn that historizing means distancing from the past, and distancing means transforming the past into a historical past.[3] Third, there must be no interference with the object of observation. Although history creates identities, identities need an outer view to attribute authority to their formation. The concept of impartiality of history

Notes for this section begin on page 274.

and of objective truth empowers its role in identity formation. Fourth, distance requires the creation of an institutional culture, which guarantees and oversees the independence of the historian. The concepts of distance, impartiality, objectivity, neutrality and others have formed the ethos of professional history and defined the role of the historians as observers and not participants. Impartiality, neutrality and distance create the most widespread social representation of history. Of course, this contrast between historicism and all the other ways of thinking the past exists more in the self-image of the discipline and in the guidelines for the study of history and less in the existing realities of using history and the past. The landscape is more colourful and rich in hybrid forms, connected with national cultures and, also, international trends.

In this chapter, I will try to zoom in on, and then to explore, cases where all the above concepts of the historicist foundation of the discipline exist but in a different constellation: history belongs not to the past but to the future, and the historical subject is not impartial but interferes with its object. The past is respected under the condition that it proves useful for the future. It is not a closed past but a past surprisingly reversible.

The story begins in Athens, in 2008. On the evening of 6 December, a 15-year-old schoolboy, Alexis Grigoropoulos, was shot dead by police in a district crowded with young people. His death provoked a huge wave of protest overnight by teenagers around the country, and violent clashes with the police resulted in the burning of several shops and cars in central Athens. In the following days, the city became a theatre of protest movements, demonstrations, civic riots and open public assemblies.[4] The outbreak of the crisis, two years later, renewed this wave of protests, and during most of the summer of 2011, Sytagma, the central square in front of the Greek parliament, was occupied by demonstrators. Mass protest rallies and overnight occupations of central places had begun that February in Cairo, followed by Madrid, Lisbon, Athens, London, New York and Istanbul. The protests acquired different names: Arab Spring, Indignados or αγανακτισμένοι (aganaktisménoi) in Spain, Portugal and Greece, Occupy movement in London and New York and Gezi Park protests in Istanbul.[5] During these years of demonstrations in Athens (2008–2011), among the other slogans in graffiti and manifestoes, there were many references to historical terms and concepts. The question is whether there is something to understand here about the historical thinking of the protesters. What do they reveal regarding their aspirations and their views on the past, present and future? What do they say about historical thinking, not in the class and the library but in the streets? My analysis is organized in six points.

Cultural Transfer

Although these images and slogans appeared in a Greek context, they were transfers from protest, antiglobal or Occupy movements from around the world, transmitted mostly through the new social media. The term 'cultural transfer', coined by Michel Espagne for the open cultural exchanges between France and Germany in the eighteenth century, might be useful for our analysis.[6] Espagne's term does not imply a system of exchanges but an open and dispersed circulation of cultural elements and ideas. In the technological environment of the twenty-first century, this exchange also regards technologies of communicating. For example, in the 2008 riots, SMS was the main tool of mobilization. Three years later, Facebook took the primary role. These transfers belong to two types. The first regards transfers from one country to the other; and the second from one literary genre to the other. An example of the transfers of the first type is the slogan 'Fuck 1968, act now!' This is one of many variants with the same meaning of calling on others not to stick to the heroic past but to take a position in the present and to act now. This imperative, with the same wording, was used in English student rallies and in Greek graffiti at the same time.

Another example is the Guy Fawkes mask worn by Anonymous activists, inspired by the one worn by the title character of the graphic novel *V for Vendetta*, which became a global symbol of protest after the success of the homonymous film by James McTeigue in 2006. The Anonymous figure is an example of the transfer of the second type – i.e. from one genre to the other. The same film was a transfer from the graphic novel by Alan Moore and David Lloyd, which was inspired by the English gunpowder plot of 1605.[7]

Some slogans were patterns whose content was altered according to the new context. The slogan 'Remember, Remember the 5th of November', from the film *V for Vendetta* but originally from a song sung on Guy Fawkes Night, was transformed in Athens in 2008 to 'Remember, Remember the 6th of December', the day of the shooting of Grigoropoulos, and the night when the mass reaction started.

Besides the transfer of slogans, there were also transfers of pictures. The image of the slogan 'We are writing history, you are writing laws' is related ironically to the well-known picture of Iwo Jima and the related memorial at Arlington cemetery. This image, symbolizing tough collective effort and victory, retains its meaning, although it has been shifted from a patriotic to a protest context; its figures have been changed from mariners to students, and the US flag has been replaced by the symbol of autonomists. There are many variants of this slogan with the same image and meaning: 'You write memoranda, but we write history.' 'History belongs to the people.'

The Double Bond with the Past

Should the past constitute a tradition on which new protest movements ought to be grounded, or does this moment of protest, the present event, involve a break with the past, a totally new moment?

One of the central historical monuments in Athens is the bronze statue of Theodoros Kolokotronis, a hero of the 1821 Greek Revolution. He was the military chief of the rebel army in the Peloponnese, a leader with an immense popular appeal. His portrait still decorates classrooms, his statue stands in central places in many cities and towns and numerous streets around the country bear his name. He is identified as a symbol of courage, patriotism, self-sacrifice and independence from the ruling political class. His is popularly known as the 'Old Man of the Morea' (Morea being a historical name for the Peloponnese). So the monument of the Old Man became a palimpsest of contrasting slogans, where we can detect an oscillation between the rejection and the acceptance of the past.

The older graffiti on the pedestal of his statue was the phrase 'Delete the past' in English. Sometime later, this graffiti was replaced by another, in Greek, stating 'Help us, Old Man'. Again, after a while, this slogan was replaced by another, in English, saying 'Fuck heroes, fight now'. Break with the past, appeal to continuity, again rejection of the past. Such an ambivalence and oscillation between a radical break with the past and continuity is not unknown in all radical moments of European history, from the English Puritan revolt in the seventeenth century, to the French Revolution and the social and political upheavals of the twentieth century and the artist vanguards.[8] The interchange of language, from English and Greek, is noteworthy. English works here as the language of youth subcultures. The two slogans in English, 'Delete the past' and 'Fuck heroes, fight now' share the same meaning. This is a call for a clear, abrupt and violent break with the historical past. History and tradition are considered as cultural and intellectual burdens that inhibit people from aspiring to a totally new beginning and the fight for it. On the other hand, the Greek slogan 'Help us, Old Man' implies the opposite relationship with the past: continuity, where the past is a source of inspiration. Here, there is a plea to national history to give a helping hand in the hard times of the present. The national is a comforting supplement to the loss of self-confidence. This attitude was better articulated with the paradigmatic use of the past.

In a cartoon of the period, the same hero, from his equestrian statue, declares: 'We have sold our property to save our country,' to which a passer-by replies: 'They (the elites, the government) have sold the country to save their property.' The meaning is clear, although this double relationship with the Old Man is not with his history but with his myth. As we know from the historical scholarship regarding the Greek revolution, Kolokotronis was the opposite of a selfless person. His nickname among his contemporaries was 'Captain Spoiler' because upon entering a captured city he ordered his soldiers to stay back until he had finished looting for himself, first. Second, during the time of revolution, Kolokotronis advocated a military government to restrain the emerging power of politicians and notables, who had formed the first national assembly and enacted a republican constitution.[9] Nevertheless, he was the kind of charismatic popular leader whom the people trusted, beyond and above political institutions. In other words, he was an ideal symbol of populism.

The double relationship with the Kolokotronis monument is a metonymy of the relationship with the past; not any past but with the national past. The contrasting attitudes have nothing to do with contrasting interpretations but with the representation of the national past – the public commemoration and the public image of this past. The role of this past in the present is at stake. Historical symbols in the city are signs of the materiality of history, and this material history, which forms the symbolic space of the city, is the target. Civic rioters made successive efforts to place new meanings on them. Statues and monuments lost their monumental distance and coldness and were immersed with the people on the street, acquiring new life. On the other hand, their cleansing and whitening was part of the return to order and normality ideology, strongly evocated by Government and Media.

Another example of this double bind with the past is the slogan 'Fuck 1968, fight now!' We have already referred to the journey that this concept has taken. The year '1968' stands as a chronotope for student radicalism, which should be surpassed. But there is an ambivalence to this urge. On the one hand, there is the rejection of the ideas and the tradition of 1968 (and an antagonism with the generation of 1968); and on the other, there is a tendency towards the appropriation of it. The idea of the complete and radical rupture with the past was already present in the 1968 experience. '*Il nostro tempo è qui e comincia adesso*' ('Our time is here and it starts now') was one of the slogans of the Italian student movement of 1968. According to Luisa Passerini, a student activist of the 1968 movement and later historian, this idea of deleting the past was also expressed by the idea of this generation that 'chooses to be orphans'.[10] This tension between continuity and breaking with the past is common, and I would say structural in the conception of time in radical movements. '*Du passé faisons table rase*' (literally, 'Of the past let us make a clean slate') was one of the verses of the nineteenth socialist anthem *The Internationale*. But in the case of 1968, the break with time has to do with the tradition inside the movement and, more precisely, with the generational structure of experience. The generation of 1968 created its own myth – something that also gave them an identity – which absorbed new elements over time, in line with the new professional and life experiences of this generation and the changing of political attitudes towards the spirit of 1968.[11] This generation already had a double bind with its past, evocating it and at the same time criticizing it. This double evocation was transformed into a political ideology and lifestyle that became the target of the protesters. The Greek equivalent of this generation is the generation of the Athens Polytechnic occupation of 1973.[12]

Analogical Thinking and the Reversibility of History

Since it began, the Greek crisis has undergone different narrative structures. These narratives followed a dividing line according to the acceptance or the rejection of the 'memoranda', the austerity policies and the structural reforms imposed by the representatives of international lenders in Greece (the IMF, European Central Bank and European Commission), generally known as the troika. Since 2010, the memoranda have been at the focal point of all political and ideological debates in Greece. As a consequence, there were two sets of narratives marking different ways of narrating the crisis: the pro-memorandum and the anti-memorandum narratives. For the pro-memorandum camp, the most common narrative of the crisis is related to the discourse on modernization. As the story goes, Greece is not yet, and not completely, a modern country, and the crisis is the result of an incomplete or reluctant modernization. Narratives create a mental landscape, and the narrative of modernization creates a global map of modern and not-yet modern countries but also divides societies in two: a modern or aspiring-to-be-modern part and a pre-modern or modernization-resistant part. This *allochronism* that is at the core of the colonial viewpoint is used not only for former colonial societies outside Europe but also has its analogical forms in societies within Europe.[13]

Regarding the anti-memorandum narratives, the most popular and diffused one views the complexity of causes in a conspiracy narrative, blaming foreigners and the Greek political system for looting the country's wealth. Individuals or groups stand for economic or social forces. This narrative believes that Greece has once again become the target of 'foreigners', with the complicity of the Greek upper classes. Since World War II, the opposition between Greeks and foreigners has been an idea deeply rooted in the Greek historical imagination, giving rise to a binary opposition in national/popular culture and identity. Nikos Svoronos, a prominent and influential historian, who lived for a long time in exile in Paris, gave a most formal explanation of this attitude. According to Svoronos, the inherent character of Greek history is its antagonism towards foreigners, and resistance forms a constant feature of Greek identity.

Most of the followers of this narrative read the present situation through the lens of the history of World War II. So, Greeks, who suffered a lot under the Third Reich, are supposed to be victims now of the Fourth Reich. Same oppressors, same resistance. The conclusion is the need for a new version of the National Liberation Front (EAM) that would unite all political forces, from the communists to the nationalists. In this narrative, social and economic problems are representing as national problems, and the violation of national sovereignty is the common element between the 'then' and the 'now'. No surprise, therefore, when Angela Merkel visited Athens in October 2012 that banners appeared in demonstrations depicting the German chancellor with a Hitler moustache, with the images of Hitler and Merkel, or calling for 'Resistance to the 4th Reich'. The implication was 'then and now, same story'. Analogical thinking is not the privilege of historical illiterates. Even a Spanish university professor, according to the *New York Times* (28 March 2013), compared Merkel's policies to Hitler's in the online edition of the prestigious Spanish newspaper *El País*. After attracting severe criticism, much of it coming from Germany, his article was removed.

Another re-evocation of World War II had to do with the Greek Civil War and the defeat of the left. In graffiti that appeared on many walls, we could read 'Varkiza is over, Class war now' or 'December came to an end'. The meaning here can be summed up by the following: the period of peace since the surrender of the armed resistance to the state in February 1945, after the revolt the previous December in Athens, is over. The class war has resumed. Varkiza is a suburb of Athens where the surrender was signed by the EAM representatives, and since then it has been a metonymy for the humiliation of the left. EAM was the largest resistance organization during the war years. It was led by a coalition in which communists had the prominent role. Its armed wing ELAS liberated most of continental Greece. Two months after the withdrawal of the German army in October 1944, a bitter dispute broke out between the government and EAM over the disarmament and the demobilization of ELAS, which escalated into a dramatic month of civil war that December in Athens, which was a turning point in Greek history. EAM surrendered and signed a pact (at Varkiza) that, as it turned out, left the majority of its followers and activists at the mercy of their enemies, most of them former collaborators with the Nazi occupiers. As in the previous cases of analogical thinking, these graffiti lack historical precision because the period that started with the surrender of EAM finished two years later, with the outbreak of the civil war, which ran from 1946 to 1949.[14] The analogy skips these events. But an analogy does not imply exact comparisons. Nevertheless, the reference to December 1944 is not totally wrong. As in the civil war, the big cities and the urban population did not take part; they mainly had the defeat of December, which had a bigger emotional weight and more bitter consequences. The trauma for the older generation in Athens is indeed the revolt and the defeat of December 1944, and this month of this year became a *lieu du mémoire* for contemporary Greek history.

Another example of analogical thinking is the slogan 'The dictatorship didn't end in 1973'. The present situation is often compared with the 1967–1974 junta. But the dictatorship did not end in 1973 but in the following year. This inaccuracy provoked a big debate in the press, but it is not an indication of historical illiteracy on the part of the protesters. In November 1973, the uprising in the Athens Polytechnic and its bloody suppression became the symbol of the resistance against the dictatorship. The junta fell in July 1974, nine months after the Polytechnic events. Since then, two annual commemorations mark the end of this seven-year regime.

The first is the anniversary of the Polytechnic uprising, on 17 November, which for forty years has been marked by mass rallies and often clashes with the police. The second is the anniversary of the restoration of democracy, on July 24, an official event with no popular appeal, which until 2010 was celebrated by a reception in the gardens of the residence of the Greek president. It is obvious that in a comparison of the present with the past, there are symbolic dates that matter more than historical accuracy. The 17 November commemoration was used also to subvert the meaning of the official narrative of the successful transition from dictatorship to democracy. As Kostis Kornetis notes, 'the past was not necessarily present in the form of the knowledge of history, but in the form of a cultural memory that flashed up at specific moments'.[15] One moment when the past flashed up was the period of the economic crisis. The 'culture of the Metapolitefsi' (the Greek term for the transition to democracy in 1974) was considered as one of the main causes of the crisis. An extensive literature in media has identified Metapolitefsi as a period of relaxation of the social norms, of populism and leftism. The response was the re-evocation of the democratic struggles against dictatorship. At the same time, a parallel debate on the reconceptualization of this period took place in Portugal and Spain regarding their transitions from dictatorship to the crisis. In Portugal the anthem of the 1974 revolution, *Grândola, Vila Morena*, was used to connect the anti-austerity demonstrations of 2011–12 with those of 1974. The slogan '*Españoles, Franco ha vuelto!*' (Spaniards, Franco came back!) paralleled the Greek 'The dictatorship didn't end in 1973.'[16] History repeats itself in both cases, which also demonstrates the idea of reality as fragile and history as reversible. Time is conceived as a black hole that absorbs the temporal distance.

Personification of History

In numerous slogans, History (with a capital H) becomes a reality not as the past but as a living entity, different from the past. It acquires substance, its own life, transcends past, present and future and judges the present. The slogan 'You are writing laws, we are writing history' or 'You are writing memoranda, we are writing history' means that History is written by the people in the streets, in opposition to the ruling class or the governing authorities. History is popular resistance; it is written by the people, in the streets, in an act of disobedience, through class struggle.

In most cases, this staging of history means a split between the people, who 'are' history and the rulers who inhibit the course of history. This is an echo of the idea of progress, and in the place of progress stands history. This motto could also be read as a reversal of the common idea that 'History is always written by the winners.' But it is something more. These leaflets do not support the idea that history is written by the defeated, but they declare: 'We are writing our own history' and in another case, 'We are the history.' The latter slogan is also an element of a double cultural transfer. The Italian version '*La storia siamo noi*' was written on a large protest banner at the commemoration rally in Genoa in 2008 (marking the anniversary of Carlo Giuliani's killing in the antiglobalization protests in 2001), meaning that history is not what the leaders of the big economic powers (G8 and G20) decide it to be but what the people are struggling for. A strong feeling of appropriation of history. This Italian slogan is also a transfer from an older song by the 1970s *cantautore* (singer-songwriter) Francisco De Gregori.[17]

There is no distance between the subject and the object of historical thinking here. History is the unified experience of both but also a unifying image of the world in its temporality. The underlying meaning of this identification between history and the subject is the use of history as a way of making sense of the world. What has been imposed from above, and what is the reaction from below, is not something that is dispersed, contingent and without meaning and logic. All of that is History, and History has its logic, which is transfused to individual events. Through this use of the term history, the subject and his deeds are elevated to the rank of historical events. The concept of 'historical', from the nineteenth-century appropriation of the past, has changed several times in meaning ever since, oscillating between the residuals of the past (for example, when we speak about the 'historical' centre of a city) and the big, influential events. Here the term is endowed by the second meaning.[18]

History and the Future

The subject addresses History, announcing: 'History, we are coming'. There were several manifestoes and graffiti with the same motto. In one case, we read 'History, we're coming. Look towards heaven'. Looking towards the future, history is not the past but a force leading from the past to the future. The promise for the subject (or the moral imperative) is to join this course towards the future and not to stay behind or to be indifferent. This turn of history from the past to the future is interesting because it goes against the idea of the 'collapse of the future'. This idea describes a new configuration of time in the second half of the twentieth century, and this change of temporality is related with the turn to memory and with the growing inability to create progressive political visions. According to Andreas Huyssen, 'One of the most surprising cultural and political phenomena of recent years has been the emergence of memory as a key concern in Western societies, a turning towards the past that stands in stark contrast to the privileging of the future so characteristic of earlier decades of twentieth-century modernity.'[19]

Here, in these slogans, the future acquires a central place and also draws the present into its orbit. The present is connected with the future. One motto says 'Streets of December, images from the future', meaning that demonstrations and riots during December 2008 prefigure the class struggles and the social upheaval of the future. Another motto is much more explicit: 'We are coming from the future,' and, in reply to the pessimistic idea of the defeat of utopia and the 'end of history', another motto declares vigorously: 'Nothing is over. We are coming from the future.' The question is whether this trust in the future is a leftover from the ideology of progress – common to the traditional Left – or whether it is something new, accompanying the distrust in the future and the turn to the past. To understand how this concept of the future was used, we should move to the context, and particularly to the role of the future in the narratives of the Greek crisis. As we have seen above, the most common narrative, defending the official line, is that crisis is related to the lack of modernization. Greece is not yet, or not completely, a modern country, and this is the reason for the crisis. As a consequence, in order to join the future, society needs to unstick itself from past mentalities and 'do its homework', applying the structural reforms of the neoliberal agenda. Since the beginning of the crisis, an intense debate on the recent or even on the national past of Greek society has been at the core of public debates. The main argument of the government was that reaction to the reforms was due to the prevalence of the mentalities of the past. So protesters should demonstrate that they are not the defenders of the past order that have led to the crisis but are forerunners of the future. To a future different to what modernizing theories imply is the adaptation to the free market. But this appeal to the future is not defensive and is not confined to everyday political debate. The future is synonymous here with utopia, and history connects the present with the future because it is conceived as teleology.

In a number of leaflets, history exists and proceeds through time to an end (*telos*). This idea of history leading to a telos has deeply imputed historiography in various forms and degrees. It originated in the philosophy of history in the eighteenth and nineteenth centuries. Ideas of progress vs stagnation, and modernity vs tradition, were interwoven in historical narratives until the final quarter of the twentieth century. National historiographies also adopted a teleological pattern of narrating the history of the nation. Teleology and the personification of history are two ideas that are strictly and mutually tied. Through teleology, History acquires the status of a force, becomes a stream leading to a scope inherent in it. Teleology needs to depict History as a vehicle that travels, fulfils promises and accomplishes tasks. But teleology swings between two versions: one optimistic, the other pessimistic. In one leaflet we see the latter version where evolution leads from the ape to the human while neoliberal reforms in education reverses evolution, reverting humans to ape form. The optimistic version leads from apes to humans and from humans to a 'Free Galaxy', an anarchist and libertarian cosmic utopia. These uses of history engulf the whole of human evolution, giving the impression that the references to the future have a utopian flavour. They refer to a vague image of utopia, which here functions as a sign, as the desire to supersede reality.

Against Historicism

There is also the case of an open and very conscious aversion to historicism and historicity. In December 2009, a year after the Athens riots, a group of activists confiscated an album containing a collection of leaflets and graffiti from the riots of the previous year, published with the title *Restless: A Description of the Spontaneous in December 2008* by one of the major Athenian publishing houses. In the leaflet they distributed and posted online, they justified their seizure of the album on the basis that they refused to transform this 'living material' into a 'dead object' that could be placed in a museum. Museum means distance and neutralization of the documents. They did not deny the need to save the 'traces of the past' but insisted that this must be done for and by the 'movement'.

They recognized the need for historical distance, but they opposed this distance as a lack of commitment and as indifference to their cause.

They chose to publish a documented history of the events with the title *Remember December, Fight Now* (in English), and subtitled *The Experiences and Critical Account of the December Events, by the Fighting Communities of December* (in Greek).

Their attitude was clear: they were not historians free of any cause but historians with a cause. They were not indifferent to the past but believed the past served the present. This was not the past encapsulated in coffee table books but the past as a useful tool for changing the present. This concept of a tool is explicit and concrete in a leaflet published by *Archive ★71*, an autonomist library and archive in an occupied building in Athens. The text, which stated 'We try to learn and to defend the working class's past, contributing to its future,' is decorated by symbols of manual work, modern technology and intellectual jobs.

What kind of past is that? The distinction made by Hayden White between the historical and the practical past is useful here for analytical reasons, although in practice no past is totally historical.[20] In the story about the confiscation of the album containing leaflets, there is a clear statement in favour of the practical past and against the distance and indifference implied by the historical past. The past here, in the protest movements, is a past without historicity, without the sense of pastness. Historicism is based on the distinction of past, present and future. The past without historicity loses the rigidity of this distinction and becomes fluid. There is something more: an inversion of temporality, which questions the main assumptions of historical thinking.

The historicist attitude that the past is over and close to repetition has been the focus of criticism from many directions recently. Dominick LaCapra problematizes this attitude, focusing on traumatic events such as the Holocaust and arguing that historicity, which implies distance and the language of 'pastness', cannot be aware of how traumatic experiences are part of the present in conscious and unconscious ways. In the case of traumatic events, past and present cannot be separated in a clear way.[21] Bevernage and Lorenz also question the very idea of the separation of the past from the present, insisting on the social and political construction of the borderline between them. Much of this discussion has been based on the turn of historiography to victimhood and the experience of suffering. Here, we may observe the changing experience of time from a different perspective. Those reversing the order of time are not historians, or victims interrogated by historians. They are activists, who more than knowing the world desire to change it.[22] This desire for action put relating with the past on a different level to the desire to study the past on its own terms. This oscillation in confronting the past has its own history. In his 'A More Perfect Union' speech, delivered in Philadelphia in March 2008, then Senator Barack Obama, talking about racial discrimination, said 'The past isn't dead and buried. In fact, it isn't even past.'[23] He was paraphrasing the well-known aphorism of William Faulkner in his *Requiem for a Nun*: 'The past is never dead. It's not even past.' The use of this phrase by the future US president displays the importance of the immediacy of the past in political commitment. In a similar way, in protest movements, slogans regarding history and the past rearrange the constellation of past-present-future. This is not a new story. Historical consciousness has always oscillated between two poles. The first is the hic et nunc (here and how), the immediacy of political action, the politicization of the past. The past becomes a cultural, emotional and political source for the present. The second is the historization of the past (the past belongs to the past), the mediation of the past by history. In numerous circumstances, both forms of historical consciousness face the other, mainly in political movements aspiring to break with or maintain the political order and the order of time. But the same confrontation comes in civil wars and national confrontations. Here the sense of the immediacy of the past leads to the endless repetition of enmities. In those cases, the concept of historical distance, of the historicity of the past, of pastness, the 'working through' of the past, comes as a political proposal.[24]

We began this chapter as an exploration of paths outside the academic ways of making sense of the past. These paths are different but often coincide or overlap with academic paths. The last example comes from a graffiti in Athens regarding the opposition to racism: 'Our grandfathers were refugees, Our parents migrants, How can we be racists?'.
This graffiti explains to passers-by that a big part of the Greek population came here as refugees during the 1920s from Anatolia, Thrace and Black Sea coasts; that another part of the next generation were emigrants to western and northern Europe, Canada and Australia during the 1950s and 60s; so it poses the question how, with such an experience of being twice refugee and migrant, is it possible that their children and grandchildren are racist against the refugees and migrants who came here during the 1990s and the 2000 from countries at war or starvation regions? This graffiti tries to compare historical experience and to translate it into principles of behaviour. Without probably knowing it, the graffiti artist follows what Jörn Rüsen theorizes as the formation of historical consciousness.[25]

The encounter between street history and theory of history is an additional reason to deal with history outside the academy. Of course, street history is part of a wider problem. From the aspect of Greek history, the problem has to do with the question of how the crisis has changed Greeks' relationship with their past. From a theoretical aspect, the problem is how people in contemporary protest movements experiences time and history. It is interesting to contextualize the present theories on temporality and historical time to the past/present/future connections in concrete circumstances.[26]

Antonis Liakos is Emeritus Professor at the University of Athens. He is managing editor of the historical review *Historein,* and former chair of the Board of the International Commission for History and Theory of Historiography (2010–2015). His publications include writings on Italian Risorgimento, Modern Greek history, history of historiography and historical culture. During 2016 and 2017 he was president of the commission for educational reforms in Greece.

Notes

1. Klein, 'The Lay Historian: How Ordinary People Think about History', 25–45.
2. Nandy, 'History's Forgotten Doubles', 44–66; Iggers, *The German Conception of History: The National Tradition of Historical Thought from Herder to the Present.*
3. On the concept of historical distance, see *History and Theory*, 50, Theme Issue 50: Historical Distance (Jaap den Hollander, Herman Paul and Rik Peters, eds). See also Fasolt, 'Breaking up Time – Escaping from Time: Self-assertion and Knowledge of the Past', 176–96.
4. Kornetis, 'No More Heroes? Rejection and Reverberation of the Past in the 2008 Events in Greece', 173–97.
5. Simiti, 'Rage and Protest: The Case of the Greek Indignant Movement'.
6. Espagne, *Les Transferts Culturels Franco-Allemands.*
7. Buchanan et al., *Gunpowder Plots: A Celebration of 400 Years of Bonfire Night*; also the graphic novel by A. Moore, *V for Vendetta*, DC Comics (1982–1989) and the film *V for Vendetta*, directed by James McTeigue, 2006.
8. Hunt, *Measuring Time, Making History.*
9. Hering, *Die Politischen Parteien in Griechenland 1821–1936*, 61n.34.
10. Passerini, *Autobiography of a Generation: Italy, 1968*, 22–36.
11. For another encounter between historians (mostly of the '68 generation) talking about the history of '1968' and students crying 'to whom does 1968 belong, to us who realize it in the streets, or to you who study it', see Liakos, 'Contentious Historisation: The Conference on "1968, Forty Years Later"', 149–54, www.historeinonline.org/index.php/historein/issue/view/3 (last viewed 9 July 2014).
12. Kornetis, *Children of the Dictatorship: Student Resistance, Cultural Politics and The 'Long 1960s' in Greece*, 225–311.
13. Fabian, *Time and the Other: How Anthropology Makes its Object.*
14. Close, *The Greek Civil War, 1943–1950.*
15. Kornetis, 'No More Heroes', 190
16. Kornetis, '"Is there a Future in this Past?" Analyzing 15M's Intricate Relation to the Transición', 1–16.
17. De Grigoris, 'La Storia' (1997), www.youtube.com/watch?v=K-VpPGI2S50 (last viewed 8 July 2014).
18. Toews, *Becoming Historical.*
19. Cited by Assmann, 'Transformations of the Modern Time Regime', 39–56, 41.

20. White, 'The Practical Past', 10–19; and for a recent critique: Lorenz; 'It Takes Three to Tango: History between the Practical and the Historical Past', 29–46.
21. LaCapra, *Representing the Holocaust: History, Theory and Trauma*.
22. Bevernage and Lorenz, 'Breaking up Time – Negotiating the Borders between Present, Past and Future: An Introduction', 7–35.
23. 'Transcript: Barack Obama's Speech on Race', *The New York Times*, 18 March 2008, http://www.nytimes.com/2008/03/18/us/politics/18text-obama.html.
24. Ricoeur, *La Mémoire, l'Histoire, l'Oubli*.
25. Rüsen, '*Historical Consciousness: Narrative Structure, Moral Function, and Ontogenetic Development*', 63–85.
26. Hartog, *Regimes of Historicity: Presentism and Experiences of Time*.

Bibliography

Assmann, A. 'Transformations of the Modern Time Regime', in C. Lorenz and B. Bevernage (eds), *Breaking up Time: Negotiating the Borders between Present, Past and Future* (Göttingen: Vandenhoeck & Ruprecht, 2013), 39–56.
Bevernage, B. and C. Lorenz. 'Breaking up Time – Negotiating the Borders between Present, Past and Future: An Introduction', in C. Lorenz and B. Bevernage (eds), *Breaking up Time: Negotiating the Borders between Present, Past and Future* (Göttingen: Vandenhoeck & Ruprecht, 2013), 7–35.
Buchanan, B., A. Fraser and J. Champion. *Gunpowder Plots: A Celebration of 400 Years of Bonfire Night*. London: Penguin Books, 2005.
Close, D.H. *The Greek Civil War, 1943–1950*. New York: Routledge, 1993.
Den Hollander, J., H. Paul and R. Peters (eds). *History and Theory* 50, Theme Issue 50: Historical Distance (2011).
Espagne, M. *Les Transferts Culturels Franco-Allemands*. Paris: PUF, 1999.
Fabian, J. *Time and the Other: How Anthropology Makes its Object*. New York: Columbia University Press, 1983.
Fasolt, C. 'Breaking up Time – Escaping from Time: Self-assertion and Knowledge of the Past', in C. Lorenz and B. Bevernage (eds), *Breaking up Time: Negotiating the Borders between Present, Past and Future* (Göttingen: Vandenhoeck & Ruprecht, 2013), 176–96.
Hartog, F. *Regimes of Historicity: Presentism and Experiences of Time*. New York: Columbia University Press, 2015.
Hering, G. *Die Politischen Parteien in Griechenland 1821–1936*. Munich: Oldenbourg Verlag, 1992.
Hunt, L. *Measuring Time, Making History*. Budapest and New York: Central European University Press, 2008.
Iggers, G. *The German Conception of History: The National Tradition of Historical Thought from Herder to the Present*. Middletown, CT: Wesleyan University Press, 1983.
Klein, O. 'The Lay Historian: How Ordinary People Think about History', in R. Cabecinhas and L. Abadia (eds), *Narratives and Social Memory: Theoretical and Methodological Approaches* (Braga: Communication and Society Research Centre, 2013), 25–45.
Kornetis, K. 'No More Heroes? Rejection and Reverberation of the Past in the 2008 Events in Greece', *Journal of Modern Greek Studies* 28(2) (2010), 173–97.
———. *Children of the Dictatorship: Student Resistance, Cultural Politics and the 'Long 1960s' in Greece*. New York: Berghahn, 2013.
———. '"Is there a Future in this Past?" Analyzing 15M's Intricate Relation to the Transición', *Journal of Spanish Cultural Studies* 15 (2014), 1–16.

LaCapra, D. *Representing the Holocaust: History, Theory and Trauma*. Ithaca, NY: Cornell University Press, 1996.

Liakos, A. 'Contentious Historisation: The Conference on "1968, Forty Years Later"', *Historein* 9 (2009), 149–54.

Lorenz, C. 'It Takes Three to Tango: History between the Practical and the Historical Past', *Storia della Storiografia* 65(1) (2014), 29–46.

Nandy, A. 'History's Forgotten Doubles', *History and Theory* (*Theme Issue: World Historians and Their Critics*) 34(2) (1995), 44–66.

Passerini, L. *Autobiography of a Generation: Italy, 1968*. Hanover: Wesleyan University Press, 1996.

Ricoeur, P. *La Mémoire, l'Histoire, l'Oubli*. Paris: Seuil, 2000.

Rüsen, J. '*Historical Consciousness: Narrative Structure, Moral Function, and Ontogenetic Development*', in P. Seixas (eds), *Theorizing Historical* Consciousness (Toronto: University of Toronto Press, 2004), 63–85.

Simiti, M. 'Rage and Protest: The Case of the Greek Indignant Movement', *GreeSE Paper* 82 (2014), Hellenic Observatory Papers on Greece and Southeast Europe.

Toews, J.E. *Becoming Historical: Cultural Reformation and Public Memory in Early Nineteenth-century Berlin*. Cambridge: Cambridge University Press, 2004.

White, H. 'The Practical Past', *Historein* 10 (2010), 10–19.

AFTERWORD

The Historian as an Engaged Intellectual

Historical Writing and Social Criticism – A Personal Retrospective

GEORG G. IGGERS

There is no question that I have been an engaged intellectual my entire adult life, in fact since my youth. It is somewhat less immediately apparent how my social and political activism directly affected my historical writing and how my historical writing involved social criticism. In this chapter I shall attempt to establish how they are connected.

The Biographical Background of My Social Engagement as an Intellectual

To understand something about my motivations and work, it is necessary to trace the formation of my intellectual identity since my childhood. I was born in December 1926 in Hamburg into a Jewish family as Georg Gerson Igersheimer; the name was changed to Iggers against my will by our sponsors when we arrived in the United States.[1] The family, both on my father's and my mother's side, had been in Germany for centuries, considered themselves religiously Jewish, but were culturally fully German. I was brought up orthodox, but not strictly orthodox. I entered school on 3 April 1933 only two months after Hitler became Reich chancellor and

---

Notes for this section begin on page 297.

two days after the Nazi boycott of Jewish stores. My parents registered me not in the Jewish Talmud Torah school but in the normal public school in our district, the *Volksschule* for boys. I encountered no anti-Semitism from my fellow students or the teachers. This seems unusual, but contemporaries of mine had the same experience in Berlin, Göttingen and Wiesbaden, while two friends who grew up in Königsberg and Vienna, in Vienna already before the Nazi takeover, experienced harassment. The conscious dividing line in our class was between the majority of working class children and eight *bürgerlich* (middle class) children, but there was no hostility. All four Jewish pupils were bürgerlich. I felt ashamed to be bürgerlich, never ashamed of being a Jew; on the contrary, I was proud to be a Jew and still am. The teacher, Fritz Pohle, whom I liked very much, radiated the ideals of the youth movement with which he grew up. He was very much a nationalist and constantly reminded the class of the humiliation that Germany suffered from the Versailles Treaty. But he was no racist. Our neighbours and the stores with which we dealt remained friendly. The concierge of our apartment house and his wife often took me and my sister to their cottage over weekends. But outside of our immediate neighbourhood, I experienced the full impact of Nazi anti-Semitism; the pornographic hate propaganda of the Nazi yellow sheet, *Der Stürmer*, posted on billboards everywhere; and the signs on shops excluding Jews, as did one day the swimming pool to which I had regularly gone. One day I was severely beaten up by Hitler youths. All of this intensified my feeling of Jewish identity. In October 1936, I decided that I wanted to transfer to the Jewish Talmud Torah school, at a time when in most cities in Germany Jewish children could no longer attend public schools. Herr Pohle tried to persuade my parents to leave me in the school, assuring them very naively that as long as he was there I would be perfectly safe.

By that time I was a committed Zionist. Zionism to me meant socialism (although I did not know what the term meant) and not the authoritarian, state-controlled form as in the Soviet Union but the communitarian *kibbutz* as it existed in Palestine. I have long since given up my attachment to Zionism, which I came to see as a form of nationalism, but I have not given up its socialist ethos, from which Zionism increasingly distanced itself, and I gave up my orthodoxy while remaining a liberal religious Jew, identifying myself with the ethical, not the ethnic aspects of Jewish tradition. The idealistic Zionism in which I believed carried with it the conception of a 'new man' (*neue Mensch*), an idea also found in other non-Jewish youth movements of very different political persuasions: communist, Nazi, Catholic and others. The Zionist mission, as I understood it, called on Jews to leave the cities, cease their role in intellectual and commercial professions and work with their hands on the land. This agrarian romanticism as practised in the *kibbutzim* ultimately turned out to be totally unrealistic, as Israel moved far away from this early idealism to an increasingly urbanized, industrialized, capitalist society. My disillusionment with Zionism came gradually and painfully as I realized how the War of Independence involved ethnic cleansing and the Six Day War was followed by the occupation of the West Bank.

My Zionism thus involved a rejection of the bürgerlich world of my parents. This attitude was strengthened in the Jewish sports club to which I belonged, *Bar Kochba*, and the Zionist youth group affiliated with the Mizrachi Party, which was religious, Zionist and at that time socialist. I joined the youth group secretly against the will of my parents. They had very little understanding for what went on in my mind and were, moreover, very restrictive in a highly arbitrary way. So, for example, they forbade me to join the boys' choir at the Bornplatz synagogue (which I very much wanted to join and which would have paid me a small amount), arguing '*wir haben das nicht nötig*' ('we don't need that'). Tensions reached such a point that in December 1937, immediately after my eleventh birthday, they sent me to a 'Jewish Orphanage and Reform School' (*Israelitisches Waisenhaus und Erziehungsanstalt*) in Esslingen, near Stuttgart. It was actually a very progressive school, and I very quickly felt at home there, much more than with my parents. Most of the children came from the surrounding region where as Jews they could no longer attend school. There too, in preparation for emigration, we were taught that Jews must be trained to work with their hands, preferably on the land, and were taught accordingly. I was put in charge of the chicken coop. I ultimately realized that much of this romanticism was a mistake, but what remained was a social commitment that determined much of my adult life.

My parents brought me back to Hamburg in late August, several weeks before we left Germany for the United States on 7 October, only a month before the November Pogrom 1938 (Kristallnacht). I came to the United States with very mixed feelings, a country that in fundamental ways represented the extreme opposite of the Zionist world I had idealized. In retrospect, I am glad that I came to the United States and not to Palestine. We arrived in New York almost penniless. A very distant relative, a very well-to-do lawyer on Wall Street whom my father had almost miraculously discovered when in desperation he had made a trip to New York that March to find a sponsor for our immigration, helped us until the Hebrew Immigrant Aid Society (HIAS) settled us in Richmond, Virginia, in January 1939, three months after our arrival in the United States. In the meantime, I was thoroughly indoctrinated in American democracy at the school that I attended temporarily. I was disturbed by what I found in Richmond, the old capital of the Confederacy, which during the American

Civil War fought to preserve slavery. What shocked me was the treatment of the Black population, the segregation and economic exploitation, resulting in the extreme poverty of the vast majority, and their pervasive humiliation, much of which reminded me of the racial policies of the Nazis. I was quite outspoken and was reprimanded by my teachers, who told me that I should be grateful to be now living in a free country, to which I replied that I appreciated the relative freedom of white Americans but was very much aware that this freedom was denied to the Black population.

When the Freedom of Information Act enacted in the early 1970s made it possible to request copies of one's files, I obtained a document with a list of files the FBI had started on me in January of 1941, several weeks after my fourteenth birthday, but not the actual files, which they claimed no longer existed. I suspect that they dealt with my racial attitudes because the files started again in 1944, when I was very active in an interracial, intercollegiate student organization, in which students from the white University of Richmond and Black Virginia Union regularly met, and there was also interracial dancing, an absolute no-no at the time. In addition I was active in organizing a youth chapter of Union Now, an organization that advocated a world federation of democratic states. I had become not only an outspoken opponent of every form of racism but also of nationalism and colonialism; colonialism, of course, involved racism. This may also have come to the attention of the FBI. Already when I was in the Volksschule in Hamburg in early 1936, I wrote a letter to Emperor Haile Selassie, expressing my hope that Ethiopia would defeat the Italian invasion as they had done in 1896. In high school and at the University of Richmond, I had a small circle of friends: white Southerners who, like me, ardently opposed the racist status quo. I was still quite observant at that time, but none of my friends were Jewish.

My opposition to nationalism led me to turn to the study of foreign languages: French, Spanish, Italian, Russian and a not very successful attempt to learn Chinese. I began to invent an international language, Mundono, which would be easier to learn than Esperanto. At the University of Richmond, I majored in French and Spanish but was also interested in comparative literature and philosophy. I kept my German up to date and read both classical and twentieth-century literature. I took several philosophy courses but only one history course.

In 1944, at the age of 17, I completed my BA at the University of Richmond and began my graduate studies at the University of Chicago. I had wanted to study linguistics but discovered that linguistics as it was taught there was very far from the comparative study of languages, which interested me, and involved a highly analytical approach. I enrolled in the MA programme in German literature. I studied closely with Arnold

Bergstraesser, a German refugee political scientist, with whom I took courses in German literature and philosophy. Almost on my first day in the German department, I met Wilma Abeles in a seminar, my future wife, a Jewish refugee from Czechoslovakia, who was working on a doctorate in German. I did not know her well yet but was very impressed by her; at the end of the summer quarter she had to return to Canada to do civilian service, since it was still war, where she censored the correspondence of German prisoners of war interned in Canada, and for a semester after the war taught at the University of New Brunswick. There was no contact between us. In the meantime, I completed my MA with a thesis on Heinrich Heine and the French Saint-Simonians, which I wrote for Bergstraesser. I had become very interested in the history of socialism and had actually intended to write on Heine and Karl Marx in Paris but because of the wealth of material did not get beyond Heine's encounter with the Saint-Simonians immediately after he arrived as a refugee in France in 1831. I also joined a small but intensive Marx discussion group, which Stefan Brecht, the son of the playwright Berthold Brecht, organized. At the end of the academic year, I decided to spend the year at the New School for Social Research in New York City, where I took graduate courses in philosophy and sociology and met a number of leading German refugee scholars, including Albert Salomon, a student of Max Weber, who urged me to translate the Saint-Simonian *Doctrine de Saint-Simon*,[2] the economist Frieda Wunderlich, the phenomenologist Felix Kaufmann and the religious socialist and economist Eduard Heimann. I regularly went to Union Theological Seminary to hear the lectures of the German refugee and religious socialist Paul Tillich, who invited me to his office for a lengthy discussion. I attended his seminar (with Susanne Langer and John Randall) on the role of symbols in contemporary philosophy, based in part on the writings of Ernst Cassirer, the German refugee philosopher, who had just died. I also took two seminars on American intellectual history with Horace Kallen, a liberal Jew and close friend of John Dewey. I did not meet Hannah Arendt, who was not yet at the New School. Without any question, this was the most fruitful year of my university studies, one in which I was fully confronted with main currents of German, American and Jewish thought.

While in New York, I had to find part-time employment to support myself, including a temporary but very disappointing job as an office boy in the Jewish Agency for Palestine, where I first became aware of the hawkish aspects of the Zionist movement, and then in a Jewish-owned textile factory in Manhattan's Garment Center, along with mostly unskilled Jewish second-generation immigrant workers, where I had my first encounter with the working class.

Until then my life had little to do with my intellectual engagement as a historian. This changed when after my year at the New School I returned to the University of Chicago, where I entered the interdisciplinary doctoral programme under the Committee on the History of Culture, with a focus on Europe in the first half of the nineteenth century and with special fields in German history, French history, comparative literature, philosophy and religion. As my dissertation topic, I chose the political philosophy of the Saint-Simonians, which enabled me to define my own position to socialism.

My Early Involvement in Social Action

My return to Chicago in the fall of 1946 coincided with Wilma's return from Canada. This time we had a chance to get to know each other better; a friendship developed, a romance, and in December 1948 we married. In the fall of 1948, I had started my first teaching job at the University of Akron, where I taught German, German literature and Western Civilization. In the summer of 1950, I accepted an offer from Philander Smith College, an historically African American institution in Little Rock, Arkansas, to teach German, French and history. When we arrived in Little Rock in September, Wilma, too, was offered a position teaching German and French.

That fall, three months after the Korean War had begun, I taught a course 'The World since 1918'. The college library was very poor, but there was one good library, the Public Library, which was closed to Blacks. I wrote a letter to the liberal *Arkansas Gazette*, calling on the library to open its door to all readers without discrimination of race. While I expected no results, to my pleasant surprise the president of our college told me that the library board had asked him to inform me that my students could use the library. As a matter of fact, the library board had unanimously decided to desegregate the library but had not made a public announcement. Nevertheless, the decision became quickly known.

A few weeks later, a delegation from the local NAACP chapter came to see me. They were very good people: post office employees and small shop keepers who did not need to fear that they would be fired. They explained that they needed someone to do research and planning and asked me to assume the chair of the chapter's education committee. I accepted. Wilma and I became the first white members of the NAACP in Arkansas; on the national level the NAACP had always had white members. Although they were denounced by Southern racists as a movement akin in its radicalism to the communists, in fact their aims were very moderate: to gain for American Blacks the equality to which they were entitled as American citizens. They sought to achieve their goals through the courts and were actually very successful. It was only in the 1960s that the civil rights movement took the form of mass civil disobedience. Its main concern in Arkansas was to end segregation, particularly in the schools. I was able to fill an important void in undertaking the research needed for the law suits and in organizing these suits. At that time the US Supreme Court's 1896 Plessy vs Ferguson 'separate but equal' decision was still in effect, although facilities were nowhere equal. With the help of Wilma, who obtained the necessary statistics from the state education department by pretending to be a graduate student in education at the University of Chicago, I established vast inequalities in a number of Arkansas school districts.

The most important district was, of course, Little Rock. In 1952 I undertook a comparative study of the Little Rock high schools. The inequalities were striking. Appropriations for White students were nearly double those for Black students. The Black high school was so badly overcrowded that students had instruction in two shifts every day. But most shocking was the difference in curriculum. At the main White high school, students were prepared for college as well as for white-collar professions, and in addition there was a technical high school for Whites; the Black high school offered only the most elementary courses. My proposal was that Black students should be permitted to attend courses at the White high school not offered at the Black high school, an easy walking distance. The report received considerable support among liberal elements of the White community. It has sometimes been overlooked that the civil rights movement always also involved Whites. It is amazing that the School Board actually considered the plan seriously, but then was split three to three. It would have meant a first step to school desegregation. What I did was fully supported by the local NAACP chapter. Nevertheless, I had to remain in the background so that the racists could not identify me as a foreign agitator. I worked very closely with Daisy Bates, a very able and articulate Black person who became the spokesperson for the Arkansas chapter. She showed great courage in the face of repeated death threats.

Then on 17 May 1954, the US Supreme Court in its Brown vs Board of Education decision declared racial segregation in the schools unconstitutional, thereby repealing the Court's 1896 decision. I then arranged for a meeting of the local NAACP with the Little Rock School Board. The Board declared its readiness to comply with the Supreme Court decision and presented us with its desegregation plan, which we found acceptable.[3] Two high schools were under construction. When completed in 1956 they, as well as the already existing Central High School, would be opened without racial designation; the Black Dunbar High School would become a desegregated junior high school. By 1960 all schools would be desegregated. But when a second decision of the Supreme Court in 1955 declared that the desegregation of the schools should proceed 'with all deliberate speed', this was seen by the opponents of desegregation as a signal that they could delay the implementation of integration indefinitely, resulting in growing resistance to desegregation throughout the South. The Little Rock School Board caved in and announced that it would not desegregate the three high schools. We were thus reluctantly forced to file a law suit. I organized teams of two, who visited Black families in the neighbourhood of Central High School, whose children would have to walk the long way past Central High to the segregated high school on the East Side, and suggested to them that their children register at Central High School. Strikingly, almost all the parents agreed; indeed, we had to advise some parents not to participate, because their jobs would be in danger. We had expected twenty-eight pupils to attempt to register the morning the semester began; instead, over eighty showed up. They were all refused registration. Thus we had no choice but to bring a law suit, which went up to the US Supreme Court. The NAACP won the case to a limited extent. The US Supreme Court did not order the opening of Central High School as we had hoped but the admission of nine students of colour as a first step.[4] Wilma and I had visiting appointments at the University of Arkansas in Fayetteville during the academic tear 1956–1957, but I kept in close contact with the Little Rock chapter and attended the various planning meetings. Although the Attorney General of Georgia came to Little Rock to urge resistance, we expected the admission of the nine students to go peacefully.

In the meantime, I had accepted a position at Dillard University, a historically Black college in New Orleans. I wanted to stay in the South, but at Philander Smith College, with an eighteen- hour teaching load and teaching commitments in the summer, I had little opportunity to do any research. At Dillard University, Wilma and I were offered fifteen-hour teaching loads; in my case, exclusively in history. Moreover, John Snell, a noted historian of Germany who was about to become dean of the graduate school at the White Tulane University, assured me that he would see to it that Wilma and I would each teach a graduate course at Tulane each semester; Dillard University was willing to adjust our teaching obligations accordingly. At Tulane I also had access to a major research library.

We moved to New Orleans on Labor Day 1957, the day before the schools were to open in Little Rock. When we arrived in New Orleans the next day, we were shocked to learn that Arkansas governor Orval Faubus had mobilized the National Guard to prevent the admission of the nine pupils to Little Rock Central High School and that a nasty mob had threatened the children. Governor Faubus refused to honour the injunctions of the Supreme Court, and President Eisenhower finally sent US troops to Little Rock.

In New Orleans, I again became chair of the education committee of the local NAACP chapter. The racial atmosphere was much more tense than it had been in Little Rock, at least before the explosion in front of Central High School. The state of Louisiana and the local authorities were all committed to massive resistance in defiance of national legislation. There were no plans for the desegregation of the schools. The state legislature set up a commission to investigate what it defined as subversive activities. The NAACP was outlawed, although very quickly the federal courts reversed this decision. For the first and only time we and our children were threatened physically. My main project was the desegregation of a new high school, the Benjamin Franklin School for gifted children with IQs of over 130. The school authorities claimed that there were no Black children who would qualify. I believed that the school for gifted children would be a good place to begin the desegregation of the New Orleans schools. With the full support of the local branch of the NAACP and the American Civil Liberties Union, which arranged for the testing, we found students with high enough IQs to qualify; however, as expected, they were turned down. I was disappointed when in the last minute the national office of the NAACP advised against pressing the matter for the time being. In brief I was able to achieve much less in New Orleans than in Little Rock.

In both Little Rock and New Orleans, we lived in campus housing in the Black community. We had good relations with our neighbours. Our three children were born while we were living on the Philander Smith campus, and they played with the children of our neighbours. One indication that we were accepted was that in 1953 I was pledged as the first white brother into a Black fraternity. At the same time we had good white friends, in Little Rock Quakers, Unitarians and Bahai but also others, and our Tulane colleagues in New Orleans.

Although my involvement in civil rights had little to do directly with my work as a historian, I had my first excursion into historiography in the American history courses that I regularly taught at Philander Smith College and at Dillard University. I taught history not as a straight narrative but from a problem-oriented perspective. One such problem involved the interpretation of the Reconstruction after the American Civil War, when Blacks briefly played an important role in Southern politics. The students in the segregated schools had all been taught a Southern interpretation. We now read the chapter on the South Carolina legislature in James G, Randall's *Civil War and Reconstruction* (1937)[5] and in W.E.B. Du Bois's *Black Reconstruction in America* (1935).[6] Randall, not a Southerner but a Columbia University professor, who regarded himself a Rankean scholar committed to the strict reliance on sources, argued that the Black legislatures were total failures and ascribed this to their race; W.E.B. Du Bois, a distinguished African American historian and sociologist, showed the great contributions that the Black legislatures made in the areas of social reform, which survived the Reconstruction. Randall's book, notwithstanding its racist orientation, was greeted at the time as the standard work on the topic. Du Bois' was not even reviewed in the *American Historical Review*. It was clear that in both cases ideological presuppositions played a role. The question now was who relied more closely on the facts. Recent scholarship would agree with Du Bois; that the Reconstruction was by no means a catastrophe but enacted important social reform legislation.[7] In New Orleans, I had my all Black Dillard and all White Tulane classes on the world since 1918 meet together at least once a semester to the dismay of some of the hardliner Tulane faculty.

Years Devoted to Research and Teaching and Their Connection to My Social and Political Engagements

Once I was in New Orleans, I for the first time had time to devote to research and writing. I was fortunate in receiving three important research grants that enabled me to spend the period from May 1960 to August 1962 in France and Germany. Wilma and the children accompanied me. In Paris I regularly attended the lectures of Fernand Braudel at the Collège de France, the editor of the *Annales*, who repeatedly invited me for coffee after his lectures, where I met his most important colleagues. The journal was significant internationally for the way in which it opened up new ways in social history. This opened my eyes to the new directions in which historiography was going, and I began regularly to review the *Annales* articles in *Historical Abstracts*. From Paris I made a trip to Great Britain, where I discussed my work with four of the most important historical theorists in England at the time: Herbert Butterfield, Isaiah Berlin, Karl Popper and Geoffrey Barraclough. So the year in France with the side trip to England turned out to be very fruitful for my future work in the area of historiography.

In the course of my work in the *Bibliothèque Nationale*, I became increasingly interested in German historical thought, and particularly German historiography, since the beginnings of a so-called scientific school in the early nineteenth century, and in May 1961 we moved from Paris to Göttingen with Wilma and the three boys. We did so with some apprehension so shortly after the Holocaust, but the apprehensions soon dissipated as we made friends, particularly with the younger generation, who shared our critical attitude towards the German past and were committed to building a democratic Germany. Our boys went to public schools as the two older ones had done in France and had quickly learned the language. We realized that in many ways we were still culturally Central Europeans. We were soon well integrated into the Göttingen community. I ultimately reclaimed my German citizenship; Wilma, who had never been a German citizen, joined me, while we maintained our American citizenship with the intention of being active in both countries, and when the Jewish community, which had been annihilated by the Nazis, was revived I became an active member.

Towards the end of our stay in Germany, Roosevelt University in Chicago made me an offer. Roosevelt University had been founded in 1945 when a large number of students, faculty and the president walked out of George Williams College, affiliated with the YMCA, after it had barred Black students and founded this new school. We decided to go back to Dillard. But we were disappointed that Dillard, despite the changes that had taken place in New Orleans, had made no efforts to raise academic standards and programmes in a post-segregation era. It continued to view itself as an exclusively Black school. I began to think that many of the new challenges for me – and for Wilma – were in the North. The next year I accepted the offer from Roosevelt University, and Wilma found a position in modern languages at Loyola University in Chicago.

We liked Roosevelt and Loyola, but we were not very happy living in Chicago because of racial tensions also in the schools. We sent our children to Ray School, a public school near the University of Chicago. Theoretically, the school was integrated, with an about equal number of white and black students; in fact white and black students were in separate classrooms, supposedly because the black students were less advanced and less intelligent, but even gym classes, where IQ did not matter, were segregated. We participated in a group, 'Parents for Integrated Class Rooms', which demonstrated that there was considerable overlap in IQs and achievements between whites and blacks, but that did not move the Chicago school administration.

So when in 1965 I received very attractive offers from the newly opened Chicago campus of the University of Illinois and from the State University of New York at Buffalo, Wilma and I decided that I should accept the Buffalo offer, also for the sake of the children. In Buffalo, for the first time, I taught courses and seminars in my field of European intellectual history and worked with doctoral students. In the turbulent year of 1968, the department asked me to offer a seminar on Marxism as an Intellectual Tradition, which I conducted until my retirement in 1997. In 1968 and in the immediate years that followed, the seminar was a lively meeting place where students involved in the radical student movement, primarily from the philosophy and English departments, exchanged ideas with more conservative history students. Immediately after I arrived in Buffalo I succeeded in arranging a cooperative arrangement between SUNY/Buffalo and Philander Smith College, which saw Buffalo faculty members go to Philander Smith College to consult and Philander Smith College faculty coming to Buffalo for further training. This arrangement lasted only a few years, but I have continued my connection with the college to this today and was invited every two or three years to assist in the evaluation of the remedial education programmes.

Almost from my beginning in Buffalo I was chair of the education committee of the local NAACP chapter, which I gave up in 1975 because I thought the chair should be someone from the African American community, but I have continued to be an active member of the board of the chapter until now. The problems that faced the Buffalo chapter and still face it are very different from those in my days in Little Rock and New Orleans; it is not legal segregation but less visible but very real forms of discrimination in the areas of education, employment, housing, healthcare, racial profiling and criminal justice, just to mention a few. But my most important involvement during my early years in Buffalo was opposition to the Vietnam War. I had already participated in sit-ins in Chicago. In 1967, I helped to organize the Greater Buffalo Draft Counseling Center and then became one of its two directors. The Center differed from the Draft Resistance movement; while the latter urged potential draftees to destroy their draft cards and immigrate to Canada, we were for exhausting all legal alternatives, with going to Canada only as the last resort. I underwent an intensive training course conducted by the Central Committee of Conscientious Objectors and then counselled several hundred war resisters. I learned from an FBI file, which I obtained only recently, that the FBI had taped some of my counselling sessions. I regretted that only students from comfortably situated middle class families came for counselling. Almost all the persons we counselled were recognized as conscientious objectors and none went to jail; some were asked to do alternative civilian service, but in their stead, regretfully others, including African Americans, were sent to Vietnam. Our middle son Daniel, who was not recognized as a conscientious objector, although he very clearly was one, completed his education in Canada. He started a family there and did not return to the United States. Before going to Germany in 1971 on a research grant, I trained to counsel persons in the US military. After my return to Buffalo in 1972, for the first time I counselled young men, and occasionally women and members of ethnic minorities, who at a very early age had stumbled into the military.

Scholarly Contacts beyond National and Ideological Borders

So far my social and political engagements had had little to do with my role as a historian. This changed in the 1960s. They had a great deal to do with my commitment to establishing scholarly relations beyond national and, what is important, ideological divisions. Wilma and I were critical of both sides of the Cold War; not only the imperialism of both sides but also the systematic suppression of human rights in the Soviet bloc. Wilma was active during the Vietnam War in the Buffalo chapter of the International League of Peace and Freedom and its president during one year. The League rightly condemned the military dictatorship of Augusto Pinochet in Chile, but she resigned from the League when it answered to her suggestion that it should also pay attention to human rights abuses in Czechoslovakia that to do so would be red baiting.

We maintained close contacts with historians in Czechoslovakia. Wilma, who had been a Czechoslovak citizen, did not go there until 1966 because she had been afraid that she might not be permitted to leave again. In 1964, I went to visit her friends in the countryside and made contact with two historians in Prague, one of whom, Bedrich Loewenstein, is still a friend and played an important role in the Prague Spring. By 1968, we knew many of the historians, and we kept in touch with them after they had lost their jobs after the Soviet occupation.

In the summer of 1966 we decided to go to Czechoslovakia. We assumed that we would not be able to travel from Göttingen through the GDR (East Germany) to Wilma's friends in Bohemia, but I nevertheless applied for a transit visa by car for the five of us. To my surprise, we received the visa with an overnight stay in the university city of Halle. In the morning, two historians came to the hotel, took me to the university and invited me to spend a week in Halle the following summer. That afternoon, we met two historians in nearby Leipzig – Hans Schleier and Werner Berthold – who knew something about my work and who are still good friends. Berthold invited me in conjunction with my visit to Halle to spend a week at the Karl Marx University in Leipzig and to hold two lectures, one on American historiography and one on West German. An invitation to East Berlin followed. From then on I was invited to lecture regularly in Leipzig, whenever I was in West Germany, soon also at the Academy of Sciences in East Berlin and occasionally also at other universities. They apparently were quite aware that I differed from them politically, as became apparent in a letter that the Leipzig history department wrote to the authorities in 1969, asking them for permission to invite me despite these differences and stressing that the exchange of ideas was important for both sides.⁸ My talks were by no means uncritical. In Leipzig in 1967, I took issue with the East German identification of American and West German historians as 'NATO historians' and pointed at the critical stance regarding America's role on the world scene by the New Left Historians in the United States and the critical examination of the German past by West German historians such as Fritz Fischer and Hans Ulrich Wehler that simply did not fit this identification. These lectures, to my regret, always took place in a small closed circle with eminent East German historians, which included some doctoral candidates but no students. It was only in 1985 that for the first time I gave a public lecture, before students at the University of Jena, where I was asked to talk about contemporary trends in American historiography. I spoke not about what was being written but how it was written, stressing the diversity of approaches and interpretations, which led to a lively discussion.

In 1981, I suggested that the German Studies Association in the US invite not only West German, Austrian and Swiss but also East German scholars to its annual meetings. They did, and beginning in 1982 the East Germans came every year. Their first stop was always Buffalo, where I arranged a discussion between East and West German and American historians. A year later, I suggested that our department in Buffalo and the Academy of Sciences in East Berlin exchange doctoral students. We already had such an exchange with the Technical University in Darmstadt, West Germany, which I had established. I did not think that the Academy in East Berlin would agree to such an exchange but they did, and beginning in 1987 one doctoral candidate came each year from the GDR to Buffalo and one of our students went to the GDR. The following year, Werner Bramke, the chair of the history department at the Karl Marx University, expressed his interest in a broader student exchange with Buffalo, which did not come about with the end of the GDR.

In the fall of 1985, Wilma had a three-month research fellowship in Leipzig from IREX (International Research and Exchanges Board), a US-sponsored research programme that included the socialist countries. I accompanied her and devoted myself to an intensive study of historiography in the GDR. I asked Wolfgang Küttler, who headed the working circle for the history and theory of historiography at the Academy in East Berlin, to let me discuss my findings in his group, which he did. My talk contained both a critical and a very positive note. I strongly criticized the attempts of the GDR to reclaim a line from Luther to Frederick the Great and Bismarck as part of their progressive heritage and in an effort to mobilize nationalist and Prussian sentiments for its political agenda. At the same time, I was very positive about new work that was being done in the area of social and cultural history, which had been largely ignored in

West Germany. I began to edit a small volume, *Ein anderer historischer Blick* (*A Different Look at History*),[9] with contributors, all of whom were later considered sufficiently important in the reunited Germany to find positions. Although my comments were well received in Küttler's circle, Ernst Engelberg, who was considered the dean of East German historians and who had not attended the session, felt directly offended. He had presented me with a copy of the first volume of his Bismarck biography, which had just been published and was then also published by the conservative Siedler Verlag in West Berlin and acclaimed by conservative circles in West Germany. He had been in exile during the Nazi years. Referring to my remarks about Luther and Bismarck's foundation of the German Reich (*Reichsgründung*), he wrote to me that I 'was still strongly influenced by the resentments which we held in 1945 as émigrés'.[10] Yet my criticisms did not prevent my being invited to lectures thereafter. My comments were published in *Geschichte und Gesellschaft*[11] in West Germany and in *History and Theory*[12] in English. In 2007, German President Horst Köhler awarded me the Federal Cross of Merit (*Bundesverdienstkreuz 1. Klasse*) to recognize the work I did during the Cold War in building bridges between the two parts of divided Germany.

But I also established contacts with historians in other countries. Quite early on, I began to exchange visits and lectures with Jerzy Topolski in Poznan and through him came to know other Polish historians and, starting in the late 1970s, also Hungarian and Rumanian historians. I was not able to make contacts with historians in the Soviet Union until the final stages of Perestroika. However, in 1984–85 we had a young Soviet historian as a guest in our department in Buffalo, which turned out to be a very valuable experience for him, as he came to know a freer and more open society than the one he had known.

In 1980, together with Charles-Olivier Carbonell from France, from whom the idea came, and Lucian Boia from Bucharest, I co-founded the International Commission for the History of Historiography at the International Congress of the Historical Sciences in Bucharest. I saw to it that on the board of directors of seven people East and West were equally represented, with Carbonell as president. An international, multilingual journal, *Storia della Storiografia*, was founded. I was a member of the board until I retired from it in 2005, and I am still on the editorial board of the journal. From the beginning, Zhang Zhilian, a distinguished professor of European intellectual history at Beijing University, worked with us. Subsequent conferences took place in various European cities, including Poznan and Budapest, and in China and in Japan. In 1982, while I was chair of the Buffalo history department, I hosted a Chinese scholar, Qi Shirong, for half a year. Qi arranged for me and Wilma to come to his university, the Beijing Teachers College, now Capital Normal University, for six and a half weeks in 1984. I lectured and led discussions on the Annales and on Western Marxism, not only in Qi's college but also at Beijing University, at the Chinese Academy of Social Science and at Nanjing University. Several invitations to China, as well as to Taiwan, Japan and South Korea followed. All of my books except the one on the Saint-Simonians and several of my articles were translated into Chinese and some also into Japanese and Korean.

How My Ethical and Social Commitments Expressed Themselves in My Scholarly Work

All my historical writing was deeply affected by the ethical and social commitments I formed in my early years. I have already mentioned my first book, *The Cult of Authority: The Political Philosophy of the Saint-Simonians: A Chapter in the History of Totalitarianism*,[13] a revised version of my dissertation; it was published once more in 1970 with some changes after I had access to the Enfantin papers in Paris. The book reflected my belief in democratic socialism and my rejection of the Saint-Simonian authoritarian form of socialism. While in Paris in 1960–61, I turned to a new project on the role of the idea of progress in nineteenth- and twentieth-century thought. My study of the Saint-Simonians had made me aware of the discussions around the idea of progress in the nineteenth century. On the one hand, there was a tremendous optimism broadly shared, including by Marx, about the course of history; on the other hand, there was the consciousness, very important in the Saint-Simonian writings, of a crisis of modernity, not only in the economic but also in the intellectual and cultural sphere. I now began a project, intended to be a book, on the decline of the ideas of progress in nineteenth-century and contemporary Western thought. A preliminary article of mine on the idea of progress was published in the *American Historical Review*.[14] It outlined my basic theses on the decline of this idea. In the course of my work in the *Bibliothèque Nationale*, I became increasingly interested in German historical thought, and particularly German historiography, since the beginnings of the so-called scientific school in the early nineteenth century. I conceived the idea of writing a study of this tradition from its beginnings in the nineteenth century to the period following the end of the Third Reich. My motivation was clearly political. Without making the German historical profession responsible for the advent of Nazism, I nevertheless wanted to examine the extent to which their extreme nationalism and their ardent rejection of democracy helped to create a mentality that was willing to make its peace with the Nazi regime without fully identifying itself with it. At the core of their ideology was the claim of objectivity; that they had finally made history a scientific discipline – scientific not in the sense of the natural sciences but of a humanistic cultural science (*Geisteswissenschaft*), which rested its claim on scientific objectivity on its strict reliance on documentary evidence. In the course of the nineteenth and the early twentieth century, the German school of historical studies had become a model for academic disciplines of professional history in much of the world. My argument was that the historians who were part of the German professional school of historians were far from objective. Instead, they were thoroughly ideological in constructing their narratives, creating a German past going back to the middle ages that was more myth than an honest account *wie es eigentlich gewesen* (as it actually happened) as Ranke had demanded. But my critique went further to question the philosophical assumptions on which this historiography proceeded, and it represented a particular form of historicism (*Historismus*) that rightly recognized the historical context in which all aspects of the past and present had to be seen, but it denied the Enlightenment belief in universal human rights in order to justify the status quo as represented by the semi-authoritarian national state created by Bismarck. For them, the subjection of much of Germany under Prussia in 1871 represented the high point of history. For most historians in this tradition in the Weimar Republic, the defeat of Imperial Germany in World War I did not shake this conviction. My book, *The German Conception of History: The National Tradition from Herder to the Present*,[15] was thus a call on German historians to rethink their past from a democratic perspective. Shortly after the German edition was published, I received a letter from Thomas Nipperdey, a relatively conservative German historian but by no means a part of the dominant ultranationalist school I had criticized, who wrote me that I was wrong in focusing on the ideological position of the historians and not sufficiently appreciating the solid historical work they did;[16] as I replied to him, their historical work could not be separated from their ideology. This, of course, immediately raises the question as to whether my critique of the German national tradition had its roots in my own subjective experiences, including my experiences with the Nazis. Of course it did. But this did not necessarily invalidate it.

The German paperback translation of 1971[17] had a much wider circulation than the original English one of 1968 and went through several editions. It came at a time when a younger generation of historians, such as Hans-Ulrich Wehler, Jürgen Kocka, Hans Mommsen and Wolfgang Mommsen began a critical examination of the German past. This book helped me to become well acquainted with this new critical, democratically oriented generation and to participate in their discussions.

While my *The German Conception of History* was still nation-centred, even if I criticized the narrow nation-oriented focus of the German historical profession, my later work was increasingly transnational and comparative. In 1973, I published *New Directions in European Historiography*.[18] It dealt with the reorientation of historiography away from traditional event-oriented political history to social science orientations. I gave particular emphasis to the French Annales' interdisciplinary approach, aiming at an *histoire totale*, encompassing economics, sociology, anthropology and the humanities. At the time the Annales had still been relatively little received outside of France, except in Latin America, where they were already taken very seriously. In Germany, Gerhard Ritter, the dean of the conservative nationalist school, had attacked the Annales and offered a defence of the old national tradition of writing history.[19] The *Historische Zeitschrift*, at the time the most important German historical journal, to my pleasant surprise published my article on the Annales in which I attempted to clear up the misunderstandings of the Annales that dominated in Germany.[20] I also discussed at length the West German *Historische Sozialwissenschaft* (Historical Social Science), whose proponents soon afterwards founded the journal *Geschichte und Gesellschaft*. All of this had clear political implications, with a turn to democratic, social orientations in historical writing. In this way it was a continuation on a broader transnational scale of my *The German Conception of History*.

What was particularly new in my *New Directions* book was the inclusion of a chapter on Polish historiography, which reflected a turn away from orthodox Marxism to a more open economic and social history by Witold Kula in Warsaw and the historians of the Poznan school. Several of their writings were published in the *Annales*. My book was quickly translated into Italian, Danish, Greek, Chinese, Japanese and Korean. DTV, the West German paperback publisher who had published *The German Conception of History*, asked me to prepare a German edition, for which I rewrote the book completely and with the support of two of my Buffalo colleagues included a chapter on British Marxism and on American demographic approaches to urban history.[21]

In the meantime, I worked on a critical anthology of recent trends in West German social history, *The Social History of Politics*,[22] and the already mentioned *Ein anderer historischer Blick*, on innovative trends in East German social history. At the request of the German publisher Vandenhoeck & Ruprecht I wrote a comparative survey of major trends in Western historiography since the turn away from social science paradigms to the stress on cultural and semiotic aspects, *Geschichtswissenschaft im 20. Jahrhundert: Ein kritischer Überblick im internationalen Zusammenhang* (1993)[23] – revised English edition, *Historiography in the Twentieth Century: From Scientific Objectivity to* the *Postmodern Challenge* (1997).²⁴ I recognized the contribution that the cultural turn, and to a lesser extent the linguistic turn, had made in regard to in understanding the past but also criticized their radical epistemological relativism, their efforts to turn history into a form of literature, which saw all historical narratives as products of poetic imagination that would not be subjected to rational standards of inquiry, so that in the final analysis there was no clear dividing line between history and fiction. I engaged Hayden White, a leading representative of this position, in several discussions, one of which was published in *Rethinking History*, in *Geschichte und Gesellschaft*, in the post-Soviet Russian journal *Odysseus* and in China.²⁵ The book itself appeared in ten European and East Asian languages and went through a number of editions to bring it up to date. At the same time, I became very much aware of the limitations of the book; its treatment of historical thought and writing exclusively in the Western world.

My next project, a global history of modern historiography, sought to overcome this limitation. It was published by Longman, based in London, who in 1913 had published the classical *History and Historians in the Nineteenth Century*,²⁶ which was one of the few comparative works – in fact, until recently, the only one – that went beyond the common treatments of the major West European nations and the United States and also examined the smaller Eastern, Southern and Northern European nationalities, which had generally been neglected. I had had one previous incursion into global historiography, an *International Handbook of Historical Studies: Contemporary Research and Theory* (1979), which I co-edited with Harold T. Parker. This anthology was unique at the time in including not only contributions about historiography in the Western world, including countries in the Soviet sphere, but also East Asia and India and also an article about Sub-Saharan Africa by two leading Nigerian historians.²⁷ Longman expected me to write a history of modern Western historiography, but I felt that in a modern, global, postcolonial world, this was not enough, and I had neither the knowledge nor the linguistic skills to undertake such a task. I asked my Chinese friend Q. Edward Wang to cooperate and my former Indian student, Supriya Mukherjee, to take on the Indian part. I had first met Wang in 1984 in China, when he was still a student. We corresponded extensively about comparative historiographical issues. He later came to the United States, but also has an appointment at Beijing University. With Wang I organized a conference in 2000, which resulted in a book, *Turning Points in Historiography: A Cross Cultural Perspective*, which examined current trends and discussions not only in the West but also in China, Japan, India, the Islamic world and sub-Saharan Africa.

Wang and I divided the task for the book; he took East Asia and the Islamic world; I the West, Latin America and Sub-Saharan Africa; and

Mukherjee India. The problem that we set ourselves was the one that Wang had dealt with in his book on Chinese historiography in the twentieth century:[28] how to recognize the identity of indigenous historical cultures and the process of modernization they underwent without fully giving up their traditional roots, reflecting the diversities of modernization. The book appeared in 2008 as *A Global History of Modern Historiography*. An Indian edition was published soon afterwards, followed by a Chinese and a Russian translation and in 2013 a revised and updated German translation.

I was also engaged with Wang in editing an anthology, *Marxist Historiography: A Global Perspective* (2015), with contributors throughout the world. Basically, it agrees with Erik Hobsbawm that much of what Marx said is 'out of date' or 'no longer acceptable',[29] but we wanted to examine what aspects of Marx as a critical thinker still have relevance now and what role they play for historical thought and writing, particularly in the non-Western world.

Concluding Reflections

At the end of this chapter, I must ask myself whether I succeeded in answering the question of how my political and social engagement relates to my historical writing and social criticism, or whether I have given too much space to my autobiography. What I did and what I wrote as a historian cannot be understood without its roots in my life. In my early life, I was first of all a social activist, which had no direct relation to my role as a historian, although I always possessed a historical consciousness. In fact, I was not a historian in a professional sense until later. But when I wrote history, my writings reflected my commitment to social justice and peace; yet what I wrote was not meant as an expression of ideology but kept in mind standards of honest scholarship.

Georg G. Iggers (1926–2017) was a historian of modern Europe, historiography and European intellectual history. He was Distinguished Professor Emeritus at the University of Buffalo, where he had been teaching for many decades prior to his retirement. In 2007 he received the First Class Cross of the Order of Merit of the Federal Republic of Germany. He also was the recipient of the prestigious Humboldt Prize and received multiple honorary doctorate degrees from American and German universities. Among his many publications are *The German Conception of History* (Wesleyan University Press, 1968); *A Global History of Modern Historiography* (with Edward Q. Wang and Supriya Mukherjee, Longman, 2008) and, with his wife Wilma Iggers, *Two Lives in Uncertain Times: Facing the Challenges of the Twentieth Century as Scholars and Citizens* (Berghahn, 2006).

Notes

1. On my biography see W. Iggers and G. Iggers, *Two Lives in Uncertain Times: Facing the Challenges of the 20th Century as Scholars and Citizens*.
2. Iggers, *The Doctrine of Saint-Simon: An Exposition 1828–1829*.
3. This was the so-called Blossom Plan, named after the superintendent of Little Rock schools Virgil Blossom; see Freyer, 'Politics and Law in the Little Rock Crisis, 1954–1957', 199.
4. Freyer, *Little Rock on Trial: Cooper vs. Aaron and School Desegregation*.
5. Randall, 'Reconstruction Débacle: Collapse of the Radical Régime', 847–79. His assessment of the political role of Blacks in the Reconstruction was summed up in the two sentences: 'Elections in the South became a byword and a travesty. Ignorant blacks by the thousands cast ballots without knowing even the names of the men for whom they were voting', 847.
6. Du Bois, 'The Black Proletariat in South Carolina', 381–430.
7. Recent scholarship would support Du Bois' assessment of Reconstruction. See Eric Foner's review of Douglas R. Egerton, 'The Brief, Violent History of America's Most Progressive Era', 11.
8. Werner Berthold to Rektorat internationale Beziehungen der Karl-Marx-Universität, Leipzig, May 29, 1969.
9. Iggers, *Ein anderer historischer Blick: Beispiele ostdeutscher Sozialgeschichte*.
10. Ernst Engelberg to Georg G. Iggers, Berlin-Treptow, 2 May 1986.
11. Iggers, 'Einige Aspekte neuer Arbeiten in der DDR über die neuere Deutsche Geschichte', 542–51.
12. Iggers, 'New Directions in Historical Studies in the German Democratic Republic', 59–77.
13. 1958 and 1970, published by Martinus J. Nijhoff. My dissertation and the book of 1958 had been based exclusively on printed sources, since I had no access to archives. The second edition reflects my work with the Enfantin papers in the Arsenal archive in Paris. Although I kept the stress on the authoritarianism of Saint-Simonian socialism, I now felt that it was not totalitarian in the sense of twentieth-century totalitarianism. I therefore dropped that part of the subtitle in the second edition.
14. Iggers, 'The Idea of Progress: A Critical Reassessment', 1–17.
15. Iggers, *The German Conception of History: The National Tradition from Herder to the Present*.
16. Thomas Nipperdey to Georg Iggers, 15 February 1971. I no longer have a copy of my reply.
17. Iggers, *Deutsche Geschichtswissenschaft: Eine Kritik der traditionellen Geschichtsauffassung von Herder bis zur Gegenwart* (also translated into Hungarian, Chinese and Korean).
18. Iggers, *New Directions in European Historiography* (translated into Danish, Italian, Greek, Chinese, Japanese and Korean).
19. Ritter, 'Wissenschaftliche Historie einst und jetzt', 574–602.
20. Iggers, 'Die *Annales* und ihre Kritiker: Probleme französischer Sozialgeschichte', 578–608.
21. Iggers, *Neue Geschichtswissenschaft: vom Historismus zur historischen Sozialwissenschaft. Ein internationaler Vergleich*.

22. Iggers, *The Social History of Politics: Critical Perspectives on West German Historical Writing Since 1945*.
23. Iggers, *Geschichtswissenschaft im 20. Jahrhundert: ein kritischer Überblick im internationalen Zusammenhang*.
24. Iggers, *Historiography in the Twentieth Century: From Scientific Objectivity to the Postmodern Challenge* (translated into Spanish, Chinese – in Peoples Republic and Taiwan – Japanese, Korean, Greek, Turkish, Czech and Icelandic).
25. Iggers, 'Historiography Between Scholarship and Poetry: Reflections on Hayden White's Approach to Historiography'; Iggers, 'Historiographie zwischen Dichtung und Forschung', 327–40.
26. Gooch, *History and Historians in the Nineteenth Century*.
27. Ade Ajayi and Alagoa, 'Sub-Saharan Africa', 403–18.
28. Wang, *Inventing China Through History: The May Fourth Approach to Historiography*.
29. Hobsbawm, *How to Change the World: Reflections on Marx and Marxism*, 12.

Bibliography

Ade Ajayi, J.F. and E.J. Alagoa. 'Sub-Saharan Africa', in G. Iggers and H.T. Parker (eds), *International Handbook for Historical Studies: Contemporary Research and Theory* (Westport, CT: Greenwood Press, 1979), 403–18.

Du Bois, W.E.B. 'The Black Proletariat in South Carolina', *Black Reconstruction in America: An Essay toward a History of the Part which Black Folk Played in the Attempt to Reconstruct Democracy in America (1860–1880)* (New York: Harcourt: Brace and Co., 1935), 381–430.

Foner, E. Review of Douglas R. Egerton: 'The Brief, Violent History of America's Most Progressive Era', *New York Times, Book Review* (2 February 2014), 11.

Freyer, T.A. 'Politics and Law in the Little Rock Crisis, 1954–1957', *The Arkansas Historical Quarterly* 40(3) (1981), 195–219.

———. *Little Rock on Trial: Cooper vs. Aaron and School Desegregation*. Lawrence: University of Kansas Press, 2007.

Gooch, G.P. *History and Historians in the Nineteenth Century*. London: Longman, 1913.

Hobsbawm, E. *How to Change the World: Reflections on Marx and Marxism*. New Haven, CT: Yale Press, 2011.

Iggers, G. 'The Idea of Progress: A Critical Reassessment', *American Historical Review* 71(1) (1965–66), 1–17.

———. *The German Conception of History: The National Tradition from Herder to the Present*. Middletown, CT: Wesleyan University Press, 1968; 2nd revised ed. Middletown, CT: Wesleyan University Press, 1983.

———. *Deutsche Geschichtswissenschaft: Eine Kritik der traditionellen Geschichtsauffassung von Herder bis zur Gegenwart*, Munich: DTV, 1971; 2nd ed., 1972; 3rd ed., 1976; 4th revised ed., Wien: Böhlau, 1997.

———. *New Directions in European Historiography*. Middletown, CT: Wesleyan University Press, 1973.

———. 'Die *Annales* und ihre Kritiker: Probleme französischer Sozialgeschichte', *Historische Zeitschrift* 219(3) (1974), 578–608.

———. *Neue Geschichtswissenschaft: vom Historismus zur historischen Sozialwissenschaft. Ein internationaler Vergleich*. Munich: DTV, 1978.

———. 'Einige Aspekte neuer Arbeiten in der DDR über die neuere Deutsche Geschichte', *Geschichte und Gesellschaft* 14(4) (1988), 542–51.

———. 'New Directions in Historical Studies in the German Democratic Republic', *History and Theory* 28(2) (1989), 59–77.

———. *Geschichtswissenschaft im 20. Jahrhundert: ein kritischer Überblick im internationalen Zusammenhang*, Göttingen: Vandenhoeck & Ruprecht, 1993; 4th revised ed., 2007.

———. *Historiography in the Twentieth Century: From Scientific Objectivity to the Postmodern Challenge*. Middletown, CT: Wesleyan University Press, 1997; 2nd revised ed., 2005.

———. 'Historiography Between Scholarship and Poetry: Reflections on Hayden White's Approach to Historiography', *Rethinking History* 4 (2000), 373–90.

———. 'Historiographie zwischen Dichtung und Forschung', *Geschichte und Gesellschaft* 27(2) (2001), 327–40.

Iggers, G. (ed.). *The Doctrine of Saint-Simon: An Exposition 1828–1829*, Boston, MA: Beacon Press, 1958; 2nd ed., New York: Schocken Books, 1972.

———. *The Social History of Politics: Critical Perspectives on West German Historical Writing Since 1945*. Leamington Spa: Berg, 1985.

———. *Ein anderer historischer Blick: Beispiele ostdeutscher Sozialgeschichte*, Frankfurt am Main: Fischer-Taschenbuch-Verlag, 1991.

Iggers, W. and G. Iggers. *Two Lives in Uncertain Times: Facing the Challenges of the 20th Century as Scholars and Citizens*. New York: Berghahn, 2005.

Randall, J.G. 'Reconstruction Débacle: Collapse of the Radical Régime', in J.G. Randall (ed.), *Civil War and Reconstruction* (Boston, MA: D.C Heath and Company, 1937), 847–79.

Ritter, G. 'Wissenschaftliche Historie einst und jetzt', *Historische Zeitschrift* 202(3) (1966), 574–602.

Wang, E.Q. *Inventing China Through History: The May Fourth Approach to Historiography*. Albany: SUNY Press, 2001.

Wang, E.Q. and G. Iggers. *Turning Points in Historiography: A Cross Cultural Perspective*. Rochester: University of Rochester Press, 2002.

Wang, E.Q., G. Iggers and S. Mukherjee. *A Global History of Modern Historiography*. Harlow: Pearson and Longman, 2008.

Index

JANNIK KEINDORF, SEBASTIAN BRAUN AND
RICCARDA SCHIRMERS

activism, 2, 18, 277
activist, 1–2, 17, 168, 170, 233, 244, 263, 265, 267, 271–72, 296
  Historical, 18, 20, 210
Aeschylus, 80
Africa; African, 82, 295
Age of Discoveries, 8, 16
America
  Latin America; Latin American, 55, 90, 211, 217n33, 237, 294–95
  North America, 17, 111n41
  See also United States of America
Amnesty International, 82
Anatolia, 121–23, 126, 273
Anderson, Perry, 192
Annales, 15, 17, 186, 194, 292, 294
anti-Semitism; anti-Semitic, 163, 175, 178, 278
Arab Spring, 262
Arendt, Hannah, 172, 174, 177, 281
  The Origins of Totalitarianism (1951), 164
Argentina; Argentinian, 110n27, 237
Aristoteles; Aristotelian, 170, 174
Arlington, 263
Asdrachas, Spyros, 241, 245
Ash, Timothy Garton, 165–67
  The Polish Revolution: Solidarity (1984), 166
  The Uses of Adversity (1990), 166
Asia; Asian, 190

Asia Minor, 122–23
  East Asia, 295
  South Asia, 25n79
Australia; Australian, 48, 273
Austria-Hungary; Austrian-Hungarian. *See* Habsburg Empire
authority
  academic, 137, 194, 197
  anti-authoritarianism; anti-authoritarian, 164, 172, 179, 181n18
  authoritarianism; authoritarian, 15–16, 168, 189, 212–13, 221, 237, 278, 293

Babington Macaulay, Thomas, 10
Baez, Joan, 188
Balkans, 121–22
Balkan Wars. *See under* war
Barkan, Elazar, 18, 205–6, 208–10, 213–15, 217n22
  The Guilt of Nations (2000), 208
Barraclough, Geoffrey, 5, 286
BBC Radio, 155, 169
Bedarida, Francois, 2
Beijing, 12, 137–38, 140, 147n26
Belarus, 82
Ben Gurion, David, 84
Bergstraesser, Arnold, 280–81
Berlin, 34, 165, 278
  Academy of Sciences (East Berlin), 289–91

East Berlin, 289
West Berlin, 291
Bismarck, Otto von, 290–91, 293
Bloch, Marc, 15, 60n22, 194
Bokassa, Jean-Bédel, 85
Brasilia, 224
Brazil; Brazilian, 18–19, 212–14, 221–33
   Amnesty Law (1997), 211–13
   Censorship Division for Public Entertainment (DCDP), 224
   Constitution (1946), 230
   Embrafilme, 222
   Institute of Brazilian Studies (IEB), 233
   military dictatorship (*see under* military dictatorship)
   National Cinema Institute (INC), 222
   National Education Film Institute (INCE), 234n8
   National Information Service, 234
   National Security Doctrine, 224–26, 228
   New State (1937–1945), 230
   Popular Culture Center of the National Students' Union (UNE CPC)
   Post-authoritarian, 206, 210–11, 215, 218n40
   Republic, 223–24, 235n13
   Services of Public Entertainment Censorship, 223
   Special Commission on the Killed and Disappeared Political Activists, 211
   Supreme Censorship Council, 227
   truth commission (*see under* truth commission)
   War College 'ESG', 224–25, 234n10, 235n12
Bolshevism; Bolshevik, 16, 176, 191
Bourdieu, Pierre, 4
Bucharest, 291
Bulgaria; Bulgarian, 86, 122
Burckhardt, Jacob, 80–81

Cai Yuanpei, 138
Cairo, 12, 262
Caligula, 107
Cambodia; Cambodian
   Angkor Wat, 86
   Khmer Rouge, 85–86
   Phnom Penh, 85
Camus, Albert, 172, 191
Canada; Canadian, 90, 232, 273, 281–82, 288
Capitalism; capitalist, 13, 49, 144, 177, 189, 240
   capitalist society, 144, 279
   capitalist West, 13, 17
   anti-capitalism; anti-capitalist, 46
Caribbean, 89, 226
Carter, Jimmy, 90–91, 95
   Camp David Agreement (1978), 90
   The Hornet's Nest (2004), 90
Castro, Fidel, 176
Censorship
   of documentaries, 225, 229
   of films with a historical approach, 226
   of history, 18, 222, 225, 233
   as means of controlling the past, 222
Central African Republic, 85
Chartier, Roger, 253
Chiang Kai-shek, 13, 138, 143
China; Chinese, 12–13, 46, 96, 146n10, 187, 280, 291–92, 294–95
   Chinese Communist Party (CCP), 143–45
   Han Empire, 140
   historiography, 12, 136, 139–40, 142, 145, 147n18, 296
   Nationalist Party, 137, 139, 143
   Mao's China, 52
   Ministry of Education, 137
   Qing Empire, 137
   People's Republic of China, 145, 148n44
   Republican Period, 145
   Sino-Japanese War (*see under* war)
   wartime China, 136, 139
   Warring States Period, 141–44
Chongqing, 139, 141, 143–45
Churchill, Winston, 81, 83–84, 95, 111n38
Cicero, Marcus Tullius, 38, 80
Coirolo, Julio María Sanguinetti, 122n51
Cold War. *See under* war
Colonialism, 280
   anti-Colonialism; anti-colonialist, 12
commitment
   aesthetic, 37

ethical, 38, 75
and historical scholarship, 4–6, 21, 57, 67, 75, 77n16, 145
ideological, 5, 47–48
lack of, 37, 271
nationalist, 8, 11, 15
and objectivity, 34, 54, 63
political, 1, 9–10, 12–13, 37, 63, 66, 74, 273
religious, 38
social, 279, 292
See also engagement
communism; communist, 13–14, 19, 49, 55, 84, 86, 91–92, 151, 156, 164–66, 168, 170–79, 181n30, 225, 234n10, 238, 243, 267, 278, 282
anti-communism; anti-communist, 18, 46, 166, 238, 241
Communist bloc (*see* Eastern bloc)
Communist International, 191
intellectual commitment to, 3, 15–16
and totalitarianism, 53
Confucianism; Confucian, 137
Cosmopolitanism; cosmopolitan, 164, 166–67, 171, 173–74, 176–78
Costa Gavras, Constantin, 228
Missing (1982), 228
Crisis
financial crisis, 21, 262, 266, 268, 270–71, 273
national crisis, 143
political crisis, 15–16, 211
Suez Crisis, 90
Cuba, 18
Cyprus, 156–57
Resistance movement (EOKA), 156
Czechoslovakia; Czech, 17–18, 92, 281, 289
Bohemia, 92, 289

Darwin, Charles, 92
evolutionism, 92
De Baets, Antoon, 207
de Klerk, F.W., 90
Denmark; Danish, 48, 294
Dertilis, George, 243
digitization, 20, 250–51, 254–56
discourse
academic, 21, 34, 38

historical, 11, 49, 68, 119
memory, 2, 13, 120, 254
public, 47, 151, 213
social, 68
discrimination, 53, 119, 239, 254–55
racial, 273, 282
Dreyfus affair, 3
Dreyfus, Alfred, 44
Droysen, Johann Gustav, 37
Geschichte der preußischen Politik (1855–1886), 37
Du Bois, W.E.B. 285–86
Black Reconstruction in America (1935), 285
Dutch East Indies, 110n27

Eastern bloc, 152, 156, 237–38, 289
Eguchi, Bokuro, 190–91
Egypt; Egyptian, 12
engagement
ethics of, 45, 52, 57
and historical writing, 1, 3–6, 12, 33–35, 47, 206, 208, 213, 296
human rights, 205
ideological, 153, 159
and intellectuality, 45, 47, 52, 57, 124, 164–65, 208, 282
for justice, 54, 57
limits to, 238
meanings of, 33, 37, 206–207, 212, 214, 216n2
and objectivity, 34–36
political, 3, 5, 7, 11, 14–17, 37, 153, 159, 214, 242, 286, 289
problems of, 39–40
with the past, 126, 129, 251
See also commitment
Engelberg, Ernst, 291
England; English, 3, 10–11, 15, 41, 91, 194, 226, 264, 286
Enlightenment, 4, 7–8, 23n31, 45, 55–56, 61n23, 173, 179, 293
empiricism, 6, 67, 72–73
Espagne, Michael, 263
Europe; European, 4, 8, 10–13, 15–16, 87, 118–19, 138, 172–73, 179, 190–91, 209, 230, 232, 240, 261, 266, 273, 282
Central Europe, 9, 287

East-Central Europe, 179
Eastern Europe, 13, 165–68, 177–78, 187, 295
European Central Bank, 266
European Commission, 266
history, 10, 14, 155, 169, 186, 191–94, 196, 264, 287, 291
interwar Europe, 15
Western Europe, 9, 139, 154, 240, 295
United States of Europe, 108

Farkas, Thomaz, 231, 233
Brasil verdade (1968), 231–32
Fascism; fascist, 15, 53, 143–44
anti-Fascism, 13, 144
intellectual commitment to, 15–16
movement, 3
past, 2
Faubus, Orval, 284
Fawkes, Guy, 263
Filov, Bogdan, 86
Fischhoff, Baruch, 96–97
Flaubert, Gustave, 73, 77n19
Foucault, Michel, 6, 72, 207
radical empiricism, 73, 77n18
France; French, 3, 15, 17, 44, 48, 85, 122, 152, 170, 193–94, 196, 224, 241, 263, 281, 286–87, 291, 294
Alsace, 9
Bibliotheque Nationale, 286, 292
French Revolution (1789), 10, 82, 193
history, 191, 194, 282
Lorraine, 9
Great Revolution, 16, 264
Resistance, 15, 160n2
Franco, Francisco, 16, 108, 267
Frederick the Great, 79, 290
Fujimoto, Wakio, 191–92
Fukui, Norihiko, 194

Gandhi, Indira, 93
Gandhi, Mahatma, 93, 113n63
Genoa, 269
Genocide, 11
Balkan, 163
Cambodia, 46
Holocaust, 107, 272, 286
Stalinist, 165

Geremek, Bronislaw, 22, 164, 168
Germany; German, 15, 38, 141, 152, 157, 163, 165, 190, 196, 263, 267, 277–79, 281, 286–88
East Germany; East German, 19, 237, 244, 289–91, 293–94
Federal Republic, 209
German lands, 7–8, 10
German Revolution (1884), 193
revolution (1989), 19
historiography, 8, 18, 33, 286, 292, 294
history, 193–94, 282, 293
imperial Germany, 8, 34, 291, 293
memorial culture, 8
National Socialist Germany, 16–17, 207, 267, 292
November Pogrom 1938 (*Kristallnacht*), 279
Prussia; Prussian, 8, 37, 290, 293
Resistance, 165
Social Democratic Party (SPD), 194
Weimar Republic, 15, 293
West Germany; West German, 2–3, 289–91, 294
Gervinus, Georg Gottfried, 7, 33–34
Goldfarb, Jeffrey, 167, 179
Gorbachev, Mikhail, 6, 91, 94
glasnost, 91
perestroika, 291
Perestroika: New Thinking for Our Country and the World, 91
Gottingen, 7, 278, 286–87, 289
Gottingen Seven, 7
Goulart, Joao (Jango), 211
Great Britain; British, 2, 9, 17, 82, 144, 152–54, 156, 159, 242, 286
British Empire, 9, 156
Communist Party Historians' Group, 16
history, 15
British Library, 253
British Mission, 154, 156
Conservative Party, 14
Gunpowder Plot (1605), 263
Puritan Revolt, 264
Royal Institute of Foreign Affairs, 154
Great War. *See under* war

Greece; Greek, 13, 19–21, 122–25, 127, 130–31, 151–59, 237–40, 242–43, 245–46, 262–63, 266–67, 270, 273
  ancient Greece, 143
  Association of Thracian Studies, 126, 128
  Civil War (*see under* war)
  facist occupation, 13–14
  Greek Communist Party (KKE), 152, 239, 241–42
  history, 11, 19–20, 130–31, 153, 158–59, 240–41, 267–68, 273
  Ilinden Uprooting (1903), 121
  interwar Greece, 11, 118, 130
  Megali idea, 11
  Metapolitefsi, 240, 268
  military dictatorship (*see under* military dictatorship)
  National Liberation Front (EAM), 155, 267
  New Democracy, 244, 246
  resistance movement (*see under* social movements)
  revolution (1821), 154, 264–65
  Socialist Party (PASOK), 239, 242
  Society for the Study of Modern Hellenism, 241
  Thrace, 119, 122, 126, 128–30, 273
Grigogopoulos, Alexis, 262–63
Gu Jiegang, 136, 138–39

Habsburg Empire, 92
Hamburg, 277, 279–80
Hanfu, 144–45
Hara, Kiyoshi, 195
Hasegawa, Takahiko, 196
Hegel, Georg Wilhelm Friedrich, 80, 96,
historian
  as activist, 1–2, 17–18, 20, 210, 272
  amateur, 120, 124, 128
  as dissident, 163, 166–67, 178
  engaged, 52, 119, 130, 168, 171, 179, 205–206, 213–14, 218n40
  as engaged intellectual, 2, 4, 6–8, 15, 17–18, 20, 44–45, 47–48, 51–52, 56–58, 164, 196, 198, 250, 277
  exile, 7, 16, 207, 240
  and new media, 250–51, 253
  and nationalism, 9, 15, 292
  as politician, 1, 6, 14, 82, 153
  professional, 1–5, 7, 9, 12, 14, 33, 36, 45, 82, 91, 119, 120, 138–39, 145, 153–54, 157, 159, 197, 215, 239, 243, 245, 254, 257
  as public intellectual, 1, 7–9, 13–14, 21, 44–45
  responsibility, 2, 48, 58, 66, 72, 75, 139, 198
  and society, 3, 10, 14, 17, 20, 145, 241
historical consciousness, 81, 82–83, 85, 91, 94–95, 123, 125–26, 128–29, 131, 160n12, 250, 273, 296
  and political wisdom, 6, 80–81, 83–84, 86, 90
historical culture, 5, 20, 35, 40, 152, 221, 296
  dimensions of, 36, 39
historical interpretation
  conceptualization of, 39
  conflicts of, 44–45, 48, 52
  ethics of, 38, 45, 54
historical knowledge
  and new media, 255
  and political practice, 25n79, 34–35, 84
  between objectivity and subjectivity, 33, 36
historical narrative
  deconstruction of, 21, 213, 215
  and inclusion, 119–20, 123, 127
  as moral imperative, 66, 70
  multimodal, 251
  and narrative space, 73
  political implications of, 69
  shared, 210
  transformation of, 252–54
  and trustworthiness, 69–70
  See also national narrative
historical profession, 1–2, 7, 15–16, 18, 85, 137, 292, 294
historical studies
  and engagement, 3, 33
  in global perspective, 12, 138, 293
  methodology of, 35–36, 50, 251
  and objectivity, 1, 5, 138
  and politics, 5, 7, 9, 82, 138, 145
  professionalization of, 3, 11–12, 136–37

and rationality, 35–36, 46
regulation of, 137
in relation to normative positions, 18, 34, 44, 48
See also under commitment
historical truth, 5, 19, 153, 155, 157–58, 241
historical writing
and engagement, 2, 4, 206–207, 277, 292, 296
and human rights, 18, 209, 214
and Marxism (see under Marxism)
and nationalism, 12, 138, 145
politicization of, 12, 139
professional, 145, 206–207, 214
theory of, 63
See also historiography
Historicism, 33, 120, 207, 216, 262, 271–72, 293
historiography
academic, 241–42
engaged versus non-engaged, 38–39
fact versus fiction, 66
global, 295
interpretation of, 33
modern, 295
national, 125, 128
nationalist, 8, 9, 11, 13, 15, 54, 245
political, 152
professionalization of, 35
Western, 12, 17, 294–95
Whig, 10
See also historical writing
history
aestheticization of, 6, 64, 69
depoliticization of, 6, 64
from below, 193–94
of historiography, 2–3, 5, 12
intellectual, 281, 287, 291
and legitimation, 5, 8, 11, 72
national, 11, 81, 142, 158, 166, 172, 264
public, 3, 19, 21, 152, 245, 261
in relation to memory (see under memory)
social, 186, 194–96, 286, 294
social movement, 185–86, 191–92, 196–98

theory of, 71–72, 77n11, 121, 194, 196, 273
world, 93, 142, 146, 163, 190, 209
history and digital media, 20, 254, 256
implications for historical narratives, 250–51, 254
preservation, 250–52, 255
transduction, 255–56
trans-materiality, 255–56
Hitler, Adolf, 107, 163, 165, 267, 277–78
Hobsbawm, Eric, 16, 165, 180n7, 192, 296
Holocaust. See under genocide
Horvath, Mihaly, 10
Hrushevsky, Mykhailo, 8
Humanism, 73–74, 80, 92–94, 173, 179
oppositional humanism, 164, 172, 179
human rights, 18, 87, 90, 107, 170, 207, 209, 212–14, 293
advancement of, 205, 208, 214
and historical writing (see under historical writing)
and standards of historical scholarship, 206, 215
violation, 209, 211, 235n29, 289
Universal Declaration of, 86
Hungary; Hungarian, 10, 92, 291
Magyars, 10
Hu Shi, 138, 146n4
Hussein, Saddam, 85–86
Huyssen, Andreas, 256, 270

identity
collective, 137–38, 164
historical, 40, 208
integrated, 244
formation, 40, 262
national, 10, 124, 128, 139, 266
Iggers, Georg G., 17, 207
Iggers, Wilma, 18, 281–84, 286–87, 289–91
Iliou, Philippos, 241–42
imagined community, 127
impartiality, 6, 53–54, 153, 159, 245, 261–62
imperialism, 9, 89, 92, 139, 190, 289
India; Indian, 12, 96, 143, 295–96
British India, 93

intellectual
  as agent of change, 121, 124
  autonomy, 4, 46, 136–39, 145
  and the creation of narratives, 120, 124–28, 130–31
  critical, 46, 49–50, 52, 54, 58
  engaged intellectual (*see under* historian)
  as engineer of hatred, 163–64
  notion of, 3–4, 45, 165, 250
  public, 2, 11, 15
  role in society, 44, 46, 48, 51, 58, 131, 137, 166–67, 233
  and social movements, 3, 167–68, 177, 179
  See also engagement
International Commission for the History of Historiography, 291
International Criminal Court, 82
International League of Peace and Freedom, 289
International Research and Exchange Board (IREX), 290
Ireland; Irish, 11
Iron Curtain, 14
Ishii, Norie, 195
Ishizuka, Masahide, 195
Israel; Israeli, 83, 156, 279
Istanbul, 262
Italy; Italian, 2, 82, 191, 226, 228, 265, 269, 280, 294
  fascist Italy, 16
Ivory Coast, 82
Iwo Jima, 263

Japan; Japanese, 17, 140, 143, 185–86, 193–94, 291–92, 295
  General Council of Trade Unions (GCTU), 187
  historians, 186, 192
  Historical Science Society of Japan (Rekishigaku Kenkyukai), 189–90
  Historical Society of Japan (Shigakukai), 189–90
  historiography, 17, 186, 189, 195–96
  imperialism, 139
  Japanese Communist Party (JCP), 187
  Japanese Socialist Party (JSP), 187, 191
  Japan–US Security Treaty, 187–88
  National League of All Student Unions (*Zengakuren*), 187
  Postwar Japan, 186–87, 189–90, 196, 199n8
  Russian–Japanese War (*see under* war)
  Sino–Japanese War of Resistance (1937–45) (*see under* war)
  Society of Modern Society Research, 195
  Todai Struggle, 188, 191, 193
  Zenkyoto movement (*see under* social movements)
Johnson, Lyndon B., 83
journal
  American Historical Review, 209, 286, 292
  Archive of Thracian Folklore and Lingual Thesaurus, 127
  Contemporary History Quarterly, 154
  Deutsche Zeitschrift für Geschichtswissenschaft, 107
  Geschichte und Gesellschaft, 291, 294–95
  Historical Abstracts, 286
  Historische Zeitschrift, 294
  History Workshop Journal, 3
  Mnemon, 241, 245
  The New Left Review, 192
  Radical History Review, 3
  Revue Historique, 9
  Social Movement History (SMH), 17, 185–86, 189–97
  Storia della Storiografia, 291
  Ta Istorika, 241
  Thrakika, 127
  Zhuanguo ce banyue kan, 141
justice
  and historical thinking, 45, 51, 57, 131, 205, 246
  as ideal, 6, 44–45, 51, 54, 57–58, 60n13, 80, 95, 158, 170, 227, 296
  injustice, 49, 51–52, 58, 60n21, 120, 129, 144, 242
  principles of, 53

Kant, Immanuel, 79, 80, 84, 97
Kato, Haruyasu, 191–92, 195
Kefalogiannis, Ioannis, 244
Kemalism; Kemalist, 122
Kenya; Kenyan, 156

Kikuchi, Masanori, 191
Kimura, Seiji, 192–94, 196
Kingdom of Hannover, 8
King Stephen of Hungary, 10
Kinoshita, Kenichi, 193
Kissinger, Henry, 107
Kitahara, Atsushi, 191–92
Kiyasu, Akira, 190–91
   Saint Monday in Paris (1982), 191
Khrushchev, Nikita, 85, 91
Koht, Halvdan, 89
Kolokotronis, Theodoros, 264–65
Kondo, Kazuhiko, 194, 196
Konigsberg, 278
Korean War. *See under* war
Kosovo, 209
Kuomintang, 13
Kuron, Gaja, 176, 181n20
Kuron, Jacek, 14–15, 164, 166–76, 178, 181n20
   'A Christian without God', 174
   Thoughts on the Program of Action, 174
Kyi, Aung San Suu, 95
Kyrkos, Michail, 126

Labour movement. *See under* social movements
Labour Party, 3
LaCapra, Dominick, 67, 126, 272
Lange, Christian, 107
   Histoire de l'internationalisme, 107
Latvia; Latvian, 169
Lausanne Treaty (1923), 121–22
League of Nations, 92, 96, 108
Lefebvre, Georges, 192–93
the Left, 151, 177, 232, 238–39, 241–43, 246, 267
   New Left, 17, 187, 191–92, 196, 243, 290
Lei Haizong, 12, 136, 139–44, 147n18, 147n26
Leipzig, 289–90
Lenin, Wladimir Iljitsch, 85, 191, 193
Leninism, 13, 91
liberalism, 9, 12, 16, 138
Lin Tongji, 141–42, 147n24
Lipski, Jan Jozef, 172
Lisbon, 262
Lithuania; Lithuanian, 169

Little Rock, Arkansas, 282–85, 288
London, 262
   Royal Institute of Foreign Affairs, 14, 154
Lower Saxony, 8
Lucas, Robert, 96–97
Lukashenko, Aleksandr, 82
Luther, Martin, 10, 173, 290–91
Lu Xun, 138, 147n14

Macaulay, Catherine, 11
Madariaga, Salvador de, 108
Madrid, 262
Malaysia, 156
Mandela, Nelson, 83, 89–90, 111n38
Manouilidis, Filippos, 126
Maoism; Maoist, 13, 46
Mao Zedong, 53, 84, 86, 143
Marcos, Ferdinand, 84
Martens, Fyodor, 107
Maruyama, Masao, 189
Marx, Karl, 193, 281, 296
Marxism; Marxist, 13, 17, 54, 92–93, 175, 187, 194, 226–27, 287, 292
   British, 294
   and historical writing, 16, 37, 189–90, 200n47
   orthodox, 190, 294
   Western, 292
Masaryk, Thomas, 6, 92, 94
   The Social Question (1898), 92
May, Todd, 67, 73
Mazowiecki, Tadeusz, 176
McTeigue, James
   V for Vendetta (2006), 263
memory
   activist, 2
   collective, 242–43
   community of, 124, 126–27, 158
   discourse (*see under* discourse)
   interlocutor of, 121, 124–25, 128, 130, 152
   multilayered, 131, 214
   and oblivion, 120, 123, 151
   politics of, 39, 123–24, 128, 151, 214
   preservation of, 246, 254–55
   public, 48, 51, 58, 152
   in relation to history, 2, 21, 68, 80, 186, 250, 254

social, 20, 256, 270
studies, 2, 205, 254
traumatic, 20, 130, 237, 242
See also the past
Merkel, Angela, 267
Michnik, Adam, 14, 164, 166–86, 171–76, 178, 181n30, 182n40
  The Church and the Left (1979), 173–74
  From the History of Honor in Poland (1976), 174
  New Evolutionism (1976), 174
Middle East, 90, 153, 159
military dictatorship
  Brazil, 18, 221–22
  Chile, 289
  Greece, 19–20, 151–52, 268
  Portugal, 16
Mitsotakis, Konstantinos, 244
Modzelewski, Karol, 164, 166
Montaldo, Giuliano
  Sacco and Vanzetti (1971), 226
Morris-Suzuki, Tessa, 155
Munich, 153, 155
  Institut für Zeitgeschichte, 154
Munich Agreement (1938), 92
Myanmar, 95
  Rohingya, 95

Nagao, Hisashi, 192
  The History of the Russian Revolution (1968), 192
Nanjing, 137
Napoleon Bonaparte, 83, 85
national narrative, 11, 119, 130–31, 242
  See also historical narrative
nationalism; nationalist, 9, 12, 121, 124–25, 243, 278, 280
  German, 8
  historian (*see under* historian)
  and historical writing (*see under* historical writing)
  historiography (*see under* historiography)
  history of, 12
National Socialism; National Socialist (Nazi), 2, 15–16, 38, 49, 86, 92, 107, 154, 163, 189, 194, 267, 278, 280, 287, 291–93
Neo-Nazism, 47

Nehru, Jawaharlal, 6, 83, 92–94, 96
  The Discovery of India (1946), 93
  Glimpses of World History (1934), 93
New Left. See under the Left
New Orleans, 284–88
newspaper
  Der Stürmer, 278
  Eleftheria, 155
  El País, 267
New York Times
New York City, 262, 279, 281
Ninomiya, Hiroyuki, 194, 196, 200n35
Nipperdey, Thomas, 34, 293
Nobel Peace Prize, 6, 82, 86–88, 91–92, 95, 106–107
  Norwegian Nobel Committee, 87, 89, 92, 111n42, 113n63
Nora, Pierre
  Les Lieux de Mémoire, 195
Norway; Norwegian, 107
Nostalgia, 11, 123, 128–30
Nyerere, Julius, 82

Obama, Barack, 89, 91, 111n38, 273
Odanaka, Naoki
Okamoto, Michihiro
  History as Memory, Memory as History (2013), 186, 189–90, 194, 197
Ostforschung, 16
Otsuka, Hisao, 189
Ottoman Empire, 11, 118, 121–22, 128, 130
orthodox communities, 122, 124
Oxford, 153, 165

Palestine, 278–79, 281
Paris, 9, 166. 248n13, 266, 281, 286, 292
  College de France, 286
  Paris Commune, 193
  Paris Peace Accords (1973), 107
  Society for Greek Studies, 125
Papandreou, Andreas, 238–39
the past
  as burden, 96, 120
  dealing with, 123, 128, 159, 205, 208–211, 214, 237
  evaluation of, 44, 51, 56, 93, 261, 287, 290, 293

and the future, 80, 96–97, 120, 129–31, 262, 270, 273
historical, 68, 241, 246, 261, 264, 272
as history, 5, 35, 186, 261, 273
and identity, 120, 123–24, 127, 129
interpretation of, 5, 21, 35, 37–38, 45, 52
as a minefield, 212–14, 218n42
national, 6, 21, 166, 172, 262, 265, 270
nationalization of, 119, 123, 127–28, 130
(re-)negotiation of, 119–21, 125, 128, 130
as one of cancelled potentials, 11, 120, 129
and politics, 17, 21, 92, 124, 139, 141–42, 273
practical, 119–20, 129–31, 159, 246, 272
and the present, 40, 52, 67–68, 118, 120, 129, 131, 164, 246, 261, 265, 268, 271–73
in public discourse, 2–3, 6, 18, 20, 48, 60n22, 238, 245, 265
representation of, 18, 33–34, 37, 68, 121, 221–22, 233, 250
repression of, 19–20, 85, 112n51, 120, 123, 128, 152, 212–13, 241, 244–46, 264–65
and trauma, 11, 19, 130, 237–39, 243, 245–46
See also memory
Pearson, Lester, 89–90
Permanent Court of Arbitration, 89
Peru; Peruvian, 163
  Shining Path, 163
Petri, Elio
  The Working Class Goes to Heaven (1971), 228
Philadelphia, 272
Philippines; Philippine, 84
Pirenne, Henri, 15
Plato, 80, 179
  cardinal virtues, 79, 95
  The Republic, 79, 165
  The Symposium, 164
  philosopher-king, 79–80, 93

Poland; Polish, 10, 15, 166, 168–70, 172, 174–75, 291
  constitution (1791), 10
  Communist Poland, 14, 165
  Communist Party, 174, 178
  Gdan´sk shipyard Strike, 165, 174
  historiography, 10, 294
  Komandosi, 171–72
  Nazi occupation (1939–1945), 166, 172
  Partitions (1772; 1791–1818), 166, 168
  post-Communist Poland, 178
  revolution, 14, 164, 166–67, 171, 178
  Workers' Defence Committee (KOR), 14–15, 168–180
Pol Pot, 86
Pontecorvo, Gillo
  Burn! (1969), 226–27
  The Battle of Algiers (1966), 226
Popper, Karl, 80, 97, 286
  The Open Society and Its Enemies (1945), 80
Portugal; Portuguese, 16, 226, 262, 268
  Estado Novo, 16
  military dictatorship (*see under* military dictatorship)
Postcolonialism; Postcolonial, 46, 207, 295
Prague Spring, 289
Protestantism, 10

Qian Mu, 139
Quidde, Ludwig, 107

racism; racist, 53–55, 55–56, 273, 278, 280, 282–83, 286
  desegregation, 282–85
  segregation, 95, 280, 283–85, 287–88
Radio Free Europe, 169–70
Randall, James G.: 285–86
  Civil War and Reconstruction (1937), 285
Randall, John, 281, 285–86
Ranke, Leopold von, 33–34, 61n23, 293
  Rankeanism, 195, 285f
reconciliation, 3, 18–20, 209–13, 243
refugee
  and historical narrative, 11, 123–24, 130–31

and the national imaginary, 11, 119, 123, 125, 127
religion, 8, 38, 122, 144, 165, 179, 257, 282
Renaissance, 15, 173, 179, 251
  'Second European Renaissance', 165, 180
res publica literarum, 15, 165, 173
Ribbentrop-Molotov pact, 166
Richmond, Virginia, 279–80
Rio de Janeiro, 221, 223
Rocha, Glauber
  Land in Anguish (1967), 227
Rome; Roman, 107, 166
  ancient Rome, 143
Roosevelt, Theodore, 89, 91
Rosenzweig, Roy, 251–52
Russia; Russian, 85
  historiography, 16
  history, 9
  pre-revolutionary, 8
  revolution, 46, 190–92, 195
  Tsarist, 8
  Russian–Japanese War (1904–05) (*see under* war)

Sagara, Masatoshi, 193
Said, Edward, 45, 207
Saint-Simonian, 281–82, 292
Sao Paulo, 211, 221, 231
Sarno, Geraldo, 231, 233
  Viramundo (1965), 231–32
Sartre, Jean-Paul, 6, 69, 72
  committed literature, 70, 74–75
  The Family Idiot (1971–1972), 72–73
  poststructuralism, 73, 77n19
Schama, Simon, 71–72
  Dead Certainties (1991), 70
Seeley, John Robert
  Expansion of England (1883), 9
Sennett, Richard
  Together (2012), 177
Serbia; Serbian, 92
  Serbian Academy of Sciences and Arts, 163
Shanghai, 12, 137
Shang Yang, 142, 148n32
Shibata, Michio, 193–94, 196
  Babeuf's Conspiracy (1968), 193

Shotwell, James, 107
Socialism; Socialist, 10, 167–68, 172–73, 175–77, 238, 278–79, 282
  democratic, 18, 292
  French, 191
  historian, 10, 48
  history of, 281
  state, 144, 290
social movements
  '1968', 2, 16–17, 48, 52–53, 172, 188, 192, 263, 265–66, 287
  anti-Colonial movement, 156
  anti-Vietnam War movement, 18
  Civil Rights Movement, 18, 283
  Draft Resistance movement, 288
  history of (*see under* history)
  Labour movement, 3, 10, 55, 187, 189
  Left movements (1960s), 52, 55
  national movement, 8, 15
  Occupy, 21, 262–63
  protest movement, 17, 21, 262, 264, 272–73
  Solidarnosc, 15, 164–65, 167–68, 170–71, 173–78
  Pan-European movement, 108
  peace movement, 87, 107
  resistance movement (China), 144
  resistance movement (Greece), 14, 153–56
  student movement (Italy), 265
  student movement (Japan), 17, 185, 187–89, 197
  student movement (USA), 288
  women's movement, 11
  Zenkyoto movement, 187–89, 192–93, 194–95
Solovev, Sergej Michajovic, 9
South Africa, 90
  African National Congress, 90
  Apartheid, 90
  Sharpeville massacre (1960), 90
South Korea, 292
Soviet bloc. *See* Eastern bloc
Soviet Union; Soviet, 13, 16–17, 85, 144, 165, 167, 175, 178, 187, 192, 195, 278, 289, 291, 295
  Communist Party, 91, 187
Spain; Spanish, 16, 48, 108, 262, 268, 280

speech act theory, 49–50
Spengler, Oswald, 13, 142
Stalin, Josef, 16, 83, 85, 91
  crimes, 91
  Great Purge, 165, 191
  History of the All-Russian Communist Party (Bolsheviks): Short Course (1938), 83
Stuttgart, 279
Svoronos, Nikos, 248n13, 266
Sweden; Swedish, 48–49, 52–53
Sytagma, 262

Taiwan; Taiwanese, 13, 292
Tanigawa, Minoru, 194–95
Third Reich. See under Germany
Thracian Center, 126–27
Thompson, E.P., 16–17, 192, 194, 196
  The Making of the English Working Class (1963), 192
totalitarianism; totalitarian, 13, 52–53, 56, 136, 145, 164, 170, 189, 292
Treaty of Versailles, 92, 278
Treitschke, Heinrich von, 8
truth commission, 210
  and history, 19, 50
  South Africa, 90
  Brazil, 18, 211–12
Turkel, William, 256
Turkey; Turkish, 122, 156

Uehara, Senroku, 190–91
Ukraine; Ukrainian, 8–9
United Nations, 90, 108
United Kingdom. *See* Great Britain
United States of America (USA); American, 2, 18, 83, 89–90, 92, 96, 226–27, 230, 290
  African American, 282, 286, 288
  American Historical Association, 89, 91
  Black Virginia Union, 280
  Civil War (*see under* war)
  Digital Public Library of America, 253
  Founding Fathers, 111n38, 170
  FBI, 280, 288
  Freedom of Information Act, 280
  German Studies Association, 290
  Greater Buffalo Draft Counseling Center, 288
  Hebrew Immigrant Aid Society (HIAS), 279
  history, 281, 285
  historiography, 289–90
  National Association for the Advancement of Colored People (NAACP), 282–85, 288
  Pentagon, 83
  Pentagon Papers, 83
  Reconstruction, 285–86
  Revolution (1775–1783), 90
  State Department, 95
  Supreme Court, 283–85
  Union Now, 280
  Voice of America, 169–70
  YMCA, 287
University
  Academy of Athens, 125, 241
  Ain Shams (Egypt), 12
  Akron, 282
  Arkansas, 284
  Beijing, 138, 146n4, 291–92, 295
  Chicago, 12, 280, 282–83, 287
  Dillard, 284–85
  flying, 15, 166, 169–70
  Göttingen, 7
  Jena, 290
  Kyoto, 194–95
  Moscow, 9
  Nanjing, 292
  National Central University (China), 140
  New York at Buffalo, 287
  Nihon, 188
  Philander Smith College, 282, 284–85, 288
  research, 7
  Richmond, 280
  Roosevelt University, Chicago, 287
  Sao Paulo (USP), 233
  Tsinghua, 139–40
  Tokyo, 188–89, 193–94, 196
  White Tulane, 284–86
  Wuhan, 140
USSR. *See* Soviet Union
Uruguay; Uruguayan, 112n51, 237

Varkiza, 267
Versailles Peace Conference (1919), 108
Vienna, 278
Vietnam; Vietnamese, 55
Vietnam war (*see under* war)
Volksgeschichte, 16

Wajda, Andrzej
   Walesa, Man of Hope (2013), 167
War
   American Civil War (1861–65), 280, 285
   Balkan Wars, 122
   Cold War, 13–14, 18, 151–52, 156, 187, 208, 234n10, 237, 289, 291
   Greek Civil War (1946–49), 20, 151, 238, 267–68
   Greek–Turkish War (1922), 118, 121–122
   Korean War, 187, 282
   Russian–Japanese War (1904–1905), 89
   Sino–Indian War (1962), 96
   Sino–Japanese War of Resistance (1937–1945), 13, 136, 140
   Six Day War (1967), 279
   total war, 136, 139, 141–43, 145
   Vietnam War, 25n79, 83, 107, 188, 288–89
   War of Independence (Israel), 279
   World War I (1914–1918), 11, 15, 38, 92, 94, 118–20, 122, 293
   World War II (1939–1945), 2–3, 12–14, 15–16, 20, 48, 81, 86, 107, 121, 144, 151–52, 154, 158, 159, 187, 238, 266–67

Warsaw, 166, 168, 176, 294
Washington D.C., 242
Weber, Max, 3, 108n9, 189, 194, 281
Wehler, Hans-Ulrich, 34
   Das Deutsche Kaiserreiche (1973), 34, 290, 293
Wehrmacht, 15
Westforschung, 16
White, Hayden, 6, 64–65, 67, 72, 75, 186, 246, 272, 295
Wiesel, Elie, 107
Wilson, Woodrow, 6, 93–95
   as a historian, 91–92
   Fourteen Points, 92
   History of the American People (1902), 91
Windschuttle, Keith, 70–71
Woodhouse, Christopher Montague, 13–14, 153–59
   Apple of Discord (1948), 153, 157
   Zur Geschichte der Resistance in Griechenland, 154
World War I. *See under* war
World War II. *See under* war

Yamane, Tetsuya, 196
Yamamoto, Hideyuki, 194
Yan'an, 143, 145

Zhanguo Ce Clique, 12–13, 136, 141–45
   Dagong bao, 141
Zimbabwe, 46
Zionism; Zionist, 278–79, 281

www.ingramcontent.com/pod-product-compliance
Lightning Source LLC
Chambersburg PA
CBHW071333080526
44587CB00017B/2825